Right-Wing Radicalism and National Socialism in Germany

Right-Wing Radicalism and National Socialism in Germany

Confessional Factors in Support and Resistance

Ingvar Kolden

HAMILTON BOOKS
Lanham • Boulder • New York • London

Published by Hamilton Books
An imprint of The Rowman & Littlefield Publishing Group, Inc.
4501 Forbes Boulevard, Suite 200, Lanham, Maryland 20706
www.rowman.com

6 Tinworth Street, London SE11 5AL, United Kingdom

Copyright © 2021 The Rowman & Littlefield Publishing Group, Inc.

All rights reserved. No part of this book may be reproduced in any form or by any electronic or mechanical means, including information storage and retrieval systems, without written permission from the publisher, except by a reviewer who may quote passages in a review.

British Library Cataloguing in Publication Information Available

Library of Congress Control Number: 2021932123

Contents

Abbreviations	vii
Preface	xi
Introduction	1

PART I: CHRONOLOGICAL-THEMATIC

1	The Pre-1914 Breeding Ground	21
2	The Heritage of World War I Versus the Values of 1789	115
3	The Postwar Period: Change of Mentality among Protestants	215

PART II: THEMATIC

4	Other Denominations and Nazism	221
5	Agrarian Parties and Confessional Differences	225
6	Women and Nazism	229
7	Christian Youth Associations and Nazism	231
8	The Relationship of Pius XI to Totalitarianism	235
9	Conclusions as to Differences of Mentality among the Confessions	243
	Defining of Terms	249

References	251
Index	273
About the Author	291

Abbreviations

BBB	*Bayerischer Bauernbund* (The Bavarian Farmers' Association 1893–1933. Catholic dominated farmers' association. 1918–1933: also farmers' party in Bavaria)
BK	*Bekennende Kirche* (The Confessing Church 1934–1945. Church party which opposed the *Führer* principle and an Arian clause in the Protestant churches.)
BVP	*Bayerische Volkspartei* (The Bavarian People's Party 1918–1933. Catholic Christian party in Bavaria. Precursor of the CSU in 1945)
CSAP	*Christlichsoziale Arbeiterpartei* (The Christian Social Workers' Party. Anti-Semitic Protestant party 1878–1918)
CSP	*Christlichsoziale Partei* (The Christian Social Party. Catholic Christian party in Austria before 1938)
CSVD	*Christlichsozialer Volksdienst* (The Christian Social People's Service. Protestant Christian party 1929–1933)
CV	*Cartellverband der Deutschen katholischen Studentverbände* (The Cartel Association of German Catholic Students' Associations)
DAP	*Deutsche Arbeiterpartei* (The German Workers' Party. Precursor 1903–1918 for the DNSAP and 1919–1920 for the NSDAP)
DC	*Deutsche Christen* (The German Christians 1932–1945. Church party espousing the *Führer* principle and an Arian clause in the Protestant churches)
DDP	*Deutsche Demokratische Partei* (The German Democratic Party 1918–1933. Protestant-dominated liberal left-wing party)

DEKA	*Deutscher Evangelischer Kirchenausschuss* (The German Evangelical Church Committee. Umbrella body for the 28 Protestant regional *Landeskirchen*)
DGB	*Deutscher Gewerkschaftsbund* (The German Trade Unions. Nonsocialist)
DNSAP	*Deutsche Nationalsozialistische Arbeiterpartei* (The German National Socialist Workers' Party. The Austrian Nazi Party 1918–1926)
DNVP	*Deutschnationale Volkspartei* (The German Nationalist People's Party 1918–1933. Protestant dominated right-wing party)
DSTB	*Deutschvölkischer Schutz- und Trutzbund* (The German-Volkish League for Protection and Defiance. Dominant right-wing movement in Germany 1919–1923)
DVFP	*Deutschvölkische Freiheitspartei* (The German-Volkish Freedom Party 1922–1928. Nazi Party election ally in 1924)
DVP	*Deutsche Volkspartei* (The German People's Party 1918–1933. Protestant dominated right-wing liberal party)
GcG	*Gesamtverband der christlichen Gewerkschaften* (The Christian Trade Union Confederation)
KAB	*Katholische Arbeiter-Bewegung* (The Catholic Labor Movement)
KLVdDR	*Katholischer Lehrerverband des Deutschen Reiches* (Germany's Catholic (male) Teachers' Association)
KP	*Konservative Partei* (Conservative Party 1848–1918)
KPD	*Kommunistische Partei Deutschlands* (Germany's Communist Party 1919–1933)
KV	*Kartellverband der katholischen Studentvereine* (The Cartel Association of Catholic Students' Associations)
NSDAP	*Nationalsozialistische Deutsche Arbeiterpartei* (The National Socialist German Workers' Party 1920–1945. The Nazi Party.)
PNB	*Pfarrernotbund* (The Pastors' Emergency Association 1933–1945. Clergy in opposition to the DC. Precursor for the BK.)
SPD	*Sozialdemokratische Partei Deutschlands* (The German Social Democratic Party 1875/1890–1933, 1945–)
USPD	*Unabhängige sozialdemokratische Partei Deutschlands* (The German Independent Social Democratic Party 1917–1931. Left-wing socialist party)
VB	*Völkischer Beobachter* (Volkish Observer. The Nazi Party's main press organ)
WAZ	*Westdeutsche Arbeiterzeitung* (West German Workers' Paper. Catholic)

Zentrum *Deutsche Zentrumspartei* (The German Center party 1870–1933. Catholic Christian party in Germany (excluding Bavaria until 1887 and 1918–1933), also in Danzig (until 1937) and Saar (until 1935). Precursor of the CDU in 1945.)

Preface

This book is an abridged and revised version of my dissertation for *doctor philosophiae* submitted to the University of Bergen in 2014, in Norwegian, and available digitally in that language on the following BORA-website of the University library of Bergen: http://hdl.handle.net/1956/7544

My findings are relevant to History, Politics, Culture, Religion and Social Science. Subsequently I have come across more recent and relevant research and taken this into consideration in my revision, e.g. Jörg L. Spenkuch's and Philipp Tillmann's research published in 2017, whose following conclusions I endorse:

> We establish that constituencies' religious composition is a key empirical predictor of Nazi vote shares—dwarfing the explanatory power of any other demographic or socioeconomic variable. . . . Voters' religion even explains more variation in the data than *all other available variables combined* (Emphasis by the author). . . .these results are not specific to the November election in 1932. We obtain quantitatively very similar estimates when we focus on any of the Weimar Republic's last three elections, or on the increase in Nazi votes betweeen November 1932 and May 1928.[1]

This decisive religious factor does not only apply to the *increase after* 1928, but also as early as in the elections of 1924 and 1928, and to the semi-democratic election in 1933, and *even to the last multiparty election* on German soil, to the *Volkstag* in Danzig in 1935.

For the sake of brevity I omit four of my original chapters and headings: "Sources," "The structure of the Dissertation," "Watershed," and "Clerical Nazis." (The latter chapter is mainly based on Kevin P. Spicer. *Hitler's Priests*. DeKalb: Northern Illinois University Press, 2008.)

I would like to thank a number of people whose contribution has been invaluable for so many different reasons it would take too long to describe in detail. First and foremost Professors Christhard Hoffmann, former chief of Institute of Archaeology, History, Culture and Religion, University of Bergen, and Lars Gaute Jøssang, at NLA University in Bergen, must be mentioned, in addition to my deceased father, university lecturer in mathematics, Kjell Kolden, who, based on his experiences in Central Europe in the late 1930s, already more than 50 years ago was the first person to make me aware of the Catholic resistance to Nazism.

I will also thank my good friend Richard Exelby and Megan Easley-Walsh who have edited my English, Richard also for his assistance in the arrangement of the work digitally, and, lastly, my wife, Nelfrid, for her patience.

NOTE

1. Spenkuch, Jörg L. and Tillmann, Philipp. "Elite Influence? Religion and the Electoral Success of the Nazis" https:/t.co/NyXXaKZM01 *American Journal of Political Science*, First published: 10 August 2017.

Introduction

HYPOTHESIS

My claim is that German practicing Catholics were the only numerically significant group of voters to prove thoroughly resistant to Nazi election propaganda, choosing instead to vote for the Zentrum and the BVP, the only parties of Catholic Christian causes. This can be noticed as early as in 1924 and is quite obvious in multiparty elections in 1928 and in the 1930s, also in the Saar and Danzig. In the presidential election of 1932 it is also obvious that Catholics were far more benign to vote for von Hindenburg than for Hitler.

Further, albeit less definite, corroboration is seen in the elections of university representatives.[1]

Why was there the unique reluctance among Catholic churchgoers to vote Nazi? What explains this striking contrast to the Protestant affinity to Nazism?

The most likely way to find an answer would be to look into what features (i.e. short- and long-term aspects) of various Catholic social circles diverged significantly from their Protestant equivalents. What cultural, ideological, social, clerical, political and mentality factors had evolved to prevail during the Weimar Republic? Could such differences, if they existed, have had a bearing on this Catholic resistance and Protestant attraction to right-wing radicalism in general in the 1920s and Nazism in particular during the 1930s?

CURRENT THEORIES AND INTERPRETATIONS

This line of enquiry appears to have remained largely unexplored apart from an article of my own in 1998,[2] and seems to find corroboration in Helmut

Walser Smith's comment in 1995 that although the Protestant-Catholic divide had been central to life and politics in imperial Germany, historians mainly overlooked it. They focused instead on class relations and right up to the 1990s explored these factors.[3] However, Protestant-Catholic polarization expressed itself politically, for after the unification Protestants dominated virtually all party-leadership and parliamentary representation everywhere, except among socialists and the Catholic Zentrum and BVP (and—as pointed out in a later chapter—the Catholic dominated BBB).[4]

Furthermore, argues Walser Smith, confessional differences also prevailed at most levels and aspects of social life, such as dress, choice of personal names, folklore, mobility, endogamy (mandatory intermarriage within a family/clan) and fertility rates. They affected what people heard, read, experienced, their education, and—finally—their organizational life. In short: religious mistrust split Germans culturally and permeated imperial Germany ideologically and socially.[5]

In 1992 Karl Rohe published an analysis of parliamentary elections in imperial and Weimar Germany, in which he launched his *"Dreilager"* ("Three Blocs") thesis. He asserted that right from the third *Reichstag*-elections in 1877, during the imperial era, three "blocs" are discernible within the German party system and voters: "The National" bloc, made up of Protestant bourgeoisie, supplemented by secularized Catholics; "Catholic churchgoers"; and "secular socialists." This trend lasted up to the Third Reich. The decisive factor leading Rohe to his analysis was the observation that total support for parties within these three blocs was fairly stable when compared to the suffrage, i.e. the number qualified to vote. It was especially evident when investigating the Catholic bloc. In the eleven parliamentary elections between 1877 and 1912, support for the Zentrum (with its Bavarian partner, the *Patriotenpartei*, which merged with the party in 1887) fluctuated between 16.3 and 12.7 percent.

Despite all the radically new conditions on the emergence of the Weimar Republic: loss of lands; female suffrage; lower voting age (twenty); and parliamentary democracy, this tendency continued. The Catholic bloc (the Zentrum and the BVP) had a particularly successful election in the Constituent Assembly election in 1919, lost terrain in 1920,[6] and fluctuated only slightly (between 13.5 and 11.3 percent) in the eight *Reichstag*-elections from 1920 to 1933.

The success of the Nazi Party was therefore largely due to debacles within the "National Bloc" parties, and a markedly increased voter turnout. When the turnout in 1933 rose considerably, only the Zentrum among the other parties won some (200.000) of these new voters.[7] In the special areas of the Saar and Danzig, set up in the Versailles Treaty, the same tendencies also clearly manifested themselves.

Rohe asserted that, from the point of view of the "National Bloc," the Zentrum and the SPD both were pariahs of German society, ultimately because the unification in 1871 had been pushed through on the premises of a Protestant dominated Prussian majority.[8] When a new regime was established after WWI, the stigma of "traitor" then reinforced the status of a pariah. Rohe, like Walser Smith, concludes: "Religious division was the decisive aspect of life, thought, self-perception and politics in Germany."[9]

The previous century's focus on socio-economic reasons for voter behavior may be due to the predominantly materialistic and even Marxist view of historians. The consensus of present-day historians is that this research has provided little of interest in the way of an answer thus far; hence it receives little attention in this book. Christian Stögbauer has compiled a short but good survey of research conducted during the twentieth century.[10]

According to the famous researcher from the 1980s and 1990s, Professor Jürgen Falter,[11] the most prominent researchers in this century up until 2008 are Gary King and Colin Flint.[12]

The contrast in the voting behavior of Protestants and Catholics was remarked upon already in the election of 1930, though,[13] and in 1934 Rudolf Heberle made what is probably the first investigation ever into the motivation for voting Nazi. It was a regional study in one of the strongest Nazi regions: Schleswig-Holstein. Herberle's conclusion was that belonging to a Protestant denomination was one of the key factors for Nazi success at the polls.[14] Additionally, already the 1928 election statistics highlighted clearly that there was a confessional difference in voting behavior.[15]

In 1972, Walter Burnham published his thesis of "political confessionalism." His claim was that unlike the bourgeois Protestant group, Catholics and industrial workers had long been integrated into close knit social networks and, as indicated, political parties. Catholics, who were a minority, differed from Protestants because they had their own confessional kindergartens and schools, a more comprehensive association life, they attended mass regularly, and their social life was played out in restricted circles.[16]

Gary King criticizes Burnham's theory and claims "the identification of the Catholic and industrial proletariat sections of the German population was not complete."[17] This claim is relevant. However, Catholics were themselves divided into two distinct and almost equally large groups: secularized and churchgoers and Burnham's thesis is, of course, relevant only for churchgoers. Secularized Catholics voted socialist or for Protestant dominated parties such as the Nazis, in all likelihood much the same way Protestants did, but definitely not for the Zentrum/BVP, or for that matter the tiny Protestant Christian party.

Burnham's theory is undoubtedly relevant where the Catholic churchgoers are concerned, but hardly sufficient to explain voting behavior; nor has his analysis gone into the problem deeply enough. It is surely rather striking, and sociologically very interesting, that Catholic and socialist associations should prove so very much more resistant to Nazi propaganda than their bourgeois Protestant counterparts. Maybe it indicates that the "glue" binding Catholic networks and binding socialist ones may have been made of stronger stuff than a mere organization, society and tradition. In the course of this investigation, we hope to establish if this was indeed the case with the Catholics.

Ian Kershaw is much in line with Burnham. He claims socialist and Catholic parties had learnt much from Nazi propaganda technic, even though their own propaganda was more defensive and mainly directed to their own electorate. They could rely on their solid milieus and organizations.[18]

Though this could be the case in the 1930 and 1932 elections, it was almost impossible for anyone but the Nazis to do any campaigning at all in the last three weeks running up to the 1933 election. All the same, in this very election the SPD and the BVP lost only a minor part of their voters and the Zentrum won almost 200,000 new ones.

There is some present-day research that lines up with Burnham's thesis. It has been conducted by Colin Flint and associates. They emphasize that Catholics had a stronger adhesion to their organizations than the industrial proletariat had to theirs, and they are probably right in saying so. It is also worth noting that both they and Gary King agree with Spenkuch & Tillmann in rejecting unemployment as an important factor in voting behavior.[19]

As stated, King and Flint and their teams are regarded by Jürgen Falter as the most important researchers in the first decade of the 2000s.[20] Falter himself performed the most detailed statistical research in the 1980s and 1990s on the "Nazi"-elections ever, but King's research from 2008 was the most updated information I came across prior to submitting my dissertation.[21] I discussed his findings and conclusions in my original publication but will refrain here. However, I note that he emphasizes economic incentives in voting behavior, much in line with the Marxist party theory of the Swede Lennart Berntson, which assumes that a political party represents a social class in competition with other classes for political and economic power.[22] The Zentrum, however, had an especially heterogeneous electorate with regards to class, just like the Nazi Party did, according to Stanley G. Payne and Ute Schmidt.[23] The cohesive factor was *culture*, not *class*.

There have been other theories about Nazi success based on longstanding tendencies in German history, parallel with the research focusing on statistical election analysis, the effects of the WWI defeat, and the Wall Street crash.

The *Sonderweg* thesis is an old theory that made a comeback in the 1970s. It emphasizes that Germany, unlike Great Britain and France, has been characterized historically by the late establishment of a national state and of industrialization. It lacked a democratic tradition, but it did have a strong bureaucratic one, pronounced militarism, loyalty to authority, a weak liberal bourgeoisie but a strong *Junker*-class, and its liberalism was tailored specifically to Germany. Today, the thesis is regarded as somewhat obsolete; the reasoning behind it is not.[24]

Walser Smith has emphasized the continuity of the conditions which had developed in the nineteenth century as a decisive factor in explaining the scenario that ended in the Holocaust. Contrary to advocates of the *Sonderweg* thesis, who emphasize political, organizational and socio-economic conditions, Walser Smith's new perspectives integrate cultural and super-national factors.[25] Recent studies by the French Johann Chapoutot and the Norwegian Carl Müller Frøland are much in line with Walser Smith and deal specifically with the eighteenth and nineteenth centuries' German philosophers' impact on Nazi ideology.[26] In both cases, they have bearings on our own proposition.

Unlike historians who focus on the evolution of ideologies and cultures which paved the way for the emergence of Nazism, and hence restrict themselves to the Protestant dominated "National Bloc," this book will focus on cultural differences between the "National" and the "Catholic Christian" bloc, and consider to what extent the differences impacted voting behavior.

Jürgen Falter concluded that the confessional factor constituted, to a great extent, an independent and dominating factor in voting behavior for or against the Nazi Party.[27] Christian Stögbauer has concluded the same: "The most significant political line of tension within the Weimar electorate was a confessional one."[28] Falter and King explained the Catholic rejection of Nazism by appealing to the opposition of the Church to Nazism and its favoring of Catholic parties. Weighty though this factor may be, the explanation is insufficient, as Falter and King themselves admit;[29] besides which, one needs in that case to establish the reasons for the clerical opposition to the Nazis and, in addition, say why no Protestant churches raised a critical voice. My enquiry, therefore, must clarify some of those probable reasons.

The Wall Street crash as a catalyst for Nazi success is accepted as axiomatic by most historians. However, it is fair to claim that no explanation has been universally accepted or established thus far for the success of the Nazi Party, nor for the perseverance of resistance.

In one of my dissertation lectures, I discussed what researchers had found out about the support of, a) German Nazism, and b) Italian Fascism. Ugelvik Larsen et al. demonstrate that (the most important) right-wing movements in Protestant dominated countries were primarily derivatives of Nazism: in Norway, Sweden, Denmark, Iceland, Finland, Estonia, Latvia, the Netherlands and Switzerland. However, in Catholic dominated countries, (the most important) right-wing movements were primarily Fascist derivatives: in

France, Belgium, Austria, Slovakia, Ireland and Spain (with its light Falangist version). The governmental authorities of Catholic dominated Portugal and Lithuania also followed the same pattern.[30] The British were an exception: while Protestant dominated, they were classified as Fascist and had a *British Union of Fascists*. However, the party was accused of having a rather Catholic identity.[31]

Others have shown that although the European Catholic Churches and churchgoers showed a varying and ambivalent attitude to anti-Semitism and to Italian Fascism (with its national variations and authoritarian governments), aversion to Nazism was a widespread phenomenon and not restricted to Germany.[32]

This confessional difference in attitude to right-wing movements in Europe indicates that Nazism and Fascism originally clearly derived from different sources. The famous historian George Mosse explains it thus:

> the German variety came to be unique in the primacy of the ideology of the Volk, nature and race. . . . Deeply rooted, as it was, in a specific German heritage, it could hardly serve as an aid to the fascist movements in other countries. It is typical in this regard that Hitler condemned the futurism which the Duce supported in Italy . . . this unfortunate nation (i.e. Germany) came to repudiate a European heritage which was still alive elsewhere: that of rationalism of Enlightenment and the social radicalism of the French Revolution . . . this repudiation was intimately connected with a general opposition to modernity which withdrew into itself, for . . . the awakening of German individuality was both a flight from present reality and a flight from European tradition.[33]

Obviously, though, most other European right-wing *Protestants* felt this German "uniqueness" more attractive than Fascism originated in Catholic Italy.

THE APPROACH OF THE THESIS

Theoretical Approaches

At the outset of my quest the study began in 1995 with two maps. One was of the *Reichstag*-election results in German subconstituencies (rather small areas) in November 1932, and showed that the Zentrum was the biggest party in roughly one third of the area and the Nazi Party in roughly two-thirds. Plus, there were several social democratic and communist mainly urban, (and hence geographically small) areas elsewhere. Moreover, where the Zentrum dominated, it gained 50 percent or more of the vote in more than half of its dominated area, while where the Nazis dominated, this party had equivalent support in slightly less than half of its area.[34]

This awoke my attention, and knowing the Zentrum was a typically confessionally based party, i.e. for Catholics, it was natural to compare this electoral map with a second one: the distribution of confessions in Germany.[35] The comparison showed a remarkably precise concurrence: the Zentrum was the largest party in rural districts that had 95 percent Catholics, while the Nazi Party was the largest party in rural districts with 95 percent Protestants. In no Protestant district was the Zentrum largest, while the Nazi Party was largest only in a handful of 95 percent Catholic districts.

A further striking fact was that among the more than thirty political parties participating in the 1928 election, only the Zentrum and the Nazi Party, in addition to the KPD, increased their support in relation to the number qualified to vote; and this held true right up to 1933's semi-democratic election, when only the Nazis had genuine freedom to conduct a campaign. In addition, it was conspicuous that *both* the Zentrum and the Nazis suffered a slight, but temporary, setback in November 1932.

This indicates that the parties' support came from two very different groups of voters, even though they were similar in some ways—having rural districts and small towns as their strongholds and having socially and economically heterogenous supporters. Cities were socialist bastions for the main part.

My findings gave rise to my hypothesis: that the salient factor for the resistance among the Zentrum voters was confessional, and not socio-economic, occupational or geographical, which had been the prevailing explanation among twentieth century historians. For it transpired that the Zentrum was a party for Catholic churchgoers; and what is more, the party for a specific movement within Catholic ranks: the Vatican-loyal "Ultramontanists." Correspondingly, overwhelming Nazi support in rural and smalltown Protestant areas indicates that the Nazi Party was the main preference of a typical Protestant churchgoer.

Although Catholic and social democratic opinion groups demonstrably had several ideological features in common, socialist resistance has not received much of my attention even though these similarities were especially apparent during the Weimar Republic, and were, no doubt, of significance for socialist resistance to Nazism.

My research has convinced me that important factors led the Catholic churchgoer to reject the Nazi Party at the polls: e.g. longstanding cultural factors, ideological factors and mentality factors, and stubborn Church resistance to right-wing radicalism and Nazism throughout the Weimar Republic.

The conclusions of other historians and researchers have strengthened my hypothesis. Firstly, there is Falter, asserting the confessional factor had been an independent and dominating factor in the voters' response to the Nazi Party to a great extent. Secondly, Stögbauer states, "the most significant political line of tension . . . was . . . a confessional line of tension." Thirdly, Rohe states, "religious discord was the decisive reality with life, thought, self-understanding and politics in Germany" and his "Three Bloc"-thesis about the stability of the main groups. Fourthly, comes Walser Smith who asserts the proven and significantly different culture of the disparate confessions that have been ignored in twentieth century research, and emphasizes the importance of cultural development in the nineteenth century as a key to understanding voting behavior in the 1930s. Fifthly, we have Payne's and Schmidt's assertion about the socially heterogenous supporters of both the Nazi Party and the Zentrum. Finally, there is the recent research conducted by Spenkuch & Tillmann mentioned above.

All of this is in line with Max Weber: he considered that social research should be based on an analysis of conceptions and comprehensions of values in various social settings and that these provide the starting point of actions. Research should, therefore, occupy itself with real historical periods and civilizations.[36]

There were both Catholic and Protestant socialists. However, the overwhelming majority of such people were secularized and hence of little interest in this book. As mentioned, among the nonsocialist Catholics there were also secularized ones, but they were outnumbered by the churchgoers at a ratio of roughly 2:1. Even this amount is substantial enough to be a reason why research into cultural differences has been ignored, and attention to the makeup of the confessional groups has been lacking. Hence, this confessional element, overlooked as it has been, seems important if we are to understand voting behavior in the 1930s. So, it seems incumbent to illuminate the divergent voting behavior of Catholic and Protestant churchgoers and find reasons for it.

Methodical Approaches

Having discerned the divergence of the confessional groups, I became interested in ascertaining actual support for the Catholic parties and for the Nazi Party in their respective "95 percent dominant" Catholic and Protestant zones as of November 1932. Zone statistics transpired to cover 57 percent of the total electorate, and I found this percentage fairly representative of the country as a whole. Each zone was subdivided into "rural/small-town" areas, and into "urban population" (i.e. more than 50,000 people). As there were no cities that were 95 percent Catholic, I made an estimate of more than 70 percent Catholic in cities, and the result was as follows:

- Protestant rural/small-town areas: Nazi Party 42.3 percent, Catholic parties c. 2 percent
- Protestant urban areas: Nazi Party 29.2 percent, Catholic parties c. 2 percent
- Catholic rural/small-town areas: Nazi party 18.7 percent, Catholic parties 52.3 percent
- Catholic (>70 percent) urban areas: Nazi Party 23.2 percent, Catholic parties 31.4 percent

In 1998 I first time published my findings in *Historisk Tidsskrift* (Historical Magazine), No. 3, Vol. 77 (with English summary). In this article I included the radical right-wing DNVP in the "Harzburg front" alliance with the Nazi Party. This made the difference between the right-wing and the Catholic parties even more evident. The "Harzburg front" got 53.3 percent of the vote in the Protestant countryside, but only 22.1 percent in the Catholic countryside.

These figures, once ascertained, reinforced the impression of purely confessional reasons for the support for or resistance to right-wing radicalism in general and Nazism in particular. It was, therefore, natural for me to further investigate church- and cultural-historical sources. The conclusions I came to in my article in *HT* have not changed. In the meantime I have studied an immense amount of potentially relevant sources, and new sources are continually coming to light. Among them is research on the recently downgraded primary sources in Vatican archives.

Most election statisticians restrict themselves to the *Reichstag*-elections, and some even omit the notorious 1933 election, because it was not fully democratic. To get an even more extensive impression, I have considered the presidential elections in 1925 and 1932; elections in the Versailles Treaty seceded areas; a Landtag election (in Lippe); and the last multiparty elections ever in Interwar Germany: the Prussian provincial assembly elections on March 12, 1933. The information gathered from these records is too significant, interesting and valuable to be ignored.

RELATIVE STRENGTH OF OPINION GROUPS

Reichstag- and Regional Elections

Our statistics about the relative strength of opinion groups in German elections in the Interwar period to the *Reichstag*, and to the Prussian provincial assemblies must be related to the suffrage, not merely to the ballots cast. The reason for this is that many of the new Nazi voters of the 1930s had abstained from voting in the 1920s. Those voting for Catholic parties were almost exclusively people who were loyal to them in all elections, no matter what the party program or behavior of their representatives were. This was also partly the case with the socialist parties, although communists had boycotted the elections in the 1920s to a great extent. Falter, Stögbauer and King, the main researchers of election statistics since 1980, also relate party support to suffrage.[37]

The three "Weimar" parties, which formed the government 1919–1920, the SPD, the Zentrum and the DDP, had their peak support in 1919. This was the first election after WWI, and already in 1920, after the signing of the Versailles Treaty and passing of the constitution, the support of all three parties dropped.

Although the DDP–as the only of the three parties–had abstained from acknowledging the Versailles Treay, the party's loss of support was dramatic. Their predominantly Protestant voters (not their Jewish ones at first, of course) switched primarily to several bourgeois parties which popped up in the 1920s, and to the Nazi Party in the 1930s. The Zentrum, however, only went through a minor setback up until 1928.[38] The loss after 1920 might be due to a fall off in church attendance and secularization in the 1920s in general, to a breakaway of a right-wing faction, and loss of new Protestant voters.[39]

The *Reichstag*-election in 1928 is a good starting point for assessing the resistance of parties and party groupings. The Nazi Party (together with another Swastika-party, the *Völkisch(national)er Block* got only 2.6 percent when the number is adjusted to the suffrage. On the same scale, five socialist parties got 30.9 percent and the two Catholic parties received 11.5 percent.

In the 1930 election, the Nazi Party was the only extreme right-wing party and got 15 percent, the socialists 30.6 percent, and the Catholics 12 percent. In July 1932, the Nazi Party now got 31.1 percent, the socialists 30.1 percent, and the Catholics 13 percent. In November of the same year, the Nazis suffered a setback and only got 26.4 percent. Yet, the missing voters were not inclined to vote socialist (29.9 percent) or Catholic (12 percent); so none of the other "blocs" managed to profit from the Nazi loss. This is an indication that party groupings consisted of voters with different outlooks and mentalities.

The election in March 1933 was not fair and democratic, as only the Nazis were allowed to campaign freely. Nevertheless, the Catholics experienced some small progress getting 12.3 percent (although the regional BVP suffered a 2 percent setback), while the socialists continued to decline, getting 27.1 percent. The Nazi party climbed to 38.9 percent. Elections to regional assemblies confirm these national tendencies.

The last multi party election in Interwar Germany was held a week after the *Reichstag*-election, for the Prussian provincial assemblies. Even at that election, the Zentrum made progress in their total votes, increasing in ten provinces and decreasing in four.

The results indicate that roughly half of the Catholics voted for Catholic Christian parties regularly. This is corroborated by the statistics of the German Catholic Nuncio Eugenio Pacelli (later Pope Pius XII), who in the late 1920s claimed that 55 percent went to mass regularly and 57 percent participated in the obligatory Easter Communion.[40]

I pointed out in my article in *HT* that support for the Nazi Party in the November 1932 election had little or no connection to ethnicity (Germans versus Frisians, Danes, Poles); the number of Jews locally; regions especially subject to defamation and offended German national feelings; separatism; the East-Elbian "Prussian" mentality; or unemployment locally or regionally.[41]

East-Prussia makes the most remarkable example. Unemployment in the region in 1933 was unique in Germany: less than 2.5 percent! Nevertheless, this was the strongest Nazi constituency of all in November 1932 with 56.5 percent of ballots cast. Furthermore, in its Protestant, yet *Polish*-speaking Masuria district, the party got an overwhelming 77.6 percent of ballots cast!

Research into the ballots cast in rural areas in the northwestern constituency No. 14 Weser-Ems, the only place where the Nazi Party had considerable support as early as 1928, shows that in 1928, the more than 95 percent Protestant northern half of the area, the Nazi Party got 17.6 percent and the Zentrum 1 percent. But in the southern half that was more than 95 percent Catholic, the Zentrum received 68.3 percent and the Nazis only 2.6 percent.

Four years later, in November 1932, the Nazi Party got 56.6 percent and the Zentrum 0.7 percent in the Protestant area, but the Zentrum got 78.4 percent (!) in the Catholic part and the Nazis only 12.3 percent. Research has also demonstrated that there was practically no difference between the voting behavior of Calvinists in the northwestern quarter of the constituency, East Friesland, and Lutherans in the northeastern quarter of Oldenburg in both 1928 and 1932.

Both the Nazi Party and the Catholic parties had their strongholds in rural areas, and got more female votes than male in 1932 and 1933. However, in an area that was Catholic, men supporting the Nazi Party outnumbered women.[42] Research also shows that the Nazi Party already had better support among churchgoers than among secularized people.[43]

As this book will show, it is possible to claim that the Zentrum and the BVP were specifically Catholic Christian parties. They had little support from other groups. The comparison shows that in the small overwhelmingly Protestant dominated state of Lippe, where the Zentrum was not organized, the *Katholische Volksvertretung* (The Catholic People's Representation) received equivalent support in the regional elections as the Zentrum in the

Reichstag-elections when Lippe was part of a greater constituency. Elections in the German states, e.g. Prussian provinces, and elections in the Saar and Danzig also show a similar correspondence between Catholic confession and support for Catholic parties.[44]

The Zentrum made surprising progress even in the 1933 election. However, the BVP suffered a slight setback, which was probably due to the lie Goebbels circulated that the archbishop of Bavaria had announced that Catholics were obliged to vote Nazi. Media suppression made it difficult to expose the falsehood.[45]

Presidential Elections of 1925 and 1932

The confessional factor was even more prevailing in the presidential elections than in the *Reichstag*-elections.[46] The two candidates who received the most votes in the first ballot were contenders in the second and decisive one. In 1925 Hindenburg, veteran general from WWI, and Wilhelm Marx, chancellor from 1923–1924, were the contenders. Hindenburg was a Protestant, while Marx was Catholic and a candidate for the Zentrum. The election results clearly reflected this, except in Bavaria where Hindenburg, for some political reasons, experienced major support even in some Catholic areas.[47]

In the next election, in 1932, a Protestant and a Catholic were again contenders in the second ballot. Hindenburg was the Protestant, but this time Adolf Hitler was his opponent. The result was again clearly confessionally weighted, even more than in 1925. The Catholics this time voted as with one voice, not for the "Catholic" Hitler, but for Hindenburg! The 1932 election had a topsy-turvy result: Hindenburg had the strongest support from the constituencies that had been his weakest in 1925.[48] Furthermore, the Catholics of Bavaria preferred a Protestant "Prussian" from northern Germany to their "Catholic" candidate from Munich. The rivalry between the two main German states, Prussia and Bavaria, was always a fixture of German culture, history and politics. And now, paradoxically, some of the strongest support for "Catholic" Hitler came from the Prussian Protestant "East-Elbian" districts of that "*Junker*," Hindenburg!

In the election the same tendency appeared as in the elections to the *Reichstag* in the same year, that Catholic women, to a less extent than Catholic men voted for Hitler. The majority of women all together voted for Hindenburg because Catholic women so overwhelmingly did it.

If we take another look at the Catholic area in constituency No. 14 Weser-Ems which we examined earlier, it shows a striking switch in voting behavior. In 1925 the Catholic Marx got 88.1 percent, Protestant Hindenburg got 10.9 percent. But in 1932, the Protestant Hindenburg got 85.6 percent whereas Hitler, the Catholic, only got 12 percent!

The results clearly show what Catholic churchgoers thought of Hitler and Nazism, and what significance Christian *activism* had in relation to *formal* confessional membership and geographical attachment.

One Protestant clergyman asserted that many committed Protestants rejected Hindenburg in 1932, because he had been promoted by the Catholic chancellor, Heinrich Brüning, from the Zentrum. These Protestants wished to overthrow the position of power of the Zentrum in those areas where the SPD and the Zentrum were allies. A foreign observer in the Swiss newspaper *Neue Zürcher Zeitung* tells that many Protestant clergymen campaigned for Hitler, even though church leaders remained neutral. The paper further explained the Protestant benignancy to vote Nazi by asserting that "Psychologically it has its cause, partly in the fact that the bulk of the conscious Protestant part of the population, and especially among churchgoers, still reject the new state and republic, partly in the confessional feeling of grudge against the Center party and the Catholic leadership, against whom Nazis appear as the most ardent debater."[49]

Student Representative Assemblies at Universities and High Schools

The general political development is foreshadowed in the 1930 elections for student representative assemblies at universities and high schools. Nazis got more support, and earlier here than they did in the *Reichstag*-elections. Here also distinct confessional differences in voting behavior can be traced. Karl Dietrich Bracher claims that at universities and high schools in Protestant dominated cities, Nazi momentum was strong, first becoming manifest in right-wing national associations and later in moderate ones. At first, only the predominantly Catholic high schools showed some resistance. The Nazis had joint voting slips with other right-wing associations in several high schools, and most often were opposed by Catholic and republican associations.[50]

A survey of election results from 1930 and 1931 supports Bracher's claim. Except for one single high school in Protestant dominated Hannover,[51] the Nazis got between 76 percent and 41.7 percent in thirteen high schools in cities that were Protestant dominated, and far lower support (between 40 percent and 19 percent) in Catholic dominated cities. In Catholic and alleged "Nazi" Munich they received 36.6 percent.[52]

The church historian Klaus Scholder claims that in the early 1930s as many as 90 percent of theological students at several of the universities and academies of Protestant northern Germany were Nazis.[53] In fact, election statistics from some universities, like Erlangen, Freiburg, Würzburg and Hamburg, indicate that the first Nazi upsurge came among Protestant theological students.⁵⁴ The historian Geoffrey Giles concluded: "Confessional factors, then, played a decisive role in pre-1933 resistance to Hitler in the student world."⁵⁵

Even the Nazi takeover was harbingered in the student world. The last German *Studenttag* was in 1932 and held in a military barracks. Uniforms and military jargon infused the sessions, the democratic constitution was abolished, and the *Führer* principle was established.⁵⁶

Election Results in the German Special Entities of the Versailles Treaty

"Elections" and "referendums" held during the totalitarian Third Reich are, of course, of minor interest and relevance to a study of support of and resistance to Nazism. However, democracy still lingered on in the German entities cut off since the Versailles Treaty: the Saar with its *Landesrat*, Danzig with its *Volkstag* and Memel, under Lithuanian sovereignty, with its *Landtag*. German speakers were a majority in all three districts, and, except for Memel, all the main German parties were represented by equivalents. Naturally, 95 percent Protestant Memel lacked a Zentrum offshoot, and even a DDP or a Nazi Party.

In 1935 the Saar was reunited with Germany after a referendum. Its scheduled election for 1936 was never held. Elections held in 1928 and in 1932 were fairly similar to the trends in Germany at the same time, with one main difference: the area was 72 percent Catholic and hence dominated by a strong Zentrum. The Nazi Party did not participate in 1928 and got 6.7 percent (of ballots cast) in 1932. This poor result had no effect on either the Zentrum or the socialist parties, which were the other main contenders for this industrial district. Yet, in some of the few Protestant townships, the Nazi Party got as much as 80 percent of the ballot.⁵⁷

In Danzig, the Nazi Party had a feeble start in 1927. Contending on a joint list with another party, they got an unimpressive 0.7 percent (of the suffrage), the Zentrum got 12.2 percent and socialist parties got 34.3 percent. This was roughly the same as in Germany in 1928. The result was as expected since the confessional structure was similar. In the next elections, 1930 and 1933, the tendency was again similar to trends in Germany: strong Nazi progress, slight setbacks for the socialists, and the Zentrum not only holding its own but even increasing support. The final election, held in 1935 and only partly democratic because of the Nazi government's campaign restrictions, was remarkable for two reasons: it was the only (semi-) democratic election on German soil after the elections of March 1933, and it indicated the situation among socialist and Catholic opinion groups after two years of Nazi rule both in Germany and in Danzig. Nevertheless, the election has obviously been ignored by researchers. Backed by the German government, the Nazi Party got impressive 59 percent, the socialists lost out and only got 19.2 percent, but the Zentrum not only remained unaffected, but increased its support since 1927 and got 13.3 percent!

In the meantime, the entire pack of twenty Protestant bourgeois parties collapsed. In 1923, they had divided 49.4 percent of the vote between them, but by 1935 it had dwindled to a single right-wing party which only got 4.2 percent. The left liberal DDP met an even more dramatic fate than its sister party in Germany. In 1919 the DDP had got 23.8 percent but had vanished before the 1933 election.

In Memel, socialist and bourgeois parties and a Lithuanian party had all competed in 1932. In 1935 and 1938, all the German parties had amalgamated into the *Deutsche Einheitsliste* (The German Unity List). Socialist and bourgeois parties obviously merging into a single party seems an odd outcome.

The elections in Memel, and especially Danzig, give new knowledge about the collapse of the socialist resistance against Nazism after 1933, whereas the Catholic resistance still totally prevailed. This should spur on to further research.

NOTES

1. Chap. "Relative Strength of Opinion Groups."
2. Ingvar Kolden, "Konfesjonstilhørighet og oppslutning om NSDAP i Tyskland" in *Historisk Tidsskrift*, Bd. 77, Nr. 3 (Oslo: Universitetsforlaget AS, 1998) 272.
3. Helmut Walser Smith, *German Nationalism and Religious Conflict. Culture, Ideology, Politics*, 1870–1914 (Princeton, NJ: Princeton University Press, 1995) 13–14.
4. Walser Smith, *German Nationalism*, 34–35.
5. Walser Smith, *German Nationalism*, 80. 98, 113.
6. Which I analyse in chap. "Relative Strength of Opinion Groups."
7. Karl Rohe, *Wahlen und Wählertraditionen in Deutschland. Kulturelle Grundlagen deutscher Parteien und Parteiensysteme im 19. und 20. Jahrhundert* (Frankfurt/M: Suhrkamp Verlag, 1992) 92-163, 276.
8. Rohe, *Wahlen*, 96–97.
9. Rohe, *Wahlen*, 114.
10. Christian Stögbauer, *Wählerverhalten und nationalsozialistische Machtergreifung. Ökonomische, soziokulturelle, räumliche Determinanten sowie kontrafaktische Politiksimulation* (St. Katharinen: Scripta Mercaturea Verlag, 2001) 1–6.
11. Letter to author from Professor Jürgen Falter May 16, 2011.
12. Who investigated the 1930s elections.

13. Thomas Fandel, *Konfession und Nationalsozialismus. Evangelische und katholische Pfarrer in der Pfalz 1930–1939* (Paderborn: Ferdinand Schöningh, 1997) 23–25, with notes 4, 11 and 12.
14. Stögbauer, *Wählerverhalten*, 2.
15. Chap. "Relative Strength of Opinion Groups."
16. Stögbauer, *Wählerverhalten*, 3, 4, 148.
17. King, Gary, Ori Rosen, Martin Tanner & Alexander F. Wagner, "Ordinary Voting Behavior in the Extraordinary Election of Adolf Hitler" in *Journal of Economic History, Vol. 68, No. 4* (Harvard University, 2008) 955 dash.harvard.edu Access date: 06.01.2011.
18. Ian Kershaw, *Popular Opinion and Political Dissent in the Third Reich. Bavaria 1933–1945* (Oxford: Oxford University Press, 2002) 177–178.
19. John O'Loughlin, Colin Flint & Luc Anselin, *The Political Geography of the Nazi Vote: Context, Confession and Class in the 1930 Reichstag Election*. (Research Paper 9323, Year omitted. Website closed. Official issue in *Annals of the Association of American Geographers, Vol. 84, Issue 3*, 1994) 28–30; King et al., "Voting Behaviour," 961–965; Spenkuch & Tillman, *Elite Influence*?
20. Letter to the author from Professor Jürgen Falter May 16, 2011.
21. Dissertation submitted 2013.
22. Lennart Berntson, *Politiska partier och sociala klasser. En analys av partiteorin i den moderna statskunskapen och marxismen* (Lund: Bo Cavefors Bokförlag, 1974) 16.
23. Stanley Payne, *A History of Fascism 1914–1945* (London: UCL Press Ltd., 1995) 135; Ute Schmidt, *Zentrum oder CDU. Politischer Katholizismus zwischen Tradition und Anpassung* (Opladen: Westdeutscher Verlag, 1987) 106.
24. Hans-Ulrich Wehler, *The German Empire*; Interview with Jürgen Kocka, *Bergens Tidende* June 8, 2001.
25. Helmut Walser Smith, *The Continuities of German History. Nation, Religion, and Race across the Long Nineteenth Century* (N. Y.: Cambridge University Press, 2008).
26. Johann Chapoutot, *Das Gesetz des Blutes. Von der NS-Weltanschauung zum Vernichtungskrieg* (Darmstadt: Philipp von Zabern, 2016); Carl Müller Frøland, *Nazismens idéunivers* (Oslo: Vidarforlaget AS, 2017).
27. Jürgen Falter, *Hitlers Wähler* (Munich: Beck'sche Verlagsbuchhandlung, 1991) 177–181, 187, 193.
28. Stögbauer, *Wählerverhalten*, 90–91.
29. King and al., "Voting Behaviour," 959, 964.
30. Stein Ugelvik Larsen, Bernt Hagtvedt, & Jens Petter Myklebust, *Who were the Fascists? Social Roots of European Fascists* (Oslo: Universitetsforlaget, 1980) 21–22, 155–156, 180 note 14, 359–361, 702, 720, 744; Stanley Payne, "The Concept of Fascism" in Ugelvik Larsen et al., *Who were the Fascists*, 229.
31. Tom Buchanan, "Great Britain," in Tom Buchanan & Martin Conway, *Political Catholicism in Europe, 1918–1965* (Oxford: Clarendon Press, 1996) 268, with note 76.

32. Richard J. Wolff and Jörg K. Hoensch, *Catholics, the State, and the European Radical Right, 1919–1945* (N. Y.: Columbia Universtiy Press, 1987) 224–228.
33. George L. Mosse, *The Crisis of German Ideology* (N. Y.: Howard Fertig, 1998) 315–316.
34. *Westermann Grosser Atlas zur Weltgeschichte* (Braunschweig: Georg Westermann Verlag, 1972) 154.
35. *Meyers Konversationslexikon*, 5. Edition (Leipzig: 1897) Entry: Deutsches Reich. Verteilung der Konfessionen im Deutschen Reich.
36. Per Kværne & Kari Vogt, *Religionsleksikon. Religion og religiøsitet i vår tid* (Oslo: Kunnskapsforlaget, 1992) 320.
37. Falter, *Hitlers Wähler;* Stögbauer, *Wählerverhalten*, 28; King and al., "Voting Behaviour."
38. Heinrich August Winkler, *Weimar 1918–1933. Die Geschichte der ersten deutschen Demokratie* (Munich: Verlag C. H. Beck, 1994) 295.
39. Winkler, *Weimar*, 295; Hubert Wolf, *Papst und Teufel* (Munich: Verlag C. H. Beck, 2012) 71.
40. Wolf, H., *Papst*, 77.
41. Kolden, "Konfesjonstilhørighet," 268–271.
42. Jill Stephenson, "National Socialism and Women before 1933," in Peter D. Stachura, *The Nazi Machtergreifung* (London: George Allen & Unwin, 1983) 36, 44, 90; Falter, *Hitlers Wähler*, 140–146, 181–188. Besides, see chap. "WOMEN AND NAZISM."
43. Falter, *Hitlers Wähler*, 192–193; Björn Mensing, *Pfarrer und Nationalsozialismus. Geschichte einer Verstrickung am Beispiel der Evangelisch-Lutherischen Kirche in Bayern* (Göttingen: Vandenhoeck & Ruprecht, 1998) 10–11, 13–14.
44. See e.g. surveys in http://www.gonschior.de/Wahlergebnisse.
45. Ludwig Volk, *Der Bayerische Episkopat und der Naionalsozialismus* (Mainz: Matthias-Grünewald-Verlag, 1966) 52–53.
46. According to Geoffrey Pridham, *Hitler's Rise to Power* (London: Hart Davis, 1973) 269.
47. It might be due to the BVP's dissatisfaction with Zentrum's cooperation with the rather anti-Catholic parties the SPD and the DDP, both nationally and in Prussia in particular. Pridham, *Hitler's Rise*, 66–67; See also heading ""Black-Red-Gold" versus "Black-White-Red.""
48. Falter, *Hitlers Wähler*, 175; Pridham, *Hitler's Rise*, 268–269; Jürgen Falter, Thomas Lindenberger, & Siegfried Schumann, *Wahlen und Abstimmungen in der Weimarer Republik. Materialen zum Wahlverhalten 1919–1933* (Munich: Verlag C. H. Beck, 1986) 76–79.
49. Gerhard Schäfer, *Die Evangelische Landeskirche in Württemberg und der Nationalsozialismus. Eine Dokumentation zum Kirchenkampf. Bd. 1. Um das politische Engagement der Kirche 1932–1933* (Stuttgart: Calwer Verlag, 1971) 40–41; Kurt Nowak, *Evangelische Kirche und Weimarer Republik. Zum politischen Weg des deutchen Protestantismus zwischen 1918 und 1932* (Weimar: Hermann Böhlaus Nachfolger, 1981) 322, 324.

50. Dietrich Heither, *Burschenschaften* (Köln: Papy Rosa Verlag, 2013) 87; Karl Dietrich Bracher, *Die Auflösung der Weimarer Republik. Eine Studie zum Problem des Machtverfalls in der Demokratie* (Villingen/Schwarzwald: Ring-Verlag, 1964) 147.

51. Where the Nazis got a mere 15 percent.

52. Bracher, *Auflösung*, 148.

53. Klaus Scholder, *Die Kirchen und das Dritte Reich. Band 1.* (Frankfurt/M: Verlag Ullstein, 1977) 164–165.

54. *Der Theologe Nr. 4. Die evangelische Kirche und der Holocaust. Dokumentation* http://www.theologe.de/theologe4.htm 30.01.2005; Bracher, *Auflösung*, 148; See also Anders Granås Kjøstvedt, *Hitler's Metropolis? The National Socialist Movement in Berlin 1925–1933* (Oslo: PhD-thesis submitted to the Faculty of Humanities, University of Oslo, 2010) 209, note 867; Geoffrey J. Giles, "National Socialism and the Educated Elite in the Weimar Republic," in Stachura, *Machtergreiung*, 62–63.

55. Giles, "Educated Elite," 62.

56. Friedrich Heer, "Weimar—Ein religiöser und weltanschaulicher Leerraum," in Hubert Cancik (ed.), *Religions-und Geistesgeschichte der Weimarar Republik* (Düsseldorf: Patmos Verlag, 1982) 41.

57. Kurt Schöndorf, "Für Christus und Deutschland—Gegen Hitler und die Neuheiden." Zum Widerstand katholischer Geistlicher gegen Hitler in der Saarpfalz vor der Saarabstimmung 1935, in *Saarpfalz. Blätter für Geschichte und Volkskunde* Nr. 41 (Homburg: 1994) 26.

I
CHRONOLOGICAL-THEMATIC

Chapter One

The Pre-1914 Breeding Ground

Factors underlying a disparate Protestant and Catholic Response to right-wing Radicalism and National Socialism.

CONFESSIONAL FACTORS

Protestants and Catholics responded differently to right-wing radicalism and to Nazism. General differences of theology and ecclesiastical systems seem to underly this.

Theological Authority and Diversity

The differences between the Protestant and Catholic Churches are considerable, as a comparison of theology and the status of ecclesiastical authority during the past 200 years will show.

Both churches were influenced by rationalism in the eighteenth century, but in the century after, they went through a kind of "reconfessionalism" and reverted to orthodoxy. Some decades later, liberal theology influenced Protestantism, especially after Darwinism came on the scene. In Germany, these new trends had more influence than in established churches in other places in Europe.

The Catholic Church remained far less influenced, but suffered internal strife, which caused split in the German church. In the 1840s came *Deutschkatholiken* (German-Catholics), and in 1870 *Altkatholiken* (Old Catholics) seceded and established themselves as independent churches in the wake of the papal *ex cathedra* dogma.[1]

A third group, "*Reformkatholiken*" ("Reform Catholics") opposed the Vatican system but remained in the church. People from this group were heavily involved in the embryonic Nazi Party, as it turns out.[2]

The *ex cathedra* doctrine was a historic event in the Catholic Church generally, not only in Germany. Many of the Germans had originally opposed the doctrine, but Bismarck's *Kulturkampf*, which soon afterwards was to start, induced the vast majority of German Catholics to weld into a close-knit fellowship with each other and with the Vatican, and became "Ultramontanists," the pope's loyal supporters on the other side of the Alps. Hence, in matters of faith, they were far more universally oriented than the Protestants.[3]

The *ex cathedra* doctrine implied a more centralized and stronger hierarchical ecclesiastical system and a more frequent issue of papal regulations. In Germany the bishops attained a strong authoritative position and met in conferences regularly.[4] In 1914, Pope Pius X characterized the Germans as "the best Catholics in the world". His successor, Benedict XV, was partial to Germans, too.[5] "Ultramontanism" had a lesser role in Baden and Bavaria, probably because these two states, as the only ones, had a Catholic majority and were largely unaffected by Bismarck's measures. Furthermore, Bavaria was the area of the dissident "Reform Catholics." One can also trace weaker support in the two states for the Catholic parties, and in 1933 the BVP suffered a slight setback in Bavaria.

Moral universality was essential in Catholic theology, which was the direct opposite of what turned out to be central to imperial Protestantism: the ethical freedom of the national state. During WWI, however, the German Catholic Church strayed considerably from the official moral doctrines and deviated in favor of national interests.[6] Times of war are special, though.

In the Protestant states of the Holy Roman Empire, the prince in each state and the city magistrate in each free city, as head of the church, had determined the doctrines of the church in the state/city. After the abolition of the Empire, the number of states was reduced in 1815 from about 300 to thirty-nine; hence, many of the new states became more or less biconfessional. The theological authority of their princes was diminished or lost. This gave rise to the weakened authority of theological doctrines in general, allowing new ideas, liberal theology, philosophical ideologies and Social Darwinism to impinge upon Protestant theology. The variation of theological opinions proliferated throughout the 19th century to such an extent the church historian Erwin Preuschen concluded in 1905 thus: "The evangelical church is subject now to such a division and variety of opinions that it ought to cause serious Christians alarm. It seems more and more difficult to reach mutual agreement and the possibility of joint effort when the results desired are so different."[7]

Another historian, Thomas Nipperdey, having pointed out the connection between recent quasi-religious ideas and Protestantism, states:

> The Protestants were restless and pensive, subject to modernity, for what was on the agenda and trends. They had reservations about the church and the institutionalization of life; they were more subject to modernity's crises and loss; they were so strongly committed to the Lutheran dogma of the connection between knowledge and conscience that they were receptive: first for scientific criticism of religion and for Nietzsche and his quasi-scientific views. At the same time, they craved secular convictions. This is the deeper source of values held in common, that joins liberal cultural Protestantism, adherents of the practical persuasions of faith, and adherents of new religiosity.[8]

Clergymen of the Protestant churches were considerably more involved in the academic, scientific and "cultural" world than their Catholic colleagues. They were much more attached to the state, had higher wages, and were part of "the establishment."[9]

The intimate connection between church and state not only undermined the church in religious matters, but to a great extent weakened a sense of moral responsibility when it came to the measures of political authorities. With such weak foundations to build their reasoning on, even the BK in Nazi Germany had problems coming up with rational arguments.[10]

Nevertheless, in imperial Germany, Protestant clergymen preaching in conflict with the bare minimum of established Protestant theology would still have disciplinary injunctions made against them. After WWI, this institution obviously decayed. In the Catholic Church, they had continually been common.[11]

Both Catholics and Protestants had their connected organizations, such as the *Innere Mission* (the Inner Mission) and other charitable and social institutions in the case of Protestants. But they were not attached to them in the intimate way Catholics were, let alone thought of as having a Protestant Christian party favored by the clergy.[12]

All in all, Protestants were more subject to secularization than Catholics. Contrary to the original hope of the authorities, the *Kulturkampf* made Catholic churchgoers unite in close and integrated fellowship and more church attendance than among Protestants.[13]

Hence, Catholics and Protestants in imperial Germany had little in common. German Protestant theology was contextual and Catholic was universal. Nor did they have the same culture or integrated fellowships. Furthermore, collectivism had continually been a trait of the Catholic Church, while in Protestant churches individualism held sway. More than this, the *ex cathedra* doctrine bestowed a unique authority upon the pope after 1870 that was unparalleled in any Protestant church. Ultimately, these differences of approach to political authorities bore momentous fruits when the two divergent confessions were confronted with the phenomenon of Nazism.

Catholic Involvement in Politics versus Protestant "Eigengestzlichkeitsthese" (Separate Jurisdictions Dogma)

For centuries, the Catholic Church's involvement in politics had been an established fact. Half the Catholic states in the Holy Roman Empire had been ruled by ecclesiastical persons after the Reformation and this continued until 1803. The pope had himself been the ruler of the Papal State until 1870 and continued to claim sovereignty there, up until the founding of the Vatican State in 1929. The German Catholic Church was, in principle, neutral to constitutional and to political ideas and movements. However, the *Kulturkampf*, following the establishment of the Empire, caused the clergy to interfere politically by not only openly supporting, but proclaiming, their loyalty to the Zentrum.

Although not endorsing the parliamentary system of government as such, German Catholics had rejected absolutism and favored liberal rights and parliamentary codetermination ever since the 1848 revolution. This was in keeping with the official Catholic ideology that had developed over time: from Augustine, via Thomas Aquinas, via the late scholastic Spanish theologians Francisco Vitoria and Francisco Suarez,[14] and ultimately Pope Leo XIII's *Rerum Novarum* encyclical in 1891. The ideas of these men were antithetical to Machiavelli's *Il Principe*, which had been on the *Index Librorum Prohibitorum* since 1559.[15]

During the nineteenth century, the actual policy of the Vatican was not always in accordance with these official ideas, much because of the anti-clerical views and policies of the main promoters of democracy: socialists and the radical bourgeoisie. Nevertheless, the pope even acknowledged the right to strike. Consequently, the emerging Catholic parties in Germany, Austria, the Netherlands and Belgium were democratically and radically minded.[16]

One consequence of the Vatican's political involvement was the issuing of encyclicals and resolutions, especially after the arrival of the Nazi menace. Such a policy was not fully acceptable in the Protestant churches, mainly due to their intimate relationship with their political authorities. No negative resolutions were therefore ever issued by any of them concerning Nazism during the Weimar Republic. The churches remained strictly neutral, ecclesiastical institutions, even though, as mentioned, local clergymen might campaign for the Nazi Party. However, this official neutral stand was not always an obstacle for all kinds of political statements. In the same period, lots of resolutions were passed and expressions of opinion—most of them negative—were aired by Protestant church leaders against the Versailles Treaty and the Weimar constitution.[17]

The main reason Protestant church leaders did not give advice or directions about how to vote, or issue any resolutions about Nazism, was perhaps their observance of the specifically German expounding of the Lutheran dogma of Dual Regiments: the *"Eigengesetzlichkeitsthese"* (The Separate Jurisdictions dogma). This preached the separateness of the two jurisdictions (the political and the spiritual) and thereby of the right of the one sphere to involve itself in the other's laws and obligations. The government remained independent of the moral and ethical obligations of church and of theology.[18] Furthermore, such a view made it difficult for specifically Christian parties to make headway among the Protestants. It also made it futile for the Catholic parties to try and increase their base by transforming themselves into broad interconfessional parties.[19]

The Separate Jurisdiction dogma was paradoxical, as political authorities had been the spiritual authorities of the Protestant states ever since the Reformation and until the disruption of the old Empire in 1806. The local princes had been physical protectors of the churches in the brutal religious wars of the sixteenth and seventeenth centuries and later under the (Catholic) Hapsburg Emperor.

During the time of Napoleon and the ensuing fifty years, circumstances were complicated by the radical reduction of the number of states. This meant many of them were no longer confessionally homogenous and the spiritual authority of the political authorities was thereby diminished. On Unification, the emperor was attributed virtually a *summus episcopus* status which satisfied the Protestant church, at least. Deep down, however, the real principal of the church was the German *Volk* (People).[20] Consequently, this *Volk* theology dominated the evolution of theology and church policy after the abdication of the emperor at the end of WWI.[21]

Protestants had been more satisfied than Catholics and socialists with the constitution of 1871. That meant that they became less concerned about democratic development than the other two.[22] Albrecht Ritschl, the prominent liberal theologian, asserted that everyday practical religion was about work and "Faith in Providence," not about the responsibilities of society as a whole. According to him the Zentrum, left-wing liberals and social democrats were preoccupied with natural law, theories about treaties and yearning for progress. It was un-Protestant and medieval(!) Luther had defeated the legacy of Thomas Aquinas, Erasmus and the "Baptists." The historian Thomas Nipperdey sums it up as a theological condemnation of "the Enemies of the State" of the day.[23]

The relationship of Church and State, Protestant and Catholic, during the Empire is summed up this way by the Norwegian historian Arve Thorsen:

> The rather monolithic national papacy of Germany also had a strong domestic dimension, . . . with the fusion of politics and religion political opposition and distance to the official ideology of the Reich became, in the eyes of the emperor himself as of many Protestant right wing circles, equal to heresy. Hence, the ethical national tradition turned out to promote a spiritualisation of politics: either you were good or you were bad. Either you subjected to the nation of Sedan, which was the one of God, or you did not. This was national ideology which left little room for compromise, and it may help to explain the implacable attitude toward both diverging political thought and the universality of Catholicism, which was so present in imperial Germany: The ideology of the Protestant forces unconditionally worshipping the Hohenzollern dynasty tended to defend itself not as one ideology, but as the only right one, with the support of God himself. . . . Lutheran Christianity was heavily politicised and in some versions nationalised, as a mere source of national strength. Thus, a room for both Christian Darwinism and pseudo-absolutism was made. . . .[24]

Even after the republican revolution following WWI, observance of the Separate Jurisdiction dogma continued. This comes to view in the attitudes of three distinguished theologians who were very skeptical about the Nazi ideology. Their skepticism was, at least in part, due to their situation as representatives of the church and of theology. Martin Dibelius, Rudolf Bultmann and, even the Swiss Karl Barth, apparently found it improper to continue to emphasize their opposition.[25] After WWII, Dibelius and Barth regretted they had not opposed more vigorously.[26]

Even Dietrich Bonhoeffer, the wellknown and respected anti-Nazi evangelical theologian, was too entrenched in the Separate Jurisdiction dogma. After Hitler issued his first anti-Semitic decree in April 1933, Bonhoeffer commented:

> Undoubtedly the Reformed church has no right to teach the state a lesson about its specific political actions. It shall neither praise nor blame statutes, but rather give its approval to the state as the institution maintaining God's order in a Godless world. The church shall approve the obligation of the state to maintain order—whether this order is good or bad to a humanitarian view—and it must understand that this order is based on God's will in the midst of the chaotic Godlessness of the world. . . . The measures of the state remain free of encroachments of the church. . . . History is not created by the Church, but by the State.[27]

Bonhoeffer claims that besides the political aspect there is a theological one, but their treatment must be separated strictly. He, therefore, continues:

"The church is no doubt obliged to help victims of any kind of society, even in the cases they do not belong to Christendom."[28]

Protestant Religiosity and Political Mysticism: "Arteigenes Christentum" (Race-specific Christianity) and the "Völkische Bewegung" (The Volkish(/Popular) Movement)

A specific version of Protestantism emerged in Germany during the seventeenth and eighteenth centuries: *"Weltfrömmigkeit"* ("Piety of the World"). It was typified by a mysticism that promoted a form of introvert sentimental individualism, and it spiritualized the world.

Hans Joachim Hahn explains its origins this way:

> It emerged from a wrong relationship between individual piety and a new church establishing itself. Personal religious ardour, which soon was subdued by the emerging state churches, sought compensation in "Weltfrömmigkeit" by converting the personal religiosity to "secular" interests as philosophy and literature, while the public sphere of politics was pushed into the background and left to the authorities.[29]

Even Friedrich Schleiermacher, the most prominent German theologian from Luther to the 1920s, may have contributed to the development of this "free and introvert" religiosity. He tried to connect religion to human sensitivity, not to an objective revelation of infallible holy writ. It based religion upon an anthropological foundation.[30]

The logical consequence of such a view is an emphasis on a private, subjective and mystical relation to God, a relationship distinct from morals. Morals, according to Schleiermacher, should be defined as relative, subjective and individual.[31] Furthermore, Schleiermacher considered nationalism an integral part of religion and emphasized the unity of language and race.[32]

Philosophical and secular ingredients became more and more conspicuous in German Protestant theology, from the eighteenth century with two recurring concepts: *Geist* (Spirit) and *Mythus* (Myth).[33,34] *Geist* can best be rendered as "spiritual depth" and *Mythus*, according to Friedrich Gundolf, as "word and vision of people and God; of what actually happens".[35] *Mythus* was hailed and regarded as a life-empowering promoter and innovator, not just as a vehicle to reveal the deeper understanding of reality and its fundamental values: the real people and a rather vague God. The concept was embraced by Nazis, giving intellectual content to Nazism. In the preface of his famous *Der Mythus des 20. Jahrhunderts* (*The Myth of the 20th century*) Alfred Rosenberg, the Nazi philosopher, defined the obligation of the 20th century to create "a new man through a new *Mythus* of life."[36]

There was obviously an ever-increasing difference in the way the Protestant theological system(-s) functioned and the way Catholic theology functioned (to say nothing of the differences in content). Catholic theology remained relatively uniform, clear and static. It functioned primarily as a set of dogmas demanding spiritual, moral and practical commitment from churchgoers. These demands affected both individual and collective behavior, enjoining confession and attendance at the Mass. The system was reinforced further by the *ex cathedra* dogma of 1870, which enhanced an unchallenged apostolic authority, an authority supervised through a comprehensive hierarchical system.

This was not the case for the Protestant theologies and churches. The theologies seem to have functioned more like systems of ideas and subjects for discussion, more or less disconnected from obligations of practical life. Furthermore, no Protestant clergyman could in any way claim such authority as their Catholic counterparts had, not in practice and not in theory either.

Remnants of paganism were still alive in popular belief among Protestants in the 19th century. One example is the celebration of the sunrise at the Externsteine: massive "holy" rocks in the minor Protestant state of Lippe.[37] How widespread similar beliefs were is unknown, but Himmler and Hess were clearly not afraid to flaunt their pagan worship. Though similar remnants are also present within the Catholicism of Latin America and Africa, German Ultramontanism seems to have been unsullied.

No doubt, the Nazis profited from the Protestant disoriented theological mindset. Nazis could use religious phrases, but their content was unclear and often ambiguous. In addition, once socialism stood forth with militant anti-religious rhetoric and attitudes, this facilitated the guise of Nazism as the defender of Protestant Christianity. The historian Steigmann-Gall comments:

> Nazi paganism could trace its ideological origins back to apostate German intellectuals, who sought to create a new national religion "which hid beneath pious allusions to . . . the Bible, a most thoroughgoing secularization. The religious tone remained, even after the religious faith and the religious canon had disappeared.". . . Nazi paganists, like their intellectual "forefathers," poured new secular wine into the old Christian bottles: "For the National Socialists this basic form could not be abandoned, but should simply be filled with a different content."[38]

We know from more recent scholarship that in fact much of the *völkisch* content of Nazi paganist thought found a receptive home among particular varieties of Protestant belief, well before the arrival of Nazism and even before the turn of the century, and Steigmann Gall continues:

ideas of national religion had found resonance within Protestant circles as early as the Wars of Liberation. Arguably, völkisch thought had emerged within established Protestantism by WWI: . . . the particular construct of Schöpfungsglaube (Creation faith), a departure within mainstream German Lutheranism, presaged the same kind of völkisch theories for which the Nazis would later become infamous.[39]

Nazi paganists consistently showed preferences for Protestantism over Catholicism, even going so far as to make it a barometer of how being a real German. Himmler and Rosenberg both claimed Luther's anti-Semitism as the direct ideological inheritance of the Nazi movement. If their new religious system was meant as a replacement faith for Christianity, a way of pouring new anti-Christian wine into old Christian bottles, the paganists demonstrated just how much old wine they were willing to retain in the process.[40]

Among the many nineteenth century theologians that Erwin Preuschen presents in his history of the church we find Paul de Lagarde. Some historians regard him as one of the "precursors of the Third Reich."[41] His theology is imbued with racism, anti-Semitism and rejection of the Old Testament.[42] Preuschen describes him, nevertheless, without any special comment, "for the Christian family", as an ordinary theologian.[43]

De Lagarde introduced the notion of *"Nationale Religion"* (also called *"Arteigenes Christentum"*=Race-Specific Christianity). This was a highly contextualized religion built on racial premises, purpose made to function as a basic constructional element when building the new German National State.[44] Thus de Lagarde became one of the main ideologs behind the later radical nationalist *"Völkische Bewegung,"* which became inspiration for the Nazi ideolog Alfred Rosenberg.

De Lagarde attacked both classical Protestantism and Catholicism itself. Protestantism had, according to him, developed to almost assimilate with Catholicism. What he abhorred about Catholicism, among other things, was its unassailable political system; the Church's aversion of the nation, conscience, science and intellectual life; its ultramontane dependence on Rome; the militant "New Catholicism" (which he described as "Jesuitism"); the sacraments and the devotion of Mary. De Lagarde would include "Woden rather than Jahwe" and "Siegfried rather than David "in his national religion."[45]

Preuschen was not the only one to regard de Lagarde as an "ordinary" theologian. Among de Lagarde's admirers were the prominent theologian, Ernst Troeltsch, both politically and theologically liberal; the author Thomas Mann; Thomas Masaryk (subsequently the Czech president) and, paradoxically, the politically liberal leader of the Inner Mission, Friedrich Naumann.[46] Troeltsch is interesting in this connection. Despite his liberalism, he was an extreme representative of this German non-universal political religion: he claimed that the ideal way the church should evolve ought to bring about a transition from a "church era" to what he termed a "political era." In other words, the logical result would be the extinction of the church.[47] It is probable that some Nazis in the Third Reich had just such a demise in mind!

Along with another *völkisch* Protestant representative, Julius Langbehn, de Lagarde was a highly esteemed cultural figure in the German education system,[48] though probably not esteemed in the Catholic one. His opinion of the Old Testament was recognized by Adolf von Harnack, himself the most influential Protestant theologian from the end of the 19th century until his death in 1930.[49]

Typical of the *völkisch* "political religion" was the emphasis on non-universal ethics founded on *Volk*, nation and race. It also rejected all kinds of established dogmas in favor of anthropocentric leanings like Nietzschean heroic self-deliverance. It favored the concept of an imminent and pantheistic God. As to the role of Jesus and the Norse gods, there were disagreements. Some rejected Jesus altogether, while others regarded him as an Aryan and the realization of the Teutonic Divine Man. Some regarded the Norse gods as symbols of nature interpreted as spiritual principles and images of the race, while others rejected them in favor of "German Blood" as the foundation of German Faith.[50]

There were a number of other tributaries to "political religion" besides de Lagarde: the Norse Edda, the German mystics Master Eckhardt and Jakob Böhme, Martin Luther, Goethe, the German idealists and romanticists, the philosophers Kant, Schopenhauer and Nietzsche, the Monism of the biologist Ernst Haeckel, the author Felix Dahn and the historical-critical Bible researchers.[51] It was important for its adherents that their ideology harmonized with what they considered "natural law" and "scientific understanding," and Darwinism and research on race in particular. Occultism, especially theosophy, became important as well, with teachings about the evolution of "original races". Hindu and Buddhist elements, such as reincarnation, self-deliverance and the emphasis on "Gaia" filtered down from theosophy. Art was ascribed a religious role and the artist dressed in a priestly mantle. Science and art were synthesized into a "higher" unity.[52]

Elements of popular belief were integrated with the ideology. Christmas and Midsummer Eve were welded to the solstice, (emphasized by both Himmler and Hitler) and some wished to introduce a new calendar starting at the Battle of Teutoburg Forest or even the erection of Stonehenge![53]

"Race-specific Religion" was part of the even more variegated cultural phenomenon: the "*Völkische Bewegung*," whose ideological span even found room for the anthroposophy of Rudolf Steiner (say some historians), as

Steiner incorporated into his ideology Blavatsky's theories of Atlantis and odd ideas about racism, Christianity and Persian religion. Steiner was active in the *völkisch* milieu in Munich in the early 1920s.[54]

Although the *"Völkische Bewegung"* was heterogeneous, adherents had some features in common: autarchy in every field by rejection of foreign influence on German culture (which might sound paradoxical as to what is mentioned above), race and economy; curb on industrialism to the benefit of agriculture; strife as a "'life principle" for the assertion of "race survival"; and among many Protestants an "anti-Roman bias."[55] Autarchy entailed a rejection of internationalism and of organizations and phenomena that had close relationships abroad. Four "Internationals" were perceived: "the Red International" of socialism and trade unionism; "the Grey" of liberalism; "the Golden" of banks and heavy industry; and "the Black" of Ultramontanism. Jews had their finger in all of the "International" pies, as well as having their Jewish Agency to boot.[56]

The most important spokesmen of the ideology were considered to be de Lagarde, and the authors Houston Stewart Chamberlain and Julius Langbehn.[57] One of the most important *völkisch* organizations was the Austrian fanatically anti-Catholic *"Los von Rom"* ("Away from Rome") movement with its magazine, *Heimdall*.[58] Its anti-Catholicism fed conspiracy theories about Ultramontanism and papacy.[59]

Radical *völkisch* religion does not seem to have gained a foothold in the culture generally or in Protestant churches before 1918. But from then on, not just *völkisch*, but specifically Nazi ideas percolated unopposed into the culture and the church.[60] In the only Protestant Christian *Reichstag*-party in the Weimar republic, *Christlichsozialer Volksdienst* ("Christian Social Peoples' Assistance"), extreme racist ideas held sway, asserting the Aryan race was far superior to all other nations, and hailing the "front experience" as one of the pillars of the party.[61]

Völkisch culture found adherents among (former) Catholics, too, after 1900, e.g. the Austrians Guido von List and Jörg Lanz von Liebenfels. (The latter, a previous monk, had considerable influence on Hitler).[62] "Reform Catholics", a movement in the wake of the theologian Ignaz Döllinger in the late nineteenth century, were also active in the embryonic Nazi Party in Munich, but soon withered away.[63]

In George Mosse's *The Crisis of German Ideology*, research into the confessional attachment of culturally influential persons demonstrates that among those advocating some form of *völkisch* culture the bulk were Protestants.[64]

Despite the motley nature of the *"Völkische Bewegung,"* it is possible to discern three responses to Protestant Christianity.[65] One was favorable towards the church and somewhat influential in it. The core of its theology was the "*Schöpfungsglaube*" (Creation Faith), and only a handful of theologians actively opposed it![66] The view was that Germans were a superior race and dedicated to cleansing themselves spiritually and biologically of all foreign influence, especially Jewish ones.[67]

The second response was rather hostile to the church and Christianity. Only if they could prove it was possible to "Germanize" Christianity, could they be accepted.[68] The third and last response rejected Christianity outright and favored Teutonic religion. Erich Ludendorff and his wife Mathilde were the main proponents of this group until 1933, as well as the erstwhile Christian missionary Johann Wilhelm Hauer and his *Deutsche Glaubensbewegung* (German Faith Movement) after 1933. The main Nazi Party proponent was probably Ernst Bergmann. Some historians would consider Alfred Rosenberg part of this group, but others will place him among the second, the "Germanizers."[69]

Protestant opposition to *völkisch* culture may have been puny, but Catholic opposition was vigorous. As early as 1924, the Catholic clergyman Erhardt Schlund wrote *Neugermanisches Heidentum im heutigen Deutschland* (*Neo-Teutonic Paganism in Contemporary Germany*), which contained an extensive condemnation of the "*Völkische Bewegung*" and treated Nazism as a sub-species of it. It was asserted that the culture was incompatible, even with Protestantism![70] The pope warned against it in the 1930s, and the writings of Alfred Rosenberg and Ernst Bergmann were put on the *Index*.[71]

In the late 1930s, the "*Völkische Bewegung*" withered away in the face of the ascendancy of its own offspring: Nazism.[72]

German versus Anglo-Nordic Orthodoxy, Pietism, Ecumenism and Mission

Mainstream Protestant orthodoxy, without the philosophical and mystical trimmings, was prevalent in Germany until the death of Emperor Wilhelm I. The rather introvert and nationalist attitude of the church in the late Empire and in the Weimar republic becomes evident in its minimal contact and ecumenical cooperation with foreign sister churches before the Stockholm Conference of 1925. Here, and later, the German church was noted for its pronounced oppositional stance towards relations to other churches and to joint resolutions.[73]

Although pietism originated in Germany, the German variant differed considerably from the humble version found in Northwestern Europe.[74] One reason may be that it was heavily influenced by the strongly and anti-Semitic Adolf Stöcker after the 1880s.[75] Evidence of the divergency of German pietism is their weak contribution to overseas missions. Gifts to missionary associations were far lower per capita in Germany at the end of the 19th century than in Britain or Scandinavia.[76]

NATIONALISM, ANTI-SEMITISM AND RACISM

Nationalism

Following the confessional schism and the diverging historical development after the Reformation, varying forms of nationalism evolved. Popular nationalism could unite society, but equally, it could also divide it.[77] Society was steeped in religious distrust, and it divided the people socially, culturally and ideologically.[78]

Protestant Nationalism

The German nationalist pioneer, the Protestant clergyman Johann Gottfried von Herder, attacked the Catholic Church as early as the 1780s for being detrimental to the inner nature of *"Deutschtum"* ("German-ness").[79] Clerics dominated the scene of nationalist discussion, together with teachers, officials and publicists.[80] Wolfgang Altgeld and Werner Conze assert that German Protestant national sentiment has pietistic roots. Geir M. Frøland similarly claims that elements in famous nationalist Johann Gottlieb Fichte's philosophy can be understood in the light of pietistic Christianity, that Pietism made many a German receptive to German nationalism.[81]

The French Revolution and Napoleonic era intensified the evolution of German nationalism, and its spokesmen were almost exclusively Protestant.[82] Fichte's *Reden an die deutsche Nation* (Speeches to the German Nation) is considered as one of the first and main contributors to the emergence of the modern German national identity, especially in Prussia and Saxony.[83] One of the peculiarities clearly distinguishing him from Catholicism was his assertion that the State should have power to both create and execute the moral.[84] Other nationalist spokesmen of importance in the first half of the nineteenth century were the theologian Friedrich Schleiermacher, the philosopher Friedrich Hegel, Friedrich Ludwig Jahn and Ernst Moritz Arndt. All of them were Protestants and all had studied theology.[85] Arndt asserted, "Hatred of the French is the religion of the Germans."[86]

One of the main differences between French and German nationalism was that in French nationalism, Herder's *"Volksgeist"* ("Spirit of the People") was the outcome of the interaction between the people and external factors like climate, religion, government etc. In German nationalism, in accordance with the theory of organism, "*Volksgeist*," originating in prehistory, was an objective, metaphysical state. From it flowed custom, tradition, law, political processes etc. "*Volksgeist*" was, in short, elevated to a metaphysical and religious plane.[87] Via ideas of "spiritual organism" Idealism and Romanticism elevated the nationalist concept to an exclusive variant. The Germans were, in Fichte's view, on their way to liberation from traditional morality and enslaved "enthusiasm," and due to their language, only Germans had immediate access to the absolute spirit. It was barred to the French and Italians because their civilizations had been vulgarized. When the Teutonic tribes, the (southwestern) Franks, Burgundians and Lombards had invaded Roman soil, they had lost and surrendered their own languages and cultures to Latin and Roman culture.[88] Fichte also introduced a sharp distinction between the established law of the State, its morality and written law, and the spirit of the German "*Volksgeist*." Later, German nationalists and representatives of the Conservative Revolution in the Weimar era endorsed this view.[89] Furthermore, Fichte advocated imperialism. Germans ought not to intermingle with non-German inhabitants in the conquered areas, but either expel or enslave them.[90] Fichte's nationalist state bore the hallmarks of totalitarianism, and Hegel followed suit. He claimed the total sovereignty of the state and rejected all international obligations, such as universal human rights.[91] When Catholic theologians attacked Nazism in the 1930s, they claimed the ideology was coupled to the tradition from Hegel, who had maintained "the Total State" as "the highest aim of all human effort", and not Heaven, the aim of the Catholic.[92]

Protestant theologians, including their most important one, Schleiermacher, promoted the tendency to spiritualize national and *völkisch* ideologies.[93] Schleiermacher spoke out against the Napoleonic occupation and the detestable French culture following in its wake; he feared a Catholic takeover.[94] Schleiermacher has in more recent times been upheld as one of the great nation-builders of nineteenth century Europe, explicitly including Christianity in the ideology.[95] Carl Frøland asserts Schleiermacher was the first to publicly uphold a pietistically oriented nationalism.[96] Although as an old man he returned to a universal and cosmopolitan view of Christianity, at times he stuck to ideas about each people having separate access to the Biblical message. These opinions were later adopted by the "*Völkische Bewegung*," *Deutsche Christen*, and Nazis in the twentieth century.[97]

The overwhelming number of Protestants, and particularly theologians, in the nationalistic debate is conspicuous. Wolfgang Altgeld holds it had significant consequences. The language and emotions of nationalism were filled with pietistic concepts and images, and the nationhood as the highest unity in the order of Creation developed into a central part of modern, enlightened and later liberal Protestant theology.[98] George L. Mosse, even asserts that "borrowing from the Christian liturgy was especially important in Germany, where the national consciousness was set upon pietistic foundations, and where practically all its early leaders came from a pietistic Lutheran background."[99]

Important nationalist intellectuals, such as Heinrich von Sybel, the initiator and editor of the prestigious *Historische Zeitschrift* (*Historical Magazine*), and the linguist Rudolf Hildebrand, one of the initiators of *Deutscher Sprachverein* (German Language Association), were hostile to Ultramontanism. They regarded it as incompatible with German nationalism.[100]

German Protestantism during the nineteenth century underwent a considerable metamorphosis from a confession strongly attached to the local prince as sovereign in the old Holy Roman Empire, to the foundation and precondition for a self-important German nationalism.[101] The Prussian kings and later emperors prior to Wilhelm II had been rather negative to this trend, but the mentality evolved into "*Reichsnationalismus*" during the last decades of the Empire. The National State was upgraded in a Lutheran manner and Protestantism imbued with national ideology.[102]

Until 1850 the most prominent German political philosophers had to a certain extent hailed "the ideas of 1789," but thereafter abandoned them. It coincided with a confrontation with Catholicism and social democracy.[103] Protestant theological publications, such as the most prominent *Deutsche Evangelische Kirchenzeitung* (*German Evangelical Church Magazine*), accused liberalism, communism, Judaism, and Catholicism of being responsible for the 1848 revolution.[104] "The ideas of 1789" were precisely the main bone of contention between leftists and rightists in the Weimar era, and the Nazi voice on it was unanimous. Goebbels vented: "We shall expunge the year 1789 from European history." Gregor Strasser and Alfred Rosenberg followed suit.[105]

By WWI, German Nationalism had evolved from genetical, linguistic, cultural, historical and pietistic origins to an emphasis on an authoritarian "national fellowship" at the expense of individual freedom. It differed considerably from general Western European form. It was anti-western and rejected the political and moral tradition of France, Italy, Switzerland, the Netherlands, and the Anglo-Saxon world. Leopold von Ranke, the founder of the modern historical school, allegedly called German nationalism "the reaction of the Nordic-Teutonic world to the revolutionary Latin nations."[106]

The Confessional Issue in the Nationalist Debate

Arve T. Thorsen pinpoints the essence of the confessional issue in the nationalist debate:

> The tribal undercurrents in German thought were strong enough to produce not only a "closed" national community which makes it natural to place it within the tribal half of the parameter, but also a fierce often anti-Catholic contempt for universalism and an opening for Darwinian perspectives even within the field of ethics and religion. The partial drift of influential German currents toward the tribal, as opposed to the French yearning for universal appears . . . as perhaps the most striking contrast between the two national-ideological discourses.[107]

Around 1800, Herder, Fichte, Arndt, Jahn and Schleiermacher discussed the relationship between religion, church and society as a social and the internal German problem of integration, with an eye to a national frame of reference.[108]

Herder considered Charlemagne's forced christianizing of the Saxons the first catastrophe in German medieval history. 150 years later some of the Nazis, wishing to establish a new Nazi Church, shared this view.[109] Herder also introduced the term *"Volksreligon"* (people's religion) and Hegel and other philosophers later defined the content.[110]

At the outset it seemed futile to unite the traditional confessions or weld them into one single new one, because the confessional split in Germany was so entrenched. Such a process was restricted to the unification of Lutheran and Reformed Churches in most states after 1815. All the same, nationalists endeavored to build an individual, national religion which would end up a post-Christian one. The famous fairy tale collector Jakob Grimm thought the solution must be to turn to the common religion of the old Teutons, as Herder had proposed.[111]

Such ideas were, of course, rejected in the Catholic Church, and unwelcome in the Protestant one, too. But the ideas received more attention in the wake of the new anti-Semitism and the *"Völkische Bewegung"* at the turn of the century,[112] and de Lagarde's voice was especially influential in this process.[113] He was the main instigator introducing Herder and Fichte's *"Mythos des Volkes"* ("Myth of the People") to Protestant mentality. By implication, it would entail the creation of a secular *Ersatz* (Replacement) religion where eternal life could be attained by fulfilling patriotic obligations.[114] Another important proponent of *völkisch* mentality at the turn of the century was de Lagarde's earlier mentioned disciple Julius Langbehn. His most famous book was *Rembrandt als Erzieher* (*Rembrandt as Educator*, 1890) and it was one of the main sources of inspiration for the Protestant Youth Movement later on.[115] Later in life, however, Langbehn converted to Catholicism and to "western ideals."[116]

The main nationalists' opinion throughout the nineteenth century was that the religion best in keeping with the national religion was Lutheranism.[117] This was hardly likely to endear their ideas to the Catholics; even in the rationalist period of the eighteenth century, the antagonism between the confessions was so profound that observers in Catholic south Germany asserted Protestants there were more detested than "Turks."[118]

Another reason German nationalism was dominated by Protestants, and to a great extent interwoven with theology, was because it was thought that Napoleon had intended to introduce some kind of counter-reformation in the Protestant German states. Thus, the successful Liberation War had to a certain extent an element of a religious war.[119] The Wartburg festival in 1817 on the 300th anniversary of the start of the Reformation, gave impetus to the above-mentioned amalgamation of most Lutheran and Calvinist Churches, and no theological disagreements between them seem to have influenced the nationalist discourse. The festival, which even commemorated the triumph at Leipzig, was dominated by evangelical students of theology or sons of evangelical pastors. Romantic German-ness and Christian Idealism were interwoven, and Luther's burning of the papal Bull of Excommunication was re-enacted.[120] Later, occasional "Wartburg"-festivals, dominated by strongly nationalist Protestant *"Burschenschafter"* (i.e. organized Fraternity students) were celebrated, which exacerbated antagonism towards Catholics and weakened nationalism among the latter group, or—at least—the German version of nationalism.[121]

Protestant nationalist celebrations were, to a great extent, stamped with substitute religion. The Catholics had, on the other hand, their own religious festivals, processions and pilgrimages.[122] As the famous Swiss theologian Karl Barth pointed out, there was a growing tendency among Protestants up until the Nazi era to regard "Christian" and "nationalist" as synonyms,[123] which was hardly the case with Catholics![124]

This was, therefore, bound to generate disputes between confessions, and cultural-national problems eventually turned into national-political conflicts.[125] Antagonism could grow so sharp that some radical Catholic Bavarians even asserted that they were not of Teutonic, but of Celtic origin.[126] In the Rhineland, Catholics were opposed to nationalism partly because it had been incorporated into Protestant dominated Prussia in 1815 against the will of the population. The area was favorable to France, Belgium and "the West," and this had been the case even during the Liberation War.[127]

Many Protestants regarded Catholicism as anti-modernist, hindering progress and national identity, and one radical Protestant even asserted, "the core of the ultramontane menace is its hostility towards culture, in its anti-nationalism."[128] On the other hand, a popular culture evolved within Catholicism that was more or less immune to "higher" Protestant culture and the canonization of national culture, both of which were regarded as ungodly.[129] By 1923, this view had become a common Catholic attitude, when the German *Katoliktag* (National Catholic Congress) condemned nationalism as "the major heresy of the times."[130]

Protestant churches hailed the Franco-Prussian War as a renewal and the exercise of moral power.[131] When the new Empire was established in 1871, the old black-red-yellow ensign of the March Revolution was abandoned, and the black-white-red one was adopted instead. The opposition in the *Reichstag* was made up of social democrats, a small group of progressive liberals and the Zentrum with its separatist alliance partners: the Hannoverians *("Welfen")* and Poles. These groups were classified as "enemies of the *Reich*."[132] Not only were these groups the "opposition", but they even rejected the German National State, asserts historian Jürgen Kocka (possibly with a degree of exaggeration, in my view). When it came to Catholics, Kocka asserts that the tension between Catholicism and the new state had its cause in both the Catholics, with their "pre-national and supra-national church", and the new national "Prussian-Protestant" state, were craving for souls, but on extremely different terms."[133]

In the German Federation of 1815–1866, Austria had hegemony and the two confessions were equally strong. In the new Empire, there were slightly over 60 percent Protestants and slightly under 40 percent Catholics. Most Protestant churches then adopted national self-esteem and it was manifested in the churches and their theology.[134] They contributed strongly to the establishment of the new nationalism, and a slogan: "Throne, Nation, Altar"—and even "One People, one *Reich*, one God"—was introduced.[135]

Many saw the Franco-Prussian War as marking a new era in the world: the annihilation of the Papal State, the decree of papal infallibility and theological decay, and the defeat of the French Empire were all setbacks for Catholicism. Leading Protestant papers attributed Protestant German supremacy to genius and power, energy and yearning for activity.[136] On the other hand, a paper accused the Catholic Zentrum, even before its formation, as "a poisonous mushroom . . . which incessantly . . . does its destructive work" which carried out "its treason against state and culture . . . and threatens to strangle us when its time comes."[137]

During the war, France became the symbol of modern, democratic, ungodly and licentious civilization, in contrast to German traditional, authoritarian, serene and pious Christian culture. The contrast was expounded upon in Protestant Sunday sermons, along with anxiety about French influence on

German culture.[138] It is striking how Protestant clericals dealt with the war and unification in 1870 and 1871, looking back to the past and indifferently to the future political challenges, which they entrusted to imperial authorities. They paid attention instead to the "decadence of the peace," and such emanations of the "French spirit" as international social democracy.[139]

The core problems in the clash between ultramontane Catholicism and national Protestantism were not confessional disagreements, but rather the realization of national unity in a Christian-reformatory spirit. The Catholic ideal was the particularistic state (in accord with the program of the Zentrum). This logically implied alliance with the Hannoverians and Poles, the latter of whom were Catholics, except for Masurians. Alliance with the Catholic Poles gave impetus to conflict between the confessions, however, as this non-German minority was subjected to the same suppression during the Prussian *Kulturkampf*.

The modern German idea of the nation had its origin in Protestant Germany, concludes Wolfgang Altgeld, holding that the history of German Protestantism and nationalism in the nineteenth century cannot be understood independently of each other, which has been largely ignored by theologians and historians. Furthermore, this intimate connection between nationalism and Protestantism reflects a major collective process of secularization and has been profoundly marked by the intellectual elites of Protestant North Germany.[140]

Several Protestant organizations intent on fighting ultramontane Catholicism popped up in imperial Germany. Most prominent were the *Gustav Adolf Verein* and the *Evangelischer Bund* (The Evangelical Association), the former established to hail the Swedish king who had "delivered" Protestant Germany from the Counter-Reformation during the Thirty Years War.[141] The latter compared German Protestant culture with that of a number of Catholic dominated European countries or with Catholic minorities and concluded that German Protestantism was superior to Catholicism in many ways. The *Evangelischer Bund* regarded the extensive network of Catholic organizations in Germany as treacherous and working secretly to split the nation in every way.[142] During the Weimar era, it was a member of the radical right-wing *Vereinigte Vaterländische Verbände* (United Patriotic Associations). Both Protestant organizations congratulated Hitler after the arrogation of Sudetenland in 1938.[143]

German Catholics naturally did not share the Protestant view of European Catholic countries and minorities. They claimed anti-Catholic violence was widespread, not only in Germany, but in several European countries, and conflict between Church and State was the result of modern liberal ideas about nation-building. The "Almighty State" interfered with the sanctity of home and family.[144]

At the outbreak of the *Kulturkampf* in 1872 the convocation of Catholic bishops rebuffed the frontal attack launched by Protestants on their confession. They asserted they had been hated and rendered suspect ever since the Liberation War and had false accusations of unpatriotic attitudes leveled at them after the wars of Unification in 1866 and 1870–71.[145] Similar accusations were leveled at social democrats, and both groups were considered less patriotic than other Germans. To make up for this, both social democrats and Catholics apparently tried to counterbalance this widespread opinion by enthusiastically supporting German involvement in WWI.

The Austrian "*Los von Rom*" (Release from Rome) movement was welcomed by many German Protestants. Representatives asserted that "Protestantism is the religion of the powerful nations, whereas Roman Catholicism the religion for a people in decay" and hailed Protestantism as a "robust and masculine religion, and therefore essentially German Christianity." Protestantism would strengthen the nation, whereas the Latin, feminine and irrational Catholicism would weaken it, even claiming, "Germany could only survive if it became completely Protestant. The danger from Rome was not only that it was a foreign power, but it had the capacity to destroy the German national character, not least, through mixed marriages."[146]

Although the "*Los von Rom*" and other *völkisch* movements were small numerically, their ideology seeped into the mainstream German Protestant culture, predominantly the political one. This was detrimental to the Zentrum and social democrats, both of which gained representation in the democratically elected *Reichstag*. One effect of this was to cause widespread suspicion, or even detestation, of the democratic system and opposition to the alleged "destructive tendencies" of the two parties because they had international connections.[147]

In 1915, in the middle of WWI, the Swede Rudolf Kjellén introduced the notion of "the ideas of 1914" contrasted with "the ideas of 1789." "The ideas of 1914" represented "order: solidarity, self-discipline, foresighted estimation, adequate authority, but "1789" gave us "real ideas of hucksters," having "no other purposes than procuring of certain benefits, of profits and the carnal desire of the individual."[148]

In the view of the historian Klaus von See the popularity of "the ideas of 1914" contributed to the isolation of Germany and German mentality as "the ideas of 1789" was so deeply rooted in Western democracies.[149] The historian Hans-Günther Zmarzlik claims that Germans intensified the contrast of "ideas" by portraying WWI as a history-making struggle between a peculiarly German spirit battling in sharp opposition to Western European culture.[150] "The cultivation of force, and indeed the right to force was tempting in a country that was becoming both financially and militarily the new superpower of Europe," Arve Thorsen states, and further: "Conversely . . . (it) made it considerably easier for France to . . . focus not on force, but on Right. . . ."[151]

Although confessional strife temporarily was laid to rest for the duration of WWI, Germany remained a divided nation. The permanent and intensified politicizing of the confessions hindered public coherence,[152] and the conflict was even further heightened when Catholics and social democrats collaborated in the "Weimar-Coalition" and other coalition governments in the dominant Prussian State. Karl Kupisch claims many Protestants looked on the Zentrum as the spearhead of an ultramontane conspiracy undermining the interests of the German people.[153]

Catholic Nationalism

Historians have emphasized the subduing effect on nationalist aspirations among Catholics of the supra-national Catholic Church. This is true of Catholics in Protestant-dominated imperial Germany, where both the social democrats and the Catholic Zentrum were stigmatized as unpatriotic.[154] Even before the 1848 Revolution, Catholic publications had baulked at fanatical nationalist expressions among the Protestants.[155] In the Catholic view, the relationship between church and state was paramount, and issues about the constitution, social policy and states' rights were equally important as national preferences.[156] The unification wars in Europe after 1850, which greatly diminished the power of the pope and Catholic Austria, did not increase nationalist feeling among German Catholics.[157]

The main difference between Catholic and Protestant nationalism was religious: Catholics rejected the very thought of placing the nationalist idea as being on a par with religion. The issue materialized as early as 1871 in the first year of the Empire, and in the *Kulturkampf*.[158] The main benefit for Catholics in the new Empire was the adoption of the "*Rechtsstaat*," the principle of a state governed by law, and no other social group in the Empire was so bent on protecting it as the Catholics were. When Bismarck eventually called off the *Kulturkampf*, the Zentrum immediately was prepared to cooperate with the authorities.[159]

The difference between Protestant and Catholic nationalism had further consequences. The Catholics did not participate in the annual commemoration of Sedan or any other national celebrations, nor erect any national monuments. Their clergy emphasized the state rather than the nation in their moral teachings on patriotic duties. Leaders in the Zentrum bewailed that, "Life in the state was strained by incessant striving after the uniformity of a homogeneous state," and "the political and social calamity of militarism."[160]

When Bismarck instigated the *Kulturkampf,* some of his comments about the Zentrum did not make Catholic adherence to the nation any easier. He regarded the party as a "mobilization against the state" and claimed that the foundations of the state were threatened by two international parties, the Zentrum and the SPD.[161] With regards to the latter allegation, Bismarck could have a point. The demise of the Papal State provoked the pope into establishing a counter-offensive political organization among Catholic laymen, the *Comité de Genève*, which they themselves called "The Black International." As it later turned out, this proved detrimental for Catholic political activity in general, not to mention during the Nazi offensive.[162]

In 1874, the second *Reichstag*-election showed the strength of Catholic resistance to the *Kulturkampf*. The Zentrum had its best result ever, gaining 80 percent of the ballot in several constituencies. The leader, Ludwig Windthorst, asserted the party was meant to cross confessional borders and was not exclusively Catholic.[163] However, right up until the Nazi liquidation of the party in 1933, the number of Protestant followers remained minuscule.

Even before the formation of the party a network of various organizations, media, etc. had emerged: the *"Zentrumsturm."* The Catholic Church and the Zentrum were cornerstones.[164] The annual *Katoliktag* and the bishops' conferences in Munich-Freising (for southern Germany) and Fulda (for the rest of the country) bore great weight. In addition to the Zentrum, the most important organization was probably the *Volksverein für das katholische Deutschland* (The People's Association for Catholic Germany), formed in 1890.[165]

The *"Zentrumsturm"* subculture was distinct from Protestant culture, in expression and definitions of words. Catholics considered Protestant culture elitist, liberal, nationalist and guided by Enlightenment ideas.[166] The *"Zentrumsturm"* even survived—in tatters—the Nazi period.[167] Not all Catholic churchgoers were adherents of it; many students, plus adherents of "Reform Catholicism" and Old Catholicism, objected to its ultramontane character.[168] But it was precisely among these three groups of Catholics that resistance to Nazism was weakest, and Old Catholics were somewhat benign towards anti-Semitism during the Empire and Interwar period.

The *Kulturkampf* demonstrated how different the mentalities of the two confessions were. Catholics looked on it as a matter of defending religious rights, whereas it was seen by Protestants as a political response to Catholic encroachments,[169] meaning the Zentrum was thereby understood as a counterweight to the National Liberals: conservative, anti-modern and reactionary. In reality, they were not. Bismarck has been hailed as a pioneer of social policy, but to a great extent it was at the instigation of Zentrum politicians, and it was the child of a long tradition of Catholic social welfare. The Zentrum's policy was supported by Pope Leo XIII.[170] At the same time, SPD-leader August Bebel resisted Bismarck's policy, fearing the proletariat would be less interested in revolution.[171]

Adolf Stöcker, leader of the small Protestant anti-Semitic *Christlichsoziale Arbeiterpartei* (The Christian Social Workers' Party) and his Dutch colleague, Abraham Kuyper of the *Antirevolutionaire Partij*, both admitted that Christian Catholics were far more involved in social policy than their Protestant counterparts.[172] In some parts of Bavaria, the SPD and the Zentrum would occasionally cooperate to prevent liberal party victories, and the Zentrum was also accused of cooperation with the SPD in the *Reichstag* election in 1907.[173]

According to Walser Smith, French-based and Catholic-German nationalism differed from Protestant nationalism. Catholics wanted a Germany rooted in inherited traditions, not in future destinies; a nation drawing its strength from variation, not from a progressive march towards a higher cultural unity. Catholics claimed the political legitimacy to identities with older roots than the national state: kinship, region, religious communities, were given entities, self-evident and timeless.[174]

This is Werner Conze's description of Catholic nationalism:

> The national movement of the German Catholics is during the nineteenth century strong and filled with profound, historically reasoned self-consciousness, but nevertheless, always put on the defensive by "modern" Protestantism. The abolition of the German Federation and formation of the Bismarck-state under the notion "The Evangelical Empire" of the Hohenzollern dynasty delivered a serious blow to German bi-confessionality. The Catholic Austria was seceded, Catholics in the new state reduced to a minority of one third. They were injured, and felt injured, even threatened, when the "Kulturkampf" started. Not until its abolition did they feel strengthened once they had experienced their own perseverance, and then even attained a more intimate relationship to the German state.[175]

Not until the abolition of the *Kulturkampf* could ordinary Catholics take an interest in the specifically German Protestant nationalism and German cultural heritage of the new Empire.

After the end of Romanticism, Catholicism lost its cultural voice, particularly within language and poetry, so vital for Germans since the 18th century. The cultural split became obvious in the field of science. Catholics withdrew from science and education when confronted with the predominant spirit of indifference to, or even resistance to faith in high schools and universities where they met anti-Catholic education authorities and staff policies. Hence their level of education lagged. Peter Pulzer asserts that, although anti-Semitism was evident among German nationalists and imperialists in the Empire, anti-Catholicism was even more evident in the same milieus. It was especially obvious in debates about whether to discriminate against certain confessions when hiring public employees.[176] Not only the *Evangelischer Bund* and *Gustav Adolf Verein* opposed Catholics and their integration in the national fellowship. The *Reichsverband gegen die Sozialdemokratie* (National Association against social democracy), *Wehrverein* (Defense Association), *Antiultramontaner Reichsverband* (Antiultramontane National Association) and *Flottenverein* (Association of the Naval Fleet) followed suit.[177]

Catholic withdrawal from modern culture manifested itself in three fields: a bias towards tradition; fragmentation of the cultivation of culture, and a boycott of new fields of culture and science, which include the new Darwinist and racial theories. Catholics were almost absent from the fields of natural and technical science, philology and history, right up until the end of the nineteenth century.[178]

Hans Maier summarizes the relationship of German Catholics to the national movement and national State up to 1914 like this:

> It is right to claim that German Catholics in the nineteenth century, to be sure, were strong enough to re-erect the public state of the church, but they were not strong enough to attain decisive influence on the German conditions beyond their sheer defensive position. Their political program was sufficient to assert themselves, the defensive position, the protection of the minority. Beyond this, however, they did not succeed when they were confronted by mighty opponents, the national movement, or, more to the point, the shape of this movement in Germany.[179]

Both the Zentrum and the SPD supported German participation in WWI. However, whereas German nationalism was an integrated part of the nonsocialist Protestant identity and culture, it functioned as a phenomenological veneer among the subcultures of *clerical Catholicism* and *socialism*. Before the outbreak of war, Catholics were not regarded as citizens with full and equal rights.[180] During the war, Catholics loyally supported it, but a confessional split emerged anew afterwards, and a new term arose among Catholics: "Protestant National Spirit."[181]

ANTI-SEMITISM

Old and Modern Anti-Semitism

The craving for a uniform German religion led to anti-Catholicism and anti-Judaism among many of the early nationalists. It was embryonic already in the Enlightenment when rationalist Protestant theologians declared Judaism the origin of Christian orthodoxy, especially the Catholic variety. Schleiermacher, though not himself a rationalist, transferred this motif to significant parts of German nationalism.[182] Catholicism was deplored by fundamentalist nationalists as a religion both alien to the people and inspired by Jews; like Judaism, it was allegedly international and thereby hostile, both before and after unification, to the political ambitions of the nation. At the Reformation tricentennial, one theologian and historian talked matter-of-factly about the "Jewish-Pagan Theocracy" of the medieval and post-Reformation Catholic Church.[183]

Radical adherents of this view at the end of the century strongly asserted that the threat to the Empire was from the Black (Catholic), Red (socialist) and Golden (Jewish) Internationals. These were also the colors of the liberal ensign and representative of a French version of nationalism.[184] Catholicism was portrayed as the main bastion of "Jewish Christianity" in racist *völkisch* thinking.[185] "A universal Christian conspiracy against the truth was placed next to the universal Jewish conspiracy—a conspiracy documented by the *Protocols of the Elders of Zion*. With de Lagarde and others, this developed into a Catholic-Jesuit conspiracy linked, so they asserted, to the Jewish world conspiracy itself", according to George Mosse.[186]

To the amazement of Wolfgang Altgeld, even though religious, cultural and political anti-Catholicism was far more prevalent than anti-Semitism, no systematic research was done on it before the 1990s. Yet this many-faceted confessional conflict was still ongoing after the abolition of the *Kulturkampf*, dominating and straining the national-political discussion.[187]

The first step on German soil towards emancipation of Jews was made in Austria in 1782, and Prussia prepared to follow suit. However, the gradual French takeover from 1795 onwards caused a reaction and anti-French attitudes became entangled with emancipation. Many German nationalists perceived a "Gaulish and Jewish intellectuality" versus a "naive, natural, artless" German one as the reason for the differences between the two cultures. The "French-Jewish" was a superficial "*esprit*" and was in profound opposition to the German "*Geist*."[188]

Almost all nationalists envisioned disastrous consequences for German popular and national-political evolution should Jews be granted equal civil rights to Germans. Some, therefore, called for a "holy crusade" against "Frenchmen, *Junkers*, Papists, and Jews."[189] Others even proposed their extermination.[190] Anti-Semitism had become so common by the end of the nineteenth century, that *Meyers Konverstionslexikon* called fiercely anti-Semitic Jakob Fries a "man, teacher and national politician of the noblest and purest character."[191]

During the 1820s, the trends in the predominantly Protestant nationalism had become so conspicuous that the Jewish philosopher Saul Ascher predicted

Catholic Germany and the Catholic Church would prove a bastion against the "German theocracy". He claimed this despite being a declared opponent of religious dogmatism and of clerical hierarchy and a typical representative of the German late Enlightenment. As early as 1794, Ascher accused Fichte of breeding an "entirely new variant of hatred for Jews, cloaking their hatred in the philosophical guise of "critical reason" in lieu of religion, making a tremendous advance in "the science of hating Judaism and its followers."[192] Ascher's explanation of the situation in the 1820s was that the national-religious nationalism was a result of Protestant secularization and consequently of free religiosity. In Catholic Germany, however, he saw no potential for such political "mysticism" gaining a foothold, due to the presence and power of the Church with its many integrated festivals, cultic sacraments, and other religious features. No wonder Ascher's *Die Germanomanie* was one of the five books burned on the Protestant students' bonfire in 1817 at Wartburg.[193]

It has been claimed that Luther's anti-Jewish attitude provided an alibi for anti-Semitism in German Protestantism, and truly prominent Protestant cultural personages all did express the anti-Jewish sentiment. These included Herder, Kant, Schleiermacher, and Hegel. There were even racist remarks in the case of Kant and Hegel.[194] As mentioned earlier, however, Calvinists in the 1930s elections were equally pro-Nazi as the Lutherans, even though Calvin in his later years had nothing but good to say about Jews.[195]

In the course of the nineteenth century emancipation gained ground despite opposition, and the constitution of the Empire secured equal rights for all.

Modern, racist anti-Semitism began in the mid-1870s after the economic setback in the wake of the war against France because some Jews had been involved in corruption during the first years of boom. Historians disagree whether this has any connection to old-style anti-Semitism, although both were clearly Protestant based.[196] Large parts of the population were involved, and they were mobilized by media and itinerant campaigners. Intellectuals were still active and the most prominent of them was Heinrich von Treitschke, the history professor.

The strife between Treitschke and the historian Theodor Mommsen, even though the latter was also slightly anti-Semitic, left its mark on the academic milieu of the 1880s.[197] However, it was the court pastor Adolf Stöcker who managed to influence the populace. He organized the *Christlichsoziale Arbeiterpartei* (CSAP) in 1878. It had anti-Semitism as one of the main aims of the program and can be regarded as the first of the many pre-Fascist parties and organizations in Germany, combatting liberalism, capitalism and decadence. Instead, they promoted social radicalism, corporative solutions and patriotism. Theologically, however, Stöcker represented a neo-Lutheran orthodoxy, and from 1892 he edited the main Protestant magazine in Germany,

Deutsche Evangelische Kirchenzeitung. Later, this publication welcomed the arrival of Hitler to power in 1933.[198]

Although modern anti-Semitism developed into racism, Stöcker based his reasoning on neither racism nor religion. His accusation was that the Jews were void of religion, hostile to the church, liberal, materialistic and "Mammonist". This caused them to deteriorate morally in matters of marriage and charity, and allowed them to be vehicles of various unjust international economic systems. Both individualistic and internationally minded at the same time, they knew nothing of patriotism. "Modern" Jewish culture undermined the inner unity of the State, the Christian-Protestant character and conservative order of society, in short: the values of the Empire![199]

Stöcker's influence in the 1880s and 1890s was immense even if the CSAP flopped. This "uncrowned king of Berlin" campaigned in great parts of the country in a manner that would be reminiscent of Hitler's campaigns. His influence was spread over the *whole* of Protestant Germany, according to a Danish encyclopedia.[200] A Swedish encyclopedia says he "fought with burning entrancement and incomparable agitational capability, . . . was a real personality as a religious speaker," and he "had a preference for pompous display and weakness for personal ovations".[201]

Contemporaries agree that Stöcker's personality and fervor had a remarkable effect on his audiences. He was hailed as the "second Luther." "Indeed they must have had, for this alone can account for his success," writes Pulzer.[202] "The anti-Semitic bug spread in an especially rapid way" in precisely the associations of Protestant clergymen.[203] *Fischer Lexicon* asserts that Stöcker's views on socialism and Jewishness were still decisive for the public views of the Protestant churches several decades after his death in 1908.[204] A number of other historians also emphasize Stöcker's immense influence on various segments of the German Protestant population and his significance for German political and cultural development, including the disastrous polarization of society before and after WWI.[205] That all three of the bishops, Otto Dibelius, Hans Meiser and Theophil Wurm, who were harassed and imprisoned during the *Third Reich*, had been strongly influenced by him, tells a lot about the scope of his ideological bequest to German Protestantism.[206]

Partly influenced by Stöcker's efforts, several anti-Semitic organizations popped up in the 1880s and 1890s. None of them had the close relationship to the church that Stöcker had, some were even anti-Christian. Others of these parties had an anti-Catholic program and one was even based on the *Führer* principle. For the most part, they were ephemeral affairs, splitting up, reforming, fusing, changing names, and dissolving. What they had in common was that none of them had a substantial following among Ultramonanists. "Reform Catholics," however, had supported one of them.[207]

One of the main parties in the *Reichstag*, the *Konservative Partei*, also adopted an anti-Semitic program—in 1892.[208] Then in 1899, the *Deutsche Reformpartei* adopted into its program the following:

> Thanks to the development of our modern means of communication, the Jewish Question ought to be an issue of universal character. As such it should be, together with the other peoples, solved jointly and ultimately through total isolation and (if necessary) the ultimate extermination of the Jewish people. ("und als solche . . . , wenn die Notwehr es gebietet, schliessliche Vernichtung des Judenvolkes gelöst werden.")[209]

In addition to the great KP's tacit acceptance of mild anti-Semitism, it could also be traced in the rightist-liberal parties, though publicly they dissociated themselves.[210] The close voter proximity between liberals, anti-Semites (and later, the Nazis) is visible in Saxony as early as the 1890s. The two liberal parties, the *Nationalliberale* and the *Freisinnige Partei*, got 112,000 and 57,000 votes respectively in 1890, but the anti-Semites only received 4,700. Three years on, in 1893, the KP experienced a minor setback and the SPD had an upswing, but the two liberal parties now only got 35,000 and 30,000 votes, while the anti-Semites got 116,000. So, the anti-Semitic voters must have come from the ranks of the *Nationalliberale* and the *Freisinnige Partei*. Forty years on, the Nazi Party got 45 percent of the Saxony vote.

Apart from the churches, sects and political parties had little impact compared to organizations such as the *Alldeutscher Verband*, probably the most influential one. It promoted traditional "German values": Protestantism, conservatism, nationalism, militarism, and imperialism. Anti-Semitism was a contentious issue and Jews were accepted in the leadership even after Heinrich Class, an anti-Semite, became the leader in 1908.[211] However, the organization soon developed into an anti-Semitic fighting organization and was one of the most important precursors of Nazism. Heinrich Class repeated the menace of the "Black-Red-Golden/Yellow" internationals. Certainly, the "Yellow" (Jewish) was the most dangerous of them, but the "Black" (ultramontane) peril and its Zentrum had to be arraigned because it defended the rights of the minorities in society, and "in colonial matters were so bent on defending the rights of colored people that it bordered on treason against our race."[212]

The *Alldeutscher Verband* never had many members, but several of them were prominent in numerous other organizations and it functioned as a kind of umbrella-organization for them: for the anti-Catholic organizations, for the *Kolonialverein* and a lot of veterans' organizations and for the *Deutsche Arbeiterpartei* (The German Workers' Party), precursor of the Nazi Party in Hapsburg Bohemia. Several of these organizations aimed to reach the students and young people from the bourgeoisie. The members of the *All-

deutscher Verband belonged to different parties, but all of them Protestant dominated. Sixty members of it were elected to the *Reichstag* between 1894–1912, but none from parties that later became Weimar-coalition parties. An *Alldeutsche Vereinigung* was set up within the *Reichstag* in 1901 and it had 32 representatives from various parties, one of them would later become a prominent politician in the 1920s: Gustav Stresemann.[213]

The plan to reach students and youth with anti-Semitic propaganda proved a success. In the 1880s Stöcker could, with satisfaction, experience students showing up in droves at his gatherings.[214] The mood of discussions became vulgarized and radicalized to such a degree that even anti-Semitic lecturers were amazed. The first specifically anti-Semitic student association was *Kyffhäuserverband*, which had its base in the Protestant north. At first, 50 percent of the members are said to have been students of theology, but this percentage fell later and the heavy influence of Stöcker was replaced by anti-Semitic racism.[215] Later anti-Semitism gained a foothold in almost every other student association, including Christian ones. This was true even for Catholic associations, but in a milder form.[216]

Anti-Semitism soon spread to trade unions, professional bodies, sports and outdoor life organizations, in addition to the *Evangelischer Bund, Evangelische Jugend und Jungmännervereine* and *Evangelische Arbeitervereine*.[217] Church leaders in the Protestant clergymen's associations had to urge, as early as the 1890s, a curb on involvement in anti-Semitic agitation, but anti-Semitic articles became ever more common in all kinds of Christian publications, especially after WWI.[218]

Most Protestant "*Mittelstand*"-organizations were influenced by anti-Semitism, whereas among the corresponding Catholic ones it hardly existed in any of them.[219] After 1900, an outdoor scouting organization, the *Freie Deutsche Jugendbewegung* (Free German Youth Movement) was formed. It was also known as the *Wandervogel*—(Wandering Bird) movement. It was based on the ideas of *völkisch*—and Protestant—philosophers such as de Lagarde and Langbehn and had pre-Nazi features. It primarily recruited Protestants, and some historians claim it excluded Jews, although this has not been verified.[220] Several other youth organizations, both Christian and secular, also arose. They were backed by clergymen and teachers and influenced by anti-Semitism to various extents. Thus, hatred and polarization jaundiced the younger generation in the time up to the outbreak of WWI.[221] The Protestant farmers' associations, the *Bund der Landwirte, Mitteldeutscher Bauernverein*, and *Deutscher Bauernbund*, were anti-Semitic, though this was discernible in the Catholic equivalents, too.[222]

Anti-Semitism influenced public employment through open "*Berufsverbot*" (Prohibition of employment). This term was especially used about exclusion of communists as employees in the Federal Republic.) in most of the 25 (later 26) German states, against the recruitment of Jewish military officers, judges and, often, teachers. There were noteworthy exceptions. Bavaria and Baden were the only states which employed Jewish officers. Again Bavaria and Baden, in addition to Hamburg, were the only states which employed Jews as judges up until 1907, when Prussia followed suit. Prussia had a handful of Jewish teachers in primary schools, and somewhat more in high schools in some of the Prussian cities, as did Bavaria and Baden. Only in Baden was a Jew appointed minister of the state: Moritz Ellstätter, who was Minister of Finance from 1868–1893. As we see, the states giving employment to Jews in any real number were Bavaria and Baden, the only states with Catholic majorities, and Hamburg, which was strongly socialist. Besides these, only Protestant Prussia had some few meagre openings for Jews. Other states excluded Jews totally from all public employment. These included Saxony (95 percent Protestant), Brunswick (95 percent Protestant) and Hessen (67 percent Protestant). Thus, three, or at most four states gave public employment to Jews, three forbade it, and the remaining nineteen did not, in fact, employ any. In 22 states, all with a Protestant-majority, Jews experienced a *de facto* or explicit "*Berufsverbot.*"[223]

In the military, even Catholics were discriminated. Although 36 percent of the population were Catholics, only 4 percent of the higher ranks were. Hence, when it came to discrimination, Catholics and Jews found themselves in the same boat.[224] Speaking of which, the most restrictive service of all was the Navy. No Jew was ever employed as an officer, and very few Catholics were.[225]

During the years leading to 1914, a specific Protestant cultural syndrome comes into view, one we may fairly call the "The German Protestant rightist Syndrome." It was closed or alien to Jews, socialists and Catholic churchgoers and made itself gradually felt, in moderate or radical, eventually in a *völkisch* manner, in the media and even in literary and cultural associations and gatherings, but not least: in the student world.[226]

During the Empire, three parties formed the political bulwark against "the anti-Semitic flood," and rightist syndrome generally. The three were: the leftist liberal parties, which were the refuge of most Jews, the SPD, and the politically Catholic Zentrum. In the succeeding Weimar era, exactly the same pattern repeated itself.[227]

Anti-Semitism abated after the outbreak of WWI, but in 1917 the congress of the Jewish *Centralverein* anxiously commented that anti-Semitism would become widespread in the future and that the German version differed from the Russian one in that "Russia is perhaps still an uncivilized land of pogroms, but these defects will be ended after a while with its contact with the western countries. In Germany anti-Semitism is a scientific conviction, an understanding of the world. Erudite books are written there about anti-Semitism and they are more dangerous than a pogrom."[228]

Their anxiety was justified: in the wake of the post WWI chaos, anti-Semitism exploded. The racist aspect, supposedly based on modern research, came to the fore.[229] More than a hundred more or less anti-Semitic associations and armed groups mushroomed. The *Deutschvölkischer Schutz und Trutzbund* (German-Volkish League for Protection and Defiance) was the most important and numerically strong. Bavaria was the core state of early anti-Semitic harassment, probably a result of the over-representation of Jews in the Revolutionary Government in the spring of 1919, and even Catholics, especially the "Reformed," took part in harassment.[230]

This racist new anti-Semitism found some followers among Protestant clergy in the early 1920s. Organized clerical anti-Semitism based on racist principles had its origin in the 400th anniversary of the Reformation in 1917 where "95 new theses" were adopted. § 43 read: "The new research on race has ultimately opened our eyes to the detrimental effects of mixing the blood of Teutonic and non-Teutonic peoples." Some pastors were radical to the extreme; Karl Gerecke, writing in 1920, wanted the "death knell" to chime for "Judah" and "to strangle the Jews and throw them into the furnace!"[231]

The new trend of degrading the Old Testament and "purifying" the New of "Jewish" elements and amalgamating it with "Teutonic piety" was rejected by most theologians in the early 1920s,[232] but after a while the trend influenced them little by little. Even the prominent Ernst Troeltsch, who was theologically and politically liberal, expressed himself in an anti-Semitic manner.[233]

International clerical conferences were held between 1925 and 1930. Some of them were about missions among the Jews, and Jewish-friendly resolutions were made in them, but they were ignored or treated with indifference by the Germans.[234]

During the entire Weimar era, church leaders did nothing to stem the increasing anti-Semitism among clerics and laymen. Anti-Semitic expressions from prominent opponents of the Nazis and the DC, people such as Martin Niemöller, Karl Barth, Walter Künneth and the bishops Otto Dibelius and Hans Meiser, and even Heinrich Grüber, the leader of a Jewish charity organization, indicate how profoundly and comprehensively entrenched this attitude had become in the German Protestantism in the 1930s. After the Nazi breakthrough, the radical tendency was aggravated.[235] Anti-Semitism was even found in the *Rheinische Mission*.[236]

When some radical theologians indicated that extermination of the Jews could be an acceptable solution to the "problem," the American leader of *The Universal Christian Council for Life and Work* protested in a letter to German church leaders, who felt so affronted by the protest, they wished for no further contact.[237]

Nevertheless, there was some resistance to anti-Semitism that did exist among Protestant theologians and clerics. Eduard Lamparter, a pastor in Stuttgart, was the most prominent of them. He rejected the race theories and locked horns with Schleiermacher, Stöcker and even Harnack. Several theologians supported him, Karl Barth included.[238]

The Catholic-Jewish Relationship and the Catholic Parties

The Vatican and Catholic theologians generally showed an ambivalent attitude to Jewishness during the nineteenth century, and the Vatican pursued a policy which shifted between liberalizing and restriction in the relationship to Jews. Its anti-Semitism at the end of the century was partly due to prominent Jews that had been active in anticlerical measures in Rome after the unification of Italy. However, it is also obvious that the Church would not be identified with the new militant and racist anti-Semitism. Catholic anti-Semitism was primarily restricted to what they perceived as detrimental features connected with the liberal spirit in modern society, with anarchism, church hatred, Freemasonry, and ritual murder. The most important contribution to modern anti-Semitism from German Catholicism was probably anti-Talmudism, which originated among theologians.[239]

The twentieth century saw a more friendly policy towards Jews under Popes Pius X (1903–1914), Benedict XV (1914–1922) and Pius XI (1922–1939); the latter even condemned anti-Semitism publicly.[240] In 1927, Pius is said to have degraded the French Cardinal Louis Billot because of his sympathy with the anti-Semitic *Action Francaise*.[241] He had good contact with prominent Jews, and in the 1930s was involved in promoting Jewish emigration from Nazi-governed territories and resisting anti-Semitism in several ways.[242]

Hubert Wolf, who has studied the Vatican archives accessible since 2003, concludes that all nuances of relationship towards Jews were to be found within the curia in the 1920s, but that the negative statements that existed, were all void of *racist* anti-Semitism.[243]

Casual research of German papers does reveal anti-Jewish articles even in Catholic ones, primarily in *Germania* in the 1870s and 1880s. However, these petered out later, and in 1894 *Germania* changed policy and condemned anti-Semitism after criticism from other Catholic papers.[244] It is possible to discern regional differences in Catholic ranks. Catholics in Prussian Rhineland and Westphalia seemed to be more liberal than their fellows in Bavaria, which may be due to the former's proximity to a more liberal and advanced Western Europe and to themselves being a minority in a Protestant state.[245]

Mainly due to the Zentrum's first leaders, Ludwig Windthorst and his successor, Ernst Lieber, modern anti-Semitism never gained a foothold in the party when it arose in the 1870s. Windthorst bears much of the credit for the emancipation of Jews in the North German Federation in 1869. Those Catholics who did get carried away by anti-Semitism in the 1870s did so because the bulk of Jewish politicians at that time were liberals who supported the anti-Catholic *Kulturkampf*.[246] In 1880 there was a totally futile effort to organize an inter-confessionnal counterpart of Stöcker's Protestant party.[247]

The Zentrum supported Jews and their interests in the imperial *Reichstag* on several occasions in various matters:[248] The party asserted rather modernist political ideas. To the above mentioned social radical measures in the 1880s could be added such as constitutional conformity; restriction of the power of political authorities; state governance by law; democracy; tolerance and freedom of religion and equal rights of religions and races. All of these were continual hallmarks of the Zentrum up until its liquidation in 1933. After 1900, the party, together with the SPD and leftist-liberals, promoted ministers' answerability to the *Reichstag*.[249] Despite Windthorst's and Lieber's efforts, anti-Jewishness could be found in some Catholic papers after 1900, but this phenomenon differed from Protestant anti-Semitism inasmuch as it was not racist but economically based, nor directed against Jews as such but rather "Jewish spirit" and "Jewish media."[250] For Catholics, Jews were "fellow citizens" and they rejected the racist anti-Semitism that Protestants had amalgamated with nationalism. As the question of race gradually became so vital to Protestant anti-Semitism, it constituted a significant difference in the mentality of the two confessions. Catholics never conflated the "Jewish question" with nationalism.[251]

Rudolf Lill sums up the relationship of Catholics to Jews in the Empire:

> The leading political representatives for the German Catholics rejected every kind of discrimination of Jews. Supported by some bishops they fervently opposed the demagogy of radical adversaries of Jews. Racist anti-Semitism was rejected outright by all professional advocates of German Catholicism. Following different factors prevented its entry: recognition of and reverence for the Old Testament as divine revelation, the knowledge of the inclusion of the Jews in God's plan of salvation and hence respect for the orthodox Jews, and, ultimately, a cosmopolitical restraining against the radical nationalism which in its essence was connected with anti-Semitism.[252]

There were other factors hindering racist anti-Semitism creeping into Catholicism: the uniform, international and universal structure of a church with members from all continents, a clergy who moved between various countries, and the early perception by Catholics of the fundamentally anti-Christian tendencies of *völkisch* racism.[253]

Racist anti-Semites were infuriated by the Catholic resistance and attacked them by lumping them together as part of a despicable syndicate of Jews, socialists and liberals.[254]

The three non-Ultramontanist Catholic groups, German-Catholics, Old Catholics and "Reform Catholics," had varying attitudes to anti-Semitism. The German-Catholics disappeared in the 1850s and were the only Catholic group boasting no sign of anti-Semitism, and their former leaders even accused the Ultramontanists of catering to anti-Semites. The Old Catholics did as well until one of their own representatives was elected to the *Reichstag* for the strongly anti-Semitic *Reformpartei*. Both the Old and the "Reform" Catholics were influenced by the "*Völkische Bewegung*," probably partly because they wished to distance themselves from Ultramontanism. In the eyes of Old Catholic Joseph Moog, a bishop in 1912, "Romans" and Jesuits were race-desecrators.[255] The Old Catholics showed a pronounced pro-Nazi attitude during the Third Reich and favored the creation of a *Nationalkirche*, as also several Nazis did.[256]

The Zentrum's rejection of anti-Semitism became even more pronounced during the Weimar republic. As early as December 1918 the party passed a program which called for "equal treatment of the members and institutions of the various religious denominations in every field of the public life." Thanks to their efforts, these passages were included in the constitution of August 1919.[257] Because of the new circumstances after WWI, the party made a new bid to establish an inter-confessional Christian party with an opening even for Jews. Apart from partial success in the first election in 1919, the effort proved futile, but in 1930 Georg Kareski was nominated for the *Reichstag* election as the first orthodox Jew. In both the *Reichstag* and in regional state assemblies, the Zentrum made clear statements in defense of freedom of faith and conscience for all citizens, equal rights for all religious denominations, and rejection of every kind of legislative exception. Hugo am Zehnhoff from the Zentrum clamped down on anti-Semitic expressions when he was Prussian minister of Justice, which made co-workers of Nazi Alfred Rosenberg call Am Zehnhoff's directives "a special protection of rights" for Jews and evidence of "the Zentrum's absolute Jewish affiliation."[258]

In the Zentrum it was noted that the anti-Semitism of the "*Völkische Bewegung*" was to a great extent linked to anti-Catholicism or even anti-Christianity in general, and it could trace this tendency as far back as the *Kulturkampf*. Jewish organizations also noticed this.[259] In *Der Fels* (*Apologetische Rundschau*), the publication of the *Apologetische Abteilung des Volksvereins für das katholische Deutschland*, it was claimed: " The German Catholics have generally participated less in the contemporary increasing harassment of Jews, due to their political representation in the Zentrum explicitly disapproving of it and the bishops in word and deed several times have condemned it; there will hardly be any Catholic persons of note in Germany who accepts anti-Semitism". A resolution against anti-Semitism was passed at the Zentrum's national congress in 1922 where the party's *Reichskanzler* of 1920–1921, Konstantin Fehrenbach, crassly condemned anti-Semitism and *"Ariertum"* (i.e."worship of the Aryan man"). A human rights' association commented with satisfaction that the resolution was "one of the most excellent and important resolutions ever."[260]

There was at least one Protestant among the Zentrum's publicists: Adam Röder, member of the *Reichstag* from 1924–1928 and publisher of a paper. Röder was one of very few Protestants who fervently confronted every kind of racial theory.[261] Interestingly enough, even he admitted he had once been an adherent of an "ideal anti-Semitism" having feared that "the German essence" could be impaired by the Jews. However, he considered anti-Semites fanatics and ignorant people who used the Jews as scapegoats. (As it transpires, even rightist radicals corroborated this. At the end of WWI, the leader of the *Alldeutscher Verband*, Heinrich Class, encouraged members in the prevailing distress to use the Jews as lightning-rods for all injustice.)

Hardly any Catholics, apart from Hans Rost, were anxious about a Jewish detrimental effect on "the German essence," and the idea seems to have been rather irrelevant to Catholics as a whole, indicating yet another fundamental Catholic - Protestant divide in the perception of nationalism that had developed since the time of Herder. The notion of "German essence" had its origin in a slogan: *"Bei dem Deutschen Wesen wird die Welt genesen"* ("By the German essence the world will become healthy"). Adherents of the unification in 1871 had tried to define the notion in order to identify what was genuinely German about the newly unified state.[262] The following ingredients were thought of as essential: respect for tradition; the effort to preserve what had emerged over the centuries; respect for the God-willed authorities; the will to put the collective fellowship above the individual desire and to serve this fellowship in the place where one belonged.

The antithetical "un-German," and particularly "Jewish" essence comprised a belief in the existence of common ideas, equal rights for all, and the promotion of individual interests at the expense of the common good. This mentality of stereotyped and polarized thinking was probably reinforced among Protestants by the extensive discussion about "essence" after 1900.[263]

The most prominent Zentrum politician in the Weimar era was Wilhelm Marx, party leader from 1922–1928, *Reichskanzler* 1923–1924, and 1926–1928, presidential candidate in 1925, and leader of the Catholic mass organization the *Volksverein für das katholische Deutschland*. He was an outspoken opponent of anti-Semitism. However, when he was called on by anxious Jewish adherents of Zentrum soon after Hitler became *Reichskanzler*, he was too naïve. He set their minds at rest, remarking he did not think any constitutional restrictions for races would be passed in the near future. Marx's successor as party leader 1928–1933, Father Ludwig Kaas, was also an opponent of anti-Semitism. After the Nazi takeover he was a go-between for the contact between a Jewish organization and the bishop of Berlin, who then forwarded information abroad.[264]

The Zentrum supported the Jewish right to slaughter animals in accordance with Deuteronomy 12:21 and the right of soldiers to celebrate the Sabbath.[265] Together with representatives from the two other "Weimar" parties, the SPD and the DDP, politicians from the Zentrum, among them the leaders Marx and Kaas and of the successor party CDU, Konrad Adenauer, were directly involved in Zionist policies to promote Jewish immigration to Palestine.[266] From the election in 1928 until 1933, a variety of publications were issued by the Zentrum and Catholic individuals that confronted Nazi anti-Semitism specifically.[267] As one might expect, Nazis responded accordingly. In the election campaign in 1930, the Zentrum was more heavily attacked than the KPD or the "Jew-party" DDP, and after the election, where the Zentrum made gains while the DDP collapsed, a Nazi commented: "Jewry is satisfied. Since the ever more ramshackle and shrunken social democracy, and *Staatspartei* (earlier the DDP) has shrunken to a tenth and therefore has nothing to do with any "state," it has found a new group of Jew-protectors: the most Christian Zentrum!"[268] Despite the Zentrum being clearly against anti-Semitism, the Catholic Church's opposition to anti-Semitism is regarded as having carried even more weight and remained the only significant opposition after 1932.[269]

Bavarian Catholics did not originally oppose anti-Semitism as much as Catholics in other parts of the country. There were both promoters and opponents among them, though being Catholics, the proponents were not racist and definitely a minority. The American historian Robert S. Levy asserts that "The inability of the Anti-Semites to gain a foothold in Bavaria, . . . was largely a result of the Centre Party and Church hierarchy."[270] There was a temporary shift towards anti-Semitism in the BVP—the Zentrum's successor party in that state after WWI—in the wake of the revolutionary government in 1919. However, it was still not racist anti-Semitism. The secretary general of the BVP made his excuse after WWII by saying all parties in Bavaria were more or less under the influence of anti-Semitism at the time, even the leftists. Even a few Zentrum papers joined in the BVP papers' anti-Semitic rhetoric during the peak years of crisis, 1923 and 1924.[271] However, such writings later gradually vanished from Catholic papers. In addition to the reaction to the harsh Nazi anti-Semitism, the Bavarian BVP-premier Heinrich Held (1924–1933), Cardinal Michael Faulhaber and Father Erhard Schlund in Munich, all deserve credit for causing anti-Semitism among Bavarian Catholics to cease.²⁷²

During the election campaigns in 1932, several parties and organizations cooperated in joint opposition to Nazi anti-Semitism: the Jewish *Centralverein*, the BVP, the Catholic *Bayerischer Christlicher Bauernverein*, the SPD, the socialist trade unions and the greatest mass movement in Germany, the *Reichsbanner*. The secretary general of the BVP asserted: "Probably nowhere has Rosenberg more severely been combatted than in Bavaria."²⁷³ Incidentally, in its campaign the BVP referred to the absence of anti-Semitism in Fascist Italy.²⁷⁴

The study of victims of anti-Semitism is probably the most accurate way to discover the true relationship of churchgoers from the organized Catholic Church to anti-Semitism and Jews. Obviously, very few Jews regarded the Zentrum as a political alternative in the early Empire. The party's focus on Catholic rights during the *Kulturkampf* did not attract the many liberal and urban Jews. They regarded the Zentrum as rural, reactionary and unpatriotic. 60 to 70 percent preferred leftist liberal parties and 10 to 15 percent the *Nationalliberale*. Another reason was the poor relationship between Jews and Catholic Poles, who joined hands with German brothers-in-faith and were subjected to even harsher restrictions during the *Kulturkampf*.²⁷⁵

The attitude of the Jewish media to the Catholic party gradually changed during the 1880s. The *Kulturkampf* was over and modern anti-Semitism came on stage. Windthorst and Lieber rejected anti-Semitism in the Zentrum while, after the turn of the century, the *Nationalliberale* did not, or at least did not consistently, reject anti-Semitism. By the election campaign of 1912, the Jewish paper *Israelit* openly encouraged support for the Zentrum. This change of heart among German Jews with regards to political Catholicism led to increasing support from 1867 on. In the period from 1867 to 1878, which stretched from the North German Federation to unification, 1 to 2 percent of the Jews voted the Zentrum (before 1870: the *Katholische Fraktion*). From 1879 to 1892 the number was 2 to 4 percent. From 1893 to 1902 the results were 5 to 6 percent, and from 1903 to 1914 the results were 5 to 7 percent.²⁷⁶

With their friendly attitude to Jews becoming ever more pronounced after WWI, the Zentrum gained even more support from the Jewish community. (For reasons outlined above, this naturally did not apply to the BVP until 1924). Heinrich Krone, the Vice Secretary General of the Zentrum and one of the "fathers" of the CDU after WWII, became the last leader of the Jewish *Abwehrverein* before its dissolution in 1933.²⁷⁷ After 1930, several Jewish rabbis openly supported the Zentrum, probably because the Zentrum and the BVP were the only parties which still supported Jewish religious interests.²⁷⁸ In national and regional elections in 1932 organizations recommending support for Jewish-friendly parties were formed. At least 25 percent of the Jews are said to have voted the Zentrum, and in Bavaria the BVP was their main party of preference.[279]

Uwe Mazura concludes that the attitude of the Zentrum to anti-Semitism and Nazi policy towards Jews was consistent. Firstly, its representatives felt that the fight "against Judah today," would be "against Rome tomorrow," as some anti-Semitic parties during the Empire had already wished. Windhorst and Lieber gave an early warning of the danger. Secondly, from its beginning, the Zentrum had been the advocate of Jewish emancipation and constitutional rights of minorities in international law. In fact, this had already happened with its predecessor, the *Katholische Fraktion*, during the 1850s and 1860s. Thirdly, their religious convictions logically led to a condemnation of hatred campaigns when they appeared after WWI. Christianity proscribed racist agitation and proclaimed tolerance towards people. The two slogans of the Zentrum "*Mit Gott für Wahrheit, Recht und Freiheit*" (With God for truth, rights and liberty) and "*Justitia fundamentum regnorum*" (Justice is the foundation of government) sum up the attitude of political Catholicism towards the Jews.[280] Naturally, after Hitler became a dictator in March 1933, the Zentrum and the BVP were mainly concerned about their own self-preservation; the Jews were left out in the cold.[281]

RACISM

Anti-Slavism

German anti-Slavism seems to have started around 1800, and the accusation of lacking "culture" and "history" was leveled against them. Even Hegel concurred with it. This criticism was combined with anxiety about perceived "barbaric" tendencies of the "race," and specifically of the Russians. By the mid-century, anti-Slavism became a common element within German conservatism and liberalism, whereas the conservatives had been pro-Russian and the liberals pro-Polish before. Marx and Engels underwent the same change of heart as the liberals. Soon after the unification—in keeping with elements of *völkisch* ideology—repressive measures were taken against the Poles in eastern Prussian provinces, a policy which was intensified up to WWI. It would seem anti-Slavism and anti-Semitism were already combined during the Empire, especially in policies against the Polish "Eastern Jews." Even the small and isolated Sorbian minority in Prussian Lausitz was subjected to this hysteria. This minority, which was confessionally divided, was supported by Catholic clerics against efforts to Germanize them.[282]

The SPD did not follow Marx and Engels in their anti-Slavism. Together with the Zentrum it became the protector of Polish interests.[283] The Zentrum's policy was motivated both by solidarity with their Polish brothers in the faith and the support of national minorities in the Prussian state. In Upper Silesia, where both Germans and Poles were Catholics, Bismarck's policy failed in a most embarrassing way because of the obviously opposite effect it had: the "Polonization" of Germans instead of the Germanization of Poles![284]

Colonizing "the East" was later to become a core element in the Nazi "*Lebensraum*" (living space) policy. For example, after the occupation of Norway, Norwegian "Aryan" youths were recruited to settle as farmers in the western occupied parts of the Soviet Union in 1943 and 1944.[285]

It could be considered paradoxical that the Polish Masurians so overwhelmingly voted Nazi in the elections of the 1930s. It seems to be due to their integration in the Prussian state, its history and its mentality ever since the Middle Ages and the Reformation. To the astonishment of the WWI victors, when League of Nations held a referendum offering them the opportunity to join the new Polish state, only 3 percent were in favor of seceding from Germany. Thus, only the Catholic Poles, who had become Prussian citizens after the conquest of Austrian Silesia and the dismembering of the Polish state in the eighteenth century, were subject to anti-Slavism.

Racism and "Herrenmensch" (Superior Man)

In Germany, a synthesis of the static and pessimistic race theories of Gobineau and the more dynamic and optimistic theories of Darwin amalgamated.[286] The breakthrough of racist anti-Semitism came in 1881 with the Protestant Eugen Dühring's *Die Judenfrage* (The Jewish Question). The theories of the theosophist pioneer Helena Blavatsky, who was influenced by eastern mysticism and Darwin's theories, were also of great importance for the Protestants' understanding of race. She popularized the notion of a "spiritual struggle" between various races and asserted the superiority of the Aryan race. Semites (Jews and Arabs) were Aryans according to her, but belonged on a spiritually lower level than the Indo-Europeans.[287] She had a marked influence on the founders of Ariosophy and thus, the occult precursors of Nazism: Rudolf von Sebottendorff and the Austrian Catholics Guido von List and Lanz von Liebenfels, with Liebenfels as a critical member.[288]

As Darwin was on the *Index* and Blavatsky's theosophy contradicted Catholic orthodoxy, Catholics were generally less exposed than Protestants to their theories and similar theories to theirs. More specific race hygienic projects were evolved by scientists among the Protestants such as doctor and zoologist Ludwig Woltmann, anthropologist Otto Ammon and especially

Doctor Alfred Ploetz. Of Woltmann, it is said, "He hated what he called the international Catholic conspiracy." Ammon was a leading member of *Alldeutscher Verband*. Ploetz was a member of Ernst Haeckel's anti-Catholic Monist Association, the militarist *Deutsche Vaterlandspartei* in 1917 and eventually, of the Nazi Party. Nazi race hygiene and euthanasia can trace its origins to these three scientists according to Berding.[289] He further claims that most of the pre-Nazi and *völkisch* organizations were based "on a Manichaean world view of an eternal combat between the good and the evil, a view of history as Teutonic-Jewish racial opposition pervading the whole history of the West and the concept of a fatal menace to the German people through the Jewish danger."[290]

Uriel Tal mentions several representatives of political and racist anti-Semitism and claims that they had a common understanding of anti-Semitism. It was not only in the form of a rejection of Jews and Judaism but also of criticism and even rejection of Christianity and religion generally with a special emphasis on Catholicism.[291] In short, this was the same tendency seen among Protestant anti-Semites of the early nineteenth century.

The judicial expert Felix Dahn particularly made a profound impact on the spread of racism among Protestants. His family background was Protestant, but he converted to Pantheism and Monism and combatted Catholicism. Dahn also took on Herder's view of the connection between races and judicial systems. Rejecting Roman law, he concluded, "Therefore, there is no socalled natural law, no innate rights, no so-called human rights." All the rights of a human being were subjugated to his people's rights.[292] His book *Kampf um Rom* (Battle about Rome) from the 1930s became the second most read book at that time, with 110 editions. Hitler called Dahn the only professor who has "contributed something creative."[293]

The idea of Germans as superior people had seeped deeply into the mentality by the 1930s, even into the evangelical part of the population. In my view, this, together with the idea of "the German essence," was a major gulf between German Protestants and Catholics. An article in 1931 in *Volksdienst* (Service to the People), the paper of the tiny evangelical party, asserted the "*arische Völkerfamilie*" (i.e. the Aryan family of peoples) was far superior to other groups or nations, and argued against any concept of "equality" of races.[294] The *Rheinische Mission* accepted racist hierarchy in 1935,[295] and in 1936 a Protestant clergyman agitator declared, "there have been times when a Roman cleric even dared to say he felt closer to a Catholic nigger than to a Protestant German!"[296] On the other hand, in the Catholic labor movement, for example, racism was one of the main objections to Nazism.[297]

One of the things that provoked Catholic theologians most about *Mein Kampf* was its racism, just like with the second most important Nazi work of literature, Alfred Rosenberg's *Der Mythus des 20. Jahrhunderts* (The Myth of the twentieth century), and racism was condemned at bishops' conferences.[298] As early as 1922, the bishops' conference of North Germany issued a pastoral letter committing itself to combat "with all means" "the Superior Man thing." Catholic papers followed suit, warning against the Nazi idolatry of the "Aryan Super Race." A few days before the election in 1930, a statement by Cardinal Faulhaber of South Germany at the Catholic conference was issued. I "do not belong to those who regarded our German people or the Aryan race as the chosen race of world history. Neither the Aryan race generally nor the Germans specifically have the right to create its own moral code."[299] I have yet to find a Protestant cleric, ecclesiastical institution or publication of the time expressing itself likewise.

Nazis could even use racist arguments in their battle with Catholics. According to them, the bulk of the Catholics were concentrated in the South which had been the home of the so-called "ostic" race in antiquity, and it was "completely inferior" to the "so-called Nordic race" so elevated "above all heavens."[300]

It must be conceded, though, that even in the Catholic confession racism was present, in accordance with the spirit of the time. It had the anthropologist Hermann Muckermann as its predominant proponent. One special offense for Germans generally in the 1920s, even for social democrats and Jews, was Africans in the French occupational forces, which they called *Die schwarze Schmach* (The Black Dishonor). Racial hygiene persuasions were, for that matter, allegedly also found in social democratic milieus,[301] and even present after WWII among the political and medical elites in countries such as Norway, witnessed by their treatment of the Norwegian ladies who had children with German fathers.[302]

Eugenics, "Lebensborn," and Euthanasia

Francis Galton, Darwin's student, is regarded as the founder of eugenics.[303] The concept was then radicalized by the German zoologist and neo-Darwinist August Weismann.[304] However, it was Woltmann, Ammon and especially Ploetz, plus his colleague Wilhelm Schallmeyer, who are considered the theoretical founders of *"Rassenhygiene"* in Germany. All the same, it may be fair to trace the first root of the *"Lebensborn"* strategy back to the early nationalism of Fichte.[305]

Ploetz originally urged a synthesis of socialism and eugenics but abandoned socialism after WWI in favor of *völkisch* ideology. Schallmeyer was a socialist, pacifist and monist.[306] Houston Stewart Chamberlain spread the phenomenon to a wider audience during the period of the Empire, but hardly anyone other than Willibald Hentschel attempted eugenic projects in the same period; the idea of the Nazi "*Lebensborn*" strategy is ascribed to him. Hentschel was Haeckel's student and assistant, and founder of the anti-Semitic *Deutschsoziale Partei*. At the same time, he had many followers among the great Protestant dominated KP. He was also an adherent of de Lagarde and a friend of the orthodox Lutheran Stöcker and the radical *völkisch* ideolog Theodor Fritsch. After WWI he started up the *völkisch* Artamanenmovement, named after the Aryan god Artam, finally joining the Nazi Party at the end of the 1920s.[307]

In 1920, some Protestant theologians had proposed eugenic legislation and others followed suit in the following years. Among these was Reinhold Seeberg, leader of the Inner Mission after 1923. Other prominent members of the same organization were Heinrich Wichern, the son of the famous founder, Johann H. Wichern, and Hans Harmsen who was a pioneer of eugenics in Germany generally, not just among Protestants. Harmsen and the Inner Mission and most of its membership welcomed the Nazi government. They were also strong supporters of the Nazi Sterilization Law of 1933, whereas the Catholic vice-chancellor, von Papen, disliked it.[308]

In fact, several of the leaders of the most important Nazi eugenic organization NSV, *Nationalsozialistische Volkswohlfahrt*, were from the Inner Mission, while none came from the corresponding Catholic organization, the *Caritas*. The Protestant scientists Bavink and Kleinschmidt were intensely concerned about uniting faith and science in the field and also shared the Inner Mission's attitude to Nazi government and the Sterilization Law. Some of the Nazi organizations criticized Christian charity and called it "*Bolshevik*" because it could, in the long run, lead to a "Government by the *Untermenschen* (inferior people)." This criticism was directed primarily at Catholic charity and organizations like the *Caritas*.[309]

When the 35th Congress of Evangelical Spiritual Advisers discussed the Sterilization Law in 1933, views differed with some acquiescing and others hesitating. But the Catholics refused to implement it.[310]

Eugenic tendencies could also be found in the Catholic milieus, from the late 1920s, to be sure; it was the spirit of the time, and likewise was in leftist political environments. Hermann Muckermann's promotion of such ideas has already been mentioned, but the Catholic version was practically void of *völkisch*-Nazi racist ideology. Catholic theological representatives of the Nazi-inspired "*Reichstheologie*" in the 1930s were supporters of eugenics also, but were suspended from their employment in 1934, and Didriksen asserts that only a few Catholics supported sterilization. Catholic charity organizations were against it, and several Catholics protested when the law was promulgated.[311] Catholic resistance to eugenics generally, and sterilization specifically, was finally affirmed and affixed when Pius XI issued his *Encyclica Casti Conubii* (About the Chaste and Holy Matrimony), and the German bishops' conference loyally followed suit. However, the Zentrum did not take up the issue, probably in a last-ditch effort to still win Protestant voters.[312]

After the Nazi dictatorship was imposed in March 1933, Cardinal Faulhaber outlined the main causes in the defensive battle against the authorities: resistance to sterilization and protection of Catholic schools and associations. Although the Catholic rhetoric could be tough, the Church had to allow for its principles to not be strictly followed, because many Catholics were employed by the health and social departments.[313]

However, the Sterilization Law was not unique to Germany. Some Nordic countries, thirty states of the USA, two provinces in Canada and one Swiss canton had the same law. What all these places had in common was that they were either Protestant or Protestant-dominated. No Catholic dominated country passed a similar law or liberalized sterilization. Didriksen considers "this was connected to the Catholic view that you do not mess around with issues pertaining to reproduction."[314]

The Nazi euthanasia legislation was met with a mixed response from Protestants. Many church leaders, especially within the BK, were clearly against it. Others, such as leaders of ecclesiastical orphanages, were in favor. No church leader protested publicly against the practice, however, perhaps due to the strong hold of *Schöpfungsglaube's* theology within the confession. Protests did come from Catholic Church leaders, though, especially the "thunderclap" from the pulpit of Bishop Clemens von Galen in August 1941.[315]

The Nazi strategy for organizations shows that priority was given to doctors, jurists, and teachers. Nazi special organizations for these professions were formed at the end of the 1920s, whereas other occupations had to wait, because "Lawyers, doctors and teachers have been organized at Hitler's explicit command because of the recognition that these occupations have special tasks to perform in the restoration of the German "*Reich*" and renewal of the German People."[316] As to the doctors' association, Kjøstvedt asserts it "espoused an overtly anti-Semitic and racist world view, with racial hygiene as its leading principle."[317] This worldview could then be legitimated by jurists and teachers and grafted into the people, which can explain why these organizations were assigned such importance.

Ethnic Cleansing and Genocide

In the nineteenth century Protestant social scientists had occasionally favored ethnic cleansing. Starting in the Napoleonic era, the first ones were probably Johann Fichte, Heinrich Luden and Jakob Fries, all of them one-time students of theology.[318] Forty years on de Lagarde proposed either total assimilation or deportation of Jews. Before the turn of the century, his ideas were not followed up until Heinrich Class proposed ethnic cleansing of a country waging war against Germany. He synthesized anti-Semitism, racism and the elimination of ethnic groups from German soil and his ideas became popular. Walser Smith thinks his idea "is also a bridge from the long nineteenth to the short, violent twentieth century."[319]

Not only ethnic cleansing, but pure genocide was practiced in German Southwest Africa at the beginning of the twentieth century. Only the Zentrum and the SPD criticized it in the *Reichstag*, arguing for human rights. The leftist liberal *Berliner Tageblatt* later said the Protestant *Rheinische Mission* had not succeeded in its efforts after forty years in Southwest Africa and Catholic missions should replace them.[320]

Walser Smith sums up the attitude in Germany at the outset of WWI: "The elimination of peoples, not as a policy prescription but as the acceptance of a political fact, thus became inextricably paired with racial thinking, and racial thinking came to inform politics across the political spectrum, halting only hesitantly at the socialist and Catholic milieus."[321]

NORTH-SOUTH CONFRONTATION

Universalism/Internationalism—Nationalism—Particularism

Originally, Protestants generally favored particularism, but this—apart from the Hannoverian particularism—faded after unification and nationalism benefitted.[322] (Hanoverian particularism faded only after a confrontation with Nazism after 1930.) However, international connections were not popular among German Protestants, as we see from their absence at ecumenical conferences. De Lagarde and Houston Chamberlain had opposed universalism and the latter asserted it represented coercion, intolerance, opposition to nationalism and was a predominant feature of the Roman Catholic Church.[323]

Needless to say, among Catholics generally universalism had a strong position and particularly among German Catholics from the outset of the *Kulturkampf*. Their experiences from it led to more support for universal ethical principles of state ethics having tasted the effects of nationalism. State ethics should not be limited to "Christian-Teutonic" state rights but, rather, take up the traditions from the classical philosophy of antiquity and from medieval scholasticism with Aristotle and Thomas Aquinas as the most important thinkers. The neo-scholastic movement suppressed the philosophy of idealism in Catholic theology and was expressed in several papal syllabi between 1860 and WWI whose main tendency was to weaken the "national" contemporary culture and prefer a universal one.

The German Catholic *Staatslexikon*, with politicians from the Zentrum among its contributors, expressed this trend. The right had its origin in eternal basic reason: i.e. the Creator Himself, according to this encyclopedia. Natural rights needed to be recognized as the foundation and norm for the positive legislation of rights. Emphasis should be on the issues of moral rights and shaped by the connection of human laws to the individual conscience. This teaching about the state was mainly introduced into the Catholic world of ideas by the theologian of morals, Josef Mausbach. He was also a representative in the National Assembly in 1919.[324] Mausbach recognized the importance of the nation but opposed the Protestant version of nationalism. The nation was subordinated to religion and state. In 1912 he said:

> Christian universalism is the best guarantee for a proper and broad-minded respect of national characteristics, whereas the völkisch particularism, that egoistic nationalism, deprives both itself and Christianity the breath of life. While the Protestant and Eastern Orthodox churches, being "Landeskirchen" (National Churches) sharpen rather than soften antagonism between nations, the Catholic religion wraps a unique ribbon around all the peoples of the world and brings the idea of the Messianic Kingdom of Peace, once preached by the prophets; a marvellous, though earthly framed and imperfect fulfillment. The international aspect makes the church move from the outset to counter every peace destroying perversion of national feelings.[325]

Wolfram Kaiser emphasizes the contribution of Pope Pius IX (1846–1878) particularly to "the trans-nationalization of Catholicism"[326] and outlines how this had both modernist and reactionary features:

> The contribution of Pius IX to the trans-nationalization of Catholicism . . . was not limited to the organizational and doctrinal centralization of the Church, however. The increasingly ultramontane and Romanized Church also encouraged the mobilization and political engagement of Catholics for the defense of established Church rights and influence and later also for social reforms. This mobilization facilitated trans-national grassroots-activities and resulting cultural transfer."[327]

Arve Thorsen and Adrian Hastings emphasize the importance of Catholic universalism for the world order and how it was an obstacle for militant nationalism.[328] A year before the outbreak of WWII, Pope Pius XI expressing the Catholic view of nationalism and universalism said:

> To be Catholic means to be universal, not racist, nationalist or separatist. . . . It must be emphasized that there is something reprehensible in this spirit of

separatism of exaggerated nationalism that, precisely because it is not Christian, not religious, it ends up by not being human either. . . . If we forget the universal categories, it will go very badly for this world.[329]

Particularism was present in German Catholicism in the Interwar period when major efforts were made to secede Catholic Rhineland from the country. But there was a strong aspect to this particularism of strengthening the influence of France and weakening the Prussian Protestant hegemony.[330] On the other hand, Bavarian particularism has been stronger and more constant. The Bavarian *Patriotenpartei* did not amalgamate with the Zentrum until 1887, but split off in 1918 to establish the BVP and, after WWII, the CSU. Nor would Bavarian Catholic farmers join the Protestant based agrarian party, not so much for particularist as ideological and confessional reasons.[331]

German Protestant church goers were first and foremost oriented towards the state and the nation, whereas Catholics were more divided in their attentions. This tendency also may have influenced the different voting patterns of Protestants and Catholics when the hyper-nationalist Nazi Party appeared on the ballot.

Catholic papers not only recognized that *völkisch*-Nazi racism was un-Christian, but that it endangered the Catholic Church because this racism was in opposition to the universalism of the Church. The world-encompassing Catholic Church was elevated "above the states and above the races," which naturally provoked the Nazis.[332] Hitler already attacked internationalism during the early part of WWI and emphasized the importance of the fight against universalism in relation to the fight to gain territories.[333]

A distinct difference in the view of autarchy between clerical Catholics and Nazis is apparent. Between 1900 and 1930, a democratic and Catholic based Pan-Europeanism came to the fore in both trade unionism and politics, in strong opposition to the pronounced autarchy the Nazis emphasized even before their takeover, and that was confirmed in the Third Reich.[334]

Roman Law and "Blut und Boden" (Blood and Soil)

From the Napoleonic era until the Third Reich, rejection of Roman law and choosing Teutonic judicial systems instead was an integral part of the rightist syndrome.

In *Den europeiske rettens historie* (*The History of European Law*) Erik Anners writes:

> The intellectual and rationalistic attitudes to the problems of man and society which emerged within the Hellenistic cultural world contributed to the establishment of classical, Roman jurisprudence; and it was Corpus Juris Civilis, or a

product of this jurisprudence that inspired the lawyers and specialists in Canon Law during the High Middle Ages and influenced the canonists greatly. In the Medieval legist and canonist schools, a rationalistic method was crystallized in their schools. It became the mark and joint heritage of European jurists. . . . This method distinguishes European jurisprudence from others, e.g. the Oriental or Arabic.[335]

In addition, all Catholic jurists agreed that the laws should be in accordance with the natural law on the grounds that as Nature was God's creation it followed that the natural law would always be in harmony with the Divine law. Influenced by the French Revolution, and in continuation of the principles of Roman law, Napoleon made the Civil Code *("Code Napoléon"),* which became law in the French Empire. The Nazi Walter Darré asserted that only once the Napoleonic law had been introduced were the Roman principles of right, and their understanding of state, established in France.[336]

Large parts of Germany that had been included in the French Empire, not only retained but tightly held on to the right to keep the Civil Code even after Napoleon was deposed. Baden even introduced the law voluntarily after 1815. It is notable that all these areas, which largely coincided with the Rhine area, had a great Catholic majority, and the right to retain the Code was supported by people in all Catholic areas of Western and Southern Germany. In 1900, however, the Civil Code was abolished everywhere and replaced by *Bürgeliches Gesetzbuch.*[337]

The European judicial tradition differed not only from Oriental and Arabic traditions, but fundamentally from Teutonic ones as well, and German legists in the 19th century became aware of this and pointed it out. The aversion German Protestants then adopted towards Roman law and its variants related to their detestation of the French Revolution and Napoleon. In 1784 Herder had already claimed that every people throughout history had produced its own rules of law. He attacked Roman law, which, to be sure, had at one time been the expression of the "Spirit of its People" during the Roman Empire,[338] but under medieval feudalism had promoted the replacement of the Old German order of law. Herder characterized the latter such:

> The Old German axioms that each man should be judged by peers, that the leader of the court ensures that sentence is only arrived with the help of a jury, that crime is expected to be judged according to custom and not according to words on paper, but on the contrary be judged according to living appraisal; these and a number of other juridical and guild customs are witnesses of the fair and bright German spirit.[339]

Many of the Protestant nationalists mentioned in earlier chapters were adherents of Herder's views, and opposition to Roman law was later systematized and argued by Hegel and jurists of "the historical school," Otto F. Gierke and Lorenz von Savigny.[340]

The first version of *Bürgerliches Gesetzbuch* in the 1880s was influenced by Roman law, and this caused opposition. Klaus von See presents Otto von Gierke's objections:

> He refers to elements common to Teutonic law, the many feudal patrimonial and corporative institutions which organized the fellowship organically and function as a mediator between the individual and the collectivity. Gierke places the freedom of the Teutonic mentality which was built on patrimony and corporation in negative contrast to the unconditional, individualistic and egoistic liberalism of the Roman mentality which he finds in the first version of the new German Law Book. It is remarkable that his criticism of the German judicial system has fundamental similarities to the criticism being leveled at the same time by socialists.[341]

Montgomery McGovern went so far as to claim, maybe with a touch of an exaggeration, that "The German members of the Historical School were, in fact, the leading advocates of the political philosophy which later developed into Fascism and Nazism."[342]

At least three of the small anti-Semitic parties in the Empire, the *Antisemitische Volkspartei*, the *Deutsche Reformpartei* and Stöcker's CSAP, preferred Teutonic law over Roman law and even non-German anti-Semites, such Hungarian Simonyi, deplored the "legalistic hairsplitting in the un-national Roman law."[343]

It is conspicuous that in the Nazi Party Program of 1920, § 19 demanded that "Roman law, which serves the materialistic World Order, be replaced by a German Common law" several years after the abolition of Civil Code in the German states. The German Law Book of 1900 still had "Roman remnants", probably, and it seems the Nazis—in connection with the expanding "*Völkische Bewegung*" which demanded that they "fight against the Roman view of justice"—were interested in underscoring an ethical dualism: the clash between the strong and healthy Teutonic North and the decadent Roman South with its roots in what Alfred Rosenberg contemptibly called the "Syrian-Oriental-Catholic" culture.[344]

Among the Nazis, particularly Rosenberg and Walter Darré, there was concern about the change in Europe coming with feudalism in the early Middle Ages, i.e. the transition from an Old Teutonic society of free farmers to feudalized serfdom. This transition had occurred, at least in Bavaria, parallel with the abolition of the old Teutonic law systems and adoption of Roman legal systems. In Bavaria:

Under the Guelphs, the farmers lost their freedom and became serfs. Property rights were split up and the nobility, monasteries and churches lay claim to them. The farmers were only left their right to their personal belongings and homes. If they wished to till the soil, then they had to pay tributes and perform drudgery. Old Teutonic Law had to yield to Roman law.[345]

The leader of the Nazi farmers, Walter Darré, was concerned about the historical development of the judicial systems and coupled them to the "Blood and Soil" ideology. The original patrician Roman law, connected as it was to kinship and family lands, was acceptable, but had perverted the development into a society of trade and money. When the notion of kinship disintegrated, a late-Roman system of private law emerged, with "Ego" in place of prominence. As a consequence, not only had the state ended up a "porridge of peoples," understood as a mere body of "Egos," but every notion of family was destroyed. Marriage was reduced to a mere I-You relationship; the soil was a piece of the "I's" property; a judicial system in diametric opposition to a law designed for a united folk in submission to a leader; diametrically opposed, in short, to Teutonic Law and its noble badge of distinction.[346] According to Darré "The greatness of Teuton-dom has been that it derived the law of its existence from its notion of divinity, and thus held the life-bringing conditions of existence in this world, higher than laws of Economy and of the "I." In other words, "Blood"—and by extension of blood—"Soil" also, were to be esteemed high above all "egoistic" economic considerations.[347]

Rosenberg devoted a whole chapter in "*Mythus*" to a discussion of the colliding legal systems, and Gregor Strasser claimed the "ancient Teutonic idea of the right of the whole tribe to their joint-property, of the whole nation to all the means of production and the soil" was the foundation of the entire economic program of the party.[348]

Probably it was the "essence" and "spirit" of the Roman law as opposed to the "genuine, pragmatic and plain Teutonic essence" which caused a reaction among *völkisch* and Nazis. Since antiquity Roman law had been characterized by universalism, natural law and human equality. In the first decades of the twentieth century, such values came to the fore, e.g. the Nobel Peace Prize, the International Court of Justice in the Hague, President Wilson's peace proposals and the formation of League of Nations. The first years after WWI were characterized by democratic processes in both new and old countries, e.g. the Weimar constitution in Germany.

A study of the Nazi program and later structure of government reveals that many elements had their foundation in early Teutonic ideals as opposed to Roman law and practice. The influence of Teutonic law is evident already in the introduction of the 1920 program when it says that the program is *unchangeable*. This is a vital difference from Roman law: for the Teutons, the law appeared static and was eternal (Old German: ewa=right; German: ewig=eternal). Law was not subject to production—it could only be revealed in the wise words of the judicial experts. Even the famous jurist von Savigny asserted the basic principle that it was not the task of jurisprudence to create laws, but only to find the law which already existed in "the consciousness of the people."[349] It is natural to suppose that the *Führer* was meant to be the exclusive expert of law in the Third Reich.

Furthermore, the Teutonic laws were in force for *peoples*, whereas Roman law was valid for *territory*. This created some problems in the Migration Period with mixed Teutonic and Roman populations.[350] In the Nazi program, it was stated which people were regarded as true German citizens and which were not. Not all the citizens of Germany in 1920 were accepted according to § 4 in the Nazi program.

An outcome of the intellectual and rationalist feature of Roman law was the central *position of evidence*, a position which seems to have been weaker in Teutonic law. The latter would emphasize the oath of the free man and, in case of the need for evidence, the burden of proof was on the defendant, not the plaintiff/private prosecutor.[351] It seems probable that the oath of a German man would be weightier than indicia in the judicial system of the Third Reich, and especially if the opponent were non-Aryan. Closely connected to this, another tendency appeared when the German penal laws of 1935, and in 1943 in the occupied Netherlands, were revised. Up until then, the traditional principle of the Roman law of *nulla poena sine lege* (i.e. no penal verdict without justification from a specific law) had been valid. Afterwards, to this principle, an addition of the principle of analogy was included. It read that if the fundamental intention of the law—but not its written formulation—was to judge a crime, the verdict should be in accordance with the intention, if, according to a fair understanding of the law, the act ought to be punished. In reality, this meant that the principle *nullum crimen sine poena* (i.e. no crime without punishment) was favored in relationship to the Roman principle.[352] Goering's judicial advisor, Carl Schmitt, who was Catholic, though, had favored this new principle.[353]

Nazism has been considered an ideology giving women a low status; the same was obvious in Teutonic law. Ferdinand Lot writes: "German law . . . is an archaic law. In the family, the power of the father remained excessive. His *mundium* gave him full authority over his wife and children. . . . The German woman's position in law, as compared to that of the Roman woman, was very low."[354] The family father was practically omnipotent and his authority continued over his son even after the latter had married, and when the father died, his widow was under authority of one of their sons![355] Rosenberg went beyond even the family ideal when he favored the *"Männerbund"* (i.e. company of men) as being the building block of the people.[356]

A consistent feature of Teutonic law is its archaic and formalist tendencies.[357] Perhaps in connection with this, another feature is clear. According to Lot, "It did not at all aim at protecting the weak. It troubled itself as little as possible about what we call to-day the sacred rights of the individual."[358]

Generally, a study of the Nazi structure of government seems to reveal a more or less imitation of the structures in the Teutonic Migration kingdoms and the German medieval "First Reich." The Migration kingdoms were—at least formally—constituted by the person of the king. When he died, the state, in fact, had to be re-established under the new king(s). Analogously, the Nazi state was dependent on the *Führer* only, unlike Fascist Italy, where Mussolini was formally subordinate to King Victor Immanuel (and in 1943 in reality, to Fascist Gran Consiglio).

The Migration kingdoms had no government institutions, which of course also was due to the primitive stage of civilization and communications. They related instead to individuals, and to regional and local noblemen. But even this the Nazis clearly tried to imitate. After the reorganization and radicalization of the government in February 1938, the government did not assemble as a collective unit anymore. The only connection between the ministers was, apart from Hitler himself, his secretary Heinrich Lammers. In addition to this, the regional *Reichsstatthalter* were elevated to the rank of the central ministers.[359]

Some Migration kingdoms and the Holy Roman Empire lacked official capitals. To a great extent, the kings and emperors were itinerant, and the sessions of the *Reichstags* were held in various towns. Since the high Middle Ages and later various towns alternated as preferred seats of the sovereigns, e.g. Goslar, Prague, Brussels, Vienna, Frankfort, and ultimately, Berlin. Although Berlin was the official capital, there were several towns and cities with a central function, which can indicate an effort to copy the past. Nuremberg was the city of the party congress, Munich with its *"Braunes Haus"* the city of the party leadership and *"Hauptstadt der Bewegung," "Hauptstadt der Deutschen Kunst,"* and the planned *"Hauptstadt der NS-Architektur."* Frankfort a.M. was *"Stadt des Deutschen Handwerks,"* Leipzig" *Reichsmessestadt"* and seat of the Supreme Court, Goslar *"Reichsbauernstadt"* and Celle *"Reicherbhofgericht."* Second to the chancellery in Berlin, Obersalzberg became Hitler's second residence. For long periods during WWII, Hitler frequented his five *Führerhauptquartiere*, which were spread over Germany and the occupied areas. The most famous of these was *Wolfsschanze* in East Prussia, the place of the assassination attempt in July 1944. During the battles in Poland and the Balkans, he stayed in a railway "Adler."

All in all, there is clearly a logical connection between the Protestant German nationalists' rejection of the Napoleonic system with its basis in the French Revolution and Roman law and the rejection of the same by the Third Reich. Long before Darré, in the mid-nineteenth century, the opposition to Roman law and its characteristics was joined to the emergence of the "Blood and Soil"-mentality. The slogan was introduced by the poet Joseph Victor von Scheffel, who was preoccupied with Alemannic law. In one of his poems, the popular *Der Trompeter von Säckingen*, he described Roman law as "the garbage of their meal, which the Romans have thrown to us," and further: "Shall there not from the German soil blossom our own law, odorous of the forest?"[360]

Darré elevated "Blood and Soil" to a central notion in the Third Reich and became the name of a literary genre based on the belief in a mystic connection between the spiritual characteristics of a people and the natural circumstances. The landscape became an important part of the definition of a people. However, the relationship between people and landscape was different from the equivalent relationship in the French nationalism, or from the Marxist basis—superstructure dogma, for that matter. According to George Mosse in the German "Blood and Soil,"

> man was not seen as a vanquisher of nature, nor was he credited with the ability to penetrate the meaning of nature by applying the tools of reason; instead he was glorified as living in accordance with nature, at one with its mystical forces. ... instead of being encouraged to confront the problems cast up by urbanization and industrialization, man was enticed to retreat into a rural nostalgia.[361]

By the landscape, the people were connected to the power of life and cosmos. According to Scheffel, European Mediterranean peoples with their Roman law expressed the "winding plants of the buxom South," the Jews with their Mosaic law, being desert people, were spiritually dry, barren and void of creativity. The Teutons, however, settled in the gloomy and fertile forests of Northern Europe and were profound, mysterious and creative. Because they were enveloped in the dark of the forest, they strove towards the sun, becoming *Lichtmenschen* (Men of Light).[362]

Note that the same accusations about economic recession directed at the Jews were also directed at the effects of Roman law. In the recession of 1880s, Martin Fassbender included the following decisive factors: the transition from a subsistence to a monetary economy, taxes and charges, low prices for cattle and grain, the practice of speculation and usury, and Roman law.[363]

The "Blood and Soil" mystical rejection of Roman law and the "anti-Mediterranean propaganda" were coupled, according to Peter Pulzer, with German nationalism and especially among intellectuals and the "grassroots" and this was already discernible in the 1860s. The uneducated were joined in their beliefs by their fellow-citizens in the universities. Obsessed by the primacy of the blood, they were anxious to reject all values inconsistent with it considering them foreign importations. The Rights of Man were French, Christianity was Jewish (or "Etrusco-Syrian"), and sophistication was Mediterranean. Any community with loyalties outside the pale of the select group was suspect, not only Jews, but Freemasons, Catholics, or whoever was at hand. The anti-Mediterranean propaganda was particularly strong, since the Mediterranean, being generally regarded as the cradle of European civilization, was the most dangerous source of rival values. Hence (in part) the rejection of Roman law, Wagner's diatribes against Italian music, the elevation of Arminius to a national hero (The battle of the Teutoburg Forest came to be bracketed with festivals celebrating the victory of Sedan), and the warnings which the alumni of Berlin University imbibed from the lips of Treitschke about the facts of life south of the Alps: it is *"quite in accordance with Nature that the Northern temper should be deeper and fuller"* and *"the sensuality of the Southern races go hand in hand with their idleness."* Hence, too, the exaltation of instinct over reason, of the moral over the intellectual, of the physical over the cerebral, which was the meeting point for all classes, was the form the emotion of nationalism had taken by the end of our period (from the Napoleonic era to the 1860s). Inasmuch as anti-Semitism underwent changes during those approximately fifty years, the alterations match what we observe with nationalism.[364]

Julia Zernack claims that there lay a desire to defend a threatened Nordic Teutonic *"Volkstum"* against the assault from the South in the zealotry for the North.[365] This attraction of the North was visible in Kaiser Wilhelm II's frequent summer holidays in Sognefjord in Norway where he even had a huge statue of the mythical Norse hero Fridtjov erected (still there to this day).

When his 'colleague' from the North visited him in 1934, Mussolini became acquainted with this contempt for "Etruscan-Syrian" Mediterranean culture (a theme in Alfred Rosenberg's *"Mythus"*). Hitler asserted the blood of people in the Mediterranean was partly contaminated with African blood.[366]

Rosenberg identified three heroes in German history who had tried to defend "Blood and Soil" against the harmful Southern forces: Hermann against the Romans, the futile efforts of Saxon Duke Widukind against Charlemagne and the ensuing Catholic Christianization, and in modern times, Hitler.[367]

When confronted with the Weimar Constitution, Protestant theologians even included Roman law in their objections. Friedrich Brunstäd, a prominent representative of the CSVD and the anti-DC *Jungreformatorische Bewegung* in 1933, issued a long assessment.[368] "Right law" had special German traits. Roman law was "intimately related to the ideology of the Enlightenment because its origin was the sovereign power of the individual, the *homo singulus* or *privatus*, "the absolute individual." In German law, an individual's obligation to the community surpassed their isolated rights as "peers."[369]

It is probable that Nazism looked less attractive for Catholic jurists than for Protestant ones. A fundamental difference between the Protestant and Catholic understanding of law had probably evolved in the course of the nineteenth century. In the long run it could favor the Nazis in their quest for support among Protestants and result in fewer Catholic jurists in the ranks of the Nazi organization for lawyers. I am not in possession of the confessional ratio in it, just the information that the bulk of the members were from Protestant Berlin and Saxony.[370]

German Research on Antiquity and the Middle Ages

Extensive research—and speculation—about early German history was done in the wake of the German national awakening.

Arminius ("Hermann") was stereotyped as a symbolic figure of the national idea of unity because he had asserted in the Teutoburger forest (9 AD) to "free Germania" against Roman assault. The Hermann memorial was erected in 1875 to glorify this battle on the presumed site. Arminius was even proposed as "the mythical father of the future united Germany." The Norse *Edda*, the heroic ballad *Nibelungenlied* and Tacitus' *Germania* were the written main evidence used in the research, and the North was increasingly regarded as the home of racially superior heroes rather than of barbarians.[371]

The Roman cultural influence was also a subject of research, and two institutions were established in the most romanized part of the country, Catholic Rhineland. Wiwjorra asserts researchers in these institutions "were under the influence of humanist ideals, which could even conform to a conservative-national sentiment, but not to a *völkisch* one." At the end of the nineteenth century, such institutions and their adherents were increasingly opposed by the "Teutonic" researchers who contemptuously called their antiquity-oriented colleagues "*Römlinge*."[372]

Glorification of Widukind and the Donar Oak

Widukind and his Saxon resistance against the Carolingian Empire had been a central point of reference in the *völkisch*-nationalist interpretation of history since 1900. The struggle was interpreted as a nationalist, racist and anti-Christian struggle and became a favored theme among *völkisch* authors, who starting in 1922, celebrated Good Friday as a memorial day for "the 4500 martyrs for the German Faith" and "Widukind's spirit, as the old Teutonic spirit of freedom." The authors latched onto patriotic and church-hostile tendencies and accused the Carolingians of violent missionary tactics and the incorporation of Saxony (i.e. the original Lower Saxony) in their Empire. This literature generated hatred against tyrants and criticism of religion in the *völkisch* milieu and uncritical fascination for Teutonic myths and belief. Thereby, this ecstatic cult added Widukind to their melange of yearnings for freedom, nationalism, hero-worship, racism, and paganism.[373]

"Widukind" authors were appreciated by the Nazis, and in the peak years of the cult in the mid-1930s much of literature and other activities such as archeological excavations were promoted at the instigation of Rosenberg and Himmler.[374]

The campaign promoting Widukind also figured in church opposition to the Third Reich. At Christmas 1933 Cardinal Faulhaber held his famous irate sermons against the neopaganism within Nazism and the relationship between Christianity and *"Germanentum."* He took up arms against the Nazi veneration of the "Donar Oak." This tree in Hessen Bonifacius, according to legend, had chopped down in 723 inducing a breakthrough for Christianity among the non-Frankish Teuton tribes in North Germany. The oak had been incorporated into the Protestant nationalism since Arndt's and Jahn's days at the beginning of the nineteenth century. It was used to symbolize old Teutonic values, like truth and loyalty, and as a polemic argument against French rationalism allegedly alienated to nature, while the Norse gods Thor and Balder, were venerated highly in the *"Völkische Bewegung."*[375]

Darré maintained that Bonifacius' and his successors' collaboration with the Frankish authorities was the start of those detrimental church taxes and the launching of feudalism in Germany, and added:

> These missionaries were very significant contributors of un-Teutonic concepts of law and made the Frankish kings voluntarily accept that they could strengthen their power through Roman ideas. That way Roman and Christian notions working hand in hand together led to the Frankish kingdom development, from one with a king ultimately dependent on the free "Volksgenosse" (i.e. Folk-Comradeship), into a king independent of it and equipped with a source of right within himself. Hence, the earlier "Volksgenosse" became an underling; Teutonic democracy ousted by Teutonic monarchy."[376]

In the mid-1930s, an extensive debate about Widukind veneration ensued. Protestants, and even Nazis, found it controversial, but its main opponents were most probably Catholics, due to their veneration of Widukind's counterpart, Bonifacius.[377] The seat of the North German bishops' conferences was at Fulda, where Bonifacius was buried.

DISPLAY AND CEREMONY, SYMBOLS AND FÜHRER MYTH

Display and Ceremony

The Catholic Church had and still has many displays and ceremonies absent in Protestant Churches. In 1934, when Catholics were subject to their first major suppression by the Nazis, people, especially the youth, turned up *en masse* in several demonstration-like gatherings in Catholic dominated towns and cities of Western and Southern Germany.[378]

Being Catholics, Hitler and Goebbels obviously understood the potential for the Nazi Party of mobilization of such display and mass gatherings, and these were taken in hand and developed in the 1930s. As the Catholics already had their own culture, it obviously was the Protestants who became the target of Nazi arrangements. However, they must also have hoped to attract Catholics by surpassing them in pomp and display. The Nazis could also make use of the fact that the Weimar Republic left a void where the pompous parades and festivals of the Empire once had been.[379]

The Wartburg jubilee in 1817 was a kind of Protestant nationalist display and later several colossal national monuments were erected e.g the Walhalla-, Hermann-, Leipzig-battle- and, after WWI, Tannenberg-monuments. This was true even abroad, such as the Fridtjov statue in Norway. The monuments inspired awe and reverence, predominantly among Protestants,[380] as an incident at the Hermann-monument indicates. At one ceremony there, an evangelical clergyman held a sermon and Arndt's hymn to the Liberation War (1813–1814) was sung. George Mosse considers it an example of the mixture of "*Deutschtum*" and Protestantism which had been the case since that war.[381] Because of the secularization and the tendency to mysticism and syncretism prevalent within Protestantism, there clearly was a need for sacred substitutes for going to church, and this was reinforced by the intimate combination of Protestantism and nationalism that had arisen.

The Catholics, however, built no monuments during this time. They had their own already in the Western and Southern part of the land: Romanesque and Gothic cathedrals from the idealized Middle Ages, which were buildings that also staged magnificent ceremonies.

Some national festivals, whether combined with monuments or not, could contain a barb against Catholicism. For example, Catholics were reluctant to participate in the festival of the 1870 victory at Sedan and similar festivals. They regarded it as a glorification of the political party that had supported Bismarck's anti-Catholic policy. Sedan-day was the first national festival the Empire arranged for its own glorification, and the evangelical cleric Friedrich von Bodelschwingh was its main instigator. In his rigorous Protestantism, he praised the excellent disciplining effect the war had, a war God had sent to prevent the spreading decadence of peacetime. Bodelschwingh had been appalled by the debauched feasts of the France of Napoleon III.³⁸²

Obviously, Hitler and the Nazis understood the value of the magnificent ceremonies at monuments in their propaganda, using it to effect at the burial of President Hindenburg at the Tannenberg-monument. But because they were a revolutionary and progressive movement with their own "glory" to nurture, they created a pompous arena of their own with their own pompous architecture: the arena of the Nuremberg rallies.³⁸³

Derek Hastings points out how the Nazi Party, after the "martyrdom" in 1923 of Albert Leo Schlageter, utilized it to arrange Catholic dominated masses, and that celebrations of the party continued in an even more pompous style after 1925. However, secular and pseudo-sacred features waxed, while the Catholic aspects waned in these celebrations.³⁸⁴

The Swastika

The swastika *("Hakenkreuz")* is an ancient symbol found in various cultures. It was approved by Hitler in 1920 as a symbol of the Nazi Party, but already had been used as a symbol for rightist nationalist movements in Germany and Austria-Hungary for twenty years, and it was later used in the Austrian republic and in students' associations.³⁸⁵ Its occult importance was first emphasized by Helena Blavatsky.³⁸⁶ Alfred Rosenberg linked the swastika with the Parsee sun-cult and not the Teutons.³⁸⁷ Peter Levenda writes:

> When the various völkisch and German cultural societies began adopting the Swastika as their emblem, they were just as conscious of its anti-Christian potential as of their own anti-Semitic intent. This was . . . paganism as a movement set up in opposition to Judeo-Christianity as well as Communism, Capitalism and Democracy, which were all creatures of the Jewish-Masonic conspiracy. In the Listian mode (i.e. the rightist—and Catholic—philosopher Guido von List), therefore, the swastika as Hakenkreuz identifies the völkisch Nazi movement as an ideological enemy of the prevailing forces of the time but also as an enemy of the majority religions of Western Europe.³⁸⁸

There were several *Hakenkreuzlieder*, written by the early 1920s, but in 1923 an Austrian priest, Ottokar Kernstock, composed one for a subdivision of the DNSAP that had used the swastika as a symbol since its foundation in 1903. Kernstock was criticized by both the Church and the Catholic CSP, but he was allowed to continue as a priest after he publicly distanced himself from the Nazis, protesting the way they misused the text without his consent. It illustrates the way the Catholic Church and political Catholicism understood this symbol as early as 1923, and even the secularized knew of it: on

July 11, 1923, the front-page headline of the SPD paper *Vorwärts* read: "Bavarian priests adherents of the swastika. Revolt against the Pope?"[389]

In the confrontation between the BVP and the Nazi Party in the early 1920s, the BVP asserted that the swastika was evidence of the pagan roots of Nazi ideology and that the Nazis cooperated with openly anti-Christian *völkisch* organizations whose aim it was to substitute the Christian cross with the swastika. The Catholic Nazi priest, Lorenz Pieper, replied by arguing that the swastika had been used by early Christians in Rome and in medieval art. Although it had also been used in pagan cultures, it had been a stage in the development from the original Roman T-cross on which Christ had been crucified, and the later Christian cross, Pieper asserted.[390]

Also during later conflicts, the Catholic Church cited the swastika as evidence that the Nazi Party was an anti-Christian movement. Archbishop Bertram of Breslau, cardinal of North-Germany, asserted in 1930 that "the swastika is a signal to fight against the cross of Christ," and during the election campaign the Bavarian *Augsburger Postzeitung* encouraged Catholics "to take up arms" to defend the cross of Christ against "the hostile swastika."[391] In 1932, Theodor Haecker, a Catholic philosopher, wrote: "The last dishonor of our days. The sign of the Beast, the caricature of the Cross—the *Hakenkreuz*. . . .the symbol of the urge . . . effect and interaction of subjective and objective fraud which promote each other." Another Catholic, Hans Rost, called the swastika the symbol of neopaganism and when Hitler visited Mussolini after the *Anschluss*, the pope described the swastika as "a cross incompatible with the Cross of Christ."[392]

Even Protestant clerics could feel the swastika was controversial. In 1931 one called it a heathen symbol and accused the Nazis of venerating Wotan. Nevertheless, the same person changed his mind two years later.[393] Even in pietistic and BK-circles, where one would not expect esteem for the swastika, it had its adherents.[394]

Karl-Wilhelm Dahm sums up the Protestant clergy's understanding of the swastika:

> The völkisch swastika symbol was, for one group, a religious neutral confession of the German people and the needs of life of the German state; for another it was the profession of a new German-Christian, non-Jewish religion; for a third group the profession of a consciously non-Christian or even anti-Christian "Teutonic Paganism": "Völkische Bewegung" was neither organizationally nor, upon examining its ideas, a uniform entity.[395]

With such divergent views among their clergy, no wonder Protestant congregations were left in disarray, in total contrast to the Catholic churchgoers.

The Führer Myth and Nazism as Political Messianism

Several Protestants, and even the prominent theologians Emmanuel Hirsch and Paul Althaus, had wanted the slogan *"Führertum, Volk und Staat"* to be the foundation for the new constitution, and some had regarded "the *Führer* as prophet or as king," or that "the true statesman is ruler, warrior and priest all in one."[396]

The German historian Andreas Wirsching assesses the Protestant myth in this way:

> I think this (Führer myth) was something specifically German. I even think it is connected to Lutheranism. Already at unification in 1871 and then after 1918 many Protestants shared the belief that divine revelation was manifested and revealed itself in the national history. (My comment: which is the same as Schöpfungsglaube) A study of Deutsches Pfarrerblatt after 1930 reveals this: there is a constant discussion about what is interesting for Germans about Hitler and Nazism. For most Protestants January 30, 1933, meant a religious transition, because after 1918 Protestantism had, to a degree, been homeless. The monarchs, as ecclesiastical sovereigns, did not exist any longer.[397]

Hence, the *Führer* myth gets a religious tincture, which obviously did not help recruit adherents among Ultramontanists. As early as 1920, Catholic observers anxiously noticed masses stretching "their arms towards leaders," and the largest Catholic student association, the KV, rejected the *Führer* myth when the idea became popular in university milieus during the 1920s.[398] Erhard Schlund, a Catholic priest in Munich, discerned in the early 1920s that Nazism was structured along with notions of what may be termed "Political Messianism." Another Catholic, Hermann Sacher, asserted in 1931 that "something mystical, a kind of national mysticism was disguised in Nazism . . . like the spirit within sectarian elements, this national separatist movement has a fanatical belief. . . ." Even the later Catholic turncoat, Franz von Papen, asserted when he was *Reichskanzler* in the autumn of 1932 that,

> what gives Nazism the characteristic of political religion is its axiom of "the exclusivity of the All or Nothing of the political being," and its mystic Messiah-faith in the Führer's mighty words as the only one appointed to steer destiny. And it is here I really see the incompatible difference between conservative politics, rooted in faith, and Nazi faith, rooted in politics. . . .[399]

As a result of the wording of a Hitlerjugend hymn, Pope Pius XII asserted that Hitler had adopted the role of Messiah.[400]

Catholics were not the only ones to notice these tendencies in Nazism. Protestant theologian Richard Karwehl, later president Theodor Heuss, and

Jews all became aware of it.[401] Citing Karwehl's condemnation in 1931, Friedrich Graf describes the eschatological understanding in the Protestant churches in 1933 as:

> Here, he (Karwehl) said: "Jewish Messianism" was being replaced by "Germanic Messianism." But the distinction between eschatology legitimized or not legitimized by the church remained hotly disputed among theologians. So the revolution of 1933 seems like a gigantic projection screen for shaping theological fantasies. In the dynamics of self-mobilization, experienced as liberation, the theologian-intellectuals also hoped to be able to steer the revolutionary process normatively.[402]

With its allusions to religious vocabulary, the Nazi system took on a dual structure, in Uriel Tal's view: consecrated politics and secularized religion. Several rightists, plus social Darwinists who had provided the political concepts for Nazism, identified politics with "the survival of the fittest" and elevated it to a sacred level. Hitler used words like "the effecting of the fight of a nation for survival" on which rests the holiness of "a divine order."[403]

Derek Hastings portrays Hitler's mental development from the rabid leader of a violent *völkisch* organization in the 1920s to the elevated *"Retter"* (i.e. deliverer) and *"Meister"* (i.e. master) in 1926. Hitler said of himself that he was "a gift from heaven" and would be more adored than Mussolini.[404]

YOUTH AND EDUCATION

The Youth Organizations

Organized at the turn of the century, the *Freie deutsche Jugendbewegung* or the *"Wandervogel"* movement, is regarded as being a part of the *"Völkische Bewegung."* This is due to the strong influence on it of the ideas of de Lagarde, Langbehn and the educator Ludwig Gurlitt. Gurlitt had strongly denounced the effects of Christianity on the education and development of the German nation. It is also symptomatic that the movement, according to Mosse, "soon spread over most of northern (i.e. Protestant) Germany," and, according to Peter Stachura "almost all of its membership came from a solid middleclass and Protestant background, in particular, the educated, propertied bourgeoisie." Nevertheless, the attitude towards Jewish membership was not uniform. During the 1920s, the movement split into several associations and new ones appeared. An umbrella organization, the *Bündische Jugend*, was formed in 1923.[405]

These organizations were largely ignored by Catholics who had their own: the *Neudeutschland*, *Quickborn*, and the Zentrum's *Windthorstbund*, and a lot of smaller ones.[406]

After WWII, there has been a discussion about whether there was a link between the *Wandervogel/Bündische* movements and Nazism. Some associations had obvious Nazi sympathies, whereas others were reserved or even hostile to Nazism. However, both movements obviously represented a common mentality, "the sincere and uncompromising hatred of bourgeois society" and a rather radical nationalism based on romantic and, at least partly, racist tendencies. This was a mentality the Nazis could exploit, and hence make it easy for them to eradicate their competitors after the political takeover.[407] Most Catholic youths were obviously rather unfamiliar with this mentality and continued in their own associations until these, after a period of harassment, ultimately were prohibited in 1939. During WWII, Catholic youth continued to gather secretly in the woods.[408] As Peter Stachura concludes:

> No one has charged Catholic youth, for example, with major or even minor responsibility for the success of National Socialism. Catholic youth shared the general immunity to NSDAP blandishments displayed by the older generations of Catholics before 1933 because they possessed in their own organizational, social and political life revolving around the Church and the Centre Party a secure basis of support, underpinned by a certain defensive introspectiveness resulting from decades of discrimination and persecution during and after the Kulturkampf. The small minority of Catholic youths who felt the need to break out from this ghetto situation in the search for a more satisfying meaning to life usually did so by synthesizing Bündische and Christian ideals in groups like Quickborn and not by approximating to Hitler. This is not to forget, of course, that by the late 1920s anti-liberal and nationalist attitudes were increasingly apparent in Catholic youth circles. It may be proper, on the other hand, to include a relatively large percentage of Protestant youth, who shared, on the whole, the anti-democratic, nationalist authoritarian attitudes of their parents and elders. The Protestant small-town and rural-based lower Mittelstand provided, of course, the backbone of Hitler's support among both the electorate and organized followers. Groups such as Bibelkreise had strong and barely concealed pro-Nazi sympathies before 1933. Protestant youth was, therefore, a component of the broader political and cultural ethos, dating from the time of the Wilhelmine Reich, which signally assisted Hitler to power. . . ."[409]

Schools

The education system in Germany had been subject to reform from the end of the nineteenth century. In the beginning Catholic elements made their mark, but had to yield to other tendencies. After the 1890s the reform movement was dominated by the two *völkisch* educators, Ludwig Gurlitt and Hermann

Lietz, in addition to the art educator Alfred Lichtwark.[410] Both Gurlitt and Lietz originated from the Protestant milieu and, like the *Wandervogel* movement to which they were attached, had de Lagarde as an ideal; Gurlitt also had Langbehn.[411] According to Mosse "Gurlitt's philosophy of education provided the guidelines for a group that departed from the Catholic trends of the original reform movement," and "Indeed, for Gurlitt, all traditions unaffiliated to Germanism were archaic. Both the Catholic Church, that centuries-old suppressor of the Germanic spirit, and the culture of classical Greece as well, . . . were inconsistent with the flowering of the *Volk*, past or future."[412] So there is a reason to suppose the *Wandervogel* element primarily was applicable to Protestant and mixed-faith schools. Research from Bavaria indicates that.[413] Catholic schools, however, were protected to a great extent by the Church from un-Catholic teaching by several papal encyclicals between 1897 and 1931, and anxiety about Catholic education was the main reason for the Church approving the *Reichskonkordat* with the Nazi government in 1933.[414] The Nuncio Eugenio Pacelli (later Pope Pius XII) was concerned about education. He did not accept Christian mixed-faith schools where Protestant and Catholic students were educated together, and in 1920 the German bishops demanded censorship of all textbooks, and to take the world-view into consideration with ideological subjects. The bishops were thin-skinned and alert to violations, intervening on the behalf of the Catholic teachers' organizations.[415]

Only in the strongly Catholic Bavaria did the Catholic Church, in the concordat of 1924, attain the full rights they demanded. The concordats with Prussia (1929) and Baden (1932) did not contain anything about schools, only the proscribing of officials from belonging to the Nazi Party as it was a "revolutionary" party.[416]

Being Catholic parties, both the Zentrum and the BVP were in accord with the Church's educational policy, but the Zentrum was so solidly rooted in the Western democratic values of "1789," it preferred to cooperate with the democratic SPD and DDP in Prussia, despite the opposition of these parties to the Catholic policy and despite the more Catholic-friendly education policy of the rightist DNVP.[417]

Mosse asserts the traditional conservatism of the education authorities, together with the reactionary tendencies among the youth in the Empire created an atmosphere which favored the *völkish* influence on education,[418] referring to Fritz Stern who stated: "One thousand teachers in republican Germany (i.e. the Weimar Republic) who in their youth had idolized de Lagarde and Langbehn, were as important for the triumph of Nazism as all the millions of Marks which Hitler collected from German tycoons."[419] Mosse even points out that teachers who identified themselves with the Weimar Republic, basically cooperated—though maybe unaware—with the enemies of the republic by undermining confidence in its institutions and by creating confusion about the problems confronting the modern man. He mentions as an example a history textbook which was pronounced Weimar-friendly, but at the same time praised "the Teutonic prophets" de Lagarde and Langbehn.[420] Bleuel and Klinnert assert the influence within the education of de Lagarde cannot be exaggerated. He considerably contributed to "the establishment of a *völkisch-* national myth detached from reality," and a dangerous vision. A French historian already saw through it during WWI and described it this way: "It has so deeply percolated into the German people, through universities and schools and on account of monotonous repetition of its main themes, that through the power of habit the German people have reached the point of believing it as Truth."[421] Langbehn had placed the "Spiritual influences from the South and North" up against each other and asserted that Rafael and Michelangelo were Catholics and looked back to antiquity, whereas Rembrandt favored "*Deutschtum.*"[422]

Later ideas of the right-wing philosophers Oswald Spengler and Moeller van den Bruck were incorporated in the mentality. Bleuel and Klinnert characterize the situation at the beginning of the Weimar era: " The influential parade of conservative ideologs from de Lagarde to Moeller van den Bruck, imprecise in their political thoughts and phraseology, fervent in their adoration of popular German essence, full of hatred against everything from the West that originated in the ideas of 1789, made a heavy heritage for the young republic."[423]

It would seem the Catholic mentality among academics was on its way away from rightist values. An observer in 1928 said, "The number of Catholics, mostly young academics, who build their world-view by looking backwards in almost pagan adoration of the *völkisch* and in that way not managing to grasp the spirit of Catholicism, which is open for all peoples of the world, has fortunately dwindled."[424]

Erich Weymar has undertaken research into history textbooks in the senior high schools from 1815 until the Third Reich and is astonished at the impact in them, right from the outset, of *völkisch* tendencies. During the nineteenth century, even the Old Testament was harshly treated and condemned because it taught the students about "Syrian-Arabic beduins" instead of letting them learn about the more important Teutonic heritage. The Bible was outdated by Darwin, and asserts Mosse, up until the Third Reich, teachers were the most outspoken advocates of *völkisch* ideology, especially when it came to issues of race.[425]

Eighty per cent of teachers at primary school level were members of the religiously neutral and liberal *Deutscher Lehrerverein*. There was in addition, a communist, a German nationalist and from 1927, a Nazi association. Specifically, Christian associations separately existed for both confessions. There were 45,000 members in the male and female Catholic associations combined, while the Protestant one, which was for both sexes, had slightly under 4,000. This is conspicuous since the confessional ratio in the country as such was two to one in Protestantism's favor.[426]

"The teachers who joined the National Socialist Party were predominantly Protestant, from the younger generation of teachers and lived-in small towns or medium-sized cities," according to Kjøstvedt.[427] Before 1932, the Nazi teachers' association had hardly been noticed abroad, but by 1934 almost half of the publicly employed, who were Nazi *Kreisleiter*, are said to have been teachers.[428]

It is reasonable to conclude that a profound dissimilarity between the confessions had arisen in German society by the time the Nazi offensive started: in culture, mentality and probably even the textbooks. The difference most probably facilitated Nazi acceptance among Protestants and rejection among Catholic churchgoers.

Universities and High Schools

George L. Mosse informs us that the student organizations were the first battleground where Aryan, *völkisch* and Teutonic ideas were mobilized in strength and ultimately triumphed.[429] Kjøstvedt, Jahr, and Friedmann, all concur with him. Friedmann writes: "students right from the time of *"Gründer"* (the early 1870s) were strongly influenced by a German national, even *völkisch* mentality" and fifty years later "Young academics were markedly rightist. In no other part of the population could the NSDAP get so much support so early on . . . Stirred up by a mostly reactionary group of professors the universities in the Weimar Republic became bastions of rightist extremism and anti-Semitic ideas."[430]

As we saw in the previous chapter, Mosse has also noted that prior to this development there had been a significant rightist orientation in the primary and secondary schools. This took the shape of a wave motion with the voting behavior in the 1930s as an end result. Mosse does not distinguish between Protestant and Catholic dominated schools, but according to what he writes about the heavy impact of de Lagarde and Langbehn in the education,[431] together with how important Catholic confessional schools were to the Zentrum, there is reason to expect a significant divergence in school profiles between respective confessional areas. Already in 1927, members of Catholic and inter-confessional teachers' organizations had observed and been appalled by the alienation and the political radicalization of recently educated teachers.[432]

In addition to the reasons described in the previous chapter, the Nazis' problem in attracting Catholic students could be due to a special Catholic intellectual mobilization in universities in the 1920s and 1930s. Martin Conway claims: "The 1920s and 1930s were a golden age for Catholic intellectual journals and revues which, although their circulation was relatively small, often had considerable influence in terms of distributing and popularizing the ideas of the Catholic intellectual elite."[433] A Nazi observer of the student world in 1931 noted that "remnants of bourgeois ideological elements" were first and foremost to be found in the "Corps" and the Catholic associations.[434] However, the most important reason for Catholic students' rejection of Nazism probably was the general rejection in the clerical Catholic milieu, and both of the most important Catholic student associations, the CV and the KV, prohibited Nazis from joining them. Despite this, from as early as the turn of the century, nationalist and anti-Semitic tendencies can be traced in both organizations in Munich among the "Reform Catholics."[435]

In 1930 there was an umbrella organization for students in Germany, Danzig, Austria, and German-speakers of Czechoslovakia. It was made up of 26 religiously and politically neutral associations and six religious ones, among them four Catholic. It is symptomatic that only these four, the CV, the KV, the *Unitasverband* and the *Ring Katholischer Deutscher Burschenschaften*, with 32,000 members, dissociated themselves clearly from Nazism, participated in the celebrations of the Weimar constitution and accepted the Young-plan. In addition to the four was the political *Reichsverband Deutscher Zentrumsstudenten*, which in theory was open for members of other confessions, but in reality was overwhelmingly Catholic and anti-Nazi.[436]

In 1927 a Nazi became the leader of the national students' congress, the *Studententag*, and a Catholic observer resignedly noted it was no longer a forum of democratic discussion, but an arena of demagogical and propagandist sallies. When some associations demanded *"Führerstaat"* and a war of revenge, the Catholic associations refused their consent. They even protested when Frick, the Nazi minister in Thuringia, together with the *Studententag*, forced the employment of the incompetent Nazi Hans Günther on Jena University in 1930 against the will of the board.[437] It must be conceded that in 1925 the *Ring Katholischer Deutscher Burschenschafter* was formed and openly hailed *völkisch* ideals, the only Catholic one to do so.[438] Like the case of the Christian teachers' associations, the number of members in the only two evangelical associations, the *Wingolfsbund*,[439] and the *Schwarzburgbund*, with 2700 members was less than one-tenth of the number in the Catholic ones. Articles in *Wingolf*-publications revealed a rather positive attitude to Nazism, but none of the two evangelical associations issued a public view on that ideology. The bulk of clergy in the rightist radical umbrella organization the *Christlich-Deutsche Bewegung*, which also had Nazis like Goebbels as members, had been erstwhile *Wingolf*-members. Baldur von Schirach noted with satisfaction in 1929 that Nazis even had entered the *Wingolfbund.*⁴⁴⁰

One of the main focuses of the Zentrum after the culmination of the *Kulturkampf* was the battle for parity in public employment. Catholics were discriminated against in most public departments and institutions, especially within education and science. A Catholic worldview and mentality at universities was almost nonexistent, and some universities, e.g. in Berlin, almost practiced a policy of *"Berufsverbot."* Even at Strasbourg University in 75 percent Catholic Alsace, which was German from 1871–1919, only 25 percent of the students were Catholics. Out of the 48 lecturers who were fully employed only four were Jews and two Catholics, and out of the 35 part-timers only four were Catholics.⁴⁴¹ This seems to have produced sweeping consequences for the recruitment of students and the contents of what higher educational institutions taught about culture, history and ideology.

Windthorst, the first leader of the Zentrum, demanded that Catholic historians should begin to correct the prevailing German understanding of history, and Johannes Janssen responded to the challenge. He published *Geschichte des Deutschen Volkes* (*History of the German People*), which caused alarm among the prestigious Protestant historians' establishments. Many of these were engaged in the anti-Catholic activity, as they considered Catholicism a menace to the national state.⁴⁴² The two most famous, Heinrich von Treitschke and Theodor Mommsen, were both anti-Catholic even though they disagreed on anti-Semitism.⁴⁴³

Karl Kupisch describes the influence this Protestant academic impact had on the spirit of young students in WWI:

> This national-Protestant history-theology and its product, the Christian-Teutonic culture of uniformity, has been widely spread in the academic youth. Many young Germans of the WWI generation have received their patriotic ethos from men like Stoecker, von Treitschke and Pfleiderer (Protestant liberal theologian). But in the German-Protestant high schools also, the Christian-Teutonic ideal of upbringing has been the rule and had its impact through the whole of the nineteenth century up to WWI. One example of the national upbringing at the universities was Kyffhäuserverband, which was one of the associations which had recruited German students since 1881 and had as a program: "Protection of Christianity, Monarchy and 'Deutschtum.'" This national trinity of Christian observance typified the political style among German academics before 1915. The voluntary death of young Germans on the battlefield of Langemarck in the autumn of 1914 cannot be understood without this patriotic mentality rooted in the religious.⁴⁴⁴

Thus, German students were separated into two groups in the years leading to WWI: "the national ones," i.e. defenders of imperialistic policy, and "the enemies of the *Reich*," i.e. social democrats, leftist-liberals, and the "Ultramontanists."[445]

Many Catholic students were anxious about the accusations of being unpatriotic, which led to discord in their ranks and formation of two main groups that neutralized each other: students from the working class who could not be bothered, and students from the bourgeoisie who tried in some way to adapt to the German mainstream. This may explain why the student body was regarded as the most rightist and anti-Semitic part of the Catholic population, and why it was a haven for the anti-Vatican Old Catholics and for "Reform Catholics."[446]

Most students were at first friendly towards the Weimar authorities after WWI, but a marked rightist turn could be observed in the mid-1920s, unlike the general trend in national politics of calming down. The authorities did not have success checking this development, and several Catholic students felt that they had to "go with the flow" to duck the accusation of having an unpatriotic attitude.[447]

Consequently, Catholic student associations were considered the least Nazi-resistant in the *"Zentrumsturm"* after 1930. This became apparent when the CV celebrated the bishops' partial capitulation to the Nazi government on March 28, 1933, only to be disabused shortly after. The CV had to give up its Catholic identity in January 1934 and was disbanded the year after. Several of the CV members in the Austrian branch were leading members in the anti-Nazi Resistance and jailed shortly after *"Anschluss."*[448]

After the murder of Rathenau, the *Republikanisches Studentenkartell* was formed with the main purpose of combatting anti-Semitism among students and over-pronounced nationalism, and of promoting the interests of the Weimar Republic. It was made up of associations of the three "Weimar" parties, the SPD, the DDP and the Zentrum, in addition to the *Deutscher Pazifistischer Studentenbund*. The cartel cooperated with the great republican *Reichsbanner Schwarz-Rot-Gold*. Because of the relative rightist attitudes in the CV and the KV, these associations disliked the cartel.[449]

It is possible to summarize that although rightist values had a relatively strong position in the Catholic student milieu compared to Catholic organizational life in general, the same can be said of the organized student world in Germany as a whole. However, the Protestant population outnumbered the Catholic, two to one. The number of students and the level of their education were pronouncedly higher among Protestants than Catholics. Nevertheless, Christian Catholic teachers and students' organizations recruited over ten times as many as the corresponding Protestant ones, and the Catholic organizations had a pronouncedly more anti-*völkisch* and anti-Nazi attitude than the Protestant ones had.

"THE SPIRIT OF TIME" AT THE TURN OF THE CENTURY

Three books published at the turn of the century express "The Spirit of the Age" in Germany in the opinion of Karl Kupisch and Thomas Nipperdey: *Das Wesen des Christentums* (*The Essence of Christianity*) by theologian Adolf von Harnack, *Grundlagen des 19. Jahrhunderts* (*Foundations of the Nineteenth Century*) by cultural philosopher Houston Stewart Chamberlain, and *Die Welträtsel* (*The World Enigma*) by zoologist Ernst Haeckel.[450] What the three have in common is that they all were Protestants and their books provoked Catholics and theologically orthodox conservative Protestants strongly.

Harnack claimed the Christian dogma is a product of the Greek spirit, that virgin birth was alien to original Christianity, and that the objective atonement and corporal resurrection of Christ are false additions to it. The task of theology was to release Christianity from dogmatism. It attracted enormous attention and caused huge opposition.[451] Harnack must, therefore, be regarded as one of the important liberal theologians. He even participated in polemics against Judaism and deplored that Luther had not abolished the Old Testament.[452] This polemic was one of the elements that led to the comprehensive "Essence" debate among Protestant theologians, in its turn inducing a reaction among Jewish intellectuals. Not that the debate among Protestants was new. Fichte, Schleiermacher, de Lagarde and Stöcker had all discussed the theme.[453] The significance of this theme in German Protestantism became apparent when Bishop Dibelius defended the Nazi boycott of Jews in the spring of 1933. He asserted, "what is happening now in Germany will lead to a goal everyone who loves and honors the German Essence will be grateful for." Dibelius must have sincerely regretted his remark fourteen years later when the Protestant Churches issued the following resolution: "We were wrong when we began to dream the dream of a special mission, as though the German Essence could cure the world."[454]

Harnack joined Stöcker's *Evangelisch-Sozialer Kongress* but never showed any sympathy to Nazism before he died in 1930. However, there is little doubt that his works helped reinforce a pro-Nazi attitude within liberal theology and, even more importantly, clear the way for the legitimation of the Nazi view of the Old Testament.[455]

Harnack's friend, Chamberlain was influenced by his theology and referred to it often as well as honoring Schleiermacher, whom he thought had to a great extent contributed to "a living religious worldview."[456]

Chamberlain revealed an extreme rightist radical opinion in his speculations. He synthesized Eugen Dühring's and de Lagarde's anti-Semitism into diffuse theories about "Racist irrational 'Protestantism'" and developed a world view which depicted all European history as a gigantic Aryan battle against its enemies. In his own days, this was now a concealed and fateful battle between *Germanentum* and *Judentum*.[457] This battle was also against Catholicism and, by extension, Roman law. He accused the church of despotism, intolerance, assertion of primacy, fighting against science and everything Teutonic, and it was all tied into socialism. Jesuitism was linked to Jewish religion and popes to Jews. The Teutons were the best suited to hearing "the Divine Voice," and the Germans the most religious people in the world. Through Luther the Germans had created a specific German religion. Although Luther as a reformer was not interesting himself, it was his confrontation with the power of Rome that mattered. Chamberlain even asserted Jesus was not a Jew and he despised people from Southern Europe. Chandler asserts that Chamberlain delivered "the most influential diatribe on Northern superiority, anti-Semitism and anti-Catholicism of his time."[458]

Lächele asserts Chamberlain was rejected by the academic and clerical milieu, but Berg Eriksen, Harket, and Lorenz all maintain that his main work "strongly influenced the opinion of many generations of intellectuals and officials." The nationally inclined bourgeoisie are said to have identified themselves with his viewpoints to a great extent, and all Prussian teachers' seminaries and libraries were obliged to keep a volume.[459] Chamberlain found enthusiastic adherents in several anti-Catholic organizations in Germany and Austria and even representatives of pietistic revival movements and a leader of one of the Christian student associations talked positively about Chamberlain. Additionally, Chamberlain had a great impact on the emergence of the *völkisch* literature and became the main inspiration of Alfred Rosenberg with his "*Mythus.*"[460]

Haeckel „concurred in Darwin's teachings and promoted them all his life, issuing several scientific and popular scientific works. He furthered the breakthrough of Darwinism in Germany considerably." Protestants regarded him as one of the important scientists but though some Catholics of note, such as Pierre Teilhard de Chardin and the Jesuit, Wasmann, did not find incompatibilities between Darwinism and divine creation, the Catholic Church as a whole rejected the theory of evolution and Darwin's work was put on the *Index*. Antagonism between Haeckel and Catholicism was sharpened because Haeckel was an atheist and was regarded as the founder of Social Darwinism, a variant which won ground everywhere in Germany except among clerical Catholics. Social Darwinism coincided with the literary genre of Naturalism, with its main theme of "the survival of miserable people in a harsh society." In Germany, where people and race were now becoming important social concepts, this "survival of the fittest" did not apply to individuals but was a socio-ethical struggle for the German people as a common entity.[461]

The Zentrum's policies did not fit in with this way of looking at things. It followed the social ethics of the Catholic Church, and, as mentioned, its representatives were the initiators of Bismarck's social policy, although their aims were probably rather different from his anti-socialist intentions.[462]

Haeckel founded the strongly anti-Catholic *Monistenbund*. "Monism was a sort of materialistic pantheism with roots in German Romanticism's idea of the unity between mind and matter, and it preached a deified Nature replacing Christianity," explains Emberland.[463] Haeckel was also an adherent of a kind of sun cult and in this way a precursor of *völkisch* and Nazi sun-worship.[464]

There were several other "scientific" ideologies and religions in the first decades of the 20th century, most of them a melange of religion, philosophy, science, spiritism, theosophy, and other neo-occult elements. Common to them all was their opposition to orthodox Catholicism.[465]

Walser Smith also mentions three people that were "bridge-builders" between the cultural history of the nineteenth century and the twentieth century scenario: historian von Treitschke, geographer Friedrich Ratzel, and colonial administrator Paul Rohrbach. All three were important in linking anti-Semitism, racism and ethnic cleansing/genocide together, and all three were Protestants. Rohrbach was even a theologian, while Treitschke was anti-Catholic. Ratzel's contribution to the ideological development was to introduce the concept of *Lebensraum*.[466] Treitschke's importance was to establish anti-Semitism in the academic world in an "intellectual" and "decent" way, by differentiating between the "Jewish problem" in Germany and the same "problem" in Western European lands. Jewish migrants from the east had impaired "the German essence," whereas western Jews had been better integrated since antiquity and the Middle Ages.[467]

Rohrbach, a student of Treitschke and associate of Harnack's, admonished his Protestant colleagues to tackle the challenges of *Weltpolitik* by directing "their imperial attention eastward, and infuse Germany's imperial ambitions with a serum of Christian (i.e. Protestant) values". He was appointed in 1903 Commissar of Southwest Africa, so he was partly responsible for the genocide and the establishment of concentration camps in the colony, although he criticized the way von Trotha carried it out. Rohrbach warned against educating Africans, as this would lead to greater self-confidence and resistance to colonization. A commentator asserted that his book, *Der Deutsche Gedanke in der Welt* (*The German Thought in the World*), "probably inspired more Germans than any other published since 1871."[468]

The confessional differences can also be discerned in women's organizations. "Conservative, (usually) Protestant women dominated the female rightist movements during the first decades of the twentieth century," comments an observer.[469]

Because of the dominant influence of Protestants on the "spirit of the age," it is not difficult to imagine that the Catholic milieu would feel overridden in the cultural life of the late Empire, and have problems asserting themselves after the long and bitter *Kulturkampf*.

"REFORM CATHOLICISM"

"Reform Catholics" had started in the second part of the nineteenth century as an opposition to the strengthening of papal authority, but unlike the Old Catholics, who broke away and started their own denomination, the "Reform Catholics" stayed. Whereas the Old Catholics gradually oriented themselves towards nationalism and anti-Semitism, the "Reform Catholics" joined the mainstream Protestant rightist complex from the beginning and were small in number, academically intellectual, and rejected by almost all the Catholic media. Rather than recruiting support, its elitism repelled it. Nuncio Pacelli asserted in the 1920s that the "Reformers" were influenced by "modernist currents" from the turn of the century, and "their philosophy is close to Protestantism partly in the way religion becomes a totally subjective phenomenon, an exclusively inner experience."[470]

An early representative of the movement was Joseph Görres, in Derek Hastings view, but it is only possible to talk of a Munich-based variety with the arrival of theologian Ignaz von Döllinger on the scene. After that there is continuity until the early 1920s. Döllinger opposed what he considered the increasingly reactionary spirit, which he connected both with the ultramontane awakening in Germany and the dominating neo-scholastic orthodoxy within theological and intellectual circles. He believed God had given the Germans, in particular, the historic task of redefining Catholic theology for the modern world and the future. They alone were capable of this because it was self-evident that the German "National Spirit" was "supremely competent," in contrast to the incompetent and mediocre South-European, Roman cultures in their ultramontane versions. The "feminine", Roman theological conservatism was contrasted to the noble "masculine" German edition.[471] We may reasonably say this view was a form of the Catholic version of the Protestant "German Essence."

Döllinger was excommunicated in 1871, but had many adherents among Catholic nationalists in Munich, among them Gebhard Himmler, the father of Heinrich Himmler.[472] After 1890, several organizations, parties and publications based on nationalist, anti-Semitic and "Reform Catholic" ideas arose in Munich. As with the comparable Protestant activity in the same period, such enterprises were short-lived, merged, split up and changed names.[473]

What provoked the "Reform Catholics" most was the link between the Church and the Zentrum. Clerics should, out of consideration for the churchgoers, if nothing else, be politically totally neutral, and a specific Catholic Christian party was an absurdity. Also the Jesuits were discredited. The "Reformers" used terminology that later was adopted by the Nazis, such as *"positives Christentum"* and *"Nationalsozialismus."* The *völkisch* impact on the movement increased: eugenics was approved, the Old Testament rejected, Jesus was described as an Aryan, and the race-theorists Chamberlain and Arthur de Gobineau were popular, the latter because he was both a friend of Germany and a Catholic. It was a "Reformer" who introduced the theory of the primary, secondary and "parasitic" races during WWI. In pronounced contrast to the Protestant version, soon after the end of WWI, this organized Catholic Munich-based *"Völkische Bewegung"* disappeared. Some individuals, however, became prominent members of the DAP, formed in 1919.[474]

SITUATION IN 1914: VATICAN AUTHORIZED UNIVERSAL CATHOLIC THEOLOGY IN CONFRONTATION WITH CONTEXTUAL GERMAN-NATIONALIST PROTESTANT THEOLOGY

At the outbreak of WWI, the two main confessions, Protestantism and Catholicism, had each established their singularities once the process of re-confessionalization in the nineteenth century had phased out eighteenth century Rationalism. The majority of German Catholics had adopted the centralized and universal Vatican-authorized main version once the minority German-Catholics, Old Catholics and "Reform Catholics," which in any case were geographically and numerically very restricted, had asserted themselves as the Church opposition. Therefore, the overwhelming majority of Catholic churchgoers in Germany were obliged theologically by guidelines from the Vatican. Politically, however, they were loyal subjects of the German states, and of the Empire after its formation. When the clergy and the churchgoers in the 1870s and 1880s felt the secular authorities violated their spiritual rights, a confrontation followed. Even after the abolition of the *Kulturkampf*, German society was influenced by it until "Hour zero" struck in 1945.

Having no universal theological authority, the Protestants were left in an authority vacuum once the confessionally pure states died out after 1803, and even more when the Empire and princely states were abolished in 1918. There was great scope in Protestant circles for the emergence of a theological school that, in varying degrees, was independent of the Bible. To a great extent this developed within a nationalist context, in contrast to Protestant milieus in most other countries. Furthermore, this allowed not only nationalist but gradually also racist, anti-Semitic and elements from other religions, mythologies and philosophies to gain a foothold in the theological systems. There was hardly any institution with the authority to block false doctrine.

Politically, this resulted in an aversion to specifically Christian parties. Organizationally and politically, church leaders could cooperate with others holding very different theological opinions, the only limitation being that he was not a Jew, a Catholic or a socialist.

It is, therefore, possible to conclude that whereas the Protestants were modernist, the Catholics in the religious field were anti-modernist. In the political field, however, the opposite tendencies were the case. The Zentrum, together with the secular SPD, showed a more progressive and modernist bent compared to the bulk of the parties backed by Protestant churchgoers. As we have seen, Zentrum politicians were more concerned about constitution and the rights of the states and the minorities, and they were the real instigators of the famous social radical "Bismarckian" legislation in the 1880s. In addition, from 1900 onwards the party favored ministerial responsiblility and the rights of the natives in the colonies. With the exception of the Progressive party, all the other Protestant based parties favored strong imperial authority.[475]

These factors would seem to be important for the relationship of the confessions to the *"Völkische Bewegung"* and, as we shall see in the next part, to Nazism, ultimately, after the dissimilarity had become even clearer during and after WWI.

NOTES

1. *Meyers Konversationslexikon, 5. Edition* (Leipzig: 1897) Entries, "Deutschkatholiken" and "Altkatholizismus"; Hubert Jedin, "Kirche und Katholizismus im Deutschland des 19. Jahrhunderts," in Anton Rauscher (ed.) *Entwicklungslinien des deutschen Katholizismus* (Munich: Ferdinand Schöningh, 1973) 77.

2. Chap. "Reform Catholicism."

3. Jedin, "Kirche," 77–78; Thomas Nipperdey, *Religion im Umbruch. Deutschland 1870–1918* (Munich: Verlag C. H. Beck, 1988) 9–13.

4. Wolfram Kaiser, *Christian Democracy and the Origins of European Union* (Cambridge: Cambridge University Press, 2007) 12–24; Nipperdey, *Umbruch*, 15.

5. Klaus Scholder, *Die Kirchen und das Dritte Reich. Band 1.* (Frankfurt/M: Verlag Ullstein, 1977) 15.

6. Arve T. Thorsen, *The Gospel of the Fatherland. Christianity, Universality and National Thought in France and Germany in the Early 20th Century* (Oslo: Acta Humaniora, 2008) 443.

7. Erwin Preuschen, *Kirchengeschichte für das christliche Haus/die christliche Familie* (Reutlingen: Ensslin & Laiblins Verlagsbuchhandlung, 1905) 529.

8. Nipperdey, *Umbruch*, 152–153.
9. Nipperdey, *Umbruch*, 152–153.
10. Wolfgang Huber & Theodor Strohm, "Protestantismus – soziale Organisation und der Friedensauftrag der Kirche," in Wolfgang Huber & Johannes Schwerdtfeger (ed.), *Kirche zwischen Krieg und Frieden. Studien zur Geschichte des deutschen Protestantismus* (Stuttgart: Ernst Klett Verlag, 1976) 51.
11. Cfr. Scholder, *Kirchen. Band 1*. 1977, 147–148 concerning Friedrich Andersen.
12. Nipperdey, *Umbruch*, 83.
13. Helmut Walser Smith, *German Nationalism and Religious Conflict. Culture, Ideology, Politics, 1870–1914* (Princeton, N.J.: Princeton University Press, 1995), 86-91; Karl Kupisch, "Bürgerliche Frömmigkeit im Wilhelminischen Zeitalter," in Hans Joachim Schoeps (ed.) *Zeitgeist im Wandel. Band 1. Das Wilhelminische Zeitalter* (Stuttgart: Ernst Klett Verlag, 1967) 132, note 28.
14. H. Roos, "Katolsk politisk teori," in Svend Erik Stybe (ed.) *Politiske ideologier. Fra Platon til Mao* (Copenhagen: Politikens Forlag, 1979) 49.
15. Nipperdey, *Umbruch*, 43–44; Karl Buchheim, *Geschichte der christlichen Parteien in Deutschland* (Munich: Kösel Verlag KG, 1953) 297–298; Roos, "Katolsk politisk teori," 49.
16. Roos, "Katolsk politisk teori," 49–51.
17. Hans Peter Bleuel & Ernst Klinnert, *Deutsche Studenten auf dem Weg ins Dritte Reich* (Gütersloh: Sigbert Mohn Verlag, 1967) 63–137; Karl-Wilhelm Dahm, *Pfarrer und Politik. Soziale Position und politische Mentalität des deutschen evangelischen Pfarrerstandes zwischen 1918 und 1933* (Cologne: Westdeutscher Verlag, 1965)166–184.
18. *Store Norske Leksikon* (Oslo: Kunnskapsforlaget, 1978) Entry: " regimentslære"
19. See chap."Christian parties—Catholic and Protestant."
20. Thorsen, *Gospel*, 441.
21. See chap. "The Protestant Confession."
22. Nipperdey, *Umbruch*, 102–103.
23. Nipperdey, *Umbruch*, 104.
24. Thorsen, *Gospel*, 442.
25. Hans M. Bringeland, *Martin Dibelius' oppgjer med nasjonalsosialismen* (Unpublished manuscript for lecture at submission of PhD, University of Bergen, 15 December 2011); see further chap."The Weimar Constitution."
26. Bringeland, *Martin Dibelius*, 12–14, 16; see further chap."The Confessions of Guilt by the Churches."
27. Scholder, *Kirchen Band 1*, 1977, 351.
28. Scholder, *Kirchen Band 1*, 1977, 351.
29. Hans Joachim Hahn, *German Thought and Culture from the Holy Roman Empire to the Present Day* (Manchester: Manchester University Press, 1995) 30–31.
30. Letter to the author from Professor Dr. theol. Svein Rise April 2, 2001; Terje Emberland, *Religion og rase. Nyhedenskap og nazisme I Norge 1933-1945* (Oslo: Humanist Forlag, 2003) 91.

31. Poul Lübcke (ed.), *Politikens filosofi leksikon* (Copenhagen: Politikens Forlag A/S, 1995) 390.
32. R. Butler, *The Roots of National Socialism 1783–1933* (London: Missing publishing house, 1942) 48.
33. Wolfgang Altgeld, *Katholizismus, Protestantismus, Judentum. Über religiös begründete Gegensätze und nationalreligiöse Ideen in der Geschichte des deutschen Nationalismus* (Mainz: Matthias-Grünewald-Verlag, 1992) 2, note 3.
34. George L. Mosse, *The Crisis of German Ideology* (N. Y.: Howard Fertig, 1998) 52–66.
35. Hans Kohn, *The Mind of Germany, the Education of a Nation* (N. Y.: Charles Scribner's Sons, 1960) 9–10.
36. Kohn, *The Mind*, 10.
37. Peter Levenda, *Unholy Alliance. A History of Nazi Involvement with the Occult* (N. Y.: Continuum, 2002) 178.
38. Richard Steigmann-Gall, *The Holy Reich, Nazi Conceptoions of Christianity, 1919–1945* (Cambridge: Cambridge University Press, 2004) 77–78.
39. Richard Steigmann-Gall, "Rethinking Nazism and Religion: How Anti-Christian were the "Pagans,"" in *Central European History*, Vol. 36, No. 1 (Leiden: Brill Academic Publishers, March 2003) 59–60.
40. Steigmann-Gall, "Rethinking," 103.
41. Hahn, German *Thought*, 192.
42. Paul de Lagarde, *Schriften für Deutschland* (Stuttgart: Alfred Kröner Verlag, 1933) e.g. 79, 177–180.
43. Preuschen, *Kirchengeschichte*, 528–529.
44. Lagarde, *Schriften*, 56–73, 130, 143–144.
45. Ina Ulrike Paul, "Paul Anton de Lagarde," in Uwe Puschner, Walter Schmitz & Justus H. Ulbricht (ed.) *Handbuch zur "Völkischen Bewegung"* 1871–1918 (Munich: K. G. Saur Verlag, 1996) 62–65; Lagarde, *Schriften*, 9–12,.33–42, 50–51, 103, 108–109, 122–127.
46. Rainer Lächele, "Protestantismus und völkische Religion im deutschen Kaiserreich," in Puschner et al. *Handbuch*, 155.
47. Thorsen, *Gospel*, 439–440, note 976.
48. Lagarde, *Schriften*, 64–168; George L. Mosse, "Die deutsche Rechte und die Juden," in Werner E. Mosse (ed.) *Entscheidungsjahr 1932. Zur Judenfrage in der Weimarer Republik* (Tübingen: J. C. B. Mohr, 1966) 188, 191–192, Peter Viereck, *Nazismens rötter. En historisk och psykologisk överblick* (Stockholm: Natur och kultur, 1942) 164.
49. Steigmann-Gall, *The Holy Reich*, 27.
50. Stefanie von Schnurbein, "Die Suche nach einer "arteigenen" Religion in "germanisch-" und "deutschgäubigen" Gruppen," in Puschner et al. *Handbuch*, 173–175; Stefan Arvidsson, "Germania. Noen hovedlinjer i forskningen om fortidens germanere," in Terje Emberland & Jorunn Sem Fure (ed.), *Jakten på Germania. Fra Nordensvermeri til SS-arkeologi* (Oslo: Humanist forlag, 2009) 17, 26–30.

51. See chapters on "*Protestant Nationalism,*" "*Racism and "Herrenmensch*" *(Superior Man),*" "Roman Law and "*Blut und Boden*" (Blood and Soil)," and ""The Spirit of time" at the Turn of the Century."
52. Schnurbein, "Suche," 175–177; George L. Mosse, *Die Nationalisierung der Massen. Politische Symbolik und Massenbewegungen von den Befreiungskriegen bis zum Dritten Reich* (Frankfurt/M: Campus Verlag, 1993) 118–119, 127.
53. Schnurbein, "Suche," 175–176.
54. Blavatsky, Helena P., *The Secret Doctrine. The Synthesis of Science, Religion, and Philosophy*, *Vol. II*, http://www.theosociety.org/pasadena/ Theosophical University Press Online Edition (Version from 1888) 221–223; Terje Emberland, "I tvilsomt selskap," in *Dag og Tid*, No. 42, (Oslo: Oct. 16, 2009); Jan Hansen (former anthroposopher), " Steinerdisiplenes glemte budskap?" in *Vårt Land*, (Oslo: Nov. 26 2009).
55. Kurt Sontheimer, *Antidemokratisches Denken in der Weimarer Republik. Die politischen Ideen des deutschen Nationalismus zwischen 1918 und 1933* (Munich: Nymphenberger Verlagshandlung, 1964) 166–167, 287; Puschner et al., *Handbuch*, XI.
56. Puschner et al., *Handbuch*, XII, XVIII; Lagarde, *Schriften*, 146.
57. Puschner et al., *Handbuch*, XVIII–XIX.
58. Uwe Puschner, *Die völkische Bewegung im wilhelminischen Kaiserreich. Sprache—Rasse-Religion* (Darmstadt: Wissenschaftliche Buchgesellschaft, 2001) 207–208.
59. Puschner, *Bewegung*, 211–213.
60. Lächele, "völkische Religion," 161–162; Hans-Joachim Kraus, "Die evangelische Kirche," in Werner Mosse, *Entscheidungsjahr*, 256; Karl Kupisch, "Die Wandlungen des Nationalismus im liberalen deutschen Bürgertum," in Horst Zillessen (ed.), *Volk—Nation—Vaterland* (Gütersloh: Gütersloher Verlagshaus Gerd Mohn, 1970) 132; Puschner et al., *Handbuch*, XII; Emberland, *Religion*, 32.
61. Anthony Kauders, *German Politics and the Jews. Düsseldorf and Nuremberg* (Oxford: Clarendon Press, 1996) 158–159; Hans Mommsen, *Die Deutschen und der Holocaust* (Bonn: Friedrich Ebert Stiftung, 2006) 545, 547.
62. Levenda, *Unholy Alliance*, 55–72; Helmut Zander, "Sozialdarwinistische Rassentheorien auss dem okkulten Untergrund des Kaiserreichs," in Puschner et al. *Handbuch*, 233–235, 239–240; George L. Mosse, *The Fascist Revolution. Toward a General Theory of Fascism* (N. Y.: Howard Fertig, 2000) 123, 130.
63. See chap."Reform Catholicism."
64. Biographies in *Deutsche Biographie*, deutsche-biographie.de in addition to Mosse's own information.
65. Ekkehard Hieronimus, "Zur Religiosität der völkischen Bewegung," in Hubert Cancik (ed.) *Religions- und Geistegeschichte der Weimarer Republik* (Düsseldorf: Patmos Verlag, 1982) 160–163, with note 13.
66. Bringeland, *Martin Dibelius*, 5.
67. Kauders, *German Politics*,133, 158–159.
68. Hieronimus, "Religiosität," 165–167.
69. Hieronimus, "Religiosität," 168–172; Huber Cancik, "'Neuheiden' und totaler Staat. Völkische Religion am Ende der Weimarer Republik," in Cancik, *Geistesgeschichte*, 176–180, 183–184, 201–204.

70. Cancik, "Neuheiden," 183.
71. Cancik, "Neuheiden," 189.
72. Emberland, *Religion*, 11–13.
73. Karl Kupisch, "Der Protestantismus im Epochenjahr 1917," in Schoeps (ed.), *Zeitgeist*, 40–41; Kurt Meier, *Kreuz und Hakenkreuz. Die evangelische Kirche im Dritten Reich* (Munich: Deutscher Taschenbuchverlag, 2008) 17, 19; see further chap. "The International Connections of the Christian Parties: Catholic Paneuropeanism versus German Protestant Autarchy."
74. *Dagen*, (Bergen: June 20, 2005).
75. Kupisch, "Bürgerliche Frömmigkeit," 53.
76. *Meyers* 5, Entries: "Grossbritannien," "Deutschland," "Schweiz"; *Vol. 12*, 378.
77. Walser Smith, *Conflict*, 233–234.
78. Walser Smith, *Conflict*, 80, 98, 113
79. Herder, Johann Gottfried, *Ideen zur Philosophie der Geschichte der Menschheit*, http://www.textlog.de/herder/ (1784–1791) XVIII.6.7.
80. Hagen Schulze, "Die deutsche Nationalbewegung bis zur Reichseinigung," in Otto Büsch & James J. Sheehan (ed.), *Die Rolle der Nation in der deutschen Geschichte und Gegenwart* (Berlin: Colloquium Verlag, 1985) 87–88.
81. Altgeld, *Katholizismus*, 8; Werner Conze, "Deutschland" und "deutsche Nation" als historische Begriffe," in Büsch & Sheehan, *Die Rolle*, 29; Carl Müller Frøland, *Nazismens idéunivers* (Oslo: Vidarforlaget, 2017) 73.
82. Paul-Wilhelm Gennrich, *Gott und die Völker. Beiträge zur Auffassung von Volk und Volkstum in der Geschichte der Theologie* (Stuttgart: Evangelisches Verlagswerk, 1972) 48–89.
83. Helmut Walser Smith, The *Continuities of German History. Nation, Religion, and Race across the long Nineteenth Century* (N. Y.: Cambridge University Press, 2008) 224; Trond Berg Eriksen, Håkon Harket & Einhart Lorenz, *Jødehat. Antisemittismens historie fra antikken til i dag* (Oslo: Cappelen Damm, 2009) 197.
84. Walser Smith, *Continuities*, 62, 64
85. Personal entries in *Deutsche Biographie*.
86. Schulze, "Nationalbewegung," 89–90.
87. Walser Smith, *Continuities*, 69.
88. Fichte, Johann Gottlieb, *Reden an die deutsche Nation*. http://gutenberg.spiegel.de/buch/ (Leipzig: Philip Reclam jun., 1878) ch. 5, 6, 8 & 15
89. Lagarde, *Schriften*, 84–92, 192–198; see further ch. Roman Law and "Blut und Boden" (Blood and Soil)."
90. Fichte, *Reden*, ch. 12, and 14.
91. Manfred Jacobs, "Die Entwicklung des deutschen Nationalgedankens von der Reformation bis zum deutschen Idealismus," in Zillessen, *Volk*, 101–105.
92. Hubert Wolf, *Papst und Teufel. Die Archive des Vatikans und das Dritte Reich* (Munich: Verlag C. H. Beck, 2012) 260–261.
93. Jacobs, "Entwicklung," 106–107.
94. Christoph Burger, "Der Wandel in der Beurteilung von Frieden und Krieg bei Friedrich Schleiermacher, dargestellt bei drei Predigten," in Wolfgang Huber

& Johannes Schwerdtfeger (ed.), *Kirche zwischen Krieg und Frieden. Studien zur Geschichte des deutschen Protestantismus* (Stuttgart: Ernst Klett, 1976) 235–240.

95. "Jesus som nasjonsbygger?" *Vårt Land* (Oslo: May 16, 2011).

96. Frøland, *Nazismens idéunivers*, 441, note 137.

97. Jacobs, "Entwicklung," 107.

98. Wolfgang Altgeld, "Religion, Denomination, and Nationalism in Nineteenth-Century Germany," in Helmut Walser Smith (ed.), *Protestants, Catholics and Jews in Germany, 1800–1914* (Oxford: Berg, 2001) 62.

99. Mosse, *Nationalisierung*, 74.

100. Walser Smith, *Continuities*, 54–58, Herder, *Ideen*, IV.3., IX.2., 3; Klaus von See, *Die Ideen von 1789 und die Ideen von 1914. Völkisches Denken in Deutschland zwischen Französischer Revolution und Erstem Weltkrieg* (Frankfurt/M: Akademische Verlagsgesellschaft Athenaion, 1975) 102.

101. Werner Conze, "Zum Verhältnis des Luthertums zu den mitteleuropäischen Nationalbewegungen im 19. Jahrhundert," in Bernd Moeller (ed.) Luther in der *Neuzeit* (Gütersloh: Gütersloher Verlagshaus Gerd Mohn, 1983) 193.

102. Conze, "Luthertums," 182.

103. See, *Ideen*, 2

104. Glen P. Ryland, *Translating Africa for Germans: The Rhenish Mission in Southwest Africa*, 1829–1936 (PhD-thesis, University of Notre Dame, Indiana, April 2013) 97.

105. Olav A. Abrahamsen & Andreas Aase, *Portal. Verden etter 1850* (Oslo: Det norske Samlaget, 2004) 107; Sontheimer, *Denken*, 176–177; Alfred Rosenberg, *Kampf unm die Macht, Aufsätze von 1921–1932* (Munich: Franz Eher Nachfolger, 1937) 17.

106. Peter Pulzer, *The Rise of Political Anti-Semitism in Germany & Austria* (Cambridge, Mass.: Harvard University Press, 1988) 31; Jürgen Kocka, "Probleme der politischen Integration der Deutschen 1867 bis 1945," in Büsch & Sheehan, *Die Rolle*, 128.

107. Thorsen, *Gospel*, 435.

108. Altgeld, *Katholizismus*, 110, 141.

109. Herder, *Ideen*, XVIII.3.; Alfred R. Chandler, *Rosenberg's Nazi Myth* (N. Y.: Ithaca, 1945) 123–124; see further chap."Display and Ceremony."

110. Herder, Ideen, XX.4., XII.3.; Altgeld, "Religion," 54.

111. Altgeld, "Religion," 55; Arvidsson, "Germania," 13.

112. Altgeld, "Religion," 56.

113. Gennrich, *Gott*, 79.

114. Lagarde, *Schriften*, 126, 128–129; Wolfgang Tilgner, "Volk, Nation und Vaterland im protestantischen Denken zwischen Kaiserreich und Nationalsozialismus (ca. 1870–1933)," in Zillessen, Volk, 147–149.

115. Langbehn, Julius, *Rembrandt als Erzieher*, http://gutenberg.de/buch/ (Leipzig: C. L. Hirschfeld, 1922) chap.s 10.2. and 25.3.; Tilgner, "Volk," 149–150; see chap."The Youth Organizations."

116. Hahn, *German Thought*, 105; Viereck, *Nazismens rötter*, 164.

117. Altgeld, "Religion," 56.
118. Altgeld, *Katholizismus*, 116, note 107.
119. Altgeld, *Katholizismus*, 125–126
120. Kupisch, "Wandlungen," 117–117.
121. Hagen Schulze, *The Course of German Nationalism. From Fredrick the Great to Bismarck* (Cambridge: Cambridge University Press, 1990) 98; Schulze, "Nationalbewegung," 92.
122. Schulze, "Nationalbewegung," 106–107; see further chap."Display and Ceremony."
123. Pulzer, *Anti-Semitism*, 276; Dieter Schellong, "'Ein gefährlichster Augenblick.' Zur Lage der evangelischen Theologie am Ausgang der Weimarer Zeit," in Cancik, *Geistesgeschichte*, 130, 132.
124. Altgeld, *Katholizismus*, 59, note 24.
125. Altgeld, *Katholizismus*, 126.
126. Altgeld, *Katholizismus*, 131, note 14.
127. Kohn, *The Mind*, 101–102; Walser Smith, *Continuities*, 94.
128. Walser Smith, *Conflict*, 129, note 60.
129. Altgeld, *Katholizismus*, 162.
130. Rosenberg, *Kampf*, 379.
131. Nipperdey, *Umbruch*, 99.
132. Kupisch, "Wandlungen," 125, with note 20.
133. Kocka, "Integration," 120.
134. Conze, "Luthertums," 193, 182.
135. Nipperdy, *Umbruch*, 94–95; Kupisch, "Wandlungen," 137–138.
136. Günter Brakelmann, "Der Krieg 1870–71 und die Reichsgründung im Urteil des Protestantismus" in Huber & Schwerdtfeger, *Kirche*, 303–306.
137. Hermann Greive, *Theologie und Ideologie. Katholizismus und Judentum in Deutschland und Österreich 1918–1935* (Heidelberg: Verlag Lambert Schneider, 1969) 19.
138. Brakelmann, "Krieg 1870/71," 307–311; Langbehn, *Rembrandt*, chapters 4.4. and 27.
139. Brakelmann, "Krieg 1870/71," 316–318.
140. Altgeld, *Katholizismus*, 165.
141. Kevin Cramer, "The Cult of Gustavus Adolphus: Protestant Identity and German Nationalism," in Walser Smith, *Protestants*, 97–113; Walser Smith, *Conflict*, 222.
142. Walser Smith, *Conflict*, 54–57.
143. Reinhard Gaede, "Die Stellung des deutschen Protestantismus zum Problem von Krieg und Frieden während der Zeit der Weimarer Republik," in Huber & Schwerdtfeger, *Kirche*, 392, 417.
144. Walser Smith, *Conflict*, 62.
145. Albrecht Langner, "Katholizismus und nationaler Gedanke in Deutschland" in Zillessen, *Volk*, 243.
146. Walser Smith, *Conflict*, 208–210.
147. Conze, "Luthertums," 183; Gennrich, *Gott*, 82; See, *Ideen*, 92.

148. See, *Ideen*, 112; Nordisk Familjebok, Supplement Vol. 36 (Stockholm: 1908–1926) Entry, "Kjellén"; Kjellén, Rudolf, *Die Ideen von 1914. Eine Weltgeschichtliche Perspektive* http://archive.org/details/ (Leipzig: Verlag S. Hirzel, 1916) 34–40.

149. See, *Ideen*, 114.

150. Hans-Günter Zmarzlik, *Wieviel Zukunft hat unsere Vergangenheit? Aufsätze und Überlegungen eines Historikers vom Jahrgang 1922* (Munich: R. Piper & Co. Verlag, 1970) 42.

151. Thorsen, *Gospel*, 438.

152. Huber & Strohm, "Protestantismus," 53.

153. Kupisch, "Wandlungen," 144, 146.

154. Adrian Hastings, *The Constuction of Nationhood. Ethnicity, Religious Identity and Nationalism* (Cambridge: Cambridge University Press, 1997) 202; Thorsen, *Gospel*, 450; Bracher, *Auflösung*, 7.

155. Conze, "Luthertums," 180–181.

156. Nipperdey, *Umbruch*, 47.

157. Hans Maier, "Zum Standort des deutschen Katholizismus in Gesellschaft, Staat und Kultur," in Anton Rauscher (ed.) *Entwicklungslinien des deutschen Katholizismus* (Munich: Verlag Ferdinand Schöningh, 1973) 44–45.

158. Gabriele Clemens, *Martin Spahn und der Rechtskatholizismus in der Weimarer Republik* (Mainz: Matthias-Grünewald-Verlag, 1983) 9; Rudolf Morsey, "Der deutsche Katholizismus in politischen Umbruchsituationen seit dem Beginn des 19. Jahrhunderts," in Rauscher, *Entwicklungslinien*, 36; Nipperdey, *Umbruch*, 47; George G. Windell, *The Catholics and German Unity 1866–1871* (Minneapolis: University of Minnesota Press, 1954) 278.

159. Morsey, "Katholizismus," 38; Langner, "Diskussionsbericht," 108–109.

160. Nipperdey, *Umbruch*, 49; Buchheim, *Parteien*, 203; see further ch."Display and Ceremony."

161. Höfele, *Bismarckzeit*, Part II, chap. II, doc. 15, 374-376; Buchheim, *Parteien*, 208–209.

162. Kaiser, *Democracy*, 16–17, 20–21, 30.

163. Donald J. Dietrich, *Catholic Citizens in the Third Reich: Psycho-Social Principles and Moral Reasoning* (Piscataway NJ: Transaction Publishers, 1988) 11.

164. Windell, *Catholics*, 28–51.

165. Nipperdey, *Umbruch*, 21, 24–31.

166. Walser Smith, *Conflict*, 47–48.

167. See further chap."The Situation as to Mentality Groups c. 1930."

168. See chap."Reform Catholicism"; Konrad Repgen, "Entwicklungslinien von Kirche und Katholizismus in historischer Sicht," in Rauscher, *Entwicklungslinien*, 24; Jedin, "Kirche," 77; Buchheim, *Parteien*, 207.

169. Lächele, "völkische Religion," 150.

170. Nipperdey, *Umbruch*, 54, 59, 64–65; Jürgen Aretz, *Katholische Arbeiterbewegung und Nationalsozialismus. Der Verband katholischer Arbeiter-und Knappenvereine Westdeutschlands* (Mainz: Matthias-Grünewald-Verlag, 1982) 9–12; Buchheim, *Parteien*, 297–298.

171. Nipperdey, *Umbruch*, 53; Aretz, *Arbeiterbewegung*, 7–8; Buchheim, *Parteien*, 93–94, 203–204, 234, 251–252; Höfele, *Bismarckzeit*, Part I, Chap. II, Doc. 14, 129–130; 1. Die Geschichte der DEUTSCHEN ZENTRUMSPARTEI seit 1870, pp.http://www.zentrumspartei.de/html/geschichte.html; Morsey, "Katholizismus," 38.

172. Buchheim, *Parteien*, 251–252; Paul Freston, *Protestant Political Parties. A Global Survey* (Burlington US: Ashgate Publishing Limited/Company, 2004) 18.

173. Buchheim, *Parteien*, 307; Derek Hastings, *Catholicism and the Roots of Nazism* (N. Y.: Oxford University Press, 2010) 34.

174. Walser Smith, *Conflict*, 61.

175. Conze, "Luthertums," 182.

176. Pulzer, *Jews*, 54; Wilhelm Mommsen, *Deutsche Parteiprogramme* (Munich: Olzog, 1960) 178.

177. Walser Smith, *Conflict*, 50-61, 127–138, 148, 150; Pulzer, *Jews*, 176–177.

178. Maier, "Standort," 48; Bernhard Casper, "Gesichtspunkte für eine historische Darstellung der deutschen katholischen Theologie im 19. Jahrhundert," in Rauscher, *Entwicklungslinien*, 92; Jedin, "Kirche," 80; see further chap."Universities and High Schools."

179. Maier, "Standort," 45–46.

180. Clemens, *Martin Spahn*, 12.

181. Wieland Vogel, *Katholische Kirche und nationale Kampfverbände in der Weimarer Republik* (Mainz: Matthias-Grünewald-Verlag, 1989) 45; Walser Smith, *Continuities*, 225.

182. Altgeld, "Religion," 58.

183. Altgeld, *Katholizismus*, 36, 170.

184. Besides being the ensign of the Weimar Republic, and later of Germany after 1949. Altgeld, "Religion," 58–59; see further chap."'Black-Red-Gold' versus 'Black-White-Red.'"

185. Altgeld, *Katholizismus*, 3, note 5.

186. Mosse, *Nationalisierung*, 128–130.

187. Altgeld, *Katholizismus*, 4, with note 6.

188. Helmut Berding, *Moderner Antisemitismus in Deutschland* (Frankfurt/M: Suhrkamp Verlag, 1988) 60; Pulzer, *Jews*, 20; Wilhelm Dantine, "Frühromantik-Romantik-Idealismus," in Karl Heinrich Rengstorf & Siegfried von Kotzfleisch (ed.) *Kirche und Synagoge. Handbuch zur Geschichte von Christen und Juden. Darstellung mit Quellen* (Stuttgart: Ernst Klett Verlag, 1970) 180, 186–187.

189. =wealthy farmers.

190. Altgeld, *Katholizismus*, 182–183, 190.

191. *Meyers 5*, Entry, " Fries"; Altgeld, *Katholizismus*, 60, note 26; Dantine, "Frühromantik," 183–184; Eriksen, Harket & Lorenz, *Jødehat*, 199–202.

192. David Nirenberg, *Antijudaism. The History of a Way of Thinking* (London: Head of Zeus, 2013) 390.

193. Altgeld, "Religion," 59; Ascher, Saul, *Die Germanomanie. Skizze einer Zeitgemälde* http://gutenberg.spiegel.de/buch/2602/1 (1815) 24. and 27. sections; see further chap."Display and Ceremony."

194. Herder, *Ideen*, XII.3.; John Weiss, *The Politics of Hate. Anti-Semitism, History, and the Holocaust in Modern Europe* (Chicago: Ivan R. Dee, 2003) 21; Rengstorf, "Emanzipation," 164; *Franz-Heinrich Philipp*, "Protestantismus nach 1848," in Rengstorf & Kortzfleisch, *Kirche und Synagoge*, 284–285; Ryland, *Translating Africa*, 7–10. Kant and Hegel were taught in missionary schools. Ryland, *Translating Africa*, 59–60.

195. Jean Calvin, *Institutio Religionis Christianae* (Grand Rapids: English authorized version of Book II of the 1559 version, William B. Eerdmans Publishing, 1994) 538.

196. Mommsen, *Die Deutschen*; Altgeld, *Katholizismus*, 60.

197. Eriksen, Harket, & Lorenz, *Jødehat*, 290.

198. Josef & Ruth Becker, *Hitlers Machtergreifung. Dokumente vom Machtantritt Hitlers 30. Januar 1933 bis zur Besiegelung des Einparteienstaates 14. Juli* (Munich: Deutscher Taschenbuchverlag, 1983) Doc. 96., 137, 97., 137-138, 135., 185-186; Pulzer, *Anti-Semitism*, 86–89.

199. Berding, *Antisemitismus*, 93–94; Martin Greschat, "Protestantischer Antisemitismus in Wilhelminischer Zeit. Das Beispiel des Hofpredigers Adolf Stoecker," in Günter Brakelmann & Martin Rosowski (ed.) *Antisemitismus. Von religiöser Judenfeindschaft zur Rassenideologie* (Göttingen: Vandenhoeck & Ruprecht, 1989) 29–34.

200. *Salomonsens Konversationslexikon* (Copenhagen: 1927) Entry, "Stöcker." Italics by the author.

201. *Nordisk Familjebok*, Entry, "Stöcker."

202. Pulzer, *Anti-Semitism*, 95.

203. Eriksen, Harket & Lorenz, *Jødehat*, 295–295.

204. *Fischer Lexicon* (Frankfurt/M: 1982) Entry, "Stöcker."

205. *Das ökumenische Heiligenlexikon*, Entry, "Stöcker"; Greschat, "Protestantischer Antisemitismus," 35–38, 44; Berding, *Antisemitismus*, 88–89; Werner Jochmann, "Struktur und Funktion des Deutschen Antisemitismus" in Werner E. Mosse (ed.), *Juden im Wilhelminischen Deutschland 1890–1914* (Tübingen: J. C. B. Mohr, 1976) 413, 432, with note 151; Kraus, "Die evangelische Kirche," 252–253; Eriksen, Harket & Lorenz, *Jødehat*, 296.

206. Greschat, "Protestantischer Antisemitismus," 38–44.

207. *Meyers 6*, Entry " Antisemiten"; Jochmann, "Struktur," 415–418; Berding, *Antisemitismus*, 99–110; Pulzer, *Anti-Semitism*, 89–95, 98–109, 187, 329; Werner Bergmann, "Völkischer Antisemitismus im Kaiserreich" in Puschner et al. *Handbuch*, 449–460; Karl Heinrich Rengstorf, "Der Kampf um die Emanzipation," in Rengstorf & Kortzfleisch, *Kirche und Synagoge*, 306–309; see further chap. "Reform Catholicism."

208. Pulzer, *Anti-Semitism*, 112–113; Philipp, "Protestantismus," 308–309.

209. Mommsen, *Parteiprogramme*, 84.

210. Pulzer, *Anti-Semitism*, 191; Jochmann, "Struktur," 455–456.

211. Michael Peters, "Der 'Alldeutsche Verband,'" in Puschner et al. *Handbuch*, 304.

212. Uwe Mazura, *Zentrumspartei und Judenfrage 1870–1933* (Mainz: Matthias-Grünewald-Verlag, 1994) 174–175; Class, Heinrich, *Wenn* ich der *Kaiser wär. Politische Wahrheiten und Notwendigkeiten*, http://reichsarchiv.com/Buecher/ (Leipzig: Dieterich'schen Verlagsbuchhandlung, 1913) 88, 192–197.
213. Kupisch, "Wandlungen," 129–130, with note 25; Mazura, *Zentrumspartei*, 175.
214. Berding, *Antisemitismus*, 98–99.
215. Jochmann, "Struktur," 430; Berding, *Antisemitismus*, 116–118; Norbert Kampe, *Studenten und "Judenfrage" im Deutschen Kaiserreich. Die Entstehung einer akademischen Trägerschicht des Antisemitismus* (Göttingen: Vandenhoeck & Ruprecht, 1988) 146–151.
216. Kampe, *"Judenfrage,"* 164–167; Berding, *Antisemitismus*, 118.
217. Jochmann, "Struktur," 440–441; Pulzer, *Anti-Semitism*, 185, 191; Berding, *Antisemitismus*, 118–140.
218. Jochmann, "Struktur," 431, 469.
219. Jochmann, "Struktur," 440.
220. Hans-Ulrich Wehler, *The German Empire, 1871–1918* (Leaminton Spa/Dover, NH: Berg Publishers, 1985) 124–125; see further chap."The Youth Organizations."
221. Jochmann, "Struktur," 468.
222. Jochmann, "Struktur," 441–443; Berding, *Antisemitismus*, 129–133; Mosse, *Crisis*, 82–83; *Meyers 5*, entries, "Bauernvereine," "Reichstag"; See further chap. "AGRARIAN PARTIES AND CONFESSIONAL DIFFERENCES."
223. Julius H. Schoeps, "Deutsche und nichts anderes. Von Patriotismus deutscher Juden," in *SPIEGEL SPECIAL: Juden und Deutsche*, Nr. 2, 1992,104; Pulzer, "Beteiligung," 153, 170–171; Berding, *Antisemitismus*, 152; Weiss, *Hate*, 31; Bertold Spuler, *Regenten und Regierungen der Welt, Teil II, Bd. 3*, (Würzburg: A. G. Ploetz Verlag, 1962) 69–70.
224. Mazura, *Zentrumspartei*, 142.
225. Pulzer, "Beteiligung," 153, 172.
226. Jochmann, "Struktur," 444, 464–465.
227. Jochmann, "Struktur," 457–459, 475–477.
228. William W. Hagen, "Murder in the East: German-Jewish Liberal Reactions to Anti-Jewish Violence in Poland and other East European Lands, 1918–1920," in *Central European History*, Vol. 34, No. 1, 2001, 5.
229. Philipp, "Protestantismus," 321–335; Walter Hannot, *Die Judenfrage in der katholischen Tagespresse Deutschlands und Österreichs 1923–1933* (Mainz: Matthias-Grünewald-Verlag, 1990) 100–101.
230. Berding, *Antisemitismus*, 178–182; Philipp, "Protestantismus," 323; Hannot, *Tagespresse*, 73; see further chap. "The *Deutschvölkischer Schutz-und Trutzbund* (The German-Volkish League for Protection and Defiance)."
231. Philipp, "Protestantismus," 333.
232. Philipp, "Protestantismus," 325–326.
233. Philipp, "Protestantismus," 325–329; Nirenberg, *Antijudaism*, 449.

234. Philipp, "Protestantismus," 347–350.
235. Daniel Jonah Goldhagen, *Hitler's Willing Executioners. Ordinary Germans and the Holocaust* (London: Abacus, 1997) 107–109, 112–113; Wolf, "Volk," 190–191; *Der Theologe 4*, 14, 18; John Conway, "National Socialism and the Christian Churches during the Weimar Republic," in Peter D. Stachura (ed.) *The Nazi Machtergreifung* (London: George Allen & Unwin, 1983) 141.
236. Ryland, *Translating Africa*, 256.
237. Goldhagen, *Executioners*, 126–127.
238. Kraus, "Die evangelische Kirche," 261–263; Rengstorf, "Emanzipation," 338–339; Uriel Tal, *Religion, Politics and Ideology in the Third Reich* (N. Y.: Routledge, Taylor & Francis Group, 2004) 194.
239. Mazura, *Zentrumspartei*, 28–29; David I. Kertzer, *Die Päpste gegen die Juden. Der Vatikan und die Entstehung des modernen Antisemitismus* (Munich: Ullstein Buchverlage, 2004) 182–183, 192, 195–196; Rudolf Lill, "Der heilige Stuhl und die Juden," in Rengstorf & Kortzfleisch, *Kirche und Synagoge*, 358–363; Rengstorf, "Emanzipation," 362; Olaf Blaschke, *Katholizismus und Antisemitismus im Deutschen Kaiserreich* (Göttingen: Vandenhoeck & Ruprecht, 1999) 52–64, 205, 230; Jochmann, "Struktur," 230, 397–399; Hermann Greive, "Die gesellschaftliche Bedeutung der christlich-jüdischen Differenz. Zur Situation im deutschen Katholizismus," in W. Mosse, *Juden*, 354–388; Reinhard Rürup, "Emanzipation und Krise. Zur Geschichte der "Judenfrage" in Deutschland vor 1890," in W. Mosse, *Juden*, 49–50; Hannot, *Tagespresse*, 77; Eriksen, Harket, & Lorenz, *Jødehat*, 293–294.
240. Kertzer, *Päpste*, 299–300, 319–320; Blaschke, *Katholizismus*, 231; Lill, "Stuhl," 364; Konrad Repgen, "1938—Judenpogrom und katholischer Kirchenkampf," in Brakelmann & Rosowski, *Antisemitismus*, 117; Chandler, *Nazi Myth*, 329; Hannot, *Tagespresse*, 196, note 250.
241. According to Father Claes Tande, *Vårt Land*, Feb. 2, 2010.
242. Lill, "Stuhl," 364–367; See further chap."THE RELATIONSHIP OF PIUS XI TO TOTALITARIANISM."
243. Wolf, *Papst*, 137–138.
244. Pulzer, *Anti-Semitism*, 83–84; Hannot, *Tagespresse*, 77; Mazura, *Zentrumspartei*, 45–47; Rudol Lill, "Die Deutschen Katholiken und die Juden in der Zeit von 1850 bis zur Machtübernahme Hitlers," in Rengstorf & Kortzfleisch, Kirche und Synagoge, 380–383; *Encyclopaedia Britannica*, Entry, "Anti-semitism."
245. Hannot, *Tagespresse*, 76; Mazura, *Zentrumspartei*, 47–52; Lill, "Katholiken," 370, 375.
246. Hannot, *Tagespresse*, 78–79; Lill, "Katholiken," 375–376, 381–384.
247. Blaschke, *Katholizismus*, 124–125.
248. Jochmann, "Struktur," 456, with note 227; Mazura, *Zentrumspartei*, 54–55; Blaschke, *Katholizismus*, 294, with note 119.
249. Marcus Kreuzer, "Parlamentarisation and the Question of German Exceptionalism: 1867–1918," in *Central European History*, Vol. 36, Nr. 3, 2003, 338.
250. Lill, "Katholiken," 385–386.
251. Mazura, *Zentrumspartei*, 55; Lill, "Katholiken," 390; Altgeld, Katholizismus, 211

252. Lill, "Stuhl," 393
253. Hannot, *Tagespresse*, 80.
254. See chap. "The Weimar Republic"; Rudolf Lill, "NS-Ideologie und katholische Kirche," in Klaus Gotto & Konrad Repgen, *Die Katholiken und das Dritte Reich* (Mainz: Matthias-Grünewald-Verlag, 1990) 393–394.
255. Blaschke, *Katholizismus*, 195, 197, 200, 202.
256. Blaschke, *Katholizismus*, 197; Oded Heilbronner, *Catholicism, Political Culture, and the Countryside. A Social History of the Nazi Party in South Germany* (Ann Arbor: The University of Michigan Press, 1998) 104; Oded Heilbronner, "'Long live Liberty, Equality, Fraternity and Dynamite'": The German Bourgeoisie and the Constructing of Popular Liberal and National-Socialist Subcultures in Marginal Germany," in *Journal of Social History*, 39.1, 2005, 190.
257. Pulzer, *Jews*, 241; Lill, "Katholiken," 395.
258. Lill, "Katholiken," 395–396.
259. Mazura, *Zentrumspartei*, 58–59; Martin Liepach, *Das Wahlverhalten der jüdischen Bevölkerung in der Weimarer Republik* (Tübingen: J. C. Mohr, 1996) 138–139.
260. Mazura, *Zentrumspartei*, 60–62.
261. Mazura, *Zentrumspartei*, 65.
262. Liepach, *Wahlverhalten*, 15; Christoph Jahr, "Schleichendes Gift," in *SPIEGEL SPECIAL*, Nr. 1, 2008, 43; Rost, Hans, *Gedanken und Wahrheiten zur Judenfrage. Eine soziale und politische Studie*, http://archive.org/details/ (Trier: 1907) 66–68; Jochmann, "Struktur," 403.
263. See further chap. "'The Spirit of Time' at the Turn of the Century."
264. Mazura, *Zentrumspartei*, 66–67, 70, 184; Liepach, *Wahlverhalten*, 139; Jahr, "Schleichendes Gift," 45; Pulzer, *Jews*, 242.
265. Mazura, *Zentrumspartei*, 115, note 7, 141–143; Jahr, "Schleichendes Gift," 45.
266. Mazura, *Zentrumspartei*, 168–170.
267. Mazura, *Zentrumspartei*, 68; Lill, "Katholiken," 409–410.
268. Mazura, *Zentrumspartei*, 176–177, note 34; Sarah Gordon, *Hitler, Germans and the "Jewish Question"* (Princeton, NJ: Princeton University Press, 1984) 68.
269. Gordon, *"Jewish Question,"* 36.
270. Mazura, *Zentrumspartei*, 165.
271. Lill, "Katholiken," 398; Hannot, *Tagespresse*, 213; Mazura, *Zentrumspartei*, 161.
272. Mazura, *Zentrumspartei*, 16, 165–166; Lill, "Katholiken," 405.
273. Pulzer, *Jews*, 313–314; Mazura, *Zentrumspartei*, 162–163, 219; Liepach, *Wahlverhalten*, 138; Lill, "Katholiken," 399.
274. Kauders, *German Politics*, 161.
275. Pulzer, "Beteiligung," 192–194; Hannot, *Tagespresse*, 77; Jochmann, "Struktur," 397–399.
276. Mazura, *Zentrumspartei*, 188–189; Pulzer, *Jews*, 187; Greive, "Bedeutung," 384.
277. Mazura, *Zentrumspartei*, 7, note 16, 70, 183–186, 189; Hannot, *Tagespresse*, 196, note 249; Liepach, *Wahlverhalten*, 100–105, 137–139, 147–151, 157, 160.

278. Pulzer, *Jews*, 243; Hannot, *Tagespresse*, 200.

279. Arnold Paucker, "Der jüdische Abwehrkampf" in W. Mosse, *Juden*, 457, 459, note 191, 497, note 48; Mazura, *Zentrumspartei*, 189–190; Pulzer, *Jews*, 285.

280. Berding, *Antisemitismus*, 217; Mazura, *Zentrumspartei*, 71–72, 221.

281. Lill, "Katholiken," 400.

282. Wolfgang Wippermann, "Antislawismus," in Puschner et al. *Handbuch*, 513–515; Ludger Udolph, "Völkische Themen in der sorbischen Literatur" in Puschner et al., *Handbuch*, 526.

283. Wippermann, "Antislawismus," 516–519.

284. Ellen Lovell Evans, *The Cross and the Ballot. Catholic Parties in Germany, Switzerland, Austria, Belgium and the Netherlands, 1785–1985* (Boston: Humanities Press, Inc.,1999) 112–113.

285. NRK (Norwegian Broadcasting Corporation), "Spekter" September 16 2010.

286. Berding, *Antisemitismus*, 140–151.

287. Blavatsky, *Secret Doctrine*, 200, 249–250.

288. Levenda, *Alliance*, 38–40, 55, 66, 77.

289. Uwe Lohalm, *Völkischer Radikalismus*, (Hamburg: Leibniz, 1970) 36; Mosse, *Crisis*, 102; Berding, *Antisemitismus*, 143–144.

290. Berding, *Antisemitismus*, 102.

291. Tal, *Religion*, 172–173.

292. Kurt Frech, "Felix Dahn. Die Verbreitung völkischen Gedankenguts durch den historischen Roman," in Puschner et al., *Handbuch*, 686, 688, 690–693; see further chap. "Roman Law and "Blut und Boden" (Blood and Soil)."

293. Frech, "Felix Dahn," 695–697.

294. Kauders, *German Politics,* 158–159.

295. Ryland, *Translating Africa*, 257–259.

296. Thomas Fandel, *Konfession und Nationalsozialismus. Evangelische und katholische Pfarrer in der Pfalz 1930–1939* (Munich: Ferdinand Schöningh, 1997) 103.

297. Aretz, *Arbeiterbewegung*, 238.

298. Heinrich Küppers, *Der katholische Lehrerverband in der Übergangszeit von der Weimarer Republik zur Hitler-Diktatur* (Mainz: Matthias-Grünewald-Verlag, 1975) 92.

299. Vogel, *Kampfverbände*, 43, note 44; Hannot, *Tagespresse*, 237.

300. Hermann Greive, *Theologie und Ideologie. Katholizismus und Judentum in Deutschland und Österreich* (Heidelberg: Verlag Lambert Schneider, 1969) 290, note 643.

301. Hannot, *Tagespresse*, 231–232; Rolf Peter Sieferle, "Rassismus, Rassenhygiene, Menschenzuchtideale," in Puschner et al., *Handbuch*, 446.

302. *BTMAGASINET*, (Bergen: March 19 and 29 2008).

303. Joachim Riedl, "Der lange Schatten des Kreuzes. Von Golgatha zur Swastika," in Michael Ley & Julius H. Schoeps (ed.) *Der Nationalsozialismus als politische Religion* (Bodenheim bei Mainz: Philo Verlagsgesellschaft, 1997) 63.

304. Sieferle, "Rassismus," 445.

305. Walser Smith, *Continuities*, 66.

306. Sieferle, "Rassismus," 920, 924; Synnøve Didriksen, *Steriliseringsloven av 1934—et ledd i norsk befolkningspolitikk* (Bergen: Unpublished thesis for *candidatus philologiae*, University of Bergen, Autumn 1995) 31.

307. Ingo Wiwjorra, "Arkaisme og krisen i det moderne. Idee Ahnenerbe," in Emberland & Fure, *Jakten på Germania*, 40; Günter Hartung, "Völkische Ideologie," in Puschner et al., *Handbuch*, 36, 911; Ulrich Linse, "Völkisch-rassische Siedlungen der Lebensreform," in Puschner et al., *Handbuch*, 401–404; Mosse, *Crisis*, 112–116, note 17, 119.

308. Steigmann-Gall, *Reich*, 192–195.

309. Steigmann-Gall, *Reich*, 193, 197, 200.

310. Gerhard Besier, *Die Kirchen und das Dritte Reich. Band 3. Spaltungen und Abwehrkämpfe 1934–1937* (Munich: Propyläen Verlag, 2001) 868.

311. Hannot, *Tagespresse*, 228, 230; Steigmann-Gall, *Reich*, 195, with note 25; Sieferle, "Rassismus," 446; Didriksen, *Steriliseringsloven*, 35.

312. Steigmann-Gall, *Reich*, 193; Didriksen, *Steriliseringsloven*, 35, 36, 39; Besier, *Kirchen*, 870.

313. Ludwig Volk, *Der Bayerische Episkopat und der Nationalsozialismus 1930–1934* (Mainz: Matthias-Grünewald-Verlag, 1966) 79; Besier, *Kirchen*, 871.

314. Didriksen, *Steriliseringsloven*, 18–19, 39–40.

315. Steigmann-Gall, *Reich*, 200–202.

316. Anders Granås Kjøstvedt, *Hitler's Metropolis? The National Socialist Movement in Berlin 1925–1933* (Oslo: PhD-thesis submitted to the Faculty of Humanities, University of Oslo, 2010) 233–237, 244.

317. Kjøstvedt, *Hitler's Metropolis*, 248.

318. Walser Smith, *Continuities*, 206–207; *Deutsche Biographie*, Entries: Johann Fichte, Heinrich Luden, Jakob Fries.

319. Lagarde, *Schriften*, 25–27, 179–180; Walser Smith, *Continuities*, 207–210.

320. Ryland, *Translating Africa*, 178.

321. Walser Smith, *Continuities*, 168, 200–201.

322. Nipperdey, *Umbruch*, 96.

323. Lagarde, *Schriften*, 13; Houston Stuart Chamberlain, *Die Grundlagen des Neunzehnten Jahrhunderts, II. Hälfte* (Munich: Verlagsanstalt F. Bruckmann A. G., 1907) 1237–1238.

324. Langner, "nationaler Gedanke," 245–246.

325. Langner, "nationaler Gedanke," 246.

326. Kaiser, *Democracy*, 12–24.

327. Kaiser, *Democracy*, 16.

328. Thorsen, *Gospel*, 450; John W. Boyer, "Catholics and the Challenges of Democracy: The Heritage of Nineteenth Century," in Wolfram Kaiser & Helmut Wohnout (ed.), *Political Catholicism in Europe 1918–45* (N. Y.: Routledge, 2004) 31.

329. Emma Fattorini, *Hitler, Mussolini and the Vatican. Pope Pius XI and the Speech that was Never Made* (Cambridge: Polity Press, 2011) 165–166.

330. Kaiser, *Democracy*, 93–94.

331. See chap."AGRARIAN PARTIES AND CONFESSIONAL DIFFERENCES."

332. Hannot, *Tagespresse*, 238.
333. Joachim C. Fest, *Hitler, En biografi* (Oslo: Gyldendal Norsk forlag, 1979) 51–52.
334. See chap."The International Connections of the Christian Parties: Catholic Paneuropeanism versus German Protestant Autarchy."
335. Erik Anners, *Den europeiske rettens historie* (Oslo: Universitetsforlaget, 1998) 172.
336. William Montgomery McGovern, *From Luther to Hitler. The History of Fascist-Nazi Political Philosophy* (London: George G. Harrap & Co. Ltd., 1947) 42, 45; Richard Walter Darré, *Neuadel aus Blut und Boden* (Munich: J. F. Lehmanns Verlag, 1943) 25.
337. Kohn, *The Mind*, 101.
338. Herder, *Ideen*, XX.4.
339. Herder, *Ideen*, XVII.6.7.
340. Lagarde, *Schriften*, 148; Langbehn, *Rembrandt*, chap. 7.3.; Dühring, Eugen, *Cursus der Philosphie als streng wissenschaftlicher Weltanschauung und Lebensgestaltung*, http://archive.org/details/ (Leipzig: L. Heimann's Verlag, 1875) 318-319; Fichte, Johann Gottlieb, *Das System der Rechtslehre*, http://www.textlog.de/fichte/ 1. Teil, chap. "Gesetz und Natur"; Pulzer, *Anti-Semitism*, 37; Dag Michalsen, *Romerrettsideologi* (Oslo: Pax forlag, 2008) 288-290; Jon W. Iddeng et al. (7 authors), *tid og tanke. Historie og filosofi* (Oslo: H. Aschehoug & Co., 2008) 273; Montgomery McGovern, *From Luther*, 392–396; *Deutsche Biographie*, Entries, Karl F. Eichhorn, Jakob Grimm, Georg Beseler, Otto von Gierke, Puchta.
341. See, *Ideen von 1789*, 95–96.
342. Montgomery McGovern, *From Luther*, 389.
343. *Meyers 5*, Entry, "Deutsch-soziale Partei"; Pulzer, *Anti-Semitism*, 38, 329; Berding, *Antisemitismus*, 93–97; Greschat, "Protestantischer Antisemitismus," 29–34.
344. Winfried Noack, *Die NS-Ideologie* (Frankfurt/M: Europäischer Verlag der Wissenschaften, 1996) 51.
345. www.bad-kohlgrub.de/welfen.html.
346. Darré, *Neuadel*, 20-23, 65–66.
347. Darré, *Neuadel*, 68.
348. Alfred Rosenberg, *Der Mythus des 20. Jahrhunderts. Eine Wertung der seelisch-geistigen Gestaltenkämpfe unserer Zeit* (Munich: Hoheneichen-Verlag, 1942) 563–598; *Arbeidernes Leksikon* (Oslo: Pax Forlag AS, 1977) 433.
349. See, *Ideen*, 38; Anners, *rettens historie*, 89; Johann Chapoutot, *Das Gesetz des Blutes. Von NS-Weltanschauung zum Vernichtungskrieg* (Darmstadt: Philipp von Zabern, 2016) 193–194; Knut Helle, "Rettsoppfatninger og rettsendringer. Europa og Norge i middelalderen," in Geir Atle Ersland, Edgar Hovland & Ståle Dyrvik (ed.), *Festskrift til Historisk institutts 40-årsjubileum 1997* (Bergen: Historisk institutt, University of Bergen, Skrifter 2, 1997) 43–44, with reference to Fritz Kern, *Recht und Verfassung im Mittelalter* (1919).
350. Robert S. Hoyt, *Europe in the Middle Ages* (N. Y.: Harcourt, Brace & World, Inc., 1966) 72.

351. Ferdinand Lot, *The End of the Ancient World and the Beginnings of the Middle Ages* (N. Y.: Harper & Row Publishers, 1961) 398.

352. Heuch Bugge, "Rettsordningen i det nye Tyskland," in *Norsk Rikskringkasting. Foredrag om det nye Tyskland* (Oslo: J. M. Stenersen Forlag, 1940) 29; Werner Warmbrunn, *The Dutch under German Occupation 1940–1945* (London: Oxford University Press, 1963) 39; Chapoutot, *Gesetz*, 187–188.

353. Thomas Darnstädt, "Mephisto als Untertan," in *SPIEGEL SPECIAL*, Nr. 1, 2008, 34.

354. Lot, *Ancient World*, 397–398.

355. Lot, *Ancient World*, 398.

356. Noack, *NS-Ideologie*, 53.

357. Lot, *Ancient World*, 397–398.

358. Lot, *Ancient World*, 400.

359. Ian Kershaw, "Führer und Hitlerkult," in Wolfgang Benz, Hermann Graml & Hermann Weiss (ed.) *Enzyklopädie des Nationalsozialismus* (Munich: Deutscher Taschenbuchverlag, 1998) 29; Helmut Heiber, "Hitler, die Partei und die Institutionen des Führerstaates," in Martin Broszat & Norbert Frei (ed.), *PLOETZ. Das Dritte Reich* (Frechen: Komet, 1983) 153–157; Bertold Spuler, *Regenten und Regierungen der Welt, Teil II. Bd. 4, Neueste Zei 1917/18–1964* (Würzburg: A. G. Ploetz Verlag, 1964) 153–155.

360. *Nordisk Familjebok*, Entry, "Scheffel"; *J. V. Scheffels Werke*, "Der Trompeter von Säckingen," 2. Stück,"Jung Werner beim Schwarzwälder Pfarrherrn" (Leipzig: Hesse & Becker Verlag, 1853) Freiburger historische Bestände—digital dl.ub.uni-freiburg.de.

361. Mosse, *Crisis*, 15.

362. Emberland, *Religion*, 30; Joseph Victor von Scheffel, *Der Trompeter von Säckingen* http://gutenberg.spiegel.de/buch/ (Leipzig: Philip Reclam jun., 1901–1017).

363. Mazura, *Zentrumspartei*, 193, note 12.

364. Pulzer, *Anti-Semitism*, 66–67.

365. Julia Zernack, "Anschauungen vom Norden im deutschen Kaiserreich," in Puschner et al., *Handbuch*, 508–509.

366. Stanley G. Payne, *A History of Fascism 1914–1945* (London: UCL Press Ltd., 1995) 231.

367. Ernst Piper, *Alfred Rosenberg. Hitlers Chefideologe* (Munich: Karl Blessing Verlag, 2005) 418; see further chap."Glorification of Widukind- and Donar Oak."

368. Klaus Tanner, *Die fromme Verstaatlichung des Gewissens. Zur Auseinandersetzung um die Legitimität der Weimarer Reichsverfassung in Staatswissenschaft und Theologie der Zwanziger Jahre* (Göttingen: Vandenhoeck & Ruprecht, 1989) 68-70, with note 74; Buchheim, *Parteien*, 396; Ernst Wolf, "Volk, Nation, Vaterland im protestantischen Denken von 1930 bis zur Gegenwart," in Zillessen (ed.), *Volk*, 189–190.

369. Tanner, *Verstaatlichung*, 88–89.

370. Kjøstvedt, *Hitler's Metropolis*, 234–235, with note 955.

371. Ingo Wiwjorra, "Die deutsche Vorgeschichtsforschung und ihr Verhältnis zu Nationalismus und Rassismus," in Puschner et al., *Handbuch*, 187, 189-190; Arvidsson, "Germania," 17; Michael Irlenbusch-Reynard, "Interaksjon mellom vitenskap og ideologi? Tre perspektiver på den gamle norrøne kultur og litteratur i Tyskland fra 1850- til 1940-årene," in Emberland & Fure (ed.), *Jakten*, 82–86.

372. Wiwjorra, "Vorgeschichtsforschung," 191.

373. Rolf Köhn, "Kirchenfeindliche und antichristliche Mittelalter-Rezeption im völkisch-nationalsozialistischen Geschichtsbild: die Beispiele Widukind und Stedinger," in Peter Wapnewski (ed.) *Mittealter-Rezeption. Ein Symposion* (Stuttgart: Metzlersche Verlagsbuchhandlung, 1986) 599.

374. Köhn, "Mittelalter-Rezeption," 599–601; Darré, *Neuadel*, 30–31; Steigmann-Gall, *Reich*, 130–131.

375. Schulze, "Nationalbewegung," 107; Mosse, "Rechte," 77–78, 102; Arvidsson, "Germania," 28.

376. Darré, *Neuadel*, 28–29.

377. Kurt Meier, *Kreuz und Hakenkreuz. Die evangelische Kirche im Dritten Reich* (Munich: Deutscher Taschenbuchverlag, 2008) 107-116; Köhn, "Mittelalter-Rezeption," 594–597, 601–603; Steigmann-Gall, *Reich*, 130–131.

378. Barbara Schellenberger, Katholische *Jugend und Drittes Reich. Eine Geschichte des Katholischen Jungmännerverbandes 1933–1939 unter besonderer Berücksichtigung der Rheinprovinz* (Mainz: Matthias-Grünewald-Verlag, 1975) 128, with notes 300 and 301.

379. Geoffrey Pridham, *Hitler's Rise to Power* ((London: Hart Davis, 1973) 181; Piper, *Rosenberg—Chefideologe*, 226–229, 350.

380. George L. Mosse, *Die Nationalisierung der Massen. Politische Symbolik und Massenbewegungen von den Befreiungskriegen bis zum Dritten Reich* (Frankfurt/M: Campus Verlag, 1993) 62–90.

381. Mosse, *Nationalisierung*, 78.

382. Mosse, *Nationalisierung*, 111–113.

383. Mosse, *Nationalisierung*, 86–90.

384. Hastings, D., *Roots of Nazism*, 162–168, 183.

385. Ernst Nolte, *Die faschistischen Bewegungen. Die Krise des liberalen Systems und die Entwicklung der Faschismen* (Munich: Deutscher Taschenbuch Verlag, 1969) 253; Emberland, *Religion*, 31; Levenda, *Alliance*, 96; Mosse, *Crisis*, 76–77, 118, 228–229, 267; Björn Mensing, *Pfarrer und Nationalsozialismus. Geschichte einer Verstrickung am Beispiel der Evangelisch-Lutherischen Kirche in Bayern* (Göttingen: Vandenhoeck & Ruprecht, 1998) 91.

386. Levenda, *Alliance*, 38, 40; Blavatsky, *Secret Doctrine*, 98–101.

387. Piper, *Rosenberg—Chefideologe*, 205.

388. Levenda, *Alliance*, 59–60.

389. Levenda, *Alliance*, 96; Kevin P. Spicer, *Hitler's Priests. Catholic Clergy and National Socialism* (DeKalb, Ill.: Northern Illinois University Press, 2008) 33–34; Charlotte Grollegg-Edler, *Die wehrhafte Nachtigall—Ottokar Kernstock (1848–1928)* (Graz: Universitätsverlag, 2006).

390. Hastings, D., *Roots of Nazism*, 127–128.

391. Kurt Nowak, "Christuskreuz gegen Hakenkreuz. Die Ideologie des Nationalsozialismus im Urteil der Kirchen," in Günter Heydemann & Lothar Kettenacker (ed.), *Kirchen in der Diktatur. Drittes Reich und SED-Staat* (Göttingen, Vandenhoeck, & Ruprecht, 1993) 227; Pridham, *Hitler's Rise*, 156.
392. Klaus Breuning, *Die Vision des Reiches. Deutscher Katholizismus zwischen Demokratie und Diktatur (1929–1934)* (Munich: Max Hueber Verlag, 1969) 167, 171; Guido Müller, "Anticipated Exile of Catholic Democrats: The Sécretariat International des Partis Démocratiques d'Inspiration Chrétienne," in Kaiser & Wohnout, *Political Catholicism*, 44; Fattorini, *Hitler, Mussolini*, 144.
393. Fandel, *Konfession*, 136–137.
394. Mosse, *Crisis*, 121–122; http://externstein.de/religion/indexreligion.htm.
395. Dahm, *Pfarrer*, 196.
396. Sontheimer, *Denken*, 271, 275; Mensing, *Pfarrer*, 64, 270; Nowak, *Kirche*, 223–224.
397. Andreas Wirsching, "Weit entfernt von simplen Antworten," interview with A. W. in *SPIEGEL SPECIAL GESCHICHTE*, Nr. 1, 2008, 22.
398. Kurt Töpner, "Der deutsche Katholizismus zwischen 1918 und 1933," in Schoeps (ed.), *Zeitgeist*, 198, note 21; Bleuel & Klinnert, *Studenten*, 91.
399. Tal, *Religion*, 16–17.
400. Wolf, *Papst*, 257–258.
401. Friedrich Wilhelm Graf, *God's Anti-Liberal Avant-Garde: New Theologies in the Weimar Republic* ((London: German Historical Institute London Bulletin, Vol. 32, No. 2, 2010) 23; Tal, *Religion*, 16–17, with note 1, 36–37; Gerhard Schäfer, *Die evangelische Landeskirche in Württemberg und der Nationalsozialismus. Eine Dokumentation zum Kirchenkampf. Bd. 1. Um das politische Engagement der Kirche 1932–1933* (Stuttgart: Calwer Verlag, 1971) 103–104.
402. Graf, *Avant-Garde*, 23–24.
403. Tal, *Religion*, 18–19, 178–179.
404. Hastings, D., *Roots of Nazism*, 139–140, 162–164; Kjøstvedt, *Hitler's Metropolis*, 93.
405. Mosse, *Crisis*, 155, 157, 171–173, 180–181, 184; Stachura, "Nazis," 69.
406. Jedin, "Kirche," 81–82; Winfried Mogge, "Religiöse Vorstellungen in der deutschen Jugendbewegung," in Cancik (ed.), *Geistesgeschichte*, 93.
407. Stachura, "Nazis," 68–81; Mosse, *Crisis*, 276; Kjøstvedt, *Hitler's Metropolis*, 170.
408. *Tysk motstand 1933–1945* (Stuttgart: The Federal Republic's Exhibition of Information and Documentation in Norway about the German Resistance Movement, Institut für Auslandsbeziehungen, 1983) 52.
409. Stachura, "Youth," 73–74.
410. Daniel Horn, "Reform and Revolution in German Education," in *History Education Quarterly*, Vol. 19, No. 4, 1979, 485.
411. *Deutsche Biographie*.
412. Mosse, *Crisis*, 157, 159.
413. Mensing, *Pfarrer*, 31–40.
414. Küppers, *Lehrerverband*, 20–21, 37, with note 53.

415. Wolf, *Papst*, 74; Küppers, *Lehrerverband*, 21.
416. Küppers, *Lehrerverband*, 29, with note 66; Pridham, *Hitler's Rise*, 192.
417. Küppers, *Lehrerverband*, 39.
418. Mosse, "Rechte," 149–170, 262–266.
419. Mosse, "Rechte," 152.
420. Mosse, "Rechte," 269.
421. Bleuel & Klinnert, *Studenten*, 35–36.
422. Langbehn, *Rembrandt*, Ch. 3.8."Christliches."
423. Bleuel & Klinnert, *Studenten*, 40; Arthur Moeller van den Bruck, *Das dritte Reich* http://nsl-archiv.com/Buecher/ (1922/33) 23–24.
424. Greive, *Theologie*, 237, note 111.
425. Mosse, *Crisis*, 154–156.
426. Küppers, *Lehrerverband*, 15, 18, 32, 34, 36.
427. Kjøstvedt, *Hitler's Metropolis*, 237.
428. Kjøstvedt, *Hitler's Metropolis*, 237; Küppers, *Lehrerverband*, 36.
429. Emberland, *Religion*, 242; Mosse, *Crisis*, 135,153.
430. Jan Friedmann, "Macht Platz, Ihr Alten", in *SPIEGEL SPECIAL*, Nr. 1, 2008, 41; Kjøstvedt, *Hitler's Metropolis,* 203-205; Jahr, "Schleifendes Gift," 45.
431. Mosse, "Rechte," 187–196; Michael H. Kater, *Studentenschaft und Rechtsradikalismus in Deutschland 1918–1933. Eine sozialgeschichtliche Studie zur Bildungskrise in der Weimarer Republik* (Hamburg: Hoffmann und Campe Verlag, 1975) 105, 145, 202.
432. Marjorie Lamberti, "German Schoolteachers, National Socialism, and the Politics of Culture at the End of the Weimar Republic," in *Central European History, Vol. 34, No. 1*, Riverside Cal., 2001, 62-63, with note 44; Friedmann, "Macht Platz," 41.
433. Conway, Martin, *Catholic Politics in Europe 1918–1945* http://www.catholicsocialscientists.org/Article--Conley--Pius%20XI.htm (N. Y.: Routledge, 1997) 43.
434. Heither, *Burschenschaften*, 90.
435. Kater, *Studentenschaft*, 141–142; Hastings, D., *Roots of Nazism*, 28; see further chap."Reform Catholicism."
436. Bleuel & Klinnert, *Studenten*, 18, 185, 212–213, 261–262, 289–290; Heither, *Burschenschaften*, 85–86.
437. Heither, *Burschenschaften,* 83; Bleuel & Klinnert, *Studenten*, 91, 109, 119–121, 124–125, 128–129.
438. Adolf Leisen, *Die Ausbreitung des völkischen Gedankens in der Studentenschaft der Weimarer Republik* (Heidelberg: Inaugural-Dissertation at the Ruprecht-Karl University, 1964) 95–96.
439. Wingolf=the Norse mythological hall of the dead, Valhall, and a hall for goddesses.
440. Hahn, *German Thought*, 32; Bleuel & Klinnert, *Studenten*, 18, 205–213, 261–262, 289; Christoph Weiling, *Die "Christlich-deutsche Bewegung." Eine Studie zum konservativen Protestantismus in der Weimarer Republik* (Göttingen: Vandenhoeck & Ruprecht, 1998) 332.
441. Clemens, *Martin Spahn,* 19, 26, 37.

442. Clemens, *Martin Spahn*, 27–28; Walser Smith, *Conflict*, 27–34, 40, 55, with note 25.
443. Kupisch "Wandlungen," 140.
444. Kupisch "Wandlungen," 139–140; see chap. "Fronterlebnis" (The Front Experience) and Langemarck."
445. Bleuel & Klinnert, *Studenten*, 29.
446. Leisen, *Ausbreitung*, 87–88; 265–266.
447. Leisen, *Ausbreitung*, 258–268; Bleuel & Klinnert, *Studenten*, 186
448. Hastings, D., *Roots of Nazism*, 74; Erika Weinzierl, "Austria. Church, State, Politics and Ideology, 1918–1938," in Richard J. Wolff & Jörg K. Hoensch (ed.), *Catholics, the State, and the European Radical Right, 1919–1945* (N. Y.: Columbia University Press, 1987) 11.
449. Franz Walter, *Soziale Akademiker-und Intellektuellenorganisationen in der Weimarer Republik* (Bonn: Friedrich Ebert Stiftung, 1990) 70; Friedhelm Golücke, *Studentenwörterbuch* (Graz: Styria, 1987) 34, 367.
450. Kupisch, "Bürgerliche Frömmigkeit," 40; Nipperdey, *Umbruch*, 70–71.
451. *Store Norske leksikon*, Entry, "Harnack"; Adolf von Harnack, *Das Wesen des Christentums* (Leipzig: J. C. Hinrich'sche Buchhandlung, 1908) 2–22, 92–93, 100–103, 120–130.
452. Steigmann-Gall, *Reich*, 38–41.
453. Uriel Tal, "Theologische Debatte um "das Wesen des Judentums" in W. Mosse (ed.), *Juden*, 599–605, 632; Lagarde, *Schriften*, 15, 80, 139; Buchheim, *Parteien*, 253.
454. www.theologe.de ; See chap."The Confessions of Guilt by the Churches."
455. Steigmann-Gall, *Reich*, 41; Nipperdey, *Umbruch*, 111.
456. Chamberlain, *Grundlagen*, 1044, 1213.
457. Steigmann-Gall, *Reich*, 39; Kupisch, "Wandlungen," 131; Berding, *Antisemitismus*, 149.
458. Kupisch, "Bürgerliche Frömmigkeit," 41; Chamberlain, *Grundlagen*, 715, 741–773, 845, 848, 893–895, 1007–1010, 1022, 1037, 1205, 1218–1219, 1232; Chandler, *Nazi Myth*, 5.
459. Lächele, "völkische Religion," 158; Berg Eriksen, Harket & Lorenz, *Jødehat*, 298; Berding, *Antisemitismus*, 150; Kupisch, "Bürgerliche Frömmigkeit," 41.
460. Lächele, "völkische Religion," 158; Walser Smith, *Conflict*, 54; Kupisch, "Bürgerliche Frömmigkeit," 55–56, note 8; Kay Dohnke, "Völkische Literatur und Heimatliteratur 1870–1918," in Puschner et al., *Handbuch*, 666–667; Steigmann-Gall, *Reich*, 100–101.
461. Höfele, "Bismarckzeit," part II, chap. I, Doc. 8, 312-313; Walser Smith, *Continuities*, 190; Fritz Bolle, "Darwinismus und Zeitgeist," in Scoeps (ed.), *Zeitgeist*, 258, 270-281; *Catholic Encyclopaedia*, Entry, "Catholics and Evolution"; Kupisch, "Bürgerliche Frömmigkeit," 40; Zmarzlik, *Zukunft*, 59, 61.
462. Langner, "Diskussionsbericht," 101, 108.
463. Emberland, *Religion*, 179; Ernst Haeckel, *Der Welträtsel. Gemeinverständliche Studien über Monistische Philosophie* (Bonn: Verlag von Emil Strauss, 1900) IV; Frank Simon-Ritz, "Die friegeistige Bewegung im Kaiserreich," in Puschner et al., *Handbuch*, 215.

464. Haeckel, *Welträtsel*, 324–329; Emberland, *Religion*, 28–30, 321; Piper, *Rosenberg—Chefideologe*, 205.

465. Emberland, *Religion*, 179, 425, note 66; Simon-Ritz, "Bewegung," 208–222; Zander, "Rassentheorien," 224–248.

466. Walser Smith, *Continuities*, 169, 193; Biographies in *Deutsche Biographie*.

467. Heinrich von Treitschke, *Ein Wort über unser Judentum*, http://nsl-archiv.com/Buecher/ (Berlin: G. Reimer Verlag, 1880) 1–3.

468. Walser Smith, *Continuities*, 184–185, 193–195, 197–200, 202–203.

469. Elizabeth Harvey, "Visions of the Volk: German Women and the Far Right from Kaiserreich to Third Reich," in *Journal of Women's History*, Vol. 16, No. 3 (The John Hopkins University Press, 2004) 152.

470. Wolf, *Papst*, 72–73; Nipperdey, *Umbruch*, 32–38.

471. Hastings, D., *Roots of Nazism*, 20–21.

472. Höfele, "Bismarckzeit," part II, chap. II, Doc. 14, 373–374; Hastings, D., *Roots of Nazism*, 22.

473. Hastings, D., *Roots of Nazism*, 23–45; See further chap."WOMEN AND NAZISM."

474. Hastings, D., *Roots of Nazism*, 31–45; See further chap."Catholicism, Protestantism and Right-wing Radicalism in Bavaria in the 1920s."

475. Kreuzer, "Parlamentarisation," 338.

Chapter Two

The Heritage of World War I Versus the Values of 1789

THE WEIMAR REPUBLIC, THE CONFESSIONS AND THEIR POLITICAL ORGANIZATIONS

The Weimar Republic

In August 1914 the German Catholics had, for the first time, the chance to prove their nationalist attitude and spirit of self-sacrifice. The Zentrum wholeheartedly supported the declaration of war and, during its first years, their war-propaganda was hardly surpassed by the Protestants.[1] One reason for the enthusiasm could also be that Germany's closest ally was the Catholic dominated Austria-Hungary and two of the main enemies were non-Catholic Britain and orthodox Russia. Some of the few groups that were reluctant, or in opposition to the war, were Bavarians, especially the Catholic BBB, which was unanimously reluctant.[2]

The attitude to continuing the warfare began to change among more and more people early in 1917. After pressure from the pope in February Catholic politicians from Germany, Austria-Hungary, Italy and France demanded under the banner of *International Catholic Union* an end to the war. Among its members were the Zentrum politicians Matthias Erzberger and Heinrich Held, the leader of the later BVP and premier of Bavaria from 1924 to 1933.[3]

Later the same year, partly at the instigation of the pope, representatives from the SPD, the Zentrum and the leftist-liberal and Protestant dominated *Fortschrittliche Volkspartei*, proposed peace in the *Reichstag*, and the first contours of the future "Weimar Coalition" versus the Protestant-dominated rightist movement became discernible. The initiative was strongly disliked by the military and great parts of the Protestant Church milieu, especially since the pope was a strong advocate of peace. After the war the pope carelessly asserted: "it is Luther who has lost the war". It did not improve the reputation of the pope that he belonged to a group of peace activists, such as Albert Einstein, Maxim Gorki, Sigmund Freud and Eglantyne Jebb, the founder of *Save the Children*. Not all of these were friends of the Church, and Einstein and Freud were Jews.[4]

Therefore, the "truce" between political parties since 1914 was over, and old antagonisms were rekindled. Leaders of the army, the *Alldeutscher Verband* and Protestant clerical circles established the *Deutsche Vaterlandspartei*, which wished to continue the war, with the annexation of territories as its aim. The 400th anniversary of the Reformation was exploited to arouse patriotism, and it seemed that the new party was made up of the bulk of non-socialist Protestants to the right of the leftist-liberal party. Among them was Stöcker's CSAP, which wanted to fight to the bitter end to change borders, partly annex Belgium and have German control over Central-Africa.[5] Reacting to this, liberal Protestants took the initiative for the first-time-ever alliance of all kinds of trade unions to promote peace. Among the trade unions, the Christian ones were predominantly Catholic.[6] Admittedly, opinions diverged among Catholics at the end of the war. Some Zentrum voters had joined the war organizations, whereas others were almost pacifists.[7]

The armistice was welcomed with relief by most Zentrum politicians—and even with some enthusiasm. On November 7, the party demanded the abdication of the emperor and at least one regional department of the party favored a republican constitution. When the Zentrum politician Erzberger returned from Compiegne after having signed the truce, he immediately hoisted the black-red-yellow flag of the 1848 revolution, although the imperial black-white-red flag still was the legal one.[8] As things turned out the former became the official flag of the Weimar Republic and the sign of the "Weimar Coalition" in their opposition against both rightist movements and the communists.

Another Zentrum leader, Josef Wirth, minister of finance from 1920 to 1921 and *Reichskanzler* 1921 to 1922, said at a workers' and soldiers' council, two days after the truce: "Only by democracy can we save our fatherland from ruin and destruction," and at the second anniversary of the Weimar Constitution, when it was threatened from both rightists and communists, he said as *Reichskanzler*: "We hope the great democratic thoughts, which today have brought us together for the foreseeable future, will be of common benefit to the whole German people."[9]

Not all Catholics liked the revolution. Cardinal Faulhaber thought it in opposition to the proper transition of government, and a Bavarian paper originally feared the position of religion.[10]

Soon after the armistice, the pope relinquished his opposition to political liberalism, and the Zentrum participated in a coalition with the two other peace parties after the January 1919 election. Already on the day of the armistice, the Zentrum did the same in two states: Hessen and Wurttemberg, and in Baden shortly afterwards.[11] This shows both the leftist inclinations of the Zentrum and the liberals and that the SPD did not regard these parties as being representatives of the old system and this, even before the communist Spartacus rebellion.

The new constellations of government were clear indications of parliamentarism taking over political life and a result of a development set in motions twenty years earlier. Ever since 1900, the SPD and the leftist-liberals had, with reserved support from the Zentrum, favored a system of ministerial responsibility. This had been prevented either by the conservatives, the government or the Upper House, the *Bundesrat*. The SPD had even favored parliamentarism but was not supported by the liberals and the Zentrum at the time, because these parties feared the degenerating trends which had occurred in Britain and France. However, after 1917, Erzberger favored parliamentarism, though.[12]

Catholic Constitutional Discussion

Catholic churchgoers were generally fairly satisfied with the new constitution, and religious rights were better taken care of than by the imperial one. Even the bishops admitted that the constitution made a good foundation for building the future. It was in accordance with Leo XIII's encyclicals of 1881 and 1885, which asserted that a constitution could be accepted if it secured the rights of the church. The right-wing opposition within the Zentrum at the time was neither in accordance with the Church any longer, nor with the majority of the party when they exasperatedly asserted that the constitution was based on an atheistic revolutionary theory of the state in the spirit of Rousseau.[13] Generally, the Bavarian bishops, still largely being monarchists and fearful of Prussian hegemony, were more skeptical towards the constitution than their fellows in northern Germany.[14]

The small rightist group in the Zentrum left the party in the early 1920s, and most of them joined the DNVP, and later, some of them joined the Nazi Party after the takeover in 1933. They accused the Zentrum of ignoring the *völkisch* (in a more extensive meaning) aspect of its program and hence being unable to "recognize the Jewish danger." The main characteristics of this group of Catholics were the support of monarchy in opposition to "Western" democracy, a pronounced anti-liberalism, anti-socialism, a pro-Prussian attitude and opposition to Jewishness as a cultural factor. The exit of the rightists, which contributed to the setback in the election in 1920, resulted in a more solid and pronounced leftist character to the Zentrum. The party seems to have been a pioneer in political Catholicism when it came to democracy and the "values of 1789." They regarded their fellows in faith in France and Fascist Italy with a certain mistrust because of their lack of specifically Christian political interests.[15]

In a handbook for the Zentrum before the elections in December 1924 one could read:

> Our attitude to the nation does not run to a system of negative currents. It means we emphatically and with justification reject nationalism, the adoration of the national element and the nationalization of religious ideas. Rather, we will promote positive acceptance of and creation of profound moral content to the national element. . . . The church is the guardian of a comprehensive universalism which binds peoples together. When it represents such concepts, it directs the challenge to the state to direct its attention to the whole world and not be suffocated within narrow national limitations.[16]

Statements like this were in complete opposition to what became the general attitude among Protestants post 1918.

In the Weimar era, and especially after 1929 and until the first years of the Third Reich, some German and Austrian Catholic notables had maintained ideas which were described as *Reichsideologie*. The ideas differed but had some elements in common: 1. Back to *Sacrum imperium*, 2. Rejection of liberal and democratic ideas, 3. The concept of an organically and theologically elevated state, 4. The idea of Germans as a people in the center, and 5. The "Mission" of the Germans to the world. Even the individualistic Roman law was rejected. Like the corresponding Protestant rightist concepts, these had their roots in the national awakening in the Napoleonic era. Their main theoretical document before the revolution of 1848 was *Die Elemente der Staatskunst* (1809) by Adam Müller, who had converted to Catholicism in 1805. Müller attacked Montesquieu and asserted that the state must be organized according to corporative estate state principles.[17] The group was small but had some influence in the Catholic milieu.[18] In an article in 1929, the Zentrum opposed the *Reichsideologie*. The party was characterized by the Catholic Thomist doctrine of natural law, which was justified by real and concrete reason.[19]

The small *Reichsideologie* group reached the peak of its activism in 1933 and 1934 when they tried to harmonize and adapt their own system and the Nazi one to each other. These ambitions came abruptly to an end after the liquidation of Röhm & co. in the summer of 1934, when even the Catholic persons of note, Herbert von Bose and Erich Klausener, together with von Papen's Calvinist secretary Edgar Jung, were assassinated in the same process. The illusions were enhanced by the following marginalization of von Papen, the assassination of the Austrian premier Engelbert Dollfuss, the death of President Hindenburg, and the increased harassment of the Catholic Church and organizational life afterwards.[20]

The Protestant Confession

The defeat in 1918 and the revolution made a deep impression on the German people and especially the Protestants, who had the closest relationship to the old regime. As a consequence, large numbers of them rejected or showed a reserved attitude, at least, to the new regime and its supporters.[21] Towards the end of the war, Bishop Otto Dibelius had raised people's expectations about a triumph soon to come, hence the defeat had a catastrophic effect on the national Protestant morale. They were totally unprepared for the blow and this had two outcomes: either refuged into the "Stab-in-the-Back-Legend" or to a general national attitude of impenitence in its turn leading to a continuation of the national Protestant tradition. Tilgner,[22] and Karl Kupisch following suit, asserts:

> German Protestantism followed the leaders of the army to the bitter end. That the German evangelical churches even after the war have not reached an understanding of their past, and absolutely not found a path to the present democratic reality, but on the contrary, to a great extent were haunted by an awful, contagious pastoral nationalism, is part and parcel of the tragic experience of those who, from 1919 to 1933, have been waiting in vain for a positive word from the church about cooperation in the democratic building of the State.[23]

This became obvious already by the spring and early summer of 1919. In April the *Deutscher Evangelischer Kirchenausschuss*, an umbrella organization for the 28 *Landeskirchen*, issued a resolution in an aggressive tone, stating the country was treated wrongly at the peace conference. The Prussian bishops followed suit.[24] Even the successor of *Fortschrittliche Volkspartei*, the leftist-liberal and Protestant based DDP, which remained a faithful member of the "Weimar Coalition," voted against approval of the Versailles Treaty and left the government coalition for a while. The treaty was passed by the SPD, the leftist socialist USPD and a majority of the Zentrum representatives. The adoption of the black-red-yellow flag happened at almost the same time. This time it was the USPD that broke away, voting for a purely red flag, and the law adopting the revolutionary flag of 1848 was passed by the SPD and a majority of the Zentrum plus a minority of DDP representatives. The rest voted for the old imperial flag. The ultimate "Weimar Constitution" was to a great extent the product of the DDP representatives but passed by all of the SPD, the Zentrum and the DDP. For this reason, they were all called "the

Weimar parties."[25] The more reluctant attitude of DDP representatives to the new realities was later demonstrated by the treatment of the referendum in Upper Silesia. Despite the result returning a German majority, the area was seceded and given to Poland. Germans of all political groups were appalled and the DDP once more left the "Weimar Coalition" government in protest. The remaining parties in the coalition, however, felt obliged to approve the decision of the League of Nations.[26]

After the Versailles Treaty was recognized, Protestant Churches held nationwide mourning services, and up to the Nazi takeover numerous "denunciations" against the treaty were declared by clerical assemblies, organizations and publications. One clerical organization, the *Rettet die Ehre* (Save the Honor) called for a war of revenge.[27] The *Evangelischer Bund* again took up arms against Ultramontanism and social democracy, and the slogan *Kulturkampf* reappeared. Tilgner describes this mentality this way: "The antagonism to Rome had led German national Protestantism into a dangerous self-satisfaction and formed the myth of the German reformational unity of the people. As its presupposition, this myth had an understanding of the Church that blinded it to its own inclines toward a nationalist and *völkisch* ideology." Even theologians like Bishop Otto Dibelius were influenced by this mentality, asserting, "the ideal of the Evangelical Church was not an international fellowship of a Christian nature (as in Catholicism), but a mankind built up of nations in each of which a people grasp the Christian faith and influence it in their own way."[28] As one would expect, a view like this and the relationship of the Protestant Churches to the Versailles Treaty, did not promote clerical participation in international cooperation.[29] Only the theologically and politically liberal magazines, *Christliche Welt* and *Die Eiche*, together with the Christian socialists, showed a more moderate approach to peace. Both magazines were the publications of an international association for friendship among Churches.[30]

The Catholic experience of the war and the revolution of 1918 was the complete inverse of all this. They came out of the war with a Church unscathed; it's theology and organization hardly touched, not rootless or confused, while Protestant Churches were dominated by a quest for a substitute for the old order. Bishop Hans Meiser of Bavaria even stated, "the Christian state, which lasted from Clovis (the Frankish king baptized 496 AD) until 1918, has ended."[31]

Several historians, e.g. Ursula Büttner, Rudolf Lill, Günter van Norden and Jochen Jacke, have given long and erudite descriptions of how they have understood the situation in German Protestantism in the Weimar era, depicting a state of affairs where a lack of ability to have a positive outlook on the future, and a rather nostalgic reaction resulted in anti-republican opposition.[32]

Several Protestant clerics had regarded WWI almost as God's choosing of the German people to lead a crusade against materialism. They directed their moral anger towards the victors, therefore. Nationalism was strongly integrated into the theology thereafter and not only regarded as a direct product of God's creative act, but His revelation found not only in the Bible, but even in the history of the nation. Theologians representing such views did not necessarily become Nazis but paved the way for "*Politische Theologie*," which in itself was a precondition for the openness to Nazism in the Protestant clergy. The search for explanations for Germany's catastrophic defeat led to a general acceptance of a dualist worldview where the Powers of Light were assimilated with *völkisch* nationalist principles and the Powers of Darkness with Judaism, materialism and liberal internationalism. Anti-Jewish rhetoric became common in Protestant pulpits, and the evangelical media spread caricatures of the Jews as corrupt, degenerated, and eager to demolish the traditional morals of the Christian Nation State.[33] A connected variant, *Schöpfungsglaube* (Creation faith), with Paul Althaus (later a Nazi) as its most prominent representative, emphasized the nation as divine because it permeated the individual and fought against the "detrimental" powers of liberal rationalism and materialism. In accordance with this view it was also important for the Church to resist the "Jewish menace," if necessary, by "resolute action." Christianity in Germany had its own national character according to Althaus, and every international ecumenical effort at the expense of *völkisch* interests was unacceptable. *Schöpfungsglaube* was part of a more extensive "Luther-renaissance" after the 1917 jubilee, and it gained adherents among two of the most prominent Protestant theologians: Werner Elert and Walter Künneth, the latter one of the leaders of the BK and one of the main critics of Rosenberg's ideology.[34]

November 9 and June 28, the dates of the 1918 revolution and the signing of the Versailles Treaty in 1919, had very negative associations for many Protestants. Bishop Dibelius in 1927 called November 9 a day of shame when the revolutionaries, whom he called demons, had betrayed their fellow citizens. The *Deutscher Evangelischer Kirchenausschuss* on the 10th anniversary of Versailles condemned the treaty and once more arranged mourning ceremonies.[35] Several theologians believed the cause of the defeat was that people had let God down. To regain His favor people had to re-convert and prepare for the day "when the lord of history will give us the signal for a new fight of liberation" as prominent theologians like Emanuel Hirsch and Paul Althaus maintained. During the 1930s, Hirsch and Althaus obviously saw the Nazis as "the signal."[36]

The Protestant post WWI confusion caused an increased disparity of theological views among them and an interest in occultism, mysticism, theosophy and anthroposophy. Several organizations emerged out of this, such as forerunners of the DC in the Third Reich. Even in the early 1920s, such phenomena had become so dominant and challenging that it was discussed at the Catholic Congress in 1922.[37]

Considering such different attitudes among the parties towards the military, and the political events in 1918 and 1919, it is only natural that the confessional divide of Empire vintage would ferment anew in the Weimar era. Winkler asserts:

> The confessional split in the political life of the Weimar Republic can hardly be exaggerated. Believing evangelical Christians, but also secularized "cultural Protestants" still were inclined to regard Catholics as secondary Germans. Thus they reinforced the Catholic inferiority complex, which not infrequently resulted in a kind of compensatory nationalism: an effort to prove themselves as especially good Germans.[38]

Karl-Wilhelm Dahm discerns at least four political groupings the Protestant clergy could be affiliated with in the 1920s: 1) "Conservative-National" group with the DNVP as the relevant party. 2) "Religious socialist" group with the SPD and the USPD as their relevant parties. 3) "Democratic-Liberal" group with the DDP as the relevant party (and possibly even the DVP and other minor parties). 4) "*Völkisch-Deutschgläubisch*" group with the *Deutschvölkische Freiheitspartei* with its successor the *Völkischer Block*, and the Nazis as the relevant parties. The latter three groups drew 5–8 percent of the clergy, with a decline for the socialists and democrats at the end of the decade, to the benefit of the Nazi Party. In 1933, the church president of Wurttemberg, Wurm, asserted 80 percent belonged either to the "Conservative-National" or the "*Völkisch-Deutschgläubisch*" group. Kurt Nowak mentions a fifth, "Confessional Lutherans," who in spite of their conservatism and skepticism towards the Weimar Republic at the onset, were open for every kind of constitution and hence even republicanism. It favored a "strong authoritarian State" where evangelical piety could thrive better than in the Weimar Republic with its "atheist-propaganda" and campaigns from bourgeois and socialist freethinkers. In accordance with such a view Ihmels, one of the leaders of the group, hailed in March 1933 the Nazi takeover as a "Gift of God to the German people."[39]

Very few Protestant theologians were concerned about the dismal conditions within the Church. One of them, the liberal Martin Rade asserted with disillusion: "Our church sins against our people when it portrays their situation as so hopeless and dreary. When it does, it leaves its audience with only one conclusion: "Only a new war can help us!"[40]

The Weimar Constitution

The constitution mirrored the compromise of interests of the following three main social groups: the reformist Labor movement, the leftist-liberal bourgeoisie and political Catholicism. The parties of these groups, the SPD, the DDP and the Zentrum, had gained 77 percent of the vote in the election to the Constitutional Assembly in 1919. The leftist socialists with the communists and the rightists all opposed the constitution, and the three "Weimar" parties all suffered setbacks and lost their majority in the first ordinary *Reichstag* election in 1920, never to regain it. Their handiwork, however, the constitution, endured until the Third Reich.

The constitution was stamped with values from the French and 1848 revolutions: rooted in the sovereignty of the people, representative political institutions, division of powers, individual liberties, female suffrage and the relatively passive role of the State in matters economic. When the imperial flag was replaced by the 1848 flag, an expert on state rights called it "the belated German realization of the ideas of 1789."[41]

"We shall eradicate the year 1789 from European history" was one of Josef Goebbels slogans,[42] and possibly he had the Weimar constitution in mind. He was not alone in his criticism. Academic attacks on the constitution from the rightists were primarily publications written by Protestant theologians, clerics, jurists and historians, and the discussions had many parallels to the discussion of Roman and Teutonic based law in the century before. At least one of the main critics in the Roman law discussion, the theologian Friedrich Brunstäd, was active in the constitutional debate. The difference this time was that the discussions of the 1920s, unlike the other debate, which had more or less been disconnected to everyday life, were strongly connected to the aftermath of WWI.[43]

The concern common to most of the critics was that they saw the age as a fundamental time of crisis. The discussion was for that reason typified by an all-inclusive debate about the crises, and their understanding of the constitution was based on the awareness of a profound cultural predicament. There was an inner cohesion between the lack of the legitimacy of the constitution and the understanding of the situation. Liberalism and "substance-less" rationalism were considered as the very causes of the crisis. Even a Catholic, Carl Schmitt, agreed with the criticism and regarded parliamentarism as the quintessence of liberalism and rationalism.[44] Kurt Sontheimer provides a general introduction to the Weimar criticism by the rightists, and Klaus Tanner a very exhaustive and in-depth introduction and survey of the debate by the Protestant public figures about the relationship between the constitution and culture in the 1920s.[45]

It is symptomatic that most Protestant theologians participating in discussions represented similar views despite having diverse political views. One paradoxical example is Paul Tillich, one of the most prominent theologians and a socialist. He may have been allured by the notion of "state socialism" which was commonly used as a positive term in the exchanges. Swiss theologian Karl Barth represents another; he understood the "Church struggle" against the Nazis in the Third Reich as a contest with a wider context as a fight against liberalism. In 1938, Barth admitted that at the beginning, despite his personal criticism of Nazism, regarded the ideology as a political experiment which the Church should give a chance.[46] One of Barth's colleagues in the BK, Eberhard Bethge, asserted that the alliance between Lutherans and Reformed Barthians at the "Barmen-declaration," the "Constitution" of the BK, had its important foundation in the joint understanding of "hostility against Enlightenment and Emancipation." The political revolution of 1933 was regarded as being a positive campaign of the battle against "the year 1789." Karl Kupisch asserts the bulk of the representatives at the Barmen synod had their background in "conservative German-national traditions. There was not much sympathy for the Weimar Republic . . . and democracy was a product of Western-liberal ideas that should be rejected." The representatives of the Barthian dialectic theology adapted themselves easily to the culturally critical mainstream, whose collective credo was a rejection of Enlightenment, liberalism, rationalism and thereby the ideological foundation of Weimar democracy.[47] In 1932 Walter Künneth stated: "A new wave of organic thinking is breaking forth, its mighty blows can be traced on every side. . . . In reaction to individualism the movement demanding social fellowship raises a broad front with many variations moving on towards the furtherance of popular masses' will, to the unity of the Nation."[48]

The most influential of the theologians, assisted by several jurists, historians and social scientists, were Alfred de Quervain, Friedrich Gogarten, H. Ph. Ehrenberg, Emmanuel Hirsch and Friedrich Brunstäd. Among the few who opposed the mainstream understanding, were the prominent liberals Otto Baumgarten, Erich Foerster, Hermann Mulert, Otto Piper and Martin Rade.[49]

The general Protestant skepticism or rejection of the Weimar Constitution surfaced when the 5th and 10th Weimar anniversary celebrations disclosed mixed attitudes among Church leaders. On the other hand, the 60th celebration of the Empire in 1931 was celebrated with pomp and ceremony by the Churches. During the celebrations, there were still even controversies about the flag.[50]

Harald Fenske introduces the notion of "the national opposition" meaning the major group of Germans who opposed the resolution of peace, and during the Weimar Republic opposed the constitution, or had an unresolved or cool relationship to it, at least. Even a number of liberals belonged to this group. Fenske's conclusion seems to be a good description of the relationship the bulk of Protestants had to the constitution:

> 'National opposition' or 'national movement' in the Weimar Republic must be understood to mean all persons, groups and parties which had a point of view to the right of the parties of the Peace Resolution and the later Weimar coalition, and who were positive to the renewal of the Empire or a revolutionary rebirth of Germany; of national and social spirit against the system of the State which had emerged from the collapse of the monarchy and were against the parties which supported this state system. It is too narrow an understanding if only those who never at any time were prepared to be content with the republic are regarded as belonging to this movement. Attachment to the "National opposition" was not synonymous with uncompromising rejection of the Weimar Republic; it did not even mean irreconcilable political radicalism. It is possible, rather, to think of such a spectrum of attitudes as tacit expectant legitimism and almost unrestrained activism under the same umbrella. It was not merely the resolute national-revolutionary minorities who belonged to the "National movement," but all groups and currents of conservatism, and a major portion of national liberalism.[51]

This is in clear opposition to what the Zentrum expected of members, as one of the party's official declarations in 1929 shows:

> What we demand of the whole of the party, is a positive attitude to the juridical and constitutional foundation of the present system of the state, the republic. We demand not only tolerance, but, on the contrary, a warm, active participation in the life of the new state of the people. To that our consciousness of responsibility and our Christian conscience oblige us ... arising from our Confession, such is our consciousness of responsibility toward our people and our state to the republic.[52]

It is reasonable to believe that this could be regarded as the "nationalist" credo of many German Catholics in the 1920s.

Christian Parties—Catholic and Protestant

For a long time, the Zentrum, with its sister party in Bavaria, was the only specifically Christian party in Germany. It had its origin in the Prussian *Katholische Fraktion* from the 1850s, but at the formation of the real party in 1870–71, it was emphasized, despite opposition, that the party intended to be an inter-confessional Christian party.[53] Had the "*Eigengesetzlichkeits*"-thesis not prevented support from Protestants, the *Kulturkampf* would have, for the Zentrum was immediately identified. These obstacles remained for the duration of the Empire, and hence the original ambition of inter-confessionality remained unattainable.[54]

Bismarck's aversion to the party has already been mentioned,[55] but he also disliked its ideological breadth: it "comprises seven intellectual directions and reflects all the colors of the political rainbow, from the extreme right to the most radical left". He even characterized the party as a "party's mobilization against the State."[56] There is reason to think Bismarck's frustration with the Zentrum was a weighty factor in starting the *Kulturkampf*, and even a reason for Protestants' abstention from establishing Christian parties.

In the years before WWI, the party made a new—and futile—effort to attract Protestants [57], and further efforts were made after the war when it appeared with the name *Christliche Volkspartei* in the election in 1919. The BVP adopted the same open attitude when it was established in 1918, and defined itself as "a general Christian party, void of any confessional barrier." A local evangelically dominated section of the party was established in Berlin, and the election results in 1919 showed that the *Christliche Volkspartei* most probably attained several Protestant votes. The main Catholic paper *Germania* thought that as many as 500,000 Protestants had voted for the two parties.[58] That appears correct, for its 19.7 percent was never matched again in the Weimar Republic when results lay between 17.8 percent and 13.9 percent (of ballots cast). One of the causes of the setback in 1920 was obviously connected to Protestant reactions to the Zentrum's partial responsibility for the recognition of the Versailles Treaty, the constitution and their cooperation with the SPD, like the reactions of the party's seceding rightist Catholic faction mentioned above. However, the immediate cause was probably that the Protestants had been discriminated against and even been looked on with aversion by those wanting a purely Catholic party.[59] The setback was additionally due to the loss of the Catholic dominated Saar and the Polish areas. They had participated in the 1919 election but been seceded afterwards.

However, at the very end of the Weimar Republic, efforts were made to establish a party on a quite different foundation. After years of cooperation with the SPD in the biggest state, Prussia, and threatened by the overwhelming Nazi offensive, people from the Zentrum and the SPD took an initiative to establish a broad non-Marxist *Partei der Arbeit*, similar to the British Labor Party, a party with many Christian voters. A working committee gathered in January 1933, but the furthering of the process was spoiled by what happened only a few days later.[60]

The aversion among German Protestants of starting specifically Christian parties had an obvious connection with the "*Eigengesetzlichkeits*"-thesis: the lacking of a right of the Church to involve itself in state matters and the independence of political life from the ethical demands of the Church.[61] It is easy to see from the literature of the famous evangelical theologian Dietrich Bonhoeffer that this was a reason why significant conservative theologians like him did not involve themselves with any specifically Christian party even after the Nazis became dominant in 1932. Other hindrances could be uncertainty about specific Christian policies, and the lack of high-profile Christian politicians,[62] in addition, Bismarck's aforementioned dislike.

Despite the barriers, Adolf Stöcker did establish his *Christlichsoziale Arbeiterpartei* in 1878. Successful as an orator, and as inspiring as he was, Stöcker's party project failed. Nipperdey thinks in addition that the evangelicals did not constitute a solid unity and church people were not in a hazardous situation like their brethren in the Netherlands and Switzerland. In addition, the official Church regarded itself as being a mediating and mollifying body above party politics. Stöcker's own Prussian Church maintained its distance from his party asserting he was too biased, unbalanced and socially critical.[63] Even Wilhelm II opposed Christian parties, and clerics as politicians because what politics "did was none of their business."[64]

Some Protestant parties were established soon after WWI, however, after some discussion. The understanding of the political situation was obviously feeble and delusive among some of the leaders of the new parties. In one of them, they hoped to turn it into to a broad alliance of voters ranging from the swastika party, the *Völkischer Block*, to the moderate *Wirtschaftspartei*, and one of the other parties hoped to ally the SPD and the Nazis![65] Most evangelical voters spread their votes over the DNVP, the DVP and the DDP. Stribrny asserts that because the SPD was hostile to churches, and the Zentrum was passive regarding Protestant clerical interests, this exacerbated the Protestant alienation from the Weimar Republic.[66]

Four Protestant Christian parties ran in 1928, but their total result did not exceed 0.2 percent (of ballots cast). At least two of them were merged before the election in 1930 into the *Christlichsozialer Volksdienst* (CSVD), which attracted some voters from the DNVP after it elected the controversial Alfred Hugenberg as their leader. The new party got 3.5 percent (of ballots cast) in 1930, which was the greatest turnout this short-lived party ever achieved. However, like its predecessors, even the CSVD lacked a political program. Their representatives were expected to follow their Christian persuasion.[67] This could lead to comical situations with its representatives lacking political maturity and in an ideological void. In Wurttemberg, the party overthrew a coalition government they normally should have supported, and despite being strongly anti-Catholic, they helped the Zentrum to win the presidency of that state. Even worse, the leader of the CSVD in Baden pursued a campaign very similar to the Nazi campaign with the result that he ultimately went over to the Nazi Party![68] Another example is the representative Peter Petersen, a pioneer in establishing pedagogy as an independent academic faculty. He is said to have been one of the most pronouncedly Nazi-inspired educators in the Third Reich and lectured in "brainwashing" deliveries in Buchenwald concentration camp for Norwegian students in order to "Teutonize" them.[69]

The CSVD did have a profile, though. Dahm asserts that except for economic and social politics, the party hardly differed from the DNVP in their political worldview, i.e. was rightist German national. An explanation may be that one of its instigators was Pastor Richard Mumm, Stöcker's son-in-law and his successor as leader of the CSAP. On the day the party was formed, wreaths were laid on Stöcker's grave, but also—somewhat paradoxically—on the grave of Friedrich Naumann, who had been one of the founders of the leftist liberal DDP. This was an expression of the two main directions of the party, the rightist deserters from the DNVP, and the originally southwestern democratically oriented pietists and members of denominations and fellowships.[70] But because of the party's vague political profile, such strident views were clearly tolerable. The party supported the Brüning government and the re-election of Hindenburg, but was split about the Versailles Treaty. It had contacts with churches in the USA, Britain and France and tried to utilize them to revise the "War-guilt" paragraph in the Versailles Treaty.[71] But its main contact abroad was probably the Dutch *Anti-Revolutionaire partij*, a party founded, as the name indicates, as a battle organization against what the adherents understood to be the detrimental liberal and radical consequences of the French Revolution, in contrast to the Catholics who regarded 1789 rather positively. Apart from the Dutch party, which later split into several parties, there was only one other similar party in the world in the 1920s: the *Evangelische Volkspartei* in Switzerland, established 1919.[72]

One would normally expect the CSVD to have been the core of a determined evangelical Christian opposition to the Nazi offensive after 1930, but there is little evidence of any such thing. The CSVD parliamentary leader, Wilhelm Simpfendörfer, presented it in the *Reichstag* in 1930 by saying that "*Fronterlebnis*" (the front experience) and German pietism" were the original grounds for the party, and, addressing himself to the Nazi representatives, he said, "we are not only anti-liberal, . . . we take a step further backwards: we are anti-rationalistic and *therefore* (author's italics) we do not find here (i.e. in the Nazi Party) our place." In short, his only criticism of the Nazis was they were not anti-rationalistic enough. Finally, he attacked "the unrighteous international treaties," "the hypocrisy of the so-called peace policy," and "a German foreign policy which in the past often was characterized by illusion and national degradation".[73] It is sensational that Simpfendörfer did not belong to the former rightist DNVP-faction, but was one of the pioneers from the *Herrnhut* heartland in Wurttemberg, whose voters had seceded from the DNVP as early as 1920. Actually, the CSVD's mentality was such that Josef Goebbels would have liked to have their representatives of the party take part in the notorious Harzburg assembly in 1931.[74] The CSVD was negative to the ban in 1932 against SA and SS, and the party paper *Tägliche Rundschau* treated the action against the Nazis as a "real persecution of Christians" by the Prussian police, and asserted that "the precious portion of the people," who represented the Nazi movement, was too good to be subject to such "Metternich-like methods." The CSVD demanded instead that Brüning should include the Nazis in the government. This would contribute to subdue the most extremist tendencies of the party.[75]

Nevertheless, the CSVD regarded the Nazi Party as a rival party, of course, and was aware that it had gained much ground among Protestants even before 1930. To prevent further hemorrhaging to the Nazis, the party started a campaign focusing on worldview and ideology in which the swastika was confronted by the crucifix. In 1930 this might have had some effect, but two years later it obviously had not. The CSVD lost two-thirds of its voters. In the meantime, naïve CSVD-adherents had visited the Nazi headquarters in Munich and been duped by assurances about Nazi policies towards churches and Christianity. After the election in 1933 the party made a futile effort to prevent closure by voluntarily submitting and adapting to the Nazi State. All the same, in June the party was dissolved. In some regional assemblies, their representatives attained status among the Nazis as interns.[76]

We can concur with Stribrny: "The Zentrum facilitated the Catholic Yes to the state, whereas on the Evangelical side there was no strong Christian party that supported the republic."[77]

The Zentrum and the BVP were dissolved in July 1933, and seven years later the exiled Sebastian Haffner described them briefly:

> It [Zentrum] could co-operate in ruling the Kaiser's Reich as well as the Republic, always exercising a moderating influence and successfully protecting the Church and Christian education and culture. A noticeable feature was that every question that was regarded as fundamental by other parties assumed secondary importance in the Zentrum's eyes. It included Right-wing and Left-wing politicians, Nationalists and friends of the League of Nations, Revenge-jingoists and Pacifists.[78]

But having experienced the lack of support from Protestants, Haffner, could add: "The hallmark of its members was the unconditional acceptance of Catholic religious and cultural values."[79]

Haffner even made a survey of the German party system in general and regarded the Zentrum as an exception:

> None of the former political parties was in any way prepared for illegal existence . . . not even the Communists, though they always boasted of its capacity. Even in legal times these parties constituted far less practical political instruments than do parties in Western countries. They were parties with "world conception": their wont was far less to encourage in practical politics than to give expression to a political philosophy; a general and vague idea of "how things should be." Scarcely any of them, with the possible exception of the Catholic Centre, had any clear conceptions and attainable aims; not one—again with the same exception—was a school for politicians who would be ready at any time under given conditions to assume the reins of government. Rather each party (and in this the Nazis are the true heirs and guardians of the old German party spirit) was constituted so as one day to take power alone, in a state governed according to its own ideas and conceptions. As long as this day did not dawn (in secret they came to realize that it never would), they pursued politics with a kind of mental reservation, unwilling to take responsibility and always on the alert to resume as soon as possible the "vacation of opposition," as the German parliamentary expression had it. They were, in fact, less parties than temples, in which Bismarck, Rousseau, or Marx were severally preached.[80]

The strong ideological tendency within the German parties, especially the KPD, has been confirmed in our time by the historian Andreas Wirsching.[81]

The Zentrum also was a party with "world conception," but this "conception" allowed for a liberal scope to the extent that the Zentrum could cooperate with the SPD, which had a totally contrary view on school policy, even though this issue was very important to the Zentrum.

Karl Buchheim thinks that it could have been possible to prevent Nazi success had the CSVD been established earlier.[82] This is an interesting theory, but given the confusing, or rather, lacking, profile of the CSVD, it is obvious that resistance to the Nazis like what the Zentrum made, could not be found among their voters. The very fact that a statement like "the Aryan *Völkerfamilie* is far superior to other groups or nations," and arguments against any concept of "equality" of the races, which was printed in the party newspaper,[83] makes the affinity apparent and explains the extensive migration of voters to the Nazi Party. Similar statements in any Zentrum paper would have been unthinkable.

The International Connections of the Christian Parties: Catholic Pan-Europeanism versus German Protestant Autarchy

As mentioned, the CSVD had some international contacts, but these were not like the institutionalized kinds found among Zentrum contacts. An international secretariat of "Christian" (i.e. Catholic) trade unions had been established as early as 1908 with the leader of the German Christian Trade Unions, Zentrum politician Adam Stegerwald, as chairman. After the war this secretariat was replaced by two Christian unions, one Catholic, the other inter-confessional but Catholic dominated. Even a fellowship of parties emerged. The Norwegian social scientist Tore Nedrebø claims, "increased competition with internationally-oriented, class-based Socialist and Communist parties encouraged greater co-operation between such parties and the growing Catholic Trade Union and Social Reform movement. Catholic Unions and Workers' Associations played a crucial role in the attempt to bind Catholic workers to Catholic parties." Nedrebø further asserts that this collusion contributed to establishing a "social and ideological bridge" between Catholic parties, moderate socialists and leftist-liberal parties, which in its turn prevented a right-wing and Fascist orientation within the Catholic parties during the Interwar period.[84] The anti-authoritarian attitude does not only involve trade unionists. Martin Conway says that especially within the Catholic youth movement and among some intellectual groups "there was an interest in pan-Europeanism, which expressed a Catholic distrust of the liberal and Fascist cult of the secular nation-state."[85] Perhaps the situation in Germany was the most obvious example of this due to the "Weimar Coalition," the establishment of the *Reichsbanner Schwarz-Rot-Gold* and the exploratory talks between the SPD and the Zentrum about party amalgamation referred to earlier.[86]

Before WWI, the international fellowship between Catholic organizations was most visibly expressed in Belgium, the Netherlands and Germany, probably due to the strong element of leftist workers in the Catholic parties in these countries and the establishment of the organization of 1908. The Catholic parties in the Hapsburg monarchy and Switzerland were dominated by the lower bourgeoisie and peasants, and in Italy and France they did not exist. In Italy, this was predominantly due to the papal ban on Catholics participating in Italian politics, and in France, the Catholic milieu was more nationalist.[87]

The papal ban was lifted in 1920, one year after the formation of the rather leftist *Partito Popolari Italiano* (PPI). In 1924, the *Parti Démocrate Populaire* (PDP) was formed in France. Thus, the foundation of a more comprehensive European Christian democratic organization was now possible, and in 1925 the *Sécretariat Internationale des Partis Démocratique d'Inspiration Chrétienne* (SIPDIC) was founded with the participation of parties primarily from countries which later on in 1957 formed the EEC, but also from Lithuania, Austria, Switzerland, Hungary and Czechoslovakia. At its congress in 1932, the SIPDIC advocated a European Union which ought to emerge from an embryo of economic integration and a common trade market. The SIPDIC decayed after the dissolution of the Zentrum and the transfer from democratic to authoritarian regimes in many countries.[88]

The SIPDIC promoted democratic values, disarmament and international cooperation within League of Nations, but by 1926 the most leftist oriented of the parties, the Italian PPI, had been banned by the Fascist government. The relationship between the PPI leader Luigi Sturzo and the Zentrum politicians Joseph Joos and Konrad Adenauer had been particularly close.[89]

Other Catholic international organizations, such as the *Pax Romana* from 1921, were fora for European Catholic politicians. After papal resistance against political liberalism ceased, the *Internationale Démocratique* was established in 1921, as a forum for promoting peace and for pacifist democrats. Both Zentrum- and DDP-politicians took part in it.[90]

Corresponding international political organizations lacked among European Protestant political parties, both because they were so few (Dutch, German and Swiss parties only) and hence restricted to the bilateral relationship between the CSVD and the ARP, and because of the general autarchic mentality within German Protestantism. This mentality was extremely expressed in the Nazi Party even in the economic field, a field which had been an important cause in the co-operation among the Catholic parties. The Nazi Party had pursued the autarchic policy at least after the inauguration of the four-year plan in 1936. Even this phenomenon can be traced back to Fichte in his *Der geschlossene Handelsstaat* (The closed Trading-state). In line with this policy the Nazi government attended to the Mark having a price differential value, preventing fixation of value as to foreign currencies. Probably this was the reason why Hjalmar Schacht, being skeptical to this pronounced autarchic policy, had to leave his office.[91]

THE HERITAGE OF WORLD WAR I

"*Fronterlebnis*" (The Front Experience) and Langemarck

The "*Fronterlebnis*" statement made by the CSVD politician Simpfendörfer expressed a highly esteemed ingredient of the adulation of the *Volk* myth. Words like *Volk*, *völkisch* and "*Fronterlebnis*" were words of honor during the Weimar Republic—among the rightists, but far less so among socialists and Catholic churchgoers. So the CSVD was part of the rightist syndrome and not just this party, but also the *Jungreformatorische Bewegung*, the predecessor in 1933 of the PNB and the BK. This milieu emphasized how positive the wars had been for Christian life in Germany.[92]

The celebration of the battle at Flemish *Langemarck* on November 11, 1914,[93] played a central part in the *"Fronterlebnis"* veneration and contributed to the increasing opposition between leftists and rightists after the shame of the defeat in 1918 had receded. Together with the "Stab-in the-Back-Legend," it gave impetus to new national pride by the mid-1920s. To quote Bernt Hüppauf:

> The elemental imagery and elaborate, often dark code associated with the name of "Langemarck" occupied a central position in the mentality of the educated and patriotic middle classes and contributed to shaping their perception of and attitudes towards reality; which—as a result of the lost war which had left their basic beliefs and position in the social-historical world shattered—they were deeply afraid of losing. Since the dreams and attitudes, for which "Langemarck" was the suggestive name, appeared to be realized by the NS movement, they can be interpreted as a driving force behind the inclination to Fascism.[94]

It does not seem as if Hüppauf has examined the confessional terrain of these "educated and patriotic middle classes." It would have been interesting, and probably revealed that fascination with the celebration was greater among Protestants than Catholics. The celebration was perceived as a demonstration against the Weimar Republic, and the name adopted by the student association of the Protestant dominated right-wing *Stahlhelm* organization. After 1927 the *Langemarck*-day was celebrated annually by the universities, and the Nazis exploited it as best as they could for their own ends, both before and after their takeover.[95] The famous post-WWII author Wolfgang Borchert, who had fought on the eastern front, remembered with bitterness the enthusiastic celebrations in his 95 percent Protestant Hamburg.[96]

"Dolchstosslegende" (The Stab-in-the-Back-Legend)

The concept, though not the word, *"Dolchstosslegende"* was probably first laid down by the Protestant Bishop Gerhard Tolzien of Mecklenburg soon after the Resolution of Peace in 1917, when he attacked the men who had entered into negotiations and "tried to betray the country", but the word itself was launched in a sermon by the Protestant court chaplain Bruno Doehring in February 1918. Two weeks before the truce, the *Deutsche Evangelische Kirchenzeitung* called the dispositions of *Reichskanzler* Max von Baden "organized high treason." Among other things engendering the legend was that for the bulk of Protestants it was totally unthinkable that Germany, God's mission to the world, could lose the war![97]

The slogan then became "legitimized" when civilian politicians Philip Scheidemann from the SPD and Matthias Erzberger from the Zentrum, who both joined the government shortly before the armistice, were accused of having "betrayed" the army leaders by signing it. The legend gained broader scope as whole groups of society, in general, were accused of the "treachery": Jews, communists, Freemasons and Jesuits. These four with their alleged international base were treated as one perfidious bunch, not least by Alfred Rosenberg.[98] Seeing as Jesuits were lumped with this despised group, the legend naturally did not gain the same status among Catholics as Protestants. There is reason to believe that, to a great extent, Catholic churchgoers refused to accept the *"Dolchstosslegende"* as a salient concept. Rolf Hobson, with reference to Boris Barth, asserts:

> "The Stab-in-the-Back-legend" . . . spread from the military officers, the Protestant churches, the nationalist academics, armed free-corps and the völkisch milieus and made inroads into wide bourgeois circles. . . . After 1914 the Prussian Protestant churches propagated a militant war-theology that had room for no explanation of the defeat other than treachery; the pulpits played a key role in making the churchgoers receptive for "The Stab-in-the-Back-legend."
> . . . Together with the Guilt Clause in the Versailles Treaty "The Stab-in-the-Back-legend" lay the uncritically accepted basis for the political world-view of all groups of the undemocratic right-wing extending far into groups of many bourgeois social circles.[99]

Hobson and Barth go on to say that by 1920 it was impossible to gainsay the legitimacy of the legend any longer, as the view had become so firmly entrenched.[100]

VÖLKISCH ORGANIZATIONS AND THE CONFESSIONS IN THE 1920S

The *Deutschvölkischer Schutz- und Trutzbund* (The German-Volkish League for Protection and Defiance)

More than a hundred right-wing organizations emerged in the first few years after WWI. Steigmann-Gall describes the turbulent era giving rise to the phenomenon:

> The trauma of defeat in the First World War, the Guilt Clause of the Versailles Treaty, and the domestic upheaval of the failed November Revolution all conspired to produce a cacophony of rightist fringe-groups determined to overthrow the newly created Weimar Republic. Although distinct in style and organization, all these groups advocated a radical völkisch nationalism that embraced antisemitism, antimarxism, antiliberalism, and anti-Catholicism to varying degrees.[101]

The greatest and most influential among these was the *Deutschvölkischer Schutz und Trutzbund*. It had 100,000 members before it was disbanded. Established at the initiative of leaders from the old *Alldeutscher Verband*, after accusations of involvement in the assassinations of Matthias Erzberger from the Zentrum and the liberal Jewish foreign minister Walter Rathenau, and the attempt on social democrat Scheidemann, it was banned in 1923.[102]

The later Nazis Gottfried Feder and Dietrich Eckhardt were attached to the organization, and also the Lutheran clergyman Friedrich Andersen. It was extremely anti-Semitic and the leader Alfred Roth said, "When we '*deutschvölkische*' take over in the future, . . . the Jews shall be taken to the gallows."[103]

On the other hand, the DSTB does not seem to have been particularly anti-Catholic, but its most prominent members were Protestants, and Protestant Hamburg their headquarters. It had the ambition of setting up a "white international" and used the swastika as a symbol, which Catholics regarded as an anti-Christian emblem. After the ban, the organization split into smaller entities, but the main core established the strongly anti-Catholic *Deutschvölkische Freiheitspartei*, a coalition-partner of the Nazi Party in 1923 and 1924.[104]

The very character of the DSTB, not to mention their involvement in the assassination of Erzberger, should suffice to show it was hardly attractive to many Catholics. Nevertheless, two prominent Catholic publicists, Dietrich Eckhardt and Josef Roth, were attached to it at the same time when they also were active in the (NS)DAP after 1919, the latter with considerable influence among students. Eriksen, Harket and Lorenz assert that, "although the DSTB only lasted a couple of years, it has been regarded as an amplifier for the anti-Semitism that existed already, because it 'modernized' and adapted it to the postwar era. . . . At the same time the organization opposed the democratic-parliamentarian system."[105]

Catholicism, Protestantism and Right-wing Radicalism in Bavaria in the 1920s

In 2010 Derek Hastings published his pioneering *Catholicism and the Roots of Nazism* with a focus on the relationship of the confessions to the right-wing and Nazi movements in Bavaria starting with the formation of the Nazi Party in 1919. Hastings provides evidence of the, up until then, little-known fact that there was heavy ("Reform") Catholic impact on the embryonic Nazi Party and summarizes it this way:

> Between 1919 and late 1923 believing Catholics and their ideals played a central, and hitherto overlooked, role in the development of the Nazi movement in

and around Munich, before events associated with the 1923 Beerhall Putsch and its chaotic aftermath dramatically changed the movement's nature and composition. This early Catholic orientation—informal yet palpable—was central to the party's ability to transcend its initial structure as a semi-secretive discussion club and to establish a broader appeal and early political foothold within the overwhelmingly Catholic context of Munich. This enabled the movement to survive its infancy by differentiating itself from other völkisch entities with visibly divergent orientations, whether Protestant-inflected or occult-based.[106]

Hastings finds the religious identity of the small DAP in 1919 unclear, but that almost all the members at the beginning were working class Catholics. One of the leaders, Karl Harrer, was also a member of the *Thulegesellschaft* established in 1918. While Rudolf Sebottendorf was a leader, until spring 1919, this organization was not only strongly anti-Catholic, but even anti-Christian. Its membership was drawn from wealthy Protestant nationalists in Munich and was a pronounced *völkisch* organization. When Sebottendorf left, the anti-Catholicism lessened and Catholics even took over its publication, *Völkischer Beobachter*, resulting in closer cooperation between the *Thulegesellschaft* and the Nazi Party. *VB* finally became the main Nazi newspaper.[107]

One evident reason why the DAP could attract Catholics was that the confession in Munich was heavily influenced in the first years after WWI by the "Reform Catholics" we made acquaintance with earlier.[108] The two most important Catholics in the DAP, Franz Schrönghamer-Heimdal and Dietrich Eckhardt had been attached to the BVP, but this party severed contact with Schrönghamer due to his anti-Semitism, and Eckhardt left the party because of his disappointment with the BVP's internationalism and its deficient capacity to combat the revolutionary policy of the Jews and Marxists.[109] Eckhardt became *VB* editor and, to emphasize his stance, he consistently added *Katholik* to his name. Nevertheless, he would introduce himself in the paper by demanding "Tear satanism's lust-Bible to pieces:—the Old Testament!," a slogan Hitler eventually removed in 1927 as a tactic to draw more support from churchgoers, even though the Old Testament was losing its status in Germany at the time.[110] Hastings thinks the efforts of Schrönghamer-Heimdal and Eckhardt in the early Nazi movement were invaluable because it was the only Catholic-influenced organization in the *völkisch* environment.[111] Even students in the Catholic CV, KV and *Hochland* became Nazis. At the end of 1922, social democratic media thought they could show "the increasing indisputable synthesis of Nazi-oriented racism and strong Catholic piety based in Munich," and in July 1923 the social democratic *Vorwärts* asserted the energetic and openly propagandistic agitation of Catholic priests on behalf of the Nazi Party, but they thought such activity was only possible in Bavaria. The paper appealed directly to the Vatican and German bishops to intervene, but it got no response before the autumn, when the parliamentary leader of the BVP, Heinrich Held, also urgently appealed to Cardinal Faulhaber because he had been shocked to discover that "even priests have been duped by Nazi ideas". Faulhaber responded with a strongly-worded tirade against anti-Semitism and racism five days before the Beer Hall Putsch, and a thinly-veiled attack on the Nazi Party.[112]

The fears of the social democrats and of Heinrich Held seemed well-founded, because in the course of 1923 up until the Beer-Hall Putsch, the Nazi Party experienced a formidable upswing in membership among Catholics, most probably due to the agitational efforts of some priests, Lorenz Pieper being the ablest of these. He was a prominent member of the mass-organization *Volksverein für das katholische Deutschland* that his brother August was Secretary-General of. In sharp contrast to what later became the norm, in 1923 no Protestant clergymen were active Nazi agitators.[113]

The "martyrdom" of Albert Leo Schlageter promoted the attraction of Nazism among Catholics. Schlageter had been executed by the French occupational forces in the Ruhr on charges of sabotage. He had been a devout Catholic, a member of the CV, a decorated veteran, and not least: one of the founding members of the local Nazi Party in Berlin. When the Nazis held masses in his honor, church leaders objected, to the disappointment of many Catholics.[114]

The Nazis were very eager to show off their Catholic identity. *VB* published Christian poems and programs from the services and prayers to be prayed during them. The members of the *Jugendbund*, the predecessor of the *Hitlerjugend*, were encouraged to attend mass.[115]

Catholic involvement culminated at the mass gathering "*Deutscher Tag*" in Nuremberg on September 1 and 2, 1923, where several *völkisch* organizations gathered and set up the *Kampfbund* in order to prepare for the Beer Hall Putsch two months later. According to Hastings, this represented a marked shift in Nazi strategy, which up until then had been to keep the party separate from other *völkisch* groups. It was a year since Mussolini's takeover in Italy, and many people expected Hitler to become the "Mussolini of Germany." It put Hitler on the spot. He needed broader support than Bavarian Catholics alone, but that entailed cooperation with strongly anti-Catholic groups and individuals such as Erich Ludendorff. Ludendorff began to write articles in *VB*, which was by now edited by another anti-Catholic, Alfred Rosenberg, who previously had belonged to the *Thulegesellschaft*.[116]

The strategic shift soon became manifest, even in Hitler's conduct. In a speech he asserted that religious identity belonged to the private sphere, and for the first time Protestant clerics from northern Bavaria took part as prominent advocates of the broader *Kampfbund* movement. Several Catholics were disillusioned, some clerics after receiving warnings from church leaders. The case of the clever Lorenz Pieper illustrates Hitler's strategic ability. Pieper offered to defy the church leaders and continue his work for the party, but Hitler advised him to bow to the clerical directives, because "a suspended priest is of no use to me, anyway."[117]

The Catholic response to the Beer Hall Putsch was diametrically opposed to the considerable sympathy in Protestant churches. Then violent anti-Catholicism broke out among the *Kampfbund* organizations and students at Munich University, and Rosenberg wrote his book *Zentrum und Bayerische Volkspartei als Feinde des Deutschen Staatsgedanken* (*The Zentrum and the BVP as Enemies of the German Idea of State*). For the first time now the Nazi Party also attacked the church, not just the BVP. In his new year's speech Cardinal Faulhaber asserted that *deutschvölkisch* was by nature the same as hostility to Catholicism. Other *völkisch* organizations and the alliance parties of the Nazi Party in 1924 and 1925 attacked the Vatican with things like: "We *völkisch* consider Ultramontanism to be the international political activity of the pope, and we reject it, because it is and continues to be detrimental to the historical evolution and inner freedom of Germany." In several right-wing speeches, it was proclaimed that the "Putsch" had primarily been an action against "Rome" in the defense of "Wittenberg." Accordingly, the antagonism between the Catholic Church and the "*Völkische Bewegung*" became permanent, and the era of Catholic Munich as a main Nazi stronghold was over for good. In connection with the trial of Hitler, Nuncio Pacelli wrote that nationalism, meaning national socialism, was "perhaps the most dangerous heresy of the day." Catholics who still clung to Nazism did so, to a great extent, at the expense of their Catholic identity.[118]

The anti-Catholic reaction in Munich caused BVP politicians to take measures against it. It is perhaps conspicuous that Hitler himself was only subject to a small degree of Catholic criticism. His image as a loyal Catholic was unimpaired. Instead, he was accused of having mixed the party with Protestant *völkisch* and lost control. Even the Ludendorff group concurred, but with the opposite explanation: the Nazi Party had been "too Catholic" oriented and sabotaged the *völkisch*.[119]

It was not just in Munich and Bavaria that the right-wing radicals offended Catholics. The events in the south attracted the attention of the rest of the country, and the long-term damage among rightists was that anti-Catholicism once again became coupled with anti-Semitism.[120] An interesting detail from this early Nazi period is the consciousness of the fundamental difference in resistance to the anti-democratic rightist movements between representatives of the confessions. In Heinrich Held's letter to Cardinal Faulhaber shortly before the "Putsch," he doubted if Gustav von Kahr, head of law enforcement in Munich, could keep the situation under control. Despite good will, he lacked—as a *Protestant*—the power to deal with the danger threatening Bavaria from the *Kampfbund*. As it turned out, during the action, von Kahr wavered.[121]

In the election campaigns of 1924, the Zentrum/BVP and the Nazi Party attacked each other bitterly, and the latter made a lot of effort to try and convince Catholic women especially that the Nazi Party was Christian-friendly.[122] It is possible that this had some effect, because the Nazi-alliance parties did fairly well in the three Bavarian constituencies in the May-election, but it is also interesting to notice that they did better in the Protestant dominated Franconia (20.7 percent) than in the Catholic dominated, however original Nazi central constituency Upper Bavaria (17.0 percent) and considerably better than in the other Catholic dominated Lower Bavaria (10.2 percent). This tendency is even obvious in the rest of the country where the parties carried better support in *all* Protestant dominated constituences than in the three most Catholic dominated ones Westfahlen Süd (1.5 percent), Köln-Aachen (1.5 percent) and Koblenz-Trier (1.3 percent). The best support in Germany the parties carried in the purely Protestant Mecklenburg in the North with 20.8 percent (all percentages as of ballots cast).

Both *Reichstag*- and *Landtag*-election results show the Nazi-alliance parties suffered serious setbacks between the elections in the spring and in the autumn, and for some years after 1924, the Nazi Party seemed to have crumbled.

The first attack on the Nazi Party ever in a publication probably came as early as in December 1920 by the monk Augustin Bea. His article "Antisemittismus, Rassentheorie und Altes Testament" in the Jesuit magazine *Stimmen der Zeit* connected the racist anti-Semitism surfacing in the local *völkisch* milieu in Munich—the new Nazi Party included—with the Teutonic-pagan ideas about racism and religion of Houston Chamberlain, Theodor Fritsch and Artur Dinter. They all condemned the Talmud and the Old Testament. The Nazis responded in *VB* by asserting that "from a purely Aryan standpoint" they did not accept identification with the *völkisch* persons mentioned and their adherents, and encouraged Catholics to join the party.[123] A dispute ensued over three years long. Catholic individuals, organizations, publications, and BVP politicians, and party congresses in the one corner, and Nazis, especially through articles in *VB*, in the other corner. The main Catholic accusations were connected with religion, and the Nazis countered by accusing the Zentrum and the BVP of mixing religious and political Catholicism and of the seemingly paradoxical collaboration with "Jews and atheists" in the SPD. At least one Catholic association, the *Jungmännerverein* in Nuremberg, prohibited members from joining Nazi, *völkisch* and anti-Semitic organizations.[124]

A controversy in the autumn of 1921 with the Bavarian premier, Hugo Max von Lerchenfeld, caused Hitler, who rarely involved himself in religious matters, to express his personal faith by saying that he understood Christ first and foremost as a warrior in "his monumental battle against the Jewish poison, and I am mightily touched by the fact that it was because of this he had to pour out his blood on the cross." Hitler was lucky to be able to fit his declaration of faith inside the frame of the agitative work of one of his Catholic priests, Philip Haeuser, who was regarded by the Nazis as a key person for the propagation of "war Christianity." Haeuser referred to an archbishop in the 14th century, Balduin of Trier, who allegedly was an athletic and masculine "warrior" and an ideal for young Catholic Nazis.

Hastings concludes Hitler's speech was significant for two reasons: he made a clear profession which the Nazi movement could utilize to great effect in the course of 1923, and it was a well-planned programmatic expression intended to embody the timeless identity of the movement and demonstrate the genuine obligation to the party clause about "Positive Christianity." The speech took on the character of being an authoritative expression of party doctrine. Actually, none of Hitler's other speeches up until then got the same publicity or public approval as this one. Its effect was enhanced by Cardinal Faulhaber's condemnation of the Weimar Republic and slipshod negative comment about "Jewish media in Berlin" and—atypically of a Catholic—his appeal to "racially pure Catholics."[125]

In the autumn of 1923, Father Erhard Schlund made a more dangerous and extensive attack on the Nazi ideology and party. Schlund had a better understanding of the times than many, espying a "religious wave" where others only saw growing materialism, the increasing crisis of faith and nihilism. His writing confronted the ideology of the whole "*Völkische Bewegung*" and its organizations and dealt with Nazism in particular.[126]

Schlund reacted to the clause in the party program allowing freedom of faith only to those who did not threaten the state or offend the moral feelings of the Teutonic race. The feelings of a race could not possibly be a vehicle for attaining the established truths of the faith. He also suspected the Nazis of ambitions to create a super-confessional fellowship of Churches, because otherwise "Positive Christianity" could mean anything at all. Schlund asked himself if "Positive Christianity" could mean also the party was opposed to enemies of Christianity. Hitler, said Father Schlund, aimed at being the new savior, not God's Son, that is to say, but a son of his fellowship-of people, people who declared: "We shall have no other god but Germany." Schlund also observed many names "had appeared during recent years" of concepts and organizations with the *völkisch*-connoted word *Deutsch*, many of them from Protestant sources. He registered a total of 62 words. Cardinal Faulhaber recognized Schlund and appointed him the leader of a media office in 1928 with the task of keeping an eye on the "publication of books and papers" and making reports about everything of "interest and significance for religious and clerical subjects." The importance of his book resulted in re-publication in the 1970s.[127]

Somewhat contrary to Hastings, Björn Mensing asserts that even the great majority of Bavarian Protestant clergymen showed a positive attitude to the Hitler-movement both *before* and after the "Putsch". He further asserts that the "Putsch" primarily was assessed along confessional lines. The clergy hoped that, at least with the participation of Ludendorff, the "Putsch" would result in the restoration of the Protestant-Prussian dominated Empire.[128] Mensing even contends that the efforts of Protestant clergymen in the spring of 1924 considerably enhanced the election success of the *Völkischer Block* in the earlier mentioned Protestant Franconia in Northern Bavaria. In some subdivisions of the constituency, the party got more than 50 percent of the votes.[129]

However, there were some critical voices among Protestant clergy and theologians. The Bavarian Church President Friedrich Veit remained calm during the "Putsch" and criticized the clergymen who had been actively involved in it and in the 1924 election campaign. Professor Hermann Strathmann in Erlangen University, one of the main Protestant critics of Nazism after 1930, attacked the "Aryan" gospel of Artur Dinter. Other theologians countered and a debate in a publication ensued.[130]

Like the general political tendency in other matters, the involvement of Protestant clerics and theologians in *völkisch* and Nazi matters seemed to dwindle after 1924, although Hastings asserts numerous Protestant clergymen continued Nazi agitation in their districts in 1925 and 1926 in keeping with the party effort to change its image.[131]

Changing Image. Religious Policy in the Nazi Party after the "Beer Hall Putsch."

After Hitler's release from prison and the reorganization of the party in February 1925 he severed the bonds to the DVFP and Ludendorff, realizing that the alliance had had a detrimental effect on the Nazi cause. Already in *Mein Kampf* he had signaled a future showdown with the *völkisch* ideologs, whom he regarded as unrealistic dreamers of "old Teutonic heroic deeds" and "grey antiquity" wanting to fight with "spiritual weapons" but timorous in confrontation with communists. Even Schönerer's *Los-von-Rom*-movement was criticized. This movement and the *völkisch* ideologs had blocked the recruitment of Catholics to Nazism.[132]

Not all Nazis agreed with Hitler, however. One of his most loyal supporters, Artur Dinter, accused his erstwhile friend of being blind to the fact that, "the Roman Papal Church is an equally dreadful enemy as the Jew of a *völkisch* Germany—to say nothing of a *völkisch Grossdeutschland*." Alfred Rosenberg's standpoint was very close to Dinter's, but when the controversy about his literature raged in the 1930s, he made it very clear that his viewpoints were private and that Nazism—in loyal accordance with Hitler's demand—was primarily a political movement. Dinter was anomalous in that he asserted that "the history of all peoples at all times teaches us that religious revolutions always precede the political ones, it is never the opposite way around." It, therefore, seems that for Hitler—and Rosenberg—the decisive battle was primarily political. Dinter was expelled from the party. His view was taken up in Ludendorff's group, but that one dwindled almost to nothing.[133]

Hitler's new policy created a schism in the "*Völkische Bewegung*." He was attacked by several traditional Protestant *völkisch* people before both next elections, in 1928 and 1930, with accusations of not only ingratiating himself with Catholics, but, together with Italian Fascism, participating in an international Catholic conspiracy. In reaction to Hitler, Bruno Doehring, the leader of the *Evangelischer Bund* and launcher of the "Stab-in-the-Back-Legend," found it necessary to form the *Deutsche Reformationspartei*, which although it amalgamated with the former Nazi alliance partner DVFP to the *Völkisch(national)er Block*, turned out to be a fiasco. However, despite the new party policy, Julius Streicher in Nuremberg was still allowed to continue his obscene and grossly insulting anti-Catholic propaganda in his *Der Stürmer*.[134]

In *Mein Kampf*, Hitler had classified a lot of parties. The rather large group of Protestant based parties, roughly Karl Rohe's "National bloc," were "*Bürgerliche Klassenparteien*" (with the exception of *völkisch* parties). They included the parties from the leftist DDP to the rightist DNVP. Hitler did not pay much attention to these, however. He focused on the Zentrum and the BVP and their cooperation with the SPD. These parties were the "criminals of November," and one of his main complaints about the SPD and the Zentrum cooperation was that they "courted the favor of France," Germany's main opponent, and even, some would say, their deadly enemy. He accused them of being responsible for the outbreak of WWI. Additionally, Hitler accused the Zentrum of showing a "servile slave mentality" towards the "dogmatic" Catholic Church. Contrary to Alfred Rosenberg, Hitler took care not to criticize the Church itself, however.[135]

Hitler was bent on separating politics and church life and, as mentioned, he was reluctant to express religious views. In *Mein Kampf*, he, for a second time, expresses his views, which this time differ from his original statements of the early 1920s about "war religion." Although he was a Catholic, Hitler speaks about religion as "inner experience" and hence he was in harmony with the mainstream German Protestant science of religion in the tradition of Schleiermacher. This contrasts starkly with the papally authorized and authoritarian Catholic theology of dogmas.[136]

Geoffrey Pridham asserts that the official attitude of Nazis towards religion after 1925 could be described as a mixture of patriotic appeals to the Catholics, denying that the party was interested in discriminating any of the confessions ("We are all Germans"), an emphasis on traditional values which also included religion, and avoidance of the theme by concentrating on "the danger of attack" on religion from the leftists. Nevertheless, outbursts of antagonism from party members, such as "outsiders" like Streicher could happen. The Nazi propaganda did not even flinch from shameless deliberate misrepresentation. After the Lateran Treaty, the Nazis asserted that this indicated that the pope had approved Nazism, and before the election in 1930 the clerics of Ingolstadt in Bavaria had to deny Nazi campaign assertions that the Catholic clergy there supported the party.[137]

Such incidences were perhaps symptomatic of Hitler's fanatical desire to make the Nazi Party a broad popular movement. He needed both Protestants and Catholics and his somewhat reserved religious statement could even have been aimed at recruiting socialists. However, his time in prison had obviously contributed to his self-image of not only being the *Führer*, but even a kind of messiah. Along with this, the reorganized party introduced ritual activities outside any Christian frame of reference such as the elevation of the sixteen "martyrs" from 1923 to secular saints with an eternal place in the Nazi pantheon, with the memorial of *Schlageter* purged of his Catholic identity. Secular-political religiosity overshadowed all future efforts to reinstate the former Catholic orientation.[138]

This new non-Christian trend was expressed in the working program of the party in 1927: "Of course the German people will arrive at a form of cognition of God, a religious life that its Nordic blood demands; certainly, then the trinity of blood, faith and state will be perfected. Most important of all in this sphere is that the consciousness of the Nordic idea will manifest itself."

After the Nazi success in the election of 1930, (which showed that the Zentrum was untouched), the Nazis once again changed tactics, though. *Reichskanzler* Brüning was not supported by the SPD, but by conservatives and the CSVD, and Alfred Rosenberg had published his notorious "*Mythus*" shortly after the election, and the Nazis needed to minimize its ramifications. Hence the working program from 1927 was changed in 1931: "The party as such is established on the foundation of 'Positive Christianity.' All issues, hopes and desires concerning to what extent the German people will ever find a new kind of cognition of God and religious life, do not belong among party concerns." The change was visible locally, e.g. in the main party paper in Berlin, *Der Angriff*, which regularly published articles which defended the position in society of religion and the church.[139]

Kurt Nowak summarizes his opinion of the relationship of the Nazi movement to politics, culture and theology in this way: 1) A uniqueness of NS-ideology was that it made up a theoretically weakly structured conglomerate. It was a mixture of every kind of protest element against the political and cultural modernism which had dominated Germany and Europe to a great extent since the end of the nineteenth century. 2) There was a mobile relationship between worldview and political practice. Hence, the Churches had problems in assessing its ideology. 3) The NS-ideology was a mixture of pagan, Christian and non-religious elements and therefore remained unclear.[140]

Hitler had tried to change the identity of the party after 1925 in two ways. He succeeded with the political aspect: changing the party from a rabulist gang whose aim was a physically violent takeover, to a party aiming for a legal takeover. He had greater problems with the ideological change, though, which probably related to party recruitment. Almost no Catholic churchgoers joined. All in all, Hitler's policy was clearly infected with opportunism.

OTHER PARAMILITARY ORGANIZATIONS AND CATHOLICS IN THE 1920S AND 1930S

The Paramilitary Organizations and their Relationship to Catholics 1919–1928

Other right-wing—and even paramilitary—organizations were active during the "calm" Nazi period of 1925–1930. The *Jungdeutscher Orden* and the *Stahlhelm Bund der Frontsoldaten*, both established soon after the defeat in 1918, were the biggest and most important. The former had 200,000 members, at the time of the "Putsch," but membership sank afterwards. The latter had 100,000, peaking at 500,000 in 1930.[141] SA became dominant after that.

Despite the *Jungdeutscher Orden* being accused by Zentrum politicians of representing a party political, anti-Catholic and anti-Semitic attitude, it got quite a lot of Catholic members, and the Zentrum, therefore, regarded it as a threat. Two bishops in the districts with the bulk of the Catholic members made negative statements about it. Allegedly, the order was supposed to be of a "strongly neo-pagan Teutonic kind" and even represent "a kind of Teutonic cult of God" and have contact with the Nazi Party. The Catholic members of the order protested and asserted that its official program showed its moderate character whereas the opponents referred to its rather *völkisch* practice. A case of its unclear identity is the fact that some regional divisions supported the "Putsch" while the leader, Artur Mahraun, dissociated himself from it. All the same, Mahraun defended Hitler's "worldview," and several *völkisch* writers belonged among the literature favored by the order. Catholic Lorenz Pieper was a member of the order, of the DSTB, and of the Nazi Party at the same time.[142]

The *Stahlhelm* represented a rather traditional, conservative, Prussian Protestantism and was pronouncedly more right-wing oriented than the order. It was concerned about the re-erection of a proud German State. What constitution it should have was unclear, but parliamentary democracy was an unacceptable alternative. "Internationalism," especially Marxism and Jewishness, was detested, and therefore even included Catholicism. Several Protestant clerics joined, and occasional outbursts were heard that Catholics interpreted as the start of a new *Kulturkampf*.[143]

After the political assassinations, Josef Wirth, *Reichskanzler* from 1921–1922, and Zentrum politician, rhetorically declared: "This enemy is to the Right!," and both organizations had been banned together with the DSTB. Their bans were lifted in 1923, a victory for them and a loss of prestige for the "Weimar coalition." Then, leaders of the *Jungdeutscher Orden* repeatedly tried to ingratiate themselves with the Catholic clergy and win acceptance, but Cardinal Bertram of North Germany, after having initiated an inquiry, responded in March 1924 by urgently warning against it. He concluded, not least by referring to its cooperation with the *Stahlhelm*, that the fight of the order was really directed against the Catholic Church and its calling to further worldwide reconciliation among nations, and against the Church's teaching and commandments. Bertram's intervention worked, and Catholics left the order. His warning was not about the order only, though, because he used the word "etcetera" and it was obvious that the *Stahlhelm* and the numerous other similar organizations—which would also mean the Nazi Party—were included.[144]

Nevertheless, there were still Catholic members of the order, and it caused rifts in Catholic circles. In the general assembly of the *Katholische Jugend und Jungmännerverein Deutschlands* in June 1924 there was a debate between the "nationalists" and "papists" that the "papists" won, and a resolution was passed. Wieland Vogel regards it as implying the first official rejection of Nazism on a higher organizational level. Despite this, some months later, both the northern and southern German bishops' conferences issued resolutions which softened the general Catholic attitude to the *Jungdeutscher Orden*. They declared neutrality but recommended Catholics give priority to work in the organizations of the Church. It seems that this even pertained to the *Stahlhelm*, but, shortly afterwards, incidents made radical tendencies in this organization more obvious, which caused Catholics to react negatively to it. The next year's southern bishops' conference warned strongly against the *Stahlhelm*, and some clerics began to regard right-wing organizations as a more serious menace than communist movements.[145]

It seems the tension between the "Weimar coalition" and the right-wing organizations sharpened during 1924 and 1925. The fifty-year commemoration of the unveiling of the Hermann statue in Westfahlen is an indication. It had been erected in 1875 with pomp and circumstance in the presence of the *Kaiser*. In 1925 the authorities were represented at the celebration only by officials on a lower level, probably because this time the celebration was totally dominated by the *Stahlhelm* and *Jungdeutscher Orden* and largely had become a symbolic weapon for the right-wing. The event was introduced by a Lutheran bishop who talked about "the old German God" and called for a settlement of the "shame" of November 1918, and the old imperial black-white-red flag was hoisted instead of the official black-red-yellow flag of the republic.[146]

"Black—Red—Gold" versus "Black—White—Red"

People from the "Weimar" parties also established an organization, the *Reichsbanner Schwarz—Rot—Gold* (The Standard Black-Red-Gold) in February 1924. It was not an object of condemnation by the Catholic Church, and the rightist movements were eager to call attention to this in their criticism of the Church's warnings and resolutions against them. In addition to the three "Weimar" parties, the Catholic *Bayerischer Bauernbund* took a positive stand and a few representatives from the bourgeois *Wirtschaftspartei* joined the movement, despite the negative attitude of the party leaders. However, Stresemann's DVP was negative. Among the most prominent Zentrum representatives were Konstantin Fehrenbach, (*Reichskanzler* 1920–1922), and Wilhelm Marx (*Reichskanzler* 1923–1924 and 1926–1928 and the presidential candidate of the Weimar coalition in 1925). At least one Catholic cleric was a member.[147]

Representatives of the rightist organizations could not understand that the Catholic bishops could tolerate the membership of Catholics in an organization dominated by secular and atheistic social democrats, while membership in organizations based on "Positive Christianity" was not tolerated. The leaders of the *Stahlhelm* had to admit, though, that—unlike many rightist arrangements—there had never been any anti-Christian or church-hostile statements in arrangements of the *Reichsbanner*. Besides, the *Reichsbanner* was treated with contempt by the rightists with names like "*Papphelm*" ("The Pasteboard helmet") and *"Judenschutztruppe"* ("The Jew Protection Troop"). Unlike most other organizations apart from the SA, the *Reichsbanner* increased its membership after 1930 and reached an impressive 3.5 million in the early 1930s. After the election in 1930, it established an armed division, the *Schufo*, which in 1932 is said to have equaled the SA, with a membership of almost 400,000. In many ways, the power and impact of the *Reichsbanner* did not match its membership, largely due to weak leadership and skepticism among the nonsocialist "Weimar" parties. As many as 90 percent of the members seem to have been social democrats. For a short while in the middle of the 1920s, feelers were even sent out for cooperation with the communist *Roter Fronfkämpferbund*, although most of the time the relationship was hostile. The BVP and the Zentrum's sister party in the Saar did not join. The Bavarians regarded the *Reichsbanner* as a front-runner whose purpose was to set up a "Socialist Unity Republic."[148]

Catholic clerics investigated the *Reichsbanner* and the difference between it and the rightist movements. One assessment was that whereas the *Jungdeutscher Orden* was a fellowship with the aim of educating, the *Reichsbanner* was a purely political vehicle for the protection of the constitution. The rightist movements were negative to the republic and many of them aimed at an inter-confessional church, *Nationalkirche*, in Germany. Another assessment was that the rightist movements basically were un-Christian because nationalism, and not the soul, was exalted as the hallmark of man, that they were permeated by hatred of political opponents, and a conscious anti-Catholic sentiment was manifest in many of the local divisions.[149]

"Black-red-gold/yellow" originated from the yearning in the post-Napoleonic era for German unity based on a liberal constitution. Hence, they were the colors of the 1848 Revolution and were banned after the reaction in 1849. The last time it was used was by the German states that supported Austria in the war of 1866, and it functioned as the colors of the *"Grossdeutsche"* party. This caused confusion and conflict in the 1920s about who were the rightful "owners" of the colors and what they basically symbolized. "Black-white-red" were the colors of Austria's enemies in 1866 and chosen as the flag of the North German Federation of 1867 and the Empire of 1871. They represented the combination of the Black-and-White Prussian flag and the White-and-Red colors of the Hanseatic cities (Hamburg, Bremen, Lübeck) which were the dominating entities in the 1867 federation.[150]

When the Weimar Republic chose its flag, it represented a revolutionary and democratic breach with the old Empire, and it was understood in this way by both adherents and opponents alike. The colors particularly expressed the 1848 ideas of liberty, democracy and a *"grossdeutsch"* solution to the issue of nationality.[151] The last of these aims looked like a paradoxically "rightist" factor but must be understood as aversion against Bismarck's *"kleindeutsch"* Prussia-solution. After Austria had been reduced to an almost purely German-speaking state, *"Anschluss"* had, at last, become a realistic alternative, and attractive prospect for the Zentrum. By then, it was a large and almost purely Catholic state, which would bring about a Germany where the confessions would be equal in number.

The Germans were split in the 1920s into three main political groups, each having its own color or group of colors: "Black-red-yellow" for the defenders of the constitution; "Black-white-red" for the bourgeois opponents of the constitution; and red for the communists with their paramilitary organization *Roter Frontkämpferbund*. Even the DVP, the party of the moderate Foreign Minister Stresemann, favored the old imperial flag, and he deplored the right-wing tendencies of the party at the end of the decade, a tendency which became even more pronounced after his death in 1929.[152]

When Hitler introduced his swastika flag, it was based on black, white and red. That was not coincidental but indicated to which main group his movement belonged. But because symbols were so important in Nazism, Hitler explained what the colors represented for him and his movement. According to him, red represented his variant of "socialism," "the social idea of the movement," white represented nationalism and the black swastika stood for "the victorious assignment of the Aryan man." One of Hitler's first decrees after the Nazi takeover was to replace the Weimar flag with the Nazi swastika flag and the imperial flag. He had to accept the latter out of consideration for his alliance partners the DNVP and the *Stahlhelm,* which in the election of 1933 had amalgamated under the name *Kampffront Schwarz-Weiss-Rot*. But in 1935, once all rivals had been eliminated, the imperial flag was again abolished. According to Hitler, the black-red-yellow colors had been originally positive but were robbed by "Marxism and the Zentrum" in 1919, and the imperial flag represented a defunct and limited period in German history.[153]

It is probably strange to foreigners that Hitler should use the term "socialism" in a positive way, but in Germany, it had a different meaning. In 1848, Marx condemned the German understanding of the word, and Peter Pulzer asserts that since the middle of the 19th century it had a positive meaning among right-wingers. Terje Emberland explains the concept of socialism among the leftist faction of the Nazi movement as "the existence of the right kind of solidarity and spirit of fellowship, rather than a demand for profound socio-economic changes like the abolishing of private ownership of the means of production. Socialism was first and foremost an issue of disposition and could only be realized through a spiritual awakening in the people." Emberland further asserts that this "spiritual awakening" "led to a strong interest in questions about the view of life. Many within the leftist faction thought 'the second revolution' also meant a showdown with traditional Christianity and especially the Catholic Church. When the program of the Nazi Party pleaded a 'Positive Christianity,' this meant a German-Protestant faith purified of alien conceptions about racism."[154]

The term "National Socialism" had, as was to be expected, stronger impact than "socialism" in isolation. The word was used first in 1875 by the anti-Semite Eugen Dühring, and when the leftist liberal Friedrich Naumann in 1896 established his *Nationalsozialer Verein*, he had discussed the name *Nationalsozialistischer Verein* to emphasize the labor-friendly attitude in the association.[155] This indicates that the term was widely accepted in bourgeois Protestant circles. For the Nazis and other right-wing people, "Marxism" and "social democracy" were the names for the normal concept of "socialism."

The symbolic value lay in the combination of colors, not the single color alone apart from the socialist red. The three "Weimar colors" were connected with the three coalition parties in the 1920s: black for the Catholic Zentrum, red for the social democratic SPD, and yellow for the liberal DDP. Yellow was to a certain extent also connected to Jews, and the DDP was regarded as especially attractive for Jews. The "Weimar colors" were associated by the right-wing with three "Internationals": the "black international" with its Catholic Church and Catholic organizations such as the European alliance of Catholic parties, SIPDIC; the red as the "socialist international"; and the Jewish "yellow international," and the alleged conspiration between them. Such views go back among right-wings as far as the 1870s when it was demanded that "for the same reason emergency laws are made against the revolutionary Red international, we demand exception laws against the Golden (i.e. Jewish) international." At the same time, some asked if it were possible to expel the Jews the same way as the Jesuits (the Black international) were. In 1931 Rüdiger, Graf von der Goltz, leader of the *Vereinigte vaterländische Verbände*, the umbrella organization of up to 130 right-wing organizations, felt it urgent to "make people aware of the fact that great German parties established the tightest bonds to Paris, Moscow, to the international Roman Power and the International super-governmental Jewry."[156]

Alfred Rosenberg embroidered on the relationships within the "Weimar troika" further. There was a fellowship of interests among them, although concealed. Both the Catholic Church and the communist world movement were governed by international Jewry. On the surface, the Catholic Church was in opposition to communism, but there was a link in the "communism of love" of the early Christians," "the first effort to realize a super-national fellowship based on equality in a relationship to God, where all blood-restrictions are abolished." Hence, "both the Christian and atheistic communism had their origins in Jewry." The Nazis understood themselves as being in a battle against "the international, *antivölkisch*, antiracist world front" which paved the way for a Jewish World Government.[157]

Although the *Reichsbanner* was not subject to condemnation by the Catholic Church, it was felt as a rival to the church's own organizations, especially among youth, and in 1926 the bishops' conference warned against "all (predominantly political) organizations that threaten the Catholic youth organizations and which through the character of their composition (i.e. inter-confessionality) lead to the distribution of un-Catholic doctrines and promote religious indifference and that as fighting organizations, threaten the peace and unity of the people."[158]

It caused some unrest among Zentrum members of the *Reichsbanner* when it started cooperation with the Austrian purely socialist, and even armed, *Republikanischer Schutzbund*, an adversary of rightist movements, which to a certain extent, were supported by the Catholic CSP. The CSP reacted and was supported by the BVP, which had stayed out of the *Reichsbanner*. The *Reichsbanner's* cooperation with the Austrians led to involvement in international socialist cooperation, and it became a member of "The International Commission for fighting Fascism." The criticism from the CSP and the BVP led the Zentrum leaders to issue a general warning against all armed political organizations.[159] The *Reichsbanner* was also a member of the *Conference Internationale des Associations des Mutilés de Guerre et Ancient Combattants* ("Ciamac"), which worked for peace and disarmament through League of Nations and for compulsory international arbitration. This did not cause any unrest among Zentrum members.[160]

The *Reichsbanner* remained controversial among Zentrum politicians until it was dissolved in the spring of 1933. Some feared "Marxist" infiltration among Zentrum adherents, especially among workers, and its leftist attitude could threaten the unity of the party. On the other hand, the leaders dared not offend the leftist faction, and as mentioned, prominent members of the party were or had been members. A solution was to demand the dissolution of all kinds of similar organizations, and the party became an ardent advocate of this.[161]

Bracher asserts the *Reichsbanner* was unique in Europe and that its existence was based on the extremely strong antagonism within the Weimar Republic and the constant threat against democracy. Furthermore, it is interesting to note that Rohe has proved that out of all the nonsocialist anti-Fascist paramilitary organizations in Germany there were no Protestant based ones. The few and small ones in this category, the *Bayernwacht*, the *Pfalzwacht*, the *Kreuzscharen*, and the *Volksfront*, were all exclusively Catholic. The latter cooperated with the great socialist *Eiserne Front*.[162]

There were no organized connections between the Catholic parties and the four organizations mentioned above, in accordance with the party-line.

When, for example, the *Bayernwacht* offered to prevent a Nazi *coup d'etat* in Bavaria in March 1933, BVP leaders feared a massacre and refused support. The *Bayernwacht* was supported financially by clerics and the Jewish *Centralverein*.[163]

The Relationship of Catholics to Radical Right-wing Organizations after 1928

The weakening of the *Jungdeutscher Orden* and strengthening of the *Stahlhelm* in the second half of the 1920s probably indicates a general right-wing drift in the population parallel to the drift in the academic world. In 1928 the *Stahlhelm* organized a division for clerics, Protestants and Catholics alike, to show a more positive attitude to Christianity. After a short while, 208 Protestants and ten Catholics had joined it, and in 1931 there was a total of 500, without any information about confessional distribution. Cardinal Bertram disliked the Catholic involvement and threatened at least one of his subordinates with suspension, to no avail, however. Even Protestant church leaders were negative about the involvement of their clergy, but nothing is known about suspensions.[164] In March 1930, Cardinal Faulhaber strongly attacked Bolshevism in a sermon, which made the *Stahlhelm* leader of Bavaria invite him to cooperate in a "joint front against communism." But Faulhaber refused by referring to the different weapons the church and the organization used in their fight.[165]

The subsequent radicalization of the *Stahlhelm* was probably due both to the negative attitude of the Catholic Church and the breakthrough of the Nazi Party. Negative resolutions about the right-wing organizations were passed at every bishops' conference between 1924 and 1933. After the Nazi victory in the 1930 election, the *Stahlhelm* leader Franz Seldte was very direct: "We shall continue until the total annihilation of the adversary. The last one of the red and the black scoundrels must fall in this battle", and the leader of the Bavarian division: "We fight against all who in some form or other, cling to international ideas. . . . Our fight against all un-German ideas is also against them who esteem the "black" idea higher than the "black-white-and-red". . . . The Black international is more dangerous than the Red." Others in their ranks uttered similar statements, among them a Protestant clergyman.[166]

The Nazi Party emerged anew in 1929 as the leading rightist movement, and as leader of the campaign against the Young Plan. As mentioned, it had ceased cooperating with the extreme *völkisch* Protestant dominated organizations and started working with the DNVP instead and the *Stahlhelm*. The anti-Catholic stance of the latter was primarily directed towards the international orientation of the Church and not its theological profile, and this Hitler could accept.

Catholic church leaders and Zentrum politicians favored the Young Plan, not only because the Nazis and its allies were against it, but also because rejection would be hazardous for the long-term reconciliation policy of the government. The leader of the umbrella organization of the Protestant churches, the DEKA, was encouraged to issue a statement of support, but remained neutral because he would not involve the evangelical churches "in the bitter political fight about the campaign."[167]

We may say in conclusion that, generally, Catholic clerics were skeptical towards the paramilitary organizations during the Weimar Republic. What caused this, was not only the competition with, but also the menace to, the *"Zentrumsturm,"* the comprehensive network of Catholic organizations, as well as the militant character of the others. Ideologically, the skepticism or rejection of the right-wing organizations was greater than of the social democratically dominated *Reichsbanner*, due not only to attitudes to democracy, but the exposing of a worldview among the rightist movements, which occasionally let slip an anti-Catholicism.

I have not registered any aversion of the paramilitary organizations from Protestant clerics, other than the mentioned resistance to membership of clergy in the *Stahlhelm*. A ban would not be likely nor in accordance with the *"Eigengesetzlichkeits"* thesis and what has been made clear earlier about the Protestant confession. Even the most famous and respected German evangelical theologian, Dietrich Bonhoeffer, was a frequent author of articles in *Vormarsch*, the main magazine of the *Jungdeutscher Orden*.[168]

CHRISTIAN WORKERS' ASSOCIATIONS

There were a lot of organizations in the Catholic *"Zentrumsturm."* Some of these, such as the *Verband Süddeutscher Katholischer Arbeitervereine*, had already by 1921 started combatting the rightist radicals, Nazis included, and the day before the "Putsch" their leaders published a resolution reporting that "attachment to the Nazi Party is incompatible with membership in a Catholic workers' association." Half a year earlier, when the Nazi Party was hardly known outside Bavaria, the Zentrum representative in the *Reichstag* and leader of the west German *Katholische Arbeiterbewegung* (KAB), Joseph Joos, attacked the party in an article *"Deutsch-Völkisch—Nationalsozialistisch"* in the KAB's magazine, *Westdeutsche Arbeiterzeitung* (*WAZ*). With emphasis, Joos rejected the Nazis' own characteristic of themselves as *"Sozialistische Arbeiterpartei."* "Today's spiritual sign of disease" had nothing to do with socialism or the labor movement. It was not a real party, but a gathering of socially dissatisfied people without a settled background whipped up by industrial instigators, and who, like all *völkisch* groups, had its program-basis in negation, in anti-Semitism and opposition to social democracy. The movement made use of a most detestable mix of nationalist and anti-capitalist phrases.[169]

In 1923 Joos attacked nationalism in general. He described the phenomenon as a defection of spirit, a gross delusion and a sin against the Holy Spirit, and "Nationalism is this generation's burning fatal wound." These were views directly contrary to mainstream views among nonsocialist Protestants, but they were in accordance with statements at the Catholic Annual Congress with its resolution about nationalism as "Our time's greatest heresy."[170]

The KAB was not a trade union, but more of a social fellowship. In the late 1920s it and several other similar associations were joined in a national umbrella-organization which comprised more than 95 percent of local Catholic workers' associations. With 280,000 members, it was one of the most important organizations in the "*Zentrumsturm*" and an indispensable support to the party in wooing labor votes, especially during the last years of the Weimar Republic. All members of the board, except one in the youth division, were anti-Nazis to the end. Statistics from 1932 show that the members were no less ridden by unemployment than other groups: only 29 percent of them were fully employed and in some areas almost every member was unemployed. Nevertheless, their subscription dues were paid.[171]

There was a corresponding Protestant organization, the *Evangelische Arbeitervereine*, which also was not a trade union. However, in other ways, it was different from the Catholic one. Firstly, despite the number of Protestants being double the number of Catholics, the Catholic organization was much bigger. Secondly, like Stöcker's CSAP, which in many ways was a forerunner, the Protestant organization did not mainly attract workers, but people from the bourgeoisie. Thirdly, its main aim was to "fight against the Red, Black and Golden Internationals as diabolical powers of selfishness and to lift high our banner: the Evangelical Faith."[172]

Apart from these two confessional organizations, there was a larger, inter-confessional Christian traditional trade union, the *Gesamtverband der christlichen Gewerkschaften* (GcG) and it was possible to be members of both kinds of organization. In its peak year, 1920, it had 1.1 million members but shrank by half in the middle of the decade. It has been estimated that the percentage of Protestants was between 15 and 30 percent before WWI, and was probably almost the same in the 1920s, although statistics are lacking.[173]

Thus, a tendency similar to the educational, academic and political world is apparent within Christian trade unionism and workers' associations in that, despite a confessional ratio of two to one in favor of the Protestants, far more Catholics belonged to a specifically Christian organization than did

Protestants. A CSVD representative deplored that the evangelical worker, in contrast to the Catholic one, who belonged to Zentrum, was most often politically homeless. Only Stöcker had cared about the interests of workers in his time, he opined.[174]

The GcG was part of a greater cartel, the *Deutscher Gewerkschaftsbund* (DGB), where two secular, nonsocialist, Protestant-dominated trade unions were members: the *Deutscher Handlungsgehilfen-Verband* (DHV) and *Deutschnationaler Arbeiterbund*. Fascist tendencies appeared among Protestants in the cartel, whereas, on the other hand, the Catholics showed a clear negative attitude to such.[175] William Patch asserts:

> The attitudes to Fascism among the Catholic workers of western and southern Germany, the core membership of the Christian unions, was unambiguously negative. Whereas even those DHV leaders most opposed to the radical Right felt compelled to express sympathy for Mussolini and völkisch ideals, Catholic labor leaders characterised the NSDAP as part of an international Fascist movement rivalling the COMINTERN and a threat to Democracy and Unionism. When Catholic workers' clubs of Bavaria and western Germany first took notice of the Nazi party in 1923 (author's comment: as mentioned above, the Bavarians had already in 1921), they resolved to expel any member who joined it, denouncing it as a tool of reactionary industrialists and counter-revolutionary Free Corps veterans. For Joseph Joos and his colleagues, Mussolini's suppression of parliamentary democracy was sufficient to warrant categorical rejection of Italian Fascism, and they considered Hitler an even more extreme representative of such dictatorial tendencies.[176]

In the 1920s, there was disagreement between German and Austrian Catholic trade unionists as to the Austrian *Heimwehr* movement, but when the movement in 1930 openly favored Fascism, even the Austrians reacted. The Austrians were rather positive to the Lateran Treaty, however, whereas the Germans were negative.[177]

The Nazi triumph in 1930 caused a minor split in the DGB. Whereas the DHV, which at that time had several Nazi sympathizers among their members, wanted to support the trade union's friendly leftist faction in the party, the GcG would weaken the whole party. The DHV leaders disliked the "Harzburg" gathering in 1931, however, and in 1932 all the DGB leaders supported Hindenburg in the presidential election. Many of the individual members voted for Hitler, even some Catholics. A similar tendency happened in the *Reichstag* elections in 1932. After Gustav Hülser, vice leader of the CSVD and one of the leaders of the GcG, together with the leader of the CSVD, Simpfendörfer, had had a disappointing meeting with Hitler, the Protestant unions supported the CSVD. The elections results, however, showed that this time too, some individuals did not follow their leaders.[178]

THE RELATIONSHIP BETWEEN PARTIES AND OTHER ORGANIZATIONS: NATIONAL AND INTERNATIONAL

What the three parties that totally (the Zentrum/BVP) or partially (the SPD and the KPD) were resistant to the Nazi appeal had in common, was that they not only were closely attached to a wide network of associations, but they were also attached to relatively strong and active international organizations. The Zentrum had the Catholic Church, the international Christian workers' association from 1908, mentioned earlier, and the European fellowship of Christian democratic parties. The SPD had the 2. International and the KPD had the COMINTERN. The KPD had also its own paramilitary organization, the *Roter Frontkämpferbund*.

As we have seen, international connections were not liked in Protestant organizational life. (The "Weimar" party DDP and individuals from it, however, were attached to international liberal and democratic organizations in the 1920s.) Even this isolation obviously appeared as a weakness of the bourgeois Protestant parties, and probably worse for them was that they were not attached to the paramilitary organizations either (again with the exception for the DDP which was a *Reichsbanner* party). This was probably due to the aversion among rightist organizations to the Weimar system, resulting in a refusal to cooperate with parties that participated in it. The Nazi Party fit well in here after the change of strategy in 1925. The Nazis had both a party and a paramilitary organization. The bourgeois parties and paramilitary organizations discovered the Nazi advantage too late. Before the election in 1930, an obviously desperate, unexpected and short-lived effort was made to join the DDP and the *Jungdeutscher Orden*. The DNVP and the *Stahlhelm*, which had to a great extent shared their values and ideas during the 1920s, waited until the very last multi-party election in March 1933 to amalgamate and become the *Kampffront Schwarz-Weiss-Rot*. This "front" experienced a slight increase compared to the result of the DNVP in 1932, but by this time the Nazis had long established their superiority.[179]

THE SITUATION AS TO MENTALITY GROUPS C. 1930

From the 1917 Peace Resolution until 1930, the political development showed that the German electorate could be divided into three main groups based on the relationship to democracy and various kinds of relatively authoritarian governments: the Revolutionary communists, the "Weimar Coalition," and the Protestant dominated rightist parties. This division does not correspond with the Rohe's other division, earlier mentioned, into three relatively stable blocs based on confession and secularization. In Germany, the "Weimar Coalition," based on parties from all three blocks of Rohe, constructed a fairly closed front against the other two. However, it is clear that it comprised three separate political groups: social democrats, Catholic churchgoers (the "*Zentrumsturm*") and an ever-shrinking group of bourgeois liberals of primarily Protestant confession.

In the Interwar period the German "*Zentrumsturm*" was part of a European Catholic "fortress," which Martin Conway describes in this way:

> This distinctive combination of defensive and offensive concerns found its expression in the metaphorical vision of Catholicism as a fortress. No other image was as characteristic of Catholic self-representation during the 1920s and the 1930s as that of the Church and the faithful as a bastion of order and truth in a disordered and corrupt world. Represented repeatedly in papal encyclicals, election posters and the speeches of priests and politicians, the metaphor of the fortress was one that simultaneously reflected and reinforced the prevailing Weltanschauung of many European Catholics. If its origin lay in the discrimination experienced by many European Catholics before 1914, this fortress image also derived its strength from more urgent contemporary concerns. The understandable sense of dislocation felt by many amid the disruption of war, changes of political regime and economic crisis, as well as renewed attacks by state authorities and radical movements on the autonomy of the Church, served to reinforce the self-image of the Catholics as a distinct community, united by their values and alone possessed of a solution to the manifold ills of the current age.[180]

This is a generalization but fits the German situation. The embryonic "*Zentrumsturm*" of the late 1840s was developed extensively and strengthened during the *Kulturkampf* and more than matched the socialist network of the day. In addition to the Church and the party, it had in its number 280 organizations, great and small, with a total of some million members.[181]

In contrast to most (or all) other countries, these two "pillars": social democrats and Catholic churchgoers, plus leftist liberals made up an alliance defending the Weimar Republic and "the ideas of 1789." In practical politics, this produced the almost uninterrupted string of coalition-governments of the "Weimar parties" in those states where the confessional alignment made it natural (i.e. with a rather considerable number of Catholics). This meant Baden, Hessen, Oldenburg 1919–1923 (non-party governments 1923–1932), Wurttemberg 1918–1924 and in the dominant Prussia from 1919 until 1932/1933. The Weimar collaboration even was evident in Danzig. The governments between 1920 and 1928 are described as unpolitical, but the "1789" coalition governed from 1928 until the collapse of the DDP after 1930 and total Nazi government in 1933.[182]

The main cause for this unusual three-part alliance was probably the tough antagonism of the strong revolutionary communists on the one hand, and the gradually increasingly strong rightist radicals after WWI, on the other. However, Bismarck's aversion to both Catholics and socialists in the Empire had already caused occasional signs of cooperation between the two groups despite the Vatican's hostile view of Marxism.[183]

There was no corresponding network of organizations of Protestant nonsocialists. There were many reasons: the strong identification with the Empire and traditional German nationalism; the lack of theological uniformity and involvement of the Church in politics; the split in liberal, agrarian and rightist parties with voters drifting to-and-fro between the numerous and more-or-less transient bourgeois parties. For example, during the election campaign in the spring of 1924, a whole local division of Stresemann's Protestant-dominated "liberal" party, the DVP, "migrated" to the strongly anti-Semitic *Deutschsoziale Partei*.[184]

Some Protestant clergy envied the Catholics their strong uniform Church, network of organizations, youth work and media.[185] The comprehensive Catholic organizational life, with pronounced democratic parties in contact with other European parties favoring pan-European cooperation, indicates a further modernization within the Catholic camp, whereas there is little or nothing to find of equivalent tendencies within the Protestant camp. On the contrary, the Protestant drift was towards autarchy and international isolation.

The liberal Protestants showed particularly unstable political behavior. They were neither uniform nor politically loyal, as we have seen. The leftists, the DDP, had started in the "Weimar Coalition," but the overwhelming majority of their voters had deserted to the numerous bourgeois parties that had popped up during the 1920s and eventually to the Nazis after 1930. To the dismay of the Jewish voters and the *Reichsbanner* leaders, the DDP, as mentioned, shared a short-lived amalgamation with the *Jungdeutscher Orden,* to form the *Staatspartei*. The Nobel Peace Prize winner, the pacifist Ludwig Quidde, reacted by leaving the party to form the *Radikaldemokratische Partei*. But even Quidde held anti-Semitic views.[186]

The peculiar German liberalism has been studied by historians thoroughly and therefore shall only be discussed briefly. Its indecisive and ambivalent profile was apparent even early in the Empire. The political situation in the principality of Waldeck illustrates this. In the Empire, this area had one of the one-man constituencies, and in the first *Reichstag* election in 1871, the *Nastonalliberale* carried 99.9 percent(!).[187] In 1898, one of the minor anti-Semitic parties triumphed, and in 1907 the leftist-liberal *Freisinnige Vereinigung*. In 1924 II, the DNVP was the biggest party with 43 percent, in 1928 the agrarian *Landvolk* with 31 percent and in November 1932 the Nazi Party with 63.8

percent. The *Landvolk* did not run in 1924 and was reduced to 0.3 percent in November 1932! The DDP, which in 1919 had carried 23.5 percent, was reduced in 1932 to 0.8 percent. The Zentrum, however, carried 2–3 percent in this Protestant dominated area throughout the Weimar era.

The attitudes and careers of the most prominent leftist liberals during the last twenty years of the Empire, Friedrich Naumann and Max Weber, in addition to the historian Friedrich Meinecke, shed light on the atypical and contrast-filled German liberalism, and can also contribute to explain why liberals deserted to the Nazis after 1930.

Naumann had worked closely in the 1880s with Stöcker's social work and even been a member of his CSAP and expressed anti-Semitic statements. He was heavily involved in the foundation of the influential *völkisch* and anti-Semitic student association *Kyffhäuserverband*. Naumann abandoned his *völkisch* inclinations and cooperation with Stöcker in the 1890s, and in the end his anti-Semitism too, in 1903. Together with Weber, he founded the *Nationalsozialer Verein* referred to earlier. After Stöcker's death, he became a leading member of the Inner Mission and before the election in 1912 managed to unite two liberal parties.[188]

He wrote a famous book during WWI in which he advocated a Central Europe under German supervision. After the war, again together with Weber, he was one of the founders of the DDP and one of the main brains behind the Weimar constitution, though he opposed the Versailles Treaty and changing the flag. Originally, he was strongly anti-Catholic, but moderated himself after the joint Peace Resolution in 1917. His slogan was: "I am Christian, Darwinist and imperialist"[189]

Freidrich Meinecke, one of the most prominent historians in the first half of the twentieth century and co-founder of the DDP, advocated morals that were practically Machiavellian. He contended that there was a universal moral standard for individuals and an individual moral standard for the state authorities, which apparently justified state immorality. Meinecke was allegedly an anti-Semite, and before 1917, like Naumann, an adherent of plans of territorial annexations.[190]

Max Weber, one of the most prominent social scientists, was a member of the *Alldeutscher Verband* from its start in 1891 and secretary until 1899. In a speech in 1895 he said:

> It is not peace and happiness which we shall pass on to our successors, on the contrary, the eternal struggle for the maintenance and refinement of our national identity. . . . Our successors will hold us responsible, not first and foremost

because of the national-economic form of organization which we hand down to them, but on the contrary, for the amount of elbow room we gain in the world and pass on to them. . . . Only the Master-race have been called to intervene in the spokes of world development.[191]

Weber was originally anti-Catholic but, like Naumann, revised his opinions after a while and, like Stresemann, left the *Alldeutscher Verband*.[192]

The cases of Naumann and Weber (both died in 1919), Meinecke - and Stresemann - serve to shed light on imperialist, Social-Darwinist and moral attitudes and currents that were probably to a greater or lesser degree mainstream German liberalism. This may partly explain the collapse of those sharing such a mentality when they were confronted with the Nazi challenge.

There were, however, prominent classical and traditional liberals in Germany even after 1930. Theodor Wolff, the Jewish chief editor of *Berliner Tageblatt* from 1906–1933 and even he one of the co-founders of the DDP (but left in 1926), expressed his anxious thoughts about the future on the very day after Wilhelm's abdication. With extraordinary foresight, he feared that, compared to those groups with a solid social democratic and Catholic mentality, "the 1789" values were not integrated well enough in German liberalism to make these three groups strong enough together to create a stable, democratic, state run by rule of law. "The (Protestant) bourgeoisie is confused and frightened, perplexed and spineless. Most of them flap like birds fallen from their nests, and are at their wits' end," he stated.[193]

Wolff's anxiety was justified. The German "liberalism" was obviously in full disintegration during the 1920s and the electorate on their way, via an array of bourgeois mini-parties first, towards a *völkisch* mentality, and the elections mirrored it clearly.

The first part of this book mentions the early success of the Nazi Party in a new region: Northwest-Germany, far away from the party's original core in southern Bavaria. It happened almost two years before the effects of the Wall Street crash reached Germany and before Hitler received financial support from Hugenberg and other tycoons. Together with the situation in the academic world, it gives reason to wonder whether quite independent of the world situation, the Nazi Party was already gaining enough ground by the late 1920s to develop into a formidable opposition party, and even take over the government.

All in all, then, Walter Burnham's theories of political confessionalism are presumably relevant, but probably an equal or even more important factor than the organizational "glue" holding the groups resistant to Nazism together, was the ideological "adhesive."

SEPTEMBER 1930–JANUARY 1933

Catholic Reactions to the Reichstag Elections in 1930 and 1932

The election to the *Reichstag* on September 14, 1930 represented a breakthrough for the Nazi Party, which gained 18.3 percent, second only to the SPD. Although local and regional elections had shown that the party had experienced considerable increase in support, the result was obviously a surprise. The Zentrum-leaders had scented out the trend and had scrutinized the program and practice of the party systematically, and two insights had made them particularly anxious: firstly, the obvious connection between economic misery and radicalization, especially among youth, secondly, that the Nazi ideology was in a way somewhat in line with Catholic mentality. It expressed aversion to "the abstract, puritan state, because they were more confident about the idea of the hierarchy of the Church," as the magazine *Das Zentrum* put it. Furthermore, Catholics valued authority and discipline highly, especially moral authority and discipline, and they knew that some of the most important leaders like Hitler, Goebbels, Strasser and Wagner were "Catholics."[194] *Reichskanzler* Brüning from the Zentrum had also scented out the trend and was anxious after he had dissolved the *Reichstag* and announced an election in the hope of a parliamentary majority for the government. He warned against an election that might have "such effects that could lead to a total resignation towards parliamentary democracy," and the consequences it could entail.[195]

The Catholic daily media had also noticed and been increasingly concerned about Nazism after the summer of 1929. The basically anti-republican, revolutionary and radical ideas of the party and the anti-Catholic tendencies both in theory and practice were clearly realized. Catholics warned against Nazism both ahead of and after the election, even in Jewish periodicals.[196]

Nevertheless, research into the bulk of Catholic media treatment of Nazism from 1929 until March 1933 with the introduction of censorship, reveals how clever the Nazis were at veiling their real intentions. Walter Hannot summarizes the coverage in three categories: 1) The Nazi Party was assessed and considered foremost as a traditional party without realizing the novelty of the party in due time, and the suitable actions that needed to be taken. Not enough focus was put on the fact that the success of the party was due to the vagueness of the program, to a great extent. 2) The articles managed to portray the variety of ideas and statements, false and correct assessments, and due expectations and illusions, to be found in much of the other German and foreign media, filled with contrasts. All the same, the Catholic media slant on Nazism was largely negative. 3) Although Hitler as a person was criticized and occasionally even strongly attacked, he was regarded as one of the party's moderates(!).[197]

Three weeks after the election Alfred Rosenberg's main work, *Der Mythus des 20. Jahrhunderts* (*The Myth of the 20th Century*) was published. Timing the publication to after the election was probably not accidental, for the book was imbued with assertions and views which normally should have provoked, not only Catholic believers, but all Christians who accepted a minimum of Biblical authority. It would have been hazardous to make use of it as propaganda for the election campaign. The book was primarily influenced by the old *völkisch* ideologs Chamberlain, de Lagarde and Richard Wagner, and emphasized the superiority of the Nordic race, the replacement of the Old Testament with German myth and a revision of the New Testament by rejecting the concepts of sin, virgin birth, the trinity, resurrection from the dead and Christian charity.[198] Francois Bédarida asserts: "In his (Rosenberg's) eyes Rome, this radical enemy of life and life energy, had not only corrupted the German people ever since the Middle Ages through consistent "de-Germanization," but even corrupted the whole of Christianity, clinging to the principle of equality, which had resulted in a general levelling of the human race." Rosenberg favored the establishment of a *Nationalkirche* instead, founded on purity of race and blood instead of doctrines. Rosenberg also attacked European society in general as it was founded on democratic human rights regardless of race, and hence had developed into a protector of the inferior, diseased, stunted, criminal and corrupted. The book ends with a pathetic appeal to replace the many crucifixes along the roads in Catholic areas with memorials of the fallen German soldiers from WWI.[199]

All these patently heretical aspects to Rosenberg mirrored to a degree how chaotic the hotchpotch Protestant theology had become, and may explain why Rosenberg was not attacked in a serious way by Protestant theologians before the middle of the 1930s. By then it caused alarm, however, and Protestant Nazi clergymen who were opponents of neo-paganism asked Hitler to unite the denominations, in a measure to prevent Rosenberg's ideas from becoming the predominant theology.[200] However, if the "*Mythus*" was in line with phenomena in Protestant culture since the end of the nineteenth century, as published by a prominent Nazi in the 1930s it was unique. Other Nazi ideologs, who dealt with culture and church affairs, were content to demand that the Church should not take orders from abroad. Rudolf Jung, however, did go a step further by not only favoring, but demanding all Churches should unite in a *Nationalkirche*.[201] Even that demand was unacceptable to the Catholic Church. Among Kevin Spicer's 138 "brown" Catholic priests only two accepted Rosenberg's views. They were Christian Josef Huber, SA member who later abandoned celibacy and converted to Old Catholicism, and Josef Roth, Gestapo informant. Some of the other Nazi priests were ardent opponents of Rosenberg, and the most prominent among them, Abbot Schachleiter, even asked Hitler to act against Rosenberg.[202]

Rosenberg's treatment of Protestantism was ambivalent: Luther's importance had been his Teutonization of Christianity and the destruction of the priesthood. He was the precursor of German nationalism, racial purity and spiritual independence. His conflict with Rome had been especially important and saved the West from "Tibetan-Etruscan-Asiatic" influence. The negative aspect of Luther was that he retained the "Hebrew" Old Testament, and contemporary Lutherans had started to approach once more the Roman system.[203] For Rosenberg, emphasis on the individual soul and its independence was essential. God was *not* superior to man but lived in the individual soul. Rather than "surrender" to, or fear God, the inner soul must be totally free and communicate with God. In this way, the individual could follow the example of Christ who yearned towards a holy union between the divine and human natures.[204] With views like these, Rosenberg was in line with dominant trends in German Protestantism ever since Schleiermacher and may have left Protestants with the impression that he was merely a somewhat eccentric and radical theologian in the tradition of de Lagarde and Chamberlain.

By 1942, 900,000 copies of the "*Mythus*" had been printed. On account of its radical views, however, it remained controversial within the Nazi Party. It is also unclear how familiar with its contents several Nazi leaders were. Hitler remained opaque about his view, Church minister Kerrl opposed it, and Göring and Goebbels despised Rosenberg. Even the pronounced *völkisch* Ernst zu Reventlow opposed Rosenberg, and all the Nazi newspapers of Berlin spoke of the book negatively.[205]

The view of the leader of the *Hitlerjugend*, Baldur von Schirach, is probably the most important one, because in 1934 Rosenberg became the national leader of ideological education. Von Schirach was very short and outspoken: "Rosenberg's way is also the path of German youth." However, von Schirach's ideology deviated somewhat from Rosenberg's. He favored a pronounced *Führer* adoration. Hitler was almost God incarnated. Today, historians still disagree about the influence of Rosenberg and whether "*Mythus*" had authoritative status within the party.[206]

If historians cannot agree on Rosenberg's influence and authority, it was not easier for anti-Nazis in the 1930s to assess this. Reactions to Rosenberg's book as a thoroughly authoritative Nazi product soon appeared, however, from Catholics. The bulk of the German Catholic newspapers and magazines were flooded with extensive polemics against Nazism.[207] Hitler found the reaction embarrassing, especially when Catholic media continuously asserted there was no difference between Hitler's views and Rosenberg's.[208]

The Nazi defense was twofold. Firstly, Hitler stated that *"Mythus"* was Rosenberg's private work and did not represent the official party policy. This was somewhat risky because of Rosenberg's official status in the party, and because several Nazis shared his views. On the other hand, it must have seemed like a paradox that Rosenberg was not punished or even expelled from the party when one considers the fate of Ludendorff and Dinter, both of whom had expressed similar ideas.[209] Rosenberg had taken care to emphasize in the preface, that the book only expressed his private views and was not written on behalf of the party. In a newer publication after the Nazi takeover in 1933, however, the work was not *so* private anymore: "The Political Revolution has come to an end, but the transformation of the spirits has hardly begun. For this purpose, *"Mythus"* stands from now on in the front rank." This "authorization" may have provoked even Protestants to be more active in their criticism.[210]

The second kind of Nazi response was to refute the Catholic attacks point by point. These efforts, however, were rejected as cunning manipulations.[211]

Besides this Nazis used the tactic of counterattack to overshadow the Rosenberg controversy. The Zentrum was accused of cooperation with the Christian-hostile or indifferent SPD, and after 1930 the Nazi Party had participated in regional state governments and passed measures such as prayer in schools in Thüringen and abolition of the "secular Godless schools" in Brunswick. (Among the five alternative versions of schoolprayers in Thüringen could only two be described as Christian, though.) There was also controversy about concordats. The Zentrum found it strange that the Nazis were eager to achieve concordats when they had rejected such institutions earlier, and a discussion about the nature and contents of concordats arose. The Nazi leader in the Bavarian state assembly, Rudolf Buttmann, was especially active in the discussion. Catholics were not impressed by the Nazi arguments, and some would even prefer cooperation with communists before the cooperation with Nazis, because the former were at least honest, "whereas the Nazis have cloaked their intentions and pretend to protect religion."[212]

The most important result of the Rosenberg controversy was an increasing pressure on the bishops to publish an official declaration about Nazism. No bishops' conference for the two cardinal areas would be summoned before the summer of 1931, which was made use of cleverly by the Nazi propaganda to create confusion among Catholics. Nevertheless, the Vatican had shown its attitude in the following statement in *Osservatore Romano*: "Affiliation to the Nazi party is inconsistent with Catholic consciousness in the same way as general affiliation to socialism of all kinds is inconsistent with Catholic consciousness."[213] In addition, several statements had been issued on lower hierarchical levels in Germany. Already in the autumn of 1929 a Palatine priest had inquired of his bishop whether a Catholic could be a member of the Nazi Party, and he received the answer that it was acceptable unless the party was not prohibited or "not in unrighteous or violent manner wished to subvert the order of the state or appeared hostile to faith or church." Such a response was a bit vague and, in the summer of 1930, it was more precisely stated that membership in the Nazi Party was prohibited.[214]

A priest in the Mainz diocese declared in a sermon, held shortly after the 1930 election, that membership in the Nazi Party was forbidden for Catholics. This caused a reaction among local Nazi leaders who inquired into it, but were rejected by the Church authorities. The attitude of the church was too tough, and in the eyes of some Catholics—inopportune, and they asked for a statement from a higher hierarchical level. In November, a congregation of Bavarian priests together with the papal nuncio, Vassallo di Torregrossa, issued a milder statement, and in December Cardinal Bertram of North Germany issued a general statement about political radicalism, race anger and the "National Church." The bishops of the Bavarian archsee were satisfied with neither the tough and short Mainz-, nor the general Bertram-resolution, and issued a new resolution in February 1931, differentiating between the Nazi cultural and political program. The bishops could understand why people felt attracted by the patriotic and economic aims of the Nazis, yet were unaware of the cultural-political opposition of the party to Christianity and the Church. All the same, the bishops warned against involvement in the party and put a ban on clerics participating in it. Official statements from the rest of the archbishoprics, Cologne, Paderborn and Freiburg, followed in March 1931. They were almost identical to the Bavarian one. Because Cardinal Bertram had issued his personal statement, his see, Breslau, did not issue any further statement. The Nazis exploited Bertram's mild warning to maintain he was rather friendly to the ideology.[215]

The Nazis were so upset by the Catholic reaction that Göring was sent in May 1931 to the Vatican to complain, but had to return without an audience with the pope or his Secretary of state Pacelli. Göring said to a lower official that statements by Rosenberg and other radical Nazis did not represent the party attitude, but his explanation does not seem to have made much impression.[216]

In August 1931, the bishops' conference at Fulda passed an ultimate document for North Germany as an addition to the *Instructio* of 1921, which primarily had been aimed at communism. The main doctrine of *Instructio* read: "Nothing can make the Church to relinquish or weaken its rejection of all associations hostile to Christianity and Church - and ideologies, be they socialist, Freemason or other variants. It is and remains strongly prohibited to all Catholics to join such parties or associations or promote their work."[217] In accordance with this, the bishops' conference issued the following statement:

In the same way as earlier doctrines relate to socialism and communism, they relate to National Socialism also, which passes itself off per se as only being a party with justifiable national aims, but in reality, represents a sharp opposition to the fundamental truths of Christianity and with the Catholic Church created by Christ. If one looks at the work of the party, its program, and to a greater degree numerous announcements from leading representatives and orators, it becomes obvious to anybody with their eyes wide open. It concerns not mere exaggerations by individuals, but on the contrary, the sum of these proclamations and facts about the party leaves an imprint that a few apologies and denials cannot disclaim.[218]

Cardinal Bertram explained to his clerics that it was furthermore not possible to join the party and make reservations against single paragraphs. The pope was more than satisfied and even regarded it as a model for the relationship between the Church and Italian Fascism. In reality, though, hardly any measures were taken to enforce the prohibitions, and Bishop Christian Schreiber of Berlin is said to have even officially allowed Catholics to join the party.[219]

The Catholic reaction among its clergy and media must have made an impression on Rosenberg. Already in the Christmas issue of *VB*, he attacked Catholics by accusing individual clerics of harboring unpatriotic attitudes both during and after WWI and arraigning Church harassment of the few Nazi Catholic clerics. In addition, he commented on the paradox that the "Christian" Zentrum, under the leadership of the Priest Ludwig Kaas, had nominated an orthodox Jew, "the president of the Synagog in Berlin, Georg Kareski, who, in addition, is 'eastern-Jew' and a Zionist. But he is also the manager for the wealthy Jacob Michael, this rotten Jewish stock market speculator."[220]

In October 1931, the third edition of "*Mythus*" was issued. In the foreword alone Rosenberg gives five pages of attention to Catholicism in general, especially the German version and focuses attention on the paradoxical cooperation between Catholics and Marxists. He also strongly declares that "*Mythus*" is a personal confession and that Nazism had no religious dogmas and was neither for nor against any denomination.[221] Rosenberg accused the clerics of both mobilizing and sacrificing the "believing masses" in their campaign against Nazism, and in the winter of 1932, Nazi regional papers reported of almost daily fights, —even physical—by Catholic priests against Nazis. Some priests were bold whereas others lacked candor, and some were repeatedly criticized by their own laymen about why they were resolute against communists, but lacked candor when confronted with Nazis.[222]

The 1930 election result, and overwhelming Nazi offensive the year after, obviously made Catholics anxious. Before the elections in 1932 a leading

Catholic, Walter Dirks, feared that some elements and slogans in the Nazi propaganda might sound attractive to Catholic groups. He mentioned "authority," "confidence in the *Führer*," "calm and order," "solidarity," front against "liberalism and materialism" and "anti-Marxism."[223]

The Zentrum's cooperation with the "Marxists" became a prime target for Nazi recrimination during the election campaigns in 1932. They were especially upset by the great number of clergy among the politicians in the party ("*Zentrumsprälaten*"), and this was a paradox in relation to the strong anti-communism of the Church. They even referred to the anti-Christian measures taken by the red regimes in Russia and Spain. If the "Marxists" in Germany were not assaulted, the same could happen in Germany. The Nazi Party had "Positive Christianity" in their program, and their fight so far had been against communism.[224] Bishop Michael Buchberger of Regensburg (Ratisbon) responded that it was not possible "to exorcize the Devil with Beelzebub," and "Christianity can only be built by and cared for, through Christianity, not nationalism and not socialism and not with a mixture of both. The Dictatorship of the Masses cannot be driven out by another Dictatorship of the Masses. Only he who fights against *every* kind of oppression fights for freedom."[225] The Nazis were audacious and turned the utterance on its head and lied that Buchberger had said, "Had Nazism not existed, we would perhaps already have communism". Even more audacious lies were told. Rumors were put out that Hitler had visited the pope, presented the party program, changed some of the paragraphs at the pope's request and obtained the pope's blessing and acceptance on his departure. Some Nazis asserted that it was thanks to them that the process of secularization had not gone so far as in the rest of the country and that in some districts many priests were party adherents.[226]

Three days before the *Reichstag* election on July 31 a complete bishops' conference issued a pastoral letter in which they warned against, "agitators and parties which were not worthy of the confidence of the Catholic people," and some weeks afterwards, another resolution with a sharper barb against the Nazis was issued. It read:

All bishoprics have declared adherence to this party is impermissible because:

1. Parts of its official program as it reads and . . . has to be understood, contain heresy.
2. Because pronouncements by numerous leading representatives and publicists for the party are hostile to Faith and especially hostile in attitude to basic teaching and demands in the Catholic Church, and these pronouncements are not disclaimed by the party leaders. This also includes the attitude in issues about confessional schools, Christian marriage etc.

3. It is the common verdict of the Catholic clergy and the loyal Catholic champions of the ecclesiastical rights in official life that if the party attains sole governmental power, it opens up for the most somber prospects for the ecclesiastical interests of Catholics.
4. It cannot be acceptable when considerable groups of people support the party only for economic and secular-political reasons and purposes, such as are represented by the party. Because supporting the party, means that the unified aim of the party is promoted. In addition, the promises of the party seem unattainable.[227]

It was further agreed that the entire clergy should be bound by this resolution, but that each spiritual advisor ought to show proper consideration for the relationship of each individual to the party, especially with regard to simple souls who had been subject to delusion, mass psychosis and "terrorist force."[228]

As indicated in the resolution, the reaction against Nazism gradually emerged from the rest of the *"Zentrumsturm,"* the Catholic association network. Led by the workers' movement, the most important Catholic associations united in the *Staatspolitische Arbeitsgemeinschaft der katholischen Verbände Deutschlands* in order to coordinate their fight against Nazism and to support the Zentrum. In 1932, the organization was active in the support of Hindenburg in the presidential election (but turned against him when he fired Brüning, whose successor, von Papen, originally a Zentrum representative, left the party and was considered a renegade.)[229] The youth associations were also involved. At least four national associations declared that membership in the Nazi Party was incompatible with membership in theirs.[230] The reaction of the male teachers' association, the KLVdDR, was slightly more reserved than many of the other associations, partly due to them waiting for a more precisely formulated school program from the Nazis. The Nazis deliberately kept the school program vague to prevent opposition from teachers, and when it so happened in regional states where Nazis participated in government and enforced measures that Catholic teachers disliked, such as black-lists of unacceptable teachers (drawn up by the Nazi teachers' association), the Nazis asserted these "were not official party policies." Only after the firing of Brüning in May 1932 did the KLVdDR join the pronounced anti-Nazi front of Catholic associations.[231]

In 1932 the Nazi mentality had, via manipulation, spread to the purely Protestant (or Protestant-dominated) teachers' associations, among them, the *Verband evangelischer Lehrervereine Deutschlands*. The largest association, however, the inter-confessional *Deutscher Lehrerverein*, maintained neutrality until the establishment of dictatorship in March 1933. Up to the election in the same month the KLVdDR had not experienced any decrease in membership to the benefit of the Nazi association, even though the latter had increased membership from 1200 to 12,000.[232]

Hans Müller, who has collected and published several documents dealing with the relationship of the Catholic milieu to Nazism, asserts that almost all announcements, books and articles published between the election in 1930 until the takeover in 1933 contain the following accusations against Nazism:

1. According to § 24 of the party only those religions in Hitler's government will be tolerated which are not in opposition to "the moral feeling of the Teutonic race." This ambition is not only reprehensible, but on the contrary, together with other statements of leading Nazis, could be very dangerous for the Church.
2. The racial teaching of Nazism is in opposition to the views of the Church. It leads, sooner or later, to a *Nationalkirche* and secession from Rome.
3. Nazism is against concordats and hence proves its hostility towards the Church. (Author's remark: In this matter, the Nazis disproved the accusation after their takeover. The concordat of 1933, however, was of a quite different kind than the regional state concordats in the Weimar Republic.)
4. Nazism is against confessional schools. The inter-confessional schools which they favor, promote only religious indifference.
5. Nazism represents a moral danger because it does not in principle reject lies and murders as appropriate means of campaigning.

Müller remarks that some important arguments are almost totally lacking:

1. Only exceptionally are there references to Hitler's ambitions to abolish democracy to the benefit of dictatorship.
2. The possible foreign political consequences of the radical policy of revenge which Hitler will pursue after an eventual takeover is rarely dealt with.
3. The anti-Semitism of the party is not totally and unambiguously condemned.[233]

The Nazi counterattack on the Catholic election campaign was focused on the paradoxical cooperation with the SPD, and Nazis had no scruples on trespassing – in rather clumsy and obvious ways - into the Catholic domain. Some examples from the Palatinate illustrate it: *Katholische Parole* was established in 1932 as a counterbalance to the official and strongly anti-Nazi publication of the bishopric, *Christlicher Pilger*. The "*Katholische Kanzlei Schwarz-Weiss-Rot*" was the publisher and asserted openly that its aim was to shatter the "*Zentrumsturm*" "ruin." It turned out to be a fiasco. The disguise was too obvious. The official Nazi paper in the area, *NSZ Rheinfront*, tried another tactic. It asserted that the Catholic attacks on Nazism were only restricted to the agitation of few strongly politicized Zentrum priests. This could hardly be true, however, because the paper had accused fifty-two priests, in other words, the bulk of the clergy, of agitation. The paper could not name a single friendly and benign priest in the area.[234]

To sum up: it is possible to assert that the Zentrum and the BVP were well supported by both the *"Zentrumsturm"* and the Catholic Church in the campaigning year of 1932 and, to a certain degree, of 1930. This related to the fact that there were few, or no other, alternative parties representing this milieu, which was still in the 1930s a political ghetto. Many clerics agitated openly for the Zentrum/BVP, and there was a great concurrence in leadership between the party and other organizations. The influence often followed this slogan: "the bishops have spoken—we must obey." Some asserted that people were obliged to obey the pope and bishops even when they disagreed in their actions.[235] The only weak point which could be registered in the Catholic "front" in the winter of 1931 was, according to Walter Dirks, in the students' associations at some universities.[236] This situation did not change much for the next two years.

The Catholic battle with Nazism was noticed among other groups, especially Jews. Even leftist-liberal papers edited or owned by Jews, such as *Berliner Tageblatt* and *Frankfurter Zeitung* started to regard the Zentrum as a better alternative in the elections than the shrunken DDP/*Staatspartei*. This support was conspicuous; these newspapers had clearly opposed conservative Catholic clericalism ever since the nineteenth century. But in 1932, it was paramount to save the stumps of democracy, and even the SPD was supported by the papers. They also regarded Brüning more positively than they had while he was *Reichskanzler*.[237]

Klaus Scholder, the famous author of the first comprehensive church history of both the Catholic and Protestant Churches, comparing each of their relationships to Nazism, concludes:

> The impression of the general and consequent rejection of National Socialism through the Catholic Church is even more strengthened by the fact that most Catholic organizations expressly endorsed the resolutions of the bishops. And ultimately the declarations were followed and supported by a multitude of publications, which partly attacked National Socialism even politically with exceptional sharpness.[238]

Scholder also concurs with another historian, Ernst Deuerlein, when he asserts that, "no prominent persons in the official life in Germany . . . opposed the steadily increasing (Nazi) flood with more pronounced resolve" than the

Catholic persons of note.²³⁹ So, as it turned out, both in the elections and in the general Catholic behavior, Walter Dirk's anxious prospects for 1932 were uncalled for.

Protestant Reactions to the *Reichstag* Elections in 1930 and 1932

As mentioned in the chapter "The Protestant Confession," the situation among nonsocialist Protestants was very different than among Catholics in the 1920s. Herbert Christ puts it this way:

> The rejection of the "Catholic-atheistic" republic had a highly alarming effect: it was an essential reason why many Protestants hoped for Hitler and his Third Reich. For it had not been successful in eliminating the fear of the republic and dissatisfaction with the occasional cooperation between political Catholicism and social democracy—a dissatisfaction which was widespread in evangelical circles and not in any way restricted to the notoriously anti-Catholic "Evangelischer Bund." As it was not successful in instilling an understanding of the republican way of life and republican politics, many Protestants mistrusted the republic. They felt unfairly treated and left out in the cold, searching for other possibilities.²⁴⁰

The Protestant church system was also very different from the Catholic one, which made the Church, as we have seen, less resistant against the influx of alien ideas. John S. Conway puts it this way:

> In the ranks of Protestant churches, however, there were striking differences. In comparison to the Catholics, there was no authoritative hierarchy, no one political party (Author's remark: minor parties in 1920s and the CSVD after 1929, though), and no firm doctrine of ideological opposition. Instead, an enormous variety of standpoints emerged. Each church group, each local church synod, each theological party was seeking for a new orientation in order to make up their minds.²⁴¹

Since 1929 a sudden and pronounced politicization had taken place among the clergy, but before the election in 1930 various leading clerics and church bodies had declared neutrality and even advised clerics to refrain from political activism—in vain, though.²⁴²

After the election, the most prominent church leader, General Superintendent Otto Dibelius of Kurmark, revealed his optimistic views for the future, and the Nazi success strengthened the already wide-spanning discussion. Nazism was broadly debated, in the media, in conferences of clerics and of synods, in leaflets and books and many reserved voices were also raised.²⁴³ John S. Conway puts it this way:

After the 1930 elections, the theme of the church and National Socialism became one of the most frequent and controversial topics in Protestant circles. The advantage lay with those who proclaimed the necessity of working with, rather than against, the tide of events. As a result, by the early 1930s, many Protestants had come not only to accept the rightness of Hitler's political ambitions, but also to justify them in the theoretical field as well. Not only had the evident disarray of republican governments increased the longing for an authoritarian solution to Germany's problems, but also the defensive backward-looking attitudes of the many Protestant Church leaders led some of the younger more active clergy openly to support the NSDAP, and even to believe that the leadership of the Protestant Church could be reasserted in its ranks by demonstrating the commitment of the church to the Nazis' anti-Bolshevik and anti-Semitic policies.[244]

Clerics were aware of the radical *völkisch* elements in Nazi ideology, but regarded the resolute Nazi attitude towards the communist menace and the party's opposition to the detested Zentrum as weightier. Some thought that the less acceptable excesses of the party would gradually disappear when it reached maturity, and it needed the power of Christianity "to help this . . . awakening of the German soul to victory." It was God's call to the Christians to say Yes to the movement and purify it. Such attitudes were common even among conservative Lutheran theologians as Walter Künneth, later a prominent member of the BK and one of the fiercest opponents of Rosenberg after 1935. The characteristic split between theological rejection and political acclamation turned out to be a rather common way to relate to Nazism among Protestant clerics. Among publications and groups it was probably only the liberal-democratic *Christliche Welt* and the religious socialists who also opposed the *political* views of the Nazis.[245]

The Norwegian theologian Hans M. Bringeland assessed the affinity of German theologians towards Nazism:

(Martin) Dibelius (Author's remark: a relative of Otto D.) was, more or less alone with such (liberal and democratic) views, despite having some other likeminded representatives of the so called "liberal theology." For the majority of theologians, followed by the bulk of the Protestant churchgoers, wished to be "unpolitical" in principle, in practice they were—egged on by several crises in the new republic and by nostalgic anti-modernism—opposed to parliamentary democracy and increasingly hoping for a "conservative revolution." Gradually, when it became obvious that only the National Socialist movement could realize this hope, many chose directly, or at least indirectly, to support the movement, mind you: as "the lesser evil." Others, a minority of the theologians and a greater part of the church people, enthusiastically joined the Nazi-movement.[246]

In contrast to the Catholic consternation about "*Mythus*," hardly any Protestant theologians were worried about the book before the middle of the decade. There were some, however, and these were reassured when hearing the work was Rosenberg's private ideas and did not represent the official Nazi ideology.[247]

Theologians were naturally interested in finding out and acquiring a better knowledge of the Nazi ideology, and in March 1931 Gustav Scholz, a representative of *Kirchenbundesamt*, (an umbrella organization of the Protestant Churches) met with Franz Stöhr, representative of the executive committee of the Nazi Party and *Reichstag* member. Stöhr recounted that although there were many Catholics in the party, the leadership was "shaped by Protestantism," and those leaders who were members of the Catholic Church were rather nominal and showed a more sympathetic attitude to the other denomination. As to "*Mythus*" Stöhr emphasized the anti-Dinter line of the party, which was primarily secular and political. After the meeting, Scholz did not seem convinced.[248]

Scholz's skepticism hardly touched the general Protestant mentality. Some months later, the leftist liberal Hans E. Friedrich summarized his impression of the mentality in relationship to Nazism compared to the Catholic mentality:

> This much can be ascertained: Catholicism has called National Socialism to account far more energetically and clearly than Protestantism or its Church. For the Catholics, with their autocratically structured organization, it was, true, far easier to do this once and for all in a closed, so to say categorical form. The Protestant clergy, true, does not ignore National Socialism, but the Catholics have reached a uniform result. Some (Protestants) are enthusiastically carried away by the movement and believe in the salvation of Germany through National Socialism, whereas others (e.g. the religious socialists) reject it. And yet others are attracted by some of the values of the movement but appalled by the form the fight has taken. All in all, however, there is sympathy rather than antipathy to be seen.[249]

A new and far more thoroughgoing survey of the Protestant debate was published in the summer of 1932. 43 contributions were presented and showed that the opposition against Nazism was considerable: twelve were positive to Nazism, nineteen negative and twelve were ambivalent. Scholder has tried to categorize the views and found three groups of adherents of the ideology: 1) Old "national Protestants" who switched their conservative patriotism to the revolutionary Nazism. One advocate was *Allgemeine Evangelisch-Lutherische Kirchenzeitung*, the publication which in the middle of the nineteenth century had favored "*Die germanisch-christliche Staatsidee*." In the early 1930s, it was known as the largest and leading clerical periodical in evangelical Germany. 2) "The modern political theologians," who saw in

Nazism God's will being realized through the elevation of the German people to its rightful plane. To them, Nazism was a divine revelation in history, and, therefore, solidarity with the ideology was obedience to God. The prominent theologians Emmanuel Hirsch and Paul Althaus, and the core of the members in the later DC belonged to this group. 3) Adherents of *Deutschkirche/Nationalkirche*, the union of the two main confessions in one church, in addition to the representatives of *völkisch* religion.[250]

It is worth noting that most contributors were more or less skeptical to Rosenberg, but largely hailed the Nazi movement as a *political* phenomenon.[251]

A religious socialist tried to categorize all the clergy according to their relationship to Nazism and found four different attitudes: 1) neutral (in accordance with the directions of the Church to stay above party politics), 2) waiting, 3) actively confessing (this one increasingly among the younger generation), and 4) rejecting (a small minority, primarily the religious socialists).[252]

Up until the takeover in 1933, the membership in the Nazi Party is said to have been "overwhelmingly Protestant." Such a tendency must have been even stronger within the group of clerical members because only a handful of Catholics were members. The exact number is not known, but in the early 1930s the bulk of the younger Protestant clerics and theological students are said to have either been members of the party or pro-Nazi.[253] Björn Mensing has interviewed Bavarian clerics about their motives for supporting the Nazi Party, and fear of Bolshevik revolution was a central one. Compared to the Catholic clerics, however, their insight was restricted because many made no distinction between social democrats and communists. This illusory fear was allegedly their strongest reason for supporting the party.[254]

Professor Kyle Jantzen, who studied the situation in three Protestant parishes in the Third Reich, thinks there are reasons to say that the general fascination among the clergy with the Nazis was due to four factors: 1) Many believed that the national renewal of 1933 would lead to a corresponding moral renewal; 2) There was a widespread belief that Hitler called the clergy to a partnership in which they could assist him as local leaders of this renewal; 3) There was a widespread fear of communism and gratefulness to the Nazis for the destruction of the political left; 4) Protestant clerics were predisposed to authoritarian politics based on a series of important, (problematic, however) views in Lutheran theology.

Among the total of 115 clergymen employed in the three parishes during the Third Reich, only very few expressed mild reservation or skepticism towards the Nazi government during the first years.[255]

Furthermore, Jantzen discusses differences between the North German parishes Nauen and Pirna with 90 percent Protestants on the one hand, and the

South German Ravensburg with only 10 percent Protestant confession on the other. The enthusiasm for the Nazi government was markedly greater in the north than the south, but the enthusiasm gradually turned to disillusionment because of strong Nazi intervention in the parishes and growing realization that the "Positive Christianity" of the party program did not live up to the reality. The less Nazi-benign Protestant minority of Ravensburg were not subject to Nazi intervention to the same degree, and Jantzen considers it could be due to the desire to promote Protestantism in an overwhelmingly Catholic and Nazi-hostile milieu. The less Nazi-benign attitude among the Protestants in Ravensburg could have been influenced by the Catholic anti-Nazism.[256]

The Palatine clergyman Adolf Wenz is an example of the enthusiasm of Nazi clerics:

> The situation with National Socialism is that the National Socialist idea has become a great experience for us, an experience which we do not want to miss out on, any more than a religious experience we have had. This experience is so great for us that we must regard anybody as poor, almost, who has not yet had this experience. Therefore, we also feel offended when somebody questions our experience or distrustfully wants to reject it as something weird.[257]

Wenz understood those who were skeptical about Nazism because of the neo-paganism of Rosenberg, Darré and Reventlow, but he thought Hitler's statements in *Mein Kampf* overrode them. After the takeover Wenz had to admit that he had been wrong, and he was not alone in this. Several clerics had hoped their membership would influence Nazism in a Christian manner. Quite a lot of them had had reservations about anti-Semitism or other aspects of the ideology, but were reassured that the party did not represent the "extermination" policy of Julius Streicher, but the "Stöcker" policy of "only" reducing the importance of the Jews to insignificant sojourners, because the Nazi religion was "Christian" and the main enemy was Bolshevism. Furthermore, Hitler was not going to start a new war.[258]

According to Mensing, 50–60 percent of Protestant clergymen in Bavaria voted Nazi in the election of July 1932. Although many were not party members, they openly agitated for it. This was incompatible with a new prohibition passed by their leaders, but no sanctions were attached to this ordinance, so the activists did not care. The difference between the Catholic and Protestant execution of hierarchical discipline in the churches thus became obvious, although rather lax execution of sanctions also could be found in the former church, as mentioned above.[259] Bearing in mind that the bulk of the remainder of the clergy were either adherents of the DNVP or the CSVD, it is obvious that rightist-radical tendencies were exceptionally strong within the Protestant clergy. After the takeover and until November 1933, probably

80 percent of Bavarian Protestant clergymen were "enthusiastic" adherents of Nazism, and the bulk of the others had at least a similar mentality to the Nazi alliance-partner DNVP. But, perhaps paradoxically, the bulk of the clerics also belonged to the BK, as this church was "intact" and not ruled by *Reichsbischof* Ludwig Müller.[260]

The attitude of clerics and churchgoers was not very different in neighboring Wurttemberg. A few days after the takeover Wurm, its Church president, asserted that 80 percent of the "conscious" Protestants hailed the new government, and he was happy that the Church, at last, could relinquish its political neutrality. The Nazi success in Protestant parts of the state in 1932, to a great extent, had been due to the efforts of the large number of evangelical clergy.[261]

Protestant clerical Nazi-opponents seem to fall into three groups. The leftist-liberals rejected Nazism *morally*. Nevertheless, *Christliche Welt*, the main publication of the liberal theologians had since long occasionally asserted radical rightist views. Chamberlain's *"Grundlagen,"* by many regarded as one of the main ideological sources of Nazism, was characterized as "carrying an apologetic strength our Christian world should be thankful for."[262]

Another group, the religious socialists, asserted primarily *political-ideological* arguments, although even the neo-pagan elements were criticized. A little more than 1 percent, (200 of 18,000 or according to Lewy, 16,000), of the clerics, were members of *Bruderschaft sozialistischer Theologen Deutschlands*. The most prominent theologian was Paul Tillich. At least one clergyman, Erwin Eckert, was a communist. Tillich and several others emigrated, leaving the scene to Carlo Mierendorff and Adolf Reichwein as the group's best-known opponents in the Third Reich.[263]

Some representatives of the CSVD also belonged to a group who asserted political-ideological arguments. One of these, Professor Hermann Strathmann at Erlangen, gave, according to Scholder, one of "the best and most apt analyses in the Protestant camp of the National Socialist ideology. . . . Strathmann was one of the first to understand that totally new ethics necessarily would spring from the National Socialist ideology and affect both private life and life in society." Strathmann commented on the statements of several leading Nazis, Hitler and Rosenberg included, and their attitude to Christianity in relationship to Teutonic *"Volkstum"* and concluded that all of them based their arguments on an opposition between Christianity and the Teutonic way of life. Hence, "Positive Christianity" became a void concept. During the Third Reich, Strathmann showed an ambiguous relationship to Nazism, however, and as a professor, he ran into problems.[264]

The third and last anti-Nazi group was theologians influenced by the Swiss theologian Karl Barth (to a greater or lesser degree). Only this group managed in any significant way to persuade the originally neutral or wavering theologians, because they were good at clarifying that the ideological controversy was an *issue of fundamental, epoch-making ecclesiastical-theological importance.*[265]

Between the adherents and opponents was a significant group of largely neutral theologians. These, roughly 1/3 of the "national conservatives," rejected the "Blood and Soil" mythology, but hoped that the "good" people in the Nazi Party would transpire to be stronger than the *völkisch* ones and that eventually, a Christianizing of the party would take place. But their hope was not strong enough to get them to vote Nazi.[266]

Note that before the 1933 takeover, there were no groups that can be identified as "precursors" of the later DC opponents: the *Jungreformatorische Bewegung* (from the spring 1933), the *Pfarrernotbund* (PNB) (from September 1933) or the *Bekennende Kirche* (BK) (from the spring 1934), organizations in which there were also anti-Nazi theologians. Some of the leaders in these movements, the brothers Martin and Wilhelm Niemöller, Hans Asmussen, Bishop Otto Dibelius, and probably even Walter Künneth, were pro-Nazi at some time during the early 1930s.[267]

Although "*Mythus*" was not given the same attention as we find among Catholics, some theologians dealt with the work before the Nazi takeover: Friedrich Heiler (convert from Catholicism), Helmuth Schreiner, Walter Braun and Walter Künneth. The latter was also the most thorough critic of Rosenberg after the takeover. All of them, apart from Braun, considered there were both positive and negative aspects to the book. Braun put forward an objection which at that time was unusual within Protestantism, that "*Volkstum*" can, with reference to Britain and France, be established in spite of, or even by means of, a broad racial mixture.[268] Probably the strongest showdown with Rosenberg was made by the theologian Paul Bausch, because he was also one of the leaders of the CSVD and therefore felt the Nazi challenge stronger than the others.[269]

The main Protestant understanding, if we look at the pro-Nazi church rhetoric, was that Rosenberg's "private work," like Dinter's in the 1920s, had no special significance for the Nazi Party. According to Iber, this was the main reason why no proper discussion took place about the statements in "*Mythus*" before the end of 1933 when Rosenberg was appointed the leader of ideological education.[270] In the third edition of "*Mythus*," Rosenberg mentioned the reception Protestants gave his work and lamented that many had shown the same attitude to his work as the Catholic Church had shown to the Reformation.[271]

As the discussions progressed, the situation of the Church leaders became increasingly difficult and the fronts grew sharper. Prominent theologians were present in both the pro- and anti-Nazi factions. The immediate reason to issue a statement about Nazism was the attempt to involve churches directly in the propaganda and political agitation. After the autumn of 1930, Nazi members had appeared in churches in uniforms and brought flags and banners to funerals. 400 Storm-Troopers had appeared complete with flags and banners at a Mass in Regensburg (Ratisbon) Cathedral in May 1930, which promptly resulted in such display being prohibited in Catholic churches. But it was not so easy to take action for evangelical Church leaders and to take authoritarian measures. Firstly, it was the responsibility of the local parish to arrange services. Secondly, the churchgoers, especially in the countryside where attendance was best, had to a great extent been Nazified. Hence, directives from the Church leaders uniformly amounted to short declarations to the clergy calling for respect for the party-political neutrality of the Church. However, wearing uniforms was allowed. The effects of the declarations were meagre. They did not prevent the increasing Church-politicizing in any way. And it should be mentioned that the Church leaders were very surprised at the sharpness of the rejection of Nazism in the Catholic Mainz-declaration after the 1930 election.[272]

In January 1932, a new meeting was arranged between representatives of the Churches and a representative of Hitler's staff. This was at a time when the Nazis had started to make plans (through the DC), to participate in the election to church bodies in Prussia and establish a *Nationalkirche*. Church representatives were worried and wanted to meet Hitler himself to get authoritative answers. This was refused and they reported that it was difficult to discuss with the Nazi delegate, and it seemed as if he thought something "quite different" from what the Nazis said and provide as "grounds" for their statements.[273]

The Nazis in Berlin were very active through the DC in the elections to Prussian church bodies in November 1932 and carried 1/3 of the votes. Kjøstvedt asserts that this was in accordance with a general Nazi strategy of gaining influence in social settings where they had not been established before. With this in mind, it is understandable that the Berlin party disliked Rosenberg.[274]

Before the *Reichstag* election in November 1932, two of the leaders of the 28 regional Churches, the bishops of Mecklenburg-Schwerin and Brunswick, abandoned neutrality and recommended the Nazi Party. Nevertheless, the Nazi Party—and the Zentrum—suffered slight setbacks. That might be due to the negotiations between the two strong opponents in the autumn. Both Protestants and Catholics may have been upset by such talks. Besides, some Protestants may have been put off by Hitler's approval of the *Potempa* assassinations of communists by Nazis in August, and the general Nazi use of violence.[275]

In a DEKA conference after the elections to the *Reichstag* and Prussian church bodies it was evident that the practice of uniform wearing and banners in services varied from church to church. The Nazi Party had participated in the elections to synods in two states, Prussia and Baden, and done well in both. It was regretted that some Nazi clergymen had rejected the supervision of their official Church leaders to the benefit of a Nazi organization. The attitude of the CSVD was also commented on and it was regretted that this party with its "strong reformed and pietistic strain" previously had formed bonds to "the Brüning-regime at a time when the Zentrum ran the most ruthless power- and personnel-policy in Prussia," and hence could not "win any sympathy in evangelical-conscious and national-conscious circles."[276]

So, there was opposition against Nazism before the Nazi takeover and to aspects of the ideology among several Protestant theologians. But in strong contrast to the Catholic situation, no negative declaration from any national or regional church body or representative clergyman was issued, and only two declarations from local parishes. The declaration from Wuppertal-Elberfeld attacked "the falsification of the Biblical gospel," "the racial thinking," "a Teutonic Christ," "heroic piety," and "the disdain for the Old Testament." The declaration from Oldenburg was more restricted and dealt with racism and the relationship to the Jews, although it admitted that "the Christian must . . . keep and strengthen the good genes of the people," and the Church had to carefully keep an eye on "the results of the scientific research on races."[277]

Even though no negative resolutions were passed, not all Nazi clerics were satisfied. In Wurttemberg, some broke away and chose their own leaders in January 1933, because the Church would not pass a uniformly *positive* statement about Nazism.[278]

Some prominent Protestants found the situation in their own confessional group so deplorable that they regarded the Zentrum as the only real counterweight to Nazism. The historian Friedrich Thimme wrote to his brother:

> To me, the only right thing to do seemed to make the Zentrum so strong as possible. To vote for small parties as the Volksdienst seems an absurdity to me, because the elections are not a confession, but should be a practical solution for the crisis of the State. Due to this understanding I have almost always voted the Zentrum, although I had to relinquish the hope I had long entertained of seeing the Zentrum widened to become a Christian people's party with an Evangelical wing.[279]

Klaus Scholder summarizes the situation in the Protestant camp compared with the opposite confessional camp and tries to explain the difference in attitude between them to the Nazi challenge:

> In reality the German Protestantism lacked all that caused the uniform Catholic front: the basis of Natural Rights, the political party (the Zentrum and the BVP)

and the authoritative hierarchy. Instead, everything (within Protestantism) remained open; instead of a clear front, there were numerous different opinions and voices. This meant each individual, each theological faction, each clerical group and, ultimately, each separate regional church had to search for what they discovered to be the right thing and make a decision accordingly. This explains why the problem "Church and National Socialism" after the 1930 election became one of the most frequent and contested topics at clerical conferences and in publications. The open-endedness of the situation became obvious in the manner emphasis was laid all the time on the possibility of letting different views on National Socialism be expressed 'in order to contribute to real enlightenment' and hence reach a verdict.[280]

They had to wait for this "verdict." It was not reached and passed before the end of the next war. Kurt Nowak asserts that the marginalization of criticism by the liberals in the church led to a weakening of resistance to Nazism:

The causes must be sought in a developmental process connected to an eradication of certain spiritual- and social-scientific categories from Protestant aspects of science after 1918.... German Protestantism c. 1930 lacked learned people such as Ernst Troeltsch, and there was a certain lack of judgment in its opinion-forming theological groups when faced with the negative aspects of the "Revolution in Theology" after 1918, i.e. the loss of social- and spiritual-scientific competence. This competence was the strength of certain representatives of "cultural Protestantism," who were placed "out in the left" in the theological debate. With the theological protest against the "Cultural Protestant" understanding of religion and Christianity the Evangelical church during the 1920s gradually has lost political and sociological categories. The competence of the church for sociological self-criticism in the core of the state, society, culture and politics has therefore been weakened, and thereby the ability to analyze movements and powers outside the church.[281]

Ernst Troeltsch died in 1923. Among his colleagues "placed out in the left" Nowak mentions the socialist Paul Tillich, the "cultural Protestants" Hermann Mulert and Martin Rade, the leftist-liberal Hans E. Friedrich, Richard Karwehl, Hermann Sasse and Gottfried Traub. However, Troeltsch would probably not have been the right person to restrain radical rightist tendencies in Protestant theology, because of his radical secular opinion of the Church: he regarded it to be superfluous in a new kind of state.[282]

Hans Bringeland, explaining why theologians like Martin Dibelius, Karl Barth and Rudolf Bultmann or other prominent theologians did not make any real settlement with Nazism before 1933, says:

It is not possible to give any complete and general answer. But we can probably conclude that the situation up to 1933 was partly very complex, and partly uncertain. Everybody saw that a decisive turn both politically and economically in German society was on the way. But a variety of strong forces were active, various movements which promised a new and better future. Therefore, it was hard to decide who would triumph. National Socialism was only one of several branches within the strong völkisch and national-conservative segment of German politics. And communism was still a real contender for power. That the situation in reality was so complex and undecided, we see from the fact that such an enlightened and well-oriented observer as (Martin) Dibelius obviously did not see the somber prospects. Even Barth did not manage to interpret and declare the signs of the time although he should have had the qualifications. Bultmann, however, was no homo politicus; he had probably neither interest nor the schooling that a political watchman needs.[283]

THE THIRD REICH

The *Reichstag* Election in 1933

In his announcement of new elections and in his pompous speech later in Berliner Sportpalast on February 10, Hitler deliberately made use of religious rhetoric, and *VB* published reports from church services with an emphasis on the participation of tranquil SA- and other party members and their processions in the streets afterwards. At the end of February, Hitler's Secretary of State, Heinrich Lammers, tried, in vain though, to get the churches to arrange "Prayer services for People and Fatherland" in connection with the elections. All this was obviously aimed at attracting Catholic churchgoers.[284]

Soon after the appointment of Hitler as *Reichskanzler,* the leader of the Zentrum, Ludwig Kaas, instigated the mobilization of the Christian (i.e. Catholic) trade unions, the Catholic workers' and apprentices' associations and *Jungmännerverband* to act as a "general staff," the *Christlich-deutsches Volk marschiert*, in the campaign for the next elections.[285]

The appointment of the new government caused alarm and terror in the Catholic teachers' organizations, which soon appeared well-founded. On February 15, a great number of Zentrum officials were fired.[286] Together with eleven other Catholic organizations, among them, three female organizations, the two teachers' organizations published an election appeal on February 16: *Bekenntnis zur Wahrung des Rechts und der Verfassung* (i.e. Confession to the Protection of the Rights and the Constitution). It expressed not only the view on Nazism but also of communism and the relationship between these two ideologies and society in general. Having described the situation of the country as "people confused, the consciousness of rights shattered, the cleavage between the social strata more profound, hatred, animosity and violence everywhere," the organizations saw through that the government had illegally abolished the *Reichstag*, the Prussian assembly and local assemblies in order to grasp hold of all political power. The *Bekenntnis* expressed what they understood by "German" identity and the Catholic understanding of "the German essence":

> German is according to our persuasion, loyalty to the oath taken on the Constitution. German is to love freedom, also to show consideration for the freedom of the adversary and not let violent actions remain unpunished. True Christianity is to follow the founder of Christianity, who said that blessed are the peacemakers and those who hunger for righteousness.
>
> For us, German nature and Christianity are a holy obligation. The events of today show how right they were, those who demanded sufficient security for the future. Shattered to the core we now witness the delusions, which now make their entry in our people. We call it a sin against German unity when men who have shed their blood for people and nation are called traitors, just because they have fought against this development; a sin against the youth when people instigate them to thoughts of hatred and revenge and give them freedom to harass people who think differently. It is the destruction of German youth and annihilation of a healthy State.[287]

The publication of the appeal resulted in the prohibition of 600 Zentrum-publications, among them twenty daily newspapers. Originally, the prohibition was for three days but "generously" already lifted the day after and the firing of more Zentrum officials was called off. Aretz thinks Göring's "generosity" probably was due to fear of more publicity for the appeal. However, the harassment of Zentrum publications continued in other ways, threats and all kinds of obstruction, which, subsequently resulted in gradual veiling and weakening of criticism of Nazism, and eventually complete silence.[288]

According to the leader of the workers' movement, Otto Müller, the thirteen organizations behind the appeal represented somewhere between three and four million members. Hence, the bulk of the members of organizations in the *"Zentrumsturm"* had expressed their political views before the election. Also other national Catholic organizations, such as the KV, were still uniformly negative towards Nazism, as were the bishops, who on February 20 issued a pastoral letter in which they warned against voting for "agitators and parties not worthy of the confidence of Catholic people."[289]

In the Protestant DEKA conference a little later, Bishop Wurm of Wurttemberg, one of the most pronounced anti-Nazi bishops during WWII, asserted that people must realize "that the Nazi movement through great sacrifices had destroyed a terror (i.e. the "Bolshevist" danger)." Even the rest of the conference members welcomed the efforts of the new government, primarily when it came to ethics and was on the point of passing the following resolution: "The Church hails the Patriotic Movement", but in order to maintain party political neutrality the proposal was dismissed.[290]

After a while, not just the socialist parties, but the other two "Weimar" parties, the DDP/*Staatspartei* and the Zentrum also experienced disruption during their campaign. For example, Adam Stegerwald (the one-time minister and leader of the European Christian trade unions) was physically abused, and in the Rhineland Zentrum arrangements were forbidden and campaign leaflets confiscated, abetted by the police. Again, the Nazi leaders "took a step back" through the official appeals of Hitler and Göring urging disciplined behavior and explaining the harassment as something done by "provocatory elements."[291]

After the *Reichstag*-fire and the razzia against communists, the police allegedly found written material, which "proved" collaboration with the "*Reichsbanner*, the SPD or Christian (i.e. Catholic) workers for the protection of workers' residential areas and party and trade union buildings"; this excused imposing even more campaign restrictions.[292] As a countermove to campaign restrictions, the Zentrum/BVP instigated a successful boycott of Nazi arrangements in Catholic areas.[293]

To attract Catholic voters the Nazis once again set up a "Catholic" publication, *Warmia*, in East Prussia which claimed Nazism enjoyed Catholic support. But the effect was marginal because the publication came on the very day of the election, and the bishop there refuted it as a fake Catholic publication and persuaded people to vote for the Zentrum. Even other Catholic clergy, on the very day of the election, used the opportunity to urge voters to choose the Zentrum.[294]

Sebastian Haffner thinks the Weimar-loyal paramilitary organizations with their several hundred-thousands of armed men waited only for orders to intervene, but were betrayed by their leaders.[295] Ernst Deuerlein, however, concludes that until the election in March 1933, the Zentrum and the Catholic organizations used all their powers to hinder an election triumph for Hitler. Bishops, priests and organizations all implored the voters.[296]

Although the Zentrum did well and gained almost 200,000 new votes, Göring asserted that the importance of the election was that the "Harzburg" majority had been successful in eliminating the Zentrum from key positions.[297]

Factors in the Church-Nazi Relationship after the 1933 Election that Shed Light on even Deeper Issues

So far we have dealt with the confessional relationship to German right-wing radicalism and Nazism in a society with free speech. After the Hitler government took power in January 1933, Germany developed rapidly into a totalitarian society, and there were no more multiparty elections after the elections to the Prussian regional assemblies on March 12. The Catholic milieu was immediately aware of the restricted scope for speech and action, and having been anti-Nazi for a decade, behaved accordingly. Their tactics might appear as cowardly and servile, but for those involved, it was a question of pure survival both personally and for the Church as an institution.

The vast majority of Protestants, however, understood the situation quite differently. What had taken place was a great transition from a secular, even anti-Christian state to a regime with respect for, and desire to promote, "Positive Christianity." At last the German people had got a political leadership that all patriotic Germans could support. Because of this original widespread illusion, the response of some Protestant clergy appeared more open, frank, critical and extensive than the Catholic Church's, when they after some years astonished discovered that the slogan "Positive Christianity" did not match their expectations. This, in turn, could leave the impression abroad that the Catholic Church was more deferential to the Nazi regime. The Protestant illusion lasted for some years, until 1937 perhaps, when the regime chose not to keep its promise of relatively free elections to clerical assemblies of the Protestant churches.

With this strongly restricted scope for Catholic action in mind, the further development is somewhat tangential to our purpose: to examine causes of the relationship of the confessions to right-wing radicalism in a German society that had free speech. There is an enormous amount of detailed literature about the situation of the churches during the Third Reich, and in this exploration, we, in summary, are focusing on the Catholic fight for survival, and—in the case of the Protestants—the adversaries of the DC, their relationship to Nazi ideology and the Nazi counter-measures.

Catholics and the Third Reich: Retreat and Defense Policy

The triumph of the "Harzburg" government on March 5 made a deep impression and some Catholic opponents, fearing troubled times ahead if they continued their opposition, soon gave in. Not surprisingly, because of their many Protestant members, the first ones to throw in the towel were the Christian trade unions, but a little later, and even that is not surprising since it had many rightist members–one of the students' associations. Even the KLVdDR surrendered, but that was for strategic reasons.[298] According to one of the leaders of the Nazi teachers' association, only 5 percent of its new members were active Nazis. Many of the rest used their membership to camouflage the possibility of influencing their pupils. Occasionally even clergy encouraged teachers to join the Nazi association.[299] The female teachers' association, however, fervently resisted being subdued until its liquidation in 1937.[300]

One of the few critical voices still raised against Nazism was from one of the leaders in the *Jungmännerverband*. The response: a four-month ban on it being published.[301]

Because the Nazis did not achieve a majority in Bavaria, they arranged a dramatic *coup d'etat* in the state during the night of March 10. BVP ministers were woken up in the middle of the night and maltreated, and machinery in some Catholic papers was destroyed. Again, the Nazis took "a step back" and appointed the relatively moderate General von Epp as *Reichskommissar*, and formally reinstated the BVP government; however, they made sure it had no authority.[302]

When the *Reichstag* passed the enabling act on March 23, empowering Hitler with dictatorship, the Zentrum capitulated. Scholder claims it was the pope himself, assisted by the party leader, Ludwig Kaas, who instigated the capitulation process in hope of a concordat to save the Church. Following empty promises from the government, and fierce opposition among Zentrum representatives, particularly from *Reichskanzler* "emeritus" Josef Wirth and Heinrich Brüning, the party group decided to vote as a bloc in favor of the law, leaving the social democrats alone as the only opposition.[303]

Several historians have had their reflection on the Zentrum's capitulation. The Zentrum historian Karl Bachem and the DDP-politician and historian Friedrich Meinecke thought the fear of the DDP and the Zentrum of terror may have been a weighty reason for falling into line.[304] Detlef Junker relates the behavior of the Zentrum representatives to the general behavior of the party in 1932 and 1933, and thinks they were directed by an ideology that entailed a legalist understanding of being a "constitutional party." This was a stronger inclination than the tendencies considered by historians Karl Dietrich Bracher and Rudolf Morsey to have undermined foundations for the Zentrum's resistance towards Nazism in 1932 and 1933. Bracher has emphasized allegedly "rightist" inclinations in the party towards an authoritarian policy and understanding of state after 1928, whereas Morsey thinks that there were signs of "certain erodings of the democratic marrow" within the party. However, Junker thinks these explanations do not hit the mark when it comes to the Zentrum's policy. The Zentrum's demand for "authoritarian democracy" was not a clamor for the destruction of "Weimar parliamentarism," "On the contrary, the response to the acute crisis of state by amalgamating presidential government with support in the parliament." Junker further asserts that the Zentrum—apart from the election campaign in July 1932—was never in political opposition or open conflict with the Nazi Party from the firing of Brüning in May 1932 until the dissolution of the party in July 1933. Junker's reason for thinking this is his appeal to the legalist understanding he perceives, and illusions about Hitler's real intentions, plus the reactionary policy of that renegade von Papen, who succeeded Brüning as *Reichskanzler*.[305]

Before the vote on the law the party leaders of the Zentrum, the BVP, the DDP/*Staatspartei* and the CSVD issued statements for the votes of their respective parties. The representatives of the three first parties made long statements and asserted that they would approve the law though they had their doubts about it, and admonished Hitler to respect civil rights. The CSVD-representative, however, approved the law abruptly and without reservation, and asserted the party said "Yes" to "the inner political, and especially the *foreign* political aims of the Government."[306]

Whatever the motives of the Zentrum representatives were on March 23, the bishops had now been left in the lurch by both pope and party and deprived of any real room for maneuver. Even though the Bavarian bishops were not present, a bishops' conference five days later issued a new resolution, which allowed the church people to disregard former prohibitions and warnings against the Nazi Party. However, their basic criticism of Nazism was still upheld.[307] The Bavarians were somewhat surprised, but felt obliged to follow suit and added some restrictions about the use of uniforms in sermons and protection of Catholic associations.[308] In addition to the stand of pope and party the bishops were also probably influenced on the one hand by Hitler's solemn assurances on March 23 of pursuing a policy friendly towards Christianity, and on the other: the danger of mass sacking of employed officials with Zentrum/BVP membership, if episcopal opposition continued.[309]

Confusion, uncertainty and criticism against the Catholic capitulation soon arose among both clerics, organizations and individuals. But Cardinal Faulhaber excused and asserted that the Church had ended up in this tragic situation "through the attitude of Rome."[310] Josef Joos, the leader of the workers' association, wrote thinly disguised anti-Nazi articles in *WAZ*, which demonstratively published the bishops' resolutions discreetly and tardily. An Austrian bishop criticized his German colleagues, but received the response that it was easy for him to do so, from the safety of a foreign country.[311]

On the other hand the bishops' resolutions made some clerics bold enough to join the Nazi Party before the "opportunist" barrier shut in May. By then 29 clerics had joined the party, and sixteen more were allowed to join later, but six left the party after a while. In addition to the members, there were individuals Spicer describes as, "supporting NSDAP in his preaching and teaching."[312]

After the bishops' capitulation the establishment of a national concordat was an urgent and dominant priority for the Catholic Church and churchgoers. Most urgent was the need to secure the Christian education of their 1.5 million children and youth, and after that, organizational life including the youth movement and confessional schools. At the end of May leaders received alarming information about wholesale and widespread harassment of and criminal actions against organizations and their members.[313]

Historians have tried to assess who were the instigators of the concordat, the Zentrum or the Vatican. The recent opening of more Vatican archives has not yet settled the question.[314]

After Catholics, especially in Bavaria, had tasted just how brutal the new regime could be, the Concordat was ratified in July and ultimately passed in September. As the Vatican had feared, it turned out that the concessions about organizations and schools were not worth much. The Concordat only delayed the dissolutions for a while.[315]

Some regard the Concordat as almost collaboration between Nazism and Catholicism. Short commentaries of the two superiors in the Vatican, Pope Pius XI and his secretary Pacelli, tell another story of how they understood the treaty. Pius XI asserted that, "I would negotiate with the Devil himself to be able to save a single soul," and Pacelli asserted that, "a gun has been put to my head, and I have not had any alternative." Pacelli had tried three times to arrange a concordat with the Soviet Union, the enemy of the Nazis, or at least an agreement to a modicum of religious freedom and a guarantee of spiritual guidance but he was rejected thrice.[316]

The three authors/editors of one of the comprehensive histories of the churches during the Third Reich provide a short summary of the situation for the Catholic Church under the Third Reich:

> The Catholic Church was the most important part of society under the Third Reich to survive with intact institutions and own system of values. National Socialists, therefore, regarded it as a major obstacle to the completion of its aims, so they went in for the annihilation of the Church. The regime viewed the Church's reaction to this attack as opposition and even interpreted it as a campaign of insubordination and not merely self-preservation.[317]

The Nazi challenge to the Catholic Church can be divided into three phases say the three authors (Gotto, Hockerts, and Repgen).[318] The first phase lasted until 1935 or 1936 and was a partly veiled struggle about the interests of the Church in society, i.e. the destruction of the clerical scope apart from purely spiritual guidance. This was necessary for the Nazis if they wanted to achieve their aim: the standardized human being. For this reason, media, organizations and confessional schools were either dissolved or weakened so much that later attempts at dissolution caused no problem.

The phase was dominated by the strong recoil to the "Circular for the Order of religious Upbringing in the National Socialist State," which was passed in December 1933, and reactions to Rosenberg, being appointed national leader of ideological education some weeks later. One of the circulars stated that, "Roman yearning for power is not compatible with a German understanding of Christianity." Catholics, who initially had trusted Hitler's assurances and hoped for better prospects under the new regime, were disabused, and joined the opposition. This materialized in several statements by bishops and articles in publications and leaflets and even an audience with Hitler. The main publication was *Studies of the Myth of the 20th century*. Catholics in foreign countries were also involved. Demonstrative celebrations were arranged with as many as 800,000 participants in Aachen as late as in 1938, and when Rosenberg wanted to speak in the Catholic town of Münster, there were nearly riots. But skirmishes like these came to a standstill after the prominent Catholics Erich von Klausener and Adalbert Probst were assassinated together with Röhm and company in June 1934.[319]

The Catholic resistance was noticed abroad, for example at the 7th World Congress of the COMINTERN.[320] Catholics could have exploited the Saar-referendum in 1935 to relieve their situation. However, the bishops in the two adjoining areas recommended incorporation after they had received promises of reward—fake, as it turned out—or because they feared reprisals if they did not. The Vatican remained passive to prevent allegations of external intervention.[321]

The second phase, from 1935/1936 until 1940, reached its peak in 1936 to 1937. Now the struggle was over the very-identity and system-of-values of the Church! The tactic the authorities now adopted was to break up every relationship the Church had to individual and collective life in secular society. Thus, the battle took on a new dimension now; the Church should only concern itself with "the Hereafter." Clerics were tried for indecency, and the pope made a crass statement: *Mit brennender Sorge* (With burning Grief) in the spring of 1937. The Indecency trials were a fiasco, and the papal statement received widespread attention, especially because Gestapo did not manage to stop it being read from the pulpits. The Nazis were alarmed, and the exiled KPD praised the action. The pope's reproach had very little effect, however.[322]

It may be symptomatic that after Catholic-dominated Saar had successfully been re-united with Germany, several anti-Catholic publications appeared. The fiercest of these was perhaps Kurt Eggers' *Rom gegen Reich* where he declared: "Germany fights for a Rome-free North. That is its main ambition, one of its most urgent tasks and its destiny. What Bismarck did not achieve, we as the youth of the nation will undertake as an inheritance and as much as we are able, bring to a happy conclusion."[323]

The *"Kristallnacht"* with its terrorization happened at this time. What is little known is that it was extended to Catholics. The residences of two of

Germany's cardinals, Innitzer of Austria and Faulhaber of South Germany, were beleaguered by the mob, the Faulhaber's under the banner: "down with world Jewry and its *Black* and Red allies!" When Bishop Galen of Münster was asked to proclaim a resolution by Jews, he was willing to if the Jews were willing to take the consequences. They did not dare to take the chance.

But the Protestant bishop of Thüringen, Martin Sasse, welcomed the "storming of the synagogs" as fulfilment of the Lutheran cultural heritage, and declared: "World Catholicism and 'world-wide Oxford-Protestantism' together with the Western democracies raise their voices as Jew-protectors to thwart the Third Reich's resistance to Jewry." Rudolf Lill and Hans Mommsen claim that there was a common Catholic understanding that the "*Kristallnacht*" boded ill for Catholics.[324]

The third phase coincided with WWII. The last Catholic youth associations were dissolved in the summer of 1939. They were accused of pursuing communist(!) activity, so this needed to be completed *before* the Molotov-Ribbentrop Pact.[325] In spite of intensified attacks on the Church, under the guise of general wartime restrictions, churchgoers remained loyal. Unlike Protestant churches, the Catholics did not celebrate victories on the Western front in 1940 with church services.[326] The radicalization of racial policies, euthanasia and deportation—and even the alleged murder—of Jews sharpened Catholic opposition. The euthanasia action of Bishop Galen in 1941, where he risked his life, is well known. During this phase, the Church was threatened with "the Final Solution," but the Nazi leadership could not agree whether it should happen during the war or after the victory. Uriel Tal even asserts that Himmler told *Adolf Hitler Leibstandarte SS* on September 1940 "the long-term goals were deferred until the end of war, such as genocidal plans for the Church, notably the Roman Catholic." The Church's struggle in this period was not confined to the preservation of the Church only, but to the protection of human rights in general.[327]

Even during this phase, there were oppositional activities such as the crucifix-struggle in Bavaria in the autumn of 1941. Similar to the one in Oldenburg in 1936, it was successful, probably because the authorities were embarrassed that the leaders were women with male family-members fighting on the Eastern Front, which by then should already have ended in victory.[328]

Although the German bishops—in sharp contrast to the chaotic situation among Protestant church leaders—were an exceptionally uniform group of persons, opinions differed among them as to what the best strategy in the face of the destructive fight being carried out by the authorities was. Bishop Preysing of Berlin was the most prominent exponent among the hardliners and wanted to mobilize the mass of churchgoers in a mighty protest-campaign, but Cardinal Bertram of North Germany, (regarded as the Church Superior), fearing even more deadly reprisals than in the *Kulturkampf*, preferred negotiation. With exception of two incidents in 1934 and 1935, the pope did not intervene in the bishops' discussions with directives, but secretary Pacelli gently indicated that his sympathy was with the hardliners, which runs against the post-war allegations that he was *"Hitler's Pope."*[329]

In contrast to some foreign bishops, no German bishop issued any statement in connection with the *"Kristallnacht."* However, *Caritas, St. Rafaelsverein* and other organizations were actively involved in charitable work for both Catholic converts and other Jews, between 150,000 and 200,000 in total. When the bishops in mid-1940 became aware of the policy of liquidations, Cardinal Bertram issued a protest-statement, later backed by the Vatican, to no avail. When the authorities began deporting Jews in the autumn of 1941, Bertram ordered two bishops and the Nuncio Orsenigo to inquire into the matter, again without results. In the winter of 1942, rumors told that "many have been shot," and Bishop Berning wrote that, "it is probably the plan to exterminate the Jews totally." Two other bishops protested against the persecution of the Jews.[330]

The Church has been criticized for its laxity in protesting against the persecution of the Jews, but the Church leaders must have felt that every kind of intervention was totally futile. In some cases, it might irritate the authorities to sharpen its measures, as happened in the Netherlands in 1942. The Nazis were so provoked by the protest of the archbishop of Utrecht that they speeded up the deportation of the non-Aryans. For reasons like this, Margarete Sommer, who led the Catholic charitable efforts in Berlin in the background, did not demand any statement from the bishops. Soon after the war, however, several people, both lay and clergy, raised critical voices against themselves and the Church.[331]

Protestants and the Third Reich: Chaotic and Complex Situation

Konrad Repgen and Kurt Meier consider the church struggle of the Protestants very different from the Catholic one. Whereas the Catholic struggle was the defensive fight of an almost uniform Church against the suppressive policy of the authorities, the Protestant struggle, for the first four or five years at least, was a battle between two factions, the DC and the *Jungreformatorische Bewegung*/PNB/BK. It was primarily a fight about the organization of the Church and membership: centralization, the *Führer* principle and the Aryan paragraph. Only secondarily was it about theological issues. Such problems were never relevant in the Catholic Church. The political consequences remained unclear at first, and that way many could be opponents of the DC and adherents of the BK and think that they were good Nazis all at the same time.[332] Raimund Baumgärtner describes the confused situation in the Protestant Church compared with the Catholic one:

> Though the course of the history of the Catholic Church at the time of National Socialism was easy to follow, the observer of the evangelical scene is surprised, not only by the turbulence of the incidents, but by the multitude of local special developments and first and foremost by the difficulty of working out how many of the main participants could change their stances within the clerical groups.[333]

Jantzen's research about the situation in three Protestant parishes, Nauen, Pirna and Ravensburg, confirm that the relationship both between different groups and internally within the groups was more complex than earlier research has indicated.[334]

At the time of the takeover, the Swiss theologian Karl Barth asserted that, "the Protestants of Germany welcomed the new regime with real confidence, even with the greatest anticipation," and within a short time all 28 regional Lutheran, Reformed and Union-Churches issued resolutions expressing gratefulness for the "national elevation," and clerical associations, such as the *Evangelischer Bund* and the *Bund für Deutsche Kirche*, followed suit.[335] Bishop Otto Dibelius received the honor of holding the sermon at the opening of the *Reichstag* on March 21. He began by comparing it with the solemn sermon before the declaration of war by the *Reichstag* on August 4, 1914: "It was a day when the German people experienced the highest a nation possibly can experience: an elevation of patriotic feelings which bore everybody along; an inflammation of new faith in millions of hearts; a warm preparedness to sacrifice his own life in order to make Germany live—one nation, one people, one God!"[336] Dibelius described the harassment of the other parties in the election campaign this way:

> A new beginning in the history of a State is always anyway connected to violence because the State is power. New decisions, new orientations, changes and upheavals mean always the victory of one over the other. And when the life and death of a Nation is at stake, then the might of the State must be achieved in a powerful and thorough way, be it internally or abroad.[337]

Already in the spring of 1933, a conflict appeared in the Church between those who reacted to the DC's uncritical adherence to Nazi policy and those who defended it. The main bone of contention was the introduction of the *Führer* principle, the Aryan paragraph, the uniformity of church life and intimate Church-State cooperation. The opponents of the DC, the *Jungreformatorische Bewegung*, was a heterogeneous group of primarily national-conservative clerics ranging from men later prominent in the BK, such as Walter Künneth, Hanns Lilje and Martin Niemöller, to Friedrich Brunstäd, a slightly *völkisch* character. The group supported Nazism almost unconditionally within the framework of "the Metaphysics of the *Reich*," but without extreme "*Volkstum*" ideology. They were open for dialog with the DC, and based on certain declarations from both parties, it is hard to discern many differences between them.[338] Ernst Wolf characterizes the *Jungreformatorische* this way:

> The Jungreformatorische Bewegung wanted something like a national reformation, a German national evangelical church with a bishop as leader, not as uniform as the State, but, nevertheless, joined to the ethical-biological order of "Volkstum" as the order of Creation. It is the program of a "Young Church," in an intimate relationship with people and race and simultaneously in permanent confession to the "German Liberty Movement" (read: 'Nazism'), not without a certain reference to the Wars of Liberation, more precisely as Karl Holl put it in 1916: "The importance the Great Wars have had for the development of religious and ecclesiastical life within German Protestantism."[339]

The group opposed exaggerated racism, the Aryan paragraph in the Church and the plans of eugenics, but it shared the same views as DC and the authorities on the fundamental issues of "a faith based on the policy of State and People." Originally the group favored anti-Semitism, but abandoned it later, and it rejected all kinds of democratic parliamentarism. Frequently, they referred to the calling of the "*Führer*" and to "providence" as an argument for the right path for Germany. Their theology was greatly influenced by Bonhoeffer's Lutheran "*Ordnungstheologie*," which drew a sharp distinction between the order of creation and sustenance of God and the human orders of the state, people and race. It was primarily the group around Karl Barth with his influence later in the BK that opposed this theology.[340]

Some eager Nazis involved themselves frankly and offensively in the Prussian Church as early as the spring and summer of 1933. They demanded the right to appoint official commissars in the Church. This was too radical for President Hindenburg, who personally intervened. Hitler could, of course, do nothing but make a total retreat and was later less keen to get involved in church politics.[341]

Another conflict, which lasted throughout the Third Reich, arose in the summer of 1933. It was over the circumstances around the centralization of church organization and the election of the church superior, in addition to the introduction of the Aryan paragraph. Open conflict emerged between the two church parties, both promoting their own candidates for the July elections. With the help of the authorities, the DC won a great victory. Ludwig Müller was elected *Reichsbischof* and the DC was radicalized.[342] The *Jungreformatorische Bewegung* morphed into other movements such as the *Pfarrernotbund* in Prussia and similar clerical brotherhoods in other states and eventually into the *Bekennende Kirche* with its Barmen-declaration in May 1934.

In the autumn of 1933, the DC suffered a blow from which it never recovered. At a mass meeting in November in Berlin, one of the leaders had demanded a dictatorial *Nationalkirche*, de-Judaization of Christianity by purging the Old Testament and the teachings of the "rabbi Paul". The portrayal of the humble, suffering and crucified Christ must be replaced by a powerful, heroic Jesus in accordance with the "Nordic spirit." Fanatical support for Nazi "national renewal" should be the criterion of every cleric.[343] Although DC still existed in most Churches up until 1945, functioning as an opposition party to the BK, its influence remained insignificant. Members were increasingly dissatisfied with the hostile religious policy of the authorities and leaders sent crass complaints to them. After some years, the movement was almost confined to the Church in Thüringen.[344]

In May 1934, the BK Declaration of Confession was passed at the famous conference at Barmen. It was mainly a work by the Reformed Karl Barth and the Lutheran Hans Asmussen. In the important fifth article, a totalitarian understanding of the state, which stretches its power beyond its apportioned limitations, is rejected, but also a church that tries to assume secular power. Thus, it was in accordance with the Lutheran doctrine of the separated spheres. The declaration did not express any opinion on the Aryan paragraph in secular society. Apart from Karl Barth and Dietrich Bonhoeffer, most of the other leaders, the brothers Martin and Wilhelm Niemöller, Hans Asmussen, Walter Künneth and Otto Dibelius, were pro-Nazi to a varying degree, in 1933 at least, and the Niemöller brothers were ever since the 1920s.[345]

Four years after the Catholics had started their crusade against "*Mythus*," Protestants, at last, became fully aware of the work. As he was leader of an institution for apologetics, Walter Künneth was the main challenger to Rosenberg, but neither he nor several other BK personages were willing to reject "*Mythus*" altogether, leaving Barth and Bonhoeffer as probably the only BK members who totally rejected Rosenberg's ideas, the latter also criticizing Künneth's treatment of the work. DC commentators assessed the work positively, or even enthusiastically.[346] Iber tries to explain the "compromises" of the BK critics:

> ... due to their conservative-national mentality and political predisposition they were not resistant enough to the racist and nationalist fundamental Nazi statements, in that they did not discern the Fascist nature of the Nazi regime and the Nazi world-view. Thus they contributed to the stabilizing of Nazi dominion and ensuring that a comprehensive, even political, resistance by the Christian churches against Fascism did not take place.[347]

It is worth noticing that Houston Chamberlain, one of the main sources of inspiration for Rosenberg, was almost uniformly positively received by BK members.[348]

1935 was the peak year of the Protestant participation in the Rosenberg debate. Gradually, the debate became increasingly strident until the authorities ultimately banned it in 1938 in fear of criticism of the government. Up until then, many of the critics had understood *"Mythus"* as Rosenberg's private work, but this understanding was undermined by measures by the authorities.[349]

After a while, both the DC and the BK experienced splits within their ranks, which did not help lessen the chaos within the Protestant camp. On top of this, there were Churches, which were not, or almost not, influenced by the strife, such as the strongly Nazi-influenced Church in Schleswig-Holstein and the DC Church in Thüringen, the latter of which was even influenced by the theosophically dominated *Deutsche Glaubensbewegung* of Jakob Wilhelm Hauer.[350]

In sharp contrast to the Catholic focus on the independence of their youth organizations, such matters did not receive much attention from Protestants. After the famous DC conference in Berlin in November 1933, *Reichsbishof* Müller felt his position weakened, both in his Church and in the Nazi Party. To restore confidence, not the least that of Hitler himself, he dissolved the Churches' youth organizations and incorporated them in the Nazi ones. In some places, this had happened even earlier when youth associations of the Inner Mission enthusiastically transferred themselves to the *Hitlerjugend*. Even Bishop Hans Meiser of Bavaria, who had been imprisoned because his Church had not accepted Müller as bishop, welcomed the transfer process.[351] Martin Niemöller tried to save the organizations, but failed because he had contacted President Hindenburg before his audience with Hitler.[352]

One more element contributing to the chaos in Protestant church life was the small group of clerics promoting what seems to have been the ultimate aim of the Nazis: *Nationalkirche*, i.e. the unification of all the "old" confessions, a prospect of alarm for the Catholics. It was not a new idea but had come up already in the broad discussions about nationalism during the Napoleonic period, and one of its advocates had been Fichte. By the 1930s, the most prominent advocate was the good friend of Albert Schweitzer, Emil Lind, who had belonged to the BK earlier. Because the project had so few adherents—one of them being the Old Catholic bishop and one or three ordinary Catholic priests—the Nazis obviously did not find supporting it opportune until the war had been won.[353]

1937 represented a turning point in the relationship between the regime and the Protestant Churches. The regime had announced free elections to ecclesiastical assemblies but postponed them several times hoping for reconciliation between the parties. When that did not happen, they simply abolished them and the BK especially was blamed for the fiasco. Thomas Fandel asserts that only after this did the bulk of Protestant churchgoers realize that the Nazi regime and party were no friends of the Church. Research from Bavaria indicates that a lot of clergymen left the Nazi Party and others, who were not party-members, kept their distance.[354]

Hitler's invasion of Czechoslovakia in March 1939 contributed to clarifying the differences between the BK and the DC even more. The BK supported the ecumenical condemnation of the invasion whereas the DC rebuffed it. Efforts were even made by the BK to coordinate their opposition with the Catholic clergy, but failed, partly because both groups wanted to avoid being accused of conspiracy and "stab-in-the-back" allegations.[355]

The main concentration camp for clerics was Dachau. Statistics from there illustrate the different treatment Catholics and Protestants received from the Nazis. 411 of the 447 German clerics were Catholics, with only 36 Protestants. Of these eight Catholics were executed and no Protestants. Three other Catholic priests were sentenced to death, but survived; no Protestant was sentenced.[356]

Due to the strong governmental control, the theological faculties played no significant role in the church struggle. There are indications, however, of controversies within some of them. The BK established its own high schools and teachers whom their leaders could trust.[357]

Ursula Büttner asserts that even after WWII *völkisch* opinions among some Protestant clerics still lingered on as late as the 1970s.[358]

Comparison between Catholic and Protestant Theological Basis for Policy towards the Jews

Both confessions have been accused of a lukewarm attitude in connection with the first Nazi persecution of the Jews. However, it is possible to discern a fundamental confessional difference in their reactions. In both confessions, prominent church leaders: Herman Kapler, president of the DEKA, and Cardinal Faulhaber of South Germany, wrote letters to their respective contacts in the USA as a response to the reactions from abroad to the first persecutions of Jews in spring 1933. Both were negative to the far-flung media criticism of the Hitler government. But their arguments differed. Faulhaber thought the foreign "howling chorus" only had had detrimental effects for the poor Jews and would continue to make it worse for the "tens of thousands" who suffered. Kapler seems to have thought that there had not been any persecution at all, and if there had been, there would be no reason to feel pity for them anyway. The media campaign was detrimental, not only because it was based on falsehoods, but would damage clerical liaison. He summed up curtly: "the government guarantees order and security. Impartial observations of the situation here is always possible, and desirable."[359]

Konrad Repgen asserts that all the German Catholic bishops adhered to three premises in their relationship to the Nazi authorities, principles that partly explain why the church did not involve itself more actively on behalf of the Jews:

1. It is not the task of the Church as a Church to conduct a political revolution.
2. The Church is not an institution for controlling the state that must protest every injustice committed by the state.
3. Even the totalitarian state is a state and has the right to demand the loyalty of Catholic Christians within the frame of the permissible. But when the laws of the state are in variance with Natural rights and God's Commands the following is mandatory: "*You should obey God more than man.*"³⁶⁰

Naturally, there was no shared Protestant basis for a policy towards Jews. It is worth comparing the three Catholic premises with the "doctrine" of the most prominent Jewish-friendly Protestant theologian, Dietrich Bonhoeffer from spring 1933.³⁶¹

Bonhoeffer's "*Eigengesetzlichkeits*" thesis differs fundamentally from the Catholic premises. Admittedly, the Catholics acknowledge the right of the totalitarian state to exist but, at the same time and in keeping with Augustine and Thomas Aquinas, restrict the frame of actions of such a state, and for all states for that matter. The difference is not insignificant. Taken to extremes, Bonhoeffer's "dogma" could allow the authorities freedom to carry out the policy towards the Jews that they pursued after 1941. Even Martin Dibelius, although he was no Nazi, had in May 1933 defended the authorities in their actions towards the Jews, partly based on his favored "*Schicksal*" theology which was based on the Idealistic-Metaphysical theology of history which implies the obligation of submission to the *Schicksal* (i.e. "destiny").³⁶² Even that Protestant theology did not give the Jews much better security. Besides, the Catholics would not agree at all with Bonhoeffer's assertion that, "history is not created by the church." What Dibelius thought about the "motor" of history is not known.

NOTES

1. Herbert Hömig, *Das preussische Zentrum in der Weimarer Republik* (Mainz: Matthias-Grünewald-Verlag, 1979) 16; Albrecht Langner, "Katholizismus und nationaler Gedanke in Deutschland," in Horst Zillessen (ed.), *Volk—Nation—Vaterland. Der deutsche Protestantismus und der Nationalismus* (Gütersloh: Verlagshaus Gerd Mohn, 1970) 248.

2. Helmut Walser Smith, *German Nationalism and Religious Conflict. Culture, Ideology, Politics, 1870–1914* (Princeton, NJ: Princeton University Press, 1995) 165, note 108, 226.

3. Wolfram Kaiser, *Christian Democracy and the Origins of European Union* (Cambridge: Cambridge University Press, 2007) 40.

4. Wolfgang Tilgner, "Volk, Nation und Vaterland im protestantischen Denken zwischen Kaiserreich und Nationalsozialismus (ca. 1870–1933)," in Zillessen (ed.), *Volk*, 151, 154–155, 160; Peter G. Maxwell-Stuart, *Pavene. Pavedømmet gjennom 2000 år* (Oslo: Forsythia forlag, 1998) 223; *Bergens Tidende*, May 18, 2008.

5. Karl Kupisch, "Der Protestantismus im Epochenjahr 1917," in Hans Joachim Schoeps (ed.), *Zeitgeist im Wandel. Band I. Das Wilhelminische Zeitalter* (Stuttgart: Ernst Klett Verlag, 1968) 37–40; Michael Peters, "Der "Alldeutsche Verband,"" in Uwe Puschner, Walter Schmitz & Justus H. Ulbricht (ed.) *Handbuch zur "Völkischen Bewegung" 1871–1918* (Munich: K. G. Saur Verlag, 1996) 312; Thomas Nipperdey, *Religion im Umbruch. Deutschland 1870–1918* (Munich: Verlag C. H. Beck, 1988) 100; Richard Steigmann-Gall, The Holy *Reich. Nazi Conceptions of Christianity* (Cambridge: Cambridge University Press, 2004) 16, with note 9.

6. Karl Kupisch, "Bürgerliche Frömmigkeit im Wilhelminischen Zeitalter," in Schoeps (ed.). *Zeitalter*, 48.

7. Peters, "Alldeutsche," 321; Kurt Töpner, "Der deutsche Katholizismus zwischen 1918 und 1933" in Hans Joachim Schoeps (ed.), *Zeitgeist im Wandel. Zeitgeist der Weimarer Republik* (Stuttgart: Ernst Klett Verlag, 1968) 179.

8. Heinrich August Winkler, *Weimar 1918–1933. Die Geschichte der ersten deutschen Demokratie* (Munich: Verlag C. H. Beck, 1994) 29, 64; Herbert Christ, Der politische *Protestantismus in der Weimarer Republik. Eine Studie über die politische Meinungsbildung durch die evangelischen Kirchen im Spiegel der Literatur und der Presse* (Bonn: Inaugural-dissertation, Rheinische Friedrich-Wilhelm-Universität zu Bonn, 1967) 111; Dieter Groh, "Der Umsturz von 1918 im Erlebnis der Zeitgenossen," in Schoeps (ed.) *Zeitgeist*, 14.

9. Jürgen Elvert, "A Microcosm of Society or the Key to a Majority in the Reichstag? The Centre Party in Germany," in Wolfram Kaiser & Helmut Wohnout (ed.), *Political Catholicism in Europe 1918–45*, Vol. 1 (London: Routledge, 2004) 49.

10. Geoffrey Pridham, *Hitler's Rise to Power* (London: Hart Davis, 1973) 154, note 7; Christ, *Protestantismus*, 69; Hans Peter Bleuel & Ernst Klinnert, *Deutsche Studenten auf dem Weg ins Dritte Reich* (Gütersloh: Sigbert Mohn Verlag, 1967) 107.

11. Kaiser, Democracy, 43; Bertold Spuler, *Regenten und Regierungen der Welt. Bd. 4: Neueste Zeit 1917/18–1964* (Würzburg: A. G. Ploetz Verlag, 1964) 296, 646; Hömig, *Zentrum*, 19

12. Markus Kreuzer, "*Parlamentarisation* and the Question of German Exceptionalism: 1867–1918," in *Central European History*, Vol. 36, Nr. 3, 2003, 338, 350; Elvert, "Microcosm," 49

13. Gabriele Clemens, *Martin Spahn und der Rechtskatholizismus in der Weimarer Republik* (Mainz: Matthias-Grünewald-Verlag, 1983) 86; Klaus Grosse Kracht, Vom *Gottesrecht zum Menschenrecht. Das katholische Staatsdenken in Deutschland von*

der Französischen Revolution bis zum II. Vatikanischen Konzil (1789–1965) (Paderborn: Ferdinand Schöningh Verlag, 2005) 1–2.

14. Ludwig Volk, *Der Bayerische Episkopat und der Nationalsozialismus 1930–1934* (Mainz: Matthias-Grünewald-Verlag, 1966) 6–7, 9; Hans Fenske, *Konservatismus und Rechtsradikalismus in Bayern nach 1918* (Bad Homburg: Verlag Gehlen, 1969) 305–306, 311.

15. Clemens, *Martin Spahn*, 61, 80–81, 90, 168–174, 204; Langner, "nationaler Gedanke," 258–260; Hubert Wolf, *Papst und Teufel. Die Archive des Vatikan und das Dritte Reich* (Munich: Verlag C. H. Beck, 2012) 77.

16. Langner, "nationaler Gedanke," 255.

17. Langner, "nationaler Gedanke," 238–243.

18. Klaus Breuning, *Die Vision des Reiches. Deutscher Katholizismus zwischen Demokratie und Diktatur* (1929–1934) (Munich: Max Hueber Verlag, 1969) 19–151, 154; Langner, "nationaler Gedanke," 251–258.

19. Breuning, *Vision*, 152–153; Sigmund Neumann, *Die Parteien der Weimarer Republik* (Stuttgart: Verlag W. Kohlhammer, 1977) 47.

20. Breuning, *Vision*, 278–290.

21. Wolfgang Stribrny, "Evangelische Kirche und Staat in der Weimarer Republik," in Schoeps (ed.) *Zeitgeist*, 160-162.

22. Tilgner, "Volk," 157.

23. Kupisch, "Epochenjahr," 48.

24. Reinhard Gaede, "Die Stellung des deutschen Protestantismus zum Problem von Krieg und Frieden während der Zeit der Weimarar Republik" in Wolfgang Huber & Johannes Schwerdtfeger (ed.) *Kirche zwischen Krieg und Frieden. Studien zur Geschichte des deutschen Protestantismus* (Stuttgart: Ernst Klett Verlag, 1976) 376–377; Kurt Nowak, *Evangelische Kirche und Weimarer Republik. Zum politischen Weg des deutschen Protestantismus zwischen 1918 und 1932* (Göttingen: Vandenhoeck & Ruprecht, 1981) 57; Steigmann-Gall, *Reich*, 16.

25. Wolfgang Michalka & Gottfried Niedhart, *Die ungeliebte Republik. Dokumente zur Innen- und Aussenpolitik Weimars 1918–1933* (Munich: Deutscher Taschenbuchverlag, 1981) 124–132; Winkler, *Weimar*, 93–95, 105.

26. Winkler, *Weimar*, 166.

27. Nowak, *Kirche*, 62–63; Christ, *Protestantismus*, 123–127.

28. Tilgner, "Volk," 160.

29. Gaede, "Stellung," 386–391, Kurt Meier, *Kreuz und Hakenkreuz. Die evangelische Kirche im Dritten Reich* (Munich: Deutscher Taschenbucverlag, 2008) 17, 19; Franz-Heinrich Philipp, "Protestantismus nach 1848," in Karl Heinrich Rengstorf & Siegfried von Kortzfleisch (ed.) *Kirche und Synagoge. Handbuch zur Geschichte von Christen und Juden* (Stuttgart: Klett Verlag, 1970) 347–350; Klaus-Martin Beckmann, "Zur Geschichte des "Völkischen" und des "Nationalen" im Umkreis der Ökumenischen Bewegung", in Zillessen (ed.), *Volk*, 218, 220, 226; Tilgner, "Volk," 167–168.

30. Christ, Protestantismus, 123–137; Gaede, "Stellung," 377–379; Nowak, *Kirche*, 61; Günter van Norden, "Der deutsche Protestantismus zwischen Patriotismus und Bekekenntnis," in Günter Heydemann & Lothar Kettenacker (ed.), *Kirchen*

in der Diktatur. Drittes Reich und SED-Staat (Göttingen: Vandenhoeck & Ruprecht, 1993) 91; Karl-Wilhelm Dahm, *Pfarrer und Politik. Soziale Position und politische Mentalität des deutschen evangelischen Pfarrerstandes zwischen 1918 und 1933* (Cologne: Westdeutscher Verlag, 1965) 178–179, 182.

31. Martin Greschat, "Protestantischer Antisemitismus in Wilhelminischer Zeit. Das Beispiel des Hofpredigers Adolf Stoecker," in Günter Brakelmann & Martin Rosowski, *Antisemitismus. Von religiöser Judenfeindschaft zur Rassenideologie* (Göttingen: Vandenhoeck & Ruprecht, 1989) 40.

32. Ursula Büttner, "Von der Kirche verlassen: Die deutschen Protestanten und die Verfolgung der Juden und Christen jüdischer Herkunft im "Dritten Reich,"" in Ursula Büttner & Martin Greschat (ed.), *Die verlassenen Kinder der Kirche. Der Umgang mit Christen jüdischer Herkunft im "Dritten Reich"* (Göttingen: Vandenhoeck & Ruprecht, 1998) 31–33; Rudolf Lill, "NS-Ideologie und Katholische Kirche," in Klaus Gotto & Konrad Repgen (ed.), *Die Katholiken und das Dritte Reich* (Mainz: Matthias-Grünewald-Verlag, 1990) 135; Norden, "Protestantismus," 92; Jochen Jacke, *Kirche zwischen Monarchie und Republik. Der preussische Protestantismus nach dem Zusammenbruch von 1918* (Hamburg: Hans Christians Verlag, 1976) 8-9.

33. Steigmann-Gall, *Reich*, 15; John S. Conway, "National Socialism and the Christian Churches during the Weimar Republic," in Peter D. Stachura, *The Nazi Machtergreifung* (London: George Allen & Unwin, 1983) 139–140. A comprehensive description of *"Politische Theologie"* in Klaus Scholder, *Die Kirchen und das Dritte Reich, Bd. 1. Vorgeschichte und Zeit der Illusionen 1918–1934* (Frankfurt/M: Verlag Ullstein, 1977) 147–176.

34. Steigmann-Gall, *Reich*, 34.

35. Christ, *Protestantismus*, 55–137; Dahm, *Pfarrer*, 173, 177–178.

36. Steigmann-Gall, *Reich*, 16–17.

37. Kupisch, "Bürgerliche Frömmigkeit," 45, 49; Töpner, "Katholizismus," 179–181, 198, note 20 and 21; See further chap. "The *Führer* Myth and Nazism as Political Messianism."

38. Winkler, *Weimar*, 294.

39. Dahm, *Pfarrer*, 25, 92; Nowak, *Kirche*, 283, 290–293; Kyle Jantzen, *Faith and Fatherland. Parish Politics in Hitler's Germany* (Minneapolis: Fortress Press, 2008) 20.

40. Gaede, "Stellung," 391.

41. Klaus Tanner, *Die fromme Verstaatlichung des Gewissens. Zur Auseinandersetzung um die Legitimität der Weimarer Reichsverfassung und Theologie der Zwanziger Jahre* (Göttingen: Vandenhoeck & Ruprecht, 1989) 30.

42. Olav A. Abrahamsen & Andreas Aase, *Portal. Verden etter 1850* (Oslo: Det norske Samlaget, 2004) 107.

43. Tanner, *Verstaatlichung*, 88–89; Kurt Sontheimer, *Antidemokratisches Denken in der Weimarer Republik. Die politischen Ideen des deutschen Nationalismus zwischen 1918 und 1933* (Munich: Nymphenburger Verlagshandlung, 1964) 336–337.

44. Tanner, *Verstaatlichung*, 37–38, 43–47.

45. Sontheimer, *Denken*; Tanner, *Verstaatlichung*.

46. Tanner, *Verstaatlichung*, 65, 68, 73–77; Hans M. Bringeland, *Martin Dibelius' oppgjer med nasjonalsosialismen. Ei jamføring med andre teologar sin krititkk, særlig Bultmanns og Barths* (Unpublished manuscript for lecture attached to submission of PhD, University of Bergen, 12.15.2011) 11.

47. Tanner, *Verstaatlichung*, 66–67.

48. Sontheimer, *Denken*, 323.

49. Sontheimer, *Denken*, 336–337, with note 75; Tanner, *Verstaatlichung*, 29, 179, 187–191, 194–196, 284–288.

50. Nowak, *Kirche*, 177–179.

51. Fenske, *Konservatismus*, 9.

52. Breuning, *Vision*, 152–153.

53. George G. Windell, *The Catholics and German Unity 1866–1871* (Minneapolis: University of Minnesota Press, 1954) 284.

54. Karl Buchheim, *Geschichte der christlichen Parteien in Deutschland* (Munich: Kösel Verlag, 1953) 205–208; Kaiser, *Democracy*, 47–48.

55. See chap."*Catholic Nationalism.*"

56. Kaiser, *Democracy*, 30; Karl Heinrich Höfele, *Geist und Gesellschaft der Bismarckzeit (1870–1890)* (Göttingen: Musterschmidt Verlag, 1967) 374–377.

57. Ute Schmidt, *Zentrum oder CDU. Politischer Katholizismus zwischen Tradition und Anpassung* (Opladen: Westdeutscher Verlag, 1987) 76–84.

58. Günter Grünthal, *Reichsschulgesetz und Zentrumspartei in der Weimarer Republik* (Düsseldorf: Droste Verlag, 1968) 22–26; Klaus Schönhoven, *Die Bayerische Volkspartei 1924–1932* (Düsseldorf: Droste Verlag, 1972) 22, 252; Scholder, *Kirchen. Band 1. 1977*, 5–6; Nowak, *Kirche*, 27–28.

59. Nowak, *Kirche*, 93–94; Kaiser, *Democracy*, 47–48.

60. Buchheim, *Parteien*, 415–416.

61. See chap. "Catholic Involvement in Politics versus Protestant "*Eigengesetzlichkeitsthese*" (Separate Jurisdictions Dogma)."

62. Dahm, *Pfarrer*, 111–112.

63. Nipperdey, *Umbruch*, 110–111.

64. Buchheim, *Parteien*, 282.

65. Nowak, *Kirche*, 152–154.

66. Stribrny, "*Kirche*," 164, 167–168, 173.

67. Hans Mommsen, *Die Deutschen und der Holocaust* (Bonn: Friedrich Ebert Stiftung, 2006) 545; Dahm, *Pfarrer*, 110; Buchheim, *Parteien*, 396–400; Nowak, *Kirche*, 263–264.

68. Nowak, *Kirche*, 149–150.

69. Ernst Klee, *Personenlexikon zum Dritten Reich* (Frankfurt/M: Fischer, 2005) 456.

70. Gerhard Schäfer, *Die evangelische Landeskirche in Württemberg und der Nationalsozialismus. Eine Dokumentation zum Kirchenkampf. Bd. 1 Um das politische Engagement der Kirche 1932–1933* (Stuttgart: Calwer Verlag, 1971) 134; Buchheim, *Parteien*, 292–293, 375–394.

71. Dahm, *Pfarrer*, 110, with note 263; Neumann, *Parteien*, 70; Nowak, *Kirche*, 263–267; Scholder, *Kirchen. Band 1*. 1977, 176.

72. Buchheim, *Parteien*, 177–182, 293–294.
73. Wilhelm Mommsen, *Deutsche Parteiprogramme* (Munich: Olzog, 1960) 545, 547.
74. Buchheim, *Parteien*, 377; Josef Goebbels, *Wetterleuchten. Aufsätze aus der Kampfzeit (2. Band "der Angriff")* (Munich: Franz Eher Nachfolger, 1939) 211.
75. Nowak, *Kirche*, 268.
76. Nowak, *Kirche*, 265, 268–269, with note 37, 270; Schäfer, *Württemberg*, 118.
77. Stribrny, "Kirche, 173.
78. Sebastian Haffner, *Germany, Jekyll and Hyde. An Eyewitness of Nazi Germany* (London: Abacus, 2008), 188.
79. Haffner, *Jekyll*, 188.
80. Haffner, *Jekyll*, 166–167.
81. Andreas Wirsching, "Weit entfernt von simplen Antworten," Interview mit A. W. in *SPIEGEL SPECIAL*, Nr. 1, 2008, 22.
82. Buchheim, *Parteien*, 406.
83. Anthony Kauders, *German Politics and the Jews. Düsseldorf and Nuremberg 1910–1933* (Oxford: Clarendon Press, 1996) 158–159.
84. Kaiser, *Democracy*, 25, 64; Tore Nedrebø, *Past and Present Sources of European Union. A Comparative Historical-Institutional Analysis* (Dissertation for the degree of *doctor philosophiae* (Dr. Philos), University of Bergen, 2010) 278–279.
85. Martin Conway, "Catholic Politics or Christian Democracy? The Evolution of Inter-war Political Catholicism," in Kaiser & Wohmout, *Political Catholicism*, 237.
86. See further chap.""Black-Red-Gold" versus"Black-White-Red.""
87. Kaiser, *Democracy*, 36–37.
88. Nedrebø, *European Union*, 298; Guido Müller, "Anticipated Exile of Catholic Democrats: The Sécretariat International des Partis Démocratiques d'Inspiration Chrétienne," in Kaiser & Wohnout, *Political Catholicism*, 252, with note 1; Kaiser, *Democracy*, 86, 91, 103, 111.
89. Nedrebø, *European Union*, 278–279; Kaiser, *Democracy*, 76–78, 99–100.
90. Kaiser, *Democracy*, 43, 62–63, 65.
91. Helmut Walser Smith, *The Continuities of German History. Nation, Religion, and Race across the Long Nineteenth Century* (N. Y.: Cambridge University Press, 2008) 61; Gary King, Ori Rosen, Martin Tanner & Alexander F. Wagner, "Ordinary Voting Behaviour in the Extraordinary Election of Adolf Hitler," in *Journal of Economic History, Vol. 68, No. 4*, 2008, 962; Fichte, Johann Gottlieb, *Der geschlossene Handelsstaat. Ein philosophischer Entwurf als Anhang zur Rechtslehre und Probe einer künftig zu liefernden Politik*, http://www.zeno.org/Philosophie/ (Berlin: 1845/46) 3. *Buch*, chapters 3, 4, and 7; Eli F. Heckscher, *Industrialismen. Den ekonomiska utvecklingen sedan 1750* (Stockholm: Kooperativa förlbundets bokförlag, 1944) 344–346; Walter Anger, *Das Dritte Reich in Dokumenten* (Frankfurt/M: Europäische Verlagsanstalt, 1957) chapter V, Doc. 16., 42.
92. Ernst Wolf, "Volk, Nation, Vaterland im protestantischen Denken von 1930 bis zur Gegenwart," in Zillessen (ed.), *Volk*, 190.

93. Karl Unruh, *Langemarck. Legende und Wirklichkeit* (Bonn: Bernard & Graefe Verlag, 1997) 9.

94. Bernt Hüppauf, "The Birth of Fascist Man from the Spirit of the Front. From Langemarck to Verdun," in John Milfull (ed.), *The Attraction of Fascism. Social Psychology and Aesthetics of the "triumph of the Right"* (N. Y.: Berg Publishers, 1990) 46.

95. Bleuel & Klinnert, *Studenten*, 262; Jonathan Harwell, *Myth and Monument: Memory of the Great War in Britain and Germany* (Williamstown, Mass.: Dissertation, 1999), chapters 2 and 4; Sontheimer, *Denken*, 135.

96. Wolfgang Borchert, *Draussen vor der Tür und ausgewählte Erzählungen* (Hamburg: Rowohlt Taschenbuch Verlag, 1972) 49, 82, 115.

97. Steigmann-Gall, *Reich*, 16; Nowak, *Kirche*, 53–55.

98. Sarah Gordon, *Hitler, Germans, and the "Jewish Question"* (Princeton, NJ: Princeton University Press, 1984) 51; Scholder, *Kirchen. Band 1.* 1977, 98.

99. Rolf Hobson, *Dolchstosslegende und politische Desintegration. Das Trauma der Deutschen. Niederlage im Ersten Weltkrieg 1914–1933* (Düsseldorf: Droste Verlag, 2003) 352, 354, 356.

100. Hobson, *Dolchstosslegende*, 356.

101. Steigmann-Gall, *Reich*, 13.

102. Anders Granås Kjøstvedt, *Hitler's Metropolis? The National Socialist Movement in Berlin 1925–1933* (Oslo: PhD-thesis, University of Oslo, 2010) 25–27, with notes 26–31; Helmut Berding, *Moderner Antisemitismus in Deutschland* (Franfurt/M: Suhrkamp Verlag, 1988) 187–189.

103. Berding, *Antisemitismus*, 182–186.

104. Berding, *Antisemitismus*, 178–189; Walter Jung, *Ideologische Voraussetzungen, Inhalte und Ziele aussenpolitischer Programmatik und Propaganda in der deutschvölkischen Bewegung der Anfangsjahre der Weimarer Republik—Das Beispiel Deutschvölkischer Schutz- und Trutzbund* (Göttingen: PhD-thesis, Georg-August-Universität, 2001) Abstract; Trond Berg Eriksen, Håkon Harket & Einhart Lorenz, *Jødehat. Antisemittismens historie fra antikken til i dag* (Oslo: Cappelen Damm, 2009) 387–388.

105. Derek Hastings, *Catholicism and the Roots of Nazism. Religious Identity and National Socialism* (N. Y.: Oxford University Press, 2010) 69–70; Eriksen, Harket & Lorenz, *Jødehat*, 189

106. Hastings, *Roots of Nazism*, 4.

107. Hastings, *Roots of Nazism*, 64–67, 70–72.

108. Adrian Hastings, *The Construction of Nationhood. Ethnicity, Religion and Nationalism* (Cambridge: Cambridge University Press, 1997) 387–388; Hastings, *Roots of Nazism*, 9–12, 16–22, 33.

109. Hastings, *Roots of Nazism*, 47, 52–57, 60–67, 70–72.

110. Konrad Heiden, *A History of National Socialism* (N. Y.: Octagon Books, 1971) 99.

111. Hastings, *Roots of Nazism*, 74, 79–80.

112. Hastings, *Roots of Nazism*, 84–100, 107–110, 142.

113. Hastings, *Nationhood*, 404; Hastings, *Roots of Nazism*, 98, 115.
114. Hastings, *Roots of Nazism*, 129–135.
115. Hastings, *Nationhood*, 403; Hastings, *Roots of Nazism*, 114.
116. Hastings, *Roots of Nazism*, 135–140.
117. Hastings, *Nationhood*, 421; Kevin P. Spicer, *Hitler's Priests. Catholic Clergy and National Socialism* (DeKalb, Ill.: Northern Illinois University Press, 2008) 31, 49–50; Hastings, *Roots of Nazism*, 141–142.
118. *Der Theologe 4*, 16; Wieland Vogel, *Katholische Kirche und Nationale Kampfverbände in der Weimarer Republik* (Mainz: Matthias-Grünewald-Verlag, 1989) 39; Pridham, *Hitler's Rise*, 152; Steigmann-Gall, *Reich*, 57; Hastings, *Nationhood*, 422–423; Volk, *Episkopat*, 18–19; Wolf, *Papst*, 155; Hastings, *Roots of Nazism*, 144–146.
119. Hastings, *Roots of Nazism*, 147–149.
120. Walter Hannot, *Die Judenfrage in der katholischen Tagespresse Deutschlands und Österreichs 1923–1933* (Mainz: Matthias-Grünewald-Verlag, 1990) 103–110.
121. Volk, *Episkopat*, 17.
122. Thomas Childers, *The Nazi Voter. The Social Foundations of Fascism in Germany, 1919–1933* (Chapel Hill: The University of North Carolina Press, 1983) 113–115; Fenske, *Konservatismus*, 312.
123. Hastings, *Nationhood*, 399, note 47; Hastings, *Roots of Nazism*, 105.
124. Cremer, Douglas J., ""To avoid a new Kulturkampf": the Catholic Workers' Associations and National Socialism in Weimar-era Bavaria," http://www.highbeam.com/doc/ in *Journal of Church and State*, Sept. 1999, 1; Hastings, *Nationhood*, 400–401; Hannot, *Tagespresse*, 102; Volk, *Episkopat*, 14; Hastings, *Roots of Nazism*, 100–106.
125. Hastings, *Roots of Nazism*, 102–104, 116–117.
126. Hubert Cancik, "Erbschaft jener Zeit," in Hubert Cancik (ed.), *Religions- und Geistesgeschichte der Weimarer Republik* (Düsseldorf: Patmos Verlag, 1982) 9; Volk, Episkopat, 14–15; Kratz, Peter, "*Alles schon mal dagewesen! Zehn Thesen zu New Age und Faschismus*," http://home.snafu.de/biff/NA0.htm (Unpublished manuscript of lecture held at the first antifascist "Colloquium des DISS" Dec. 8 and 9 1989).
127. Volk, *Episkopat*, 15; Ernst Piper, *Alfred Rosenberg—Hitler's Chefideologe* (Munich: Karl Blessing Verlag, 2005) 223, 230; Kevin P. Spicer, "Working for the Führer: Father Dr. Philip Haeuser and the Third Reich," in Kevin P. Spicer (ed.), *Antisemitism, Christian Ambivalence, and the Holocaust* (Bloomington: Indiana University Press, 2007) 97.
128. Björn Mensing, *Pfarrer und Nationalsozialismus. Geschichte einer Verstrickung am Beispiel der Evangelisch-Lutherischen Kirche in Bayern* (Göttingen: Vandenhoeck & Ruprecht, 1998) 72–78, with note 19, 94.
129. Mensing, *Pfarrer*, 78–80
130. Mensing, *Pfarrer*, 72–80, with notes 19, 94.
131. Mensing, *Pfarrer*, 83–88, 91; Hastings, *Roots of Nazism*, 160–162.
132. Steigmann-Gall, *Reich*, 56–57; Terje Emberland, *Religion og rase. Nyhedenskap og nazisme i Norge 1933–1945* (Oslo: Humanist Forlag, 2003) 26; Kurt

Meier, *Evangelische Kirche in Gesellschaft, Staat und Politik 1918–1945. Aufsätze zur kirchlichen Zeitgeschichte* (Berlin: Evangelische Verlagsanstalt, 1987) 41; Adolf Hitler, *Mein Kampf* (Munich: Franz Eher Nachfolger, 1940) 631–633.

133. Steigmann-Gall, *Reich*, 89; Scholder, *Kirchen. Band 1*. 1977, 139–144; Alfred Rosenberg, *Der Mythus des 20. Jahrhunderts. Eine Wertung der seelisch-geistigen Gestaltenkämpfe unserer Zeit* (Munich: Hoheneichen-Verlag, 1942) 6–7; Emberland, *Religion*, 45–46, 57–63.

134. George L. Mosse, *The Crisis of German Ideology* (N. Y.: Howard Fertig, 1998) 229–231; Hastings, *Roots of Nazism*, 157; Emberland, *Religion*, 32; Steigmann-Gall, *Reich*, 64, with note 60, 65; Nowak, *Kirche*, 153–157; Barton, Dennis, *Hitler's Rise to Power. Part 2*, The Church in History Information Centre www.church-in-history.org X. *Sources of Prejudice*; Pridham, *Hitler's Rise*, 149; Uriel Tal, *Religion, Politics and Ideology in the Third Reich. Selected Essays* (N. Y.: Routledge, Taylor & Francis Group, 2004) 113, note 12.

135. Hitler, *Mein Kampf*, 190, 236–237, 294, 402, 553, 699, 705, 748; Steigmann-Gall, *Reich*, 65–66.

136. Meier, *Evangelische Kirche*, 41; Hitler, *Mein Kampf*, 315, 361–362; Rainer Flasche, "Religionsmodelle und Erkenntnisprinzipien der Religionswissenschaft in der Weimarer Zeit," in Cancik (ed.), *Geistesgeschichte*, 276, with note 91.

137. Pridham, *Hitler's Rise*, 150, 151, 155.

138. Hastings, *Roots of Nazism*, 157–168; See further chapter "The *Führer* Myth and Nazism as Political Messianism."

139. Meier, *Evangelische Kirche*, 41, 43–44, 48, Meier, *Hakenkreuz*, 11–12; Kjøstvedt, *Hitler's Metropolis*, 255.

140. Nowak, "Christuskreuz," 216-217

141. Vogel, *Kampfverbände*, 34

142. Vogel, *Kampfverbände*, 11-12, 14-16, 31-33, 36; Martin Liepach, *Das Wahlverhalten der jüdischen Bevölkerung in der Weimarer Republik* (Tübingen: J. C. Mohr (Paul Siebeck), 1996) 102; Kauders, *German Politics*, 118.

143. Vogel, *Kampfverbände*, 26–28; Liepach, *Wahlverhalten*, 102.

144. Vogel, *Kampfverbände*, 37, with note 18, 39, 41; Spicer, *Priests*, 50.

145. Vogel, *Kampfverbände*, 55–77, 99–102, 113–114, 159–161, 163, 165, 341.

146. Andreas Dörner, *Politischer Mythos und symbolische Politik. Sinnstiftung durch symbolische Formen am Beispiel des Hermannsmythos* (Opladen/Wiesbaden: Westdeutscher Verlag, 1995) 344–345.

147. Karl Rohe, *Das Reichsbanner Schwarz-Rot-Gold. Ein Beitrag zur Geschichte und Struktur der polistischen Kampfverbände zur Zeit der Weimarer Republik* (Düsseldorf: Droste Verlag, 1966) 312–313; Vogel, *Kampfverbände*, 218-219.

148. Vogel, *Kampfverbände*, 202–205, 208, 213–216, 220, 240; Rohe, *Reichsbanner*, 74, 288, 374, with note 3, 266–267, 279–314, 379–391; Karl Dietrich Bracher, *Die Auflösung der Weimarer Republik. Eine Studie zum Problem des Machtverfalls in der Demokratie* (Villingen/Schwarzwald: Ring Verlag, 1964) 144, 287; Bengt Hagelstein/H.-U. Ludewig, *Die Militarisierung der Gesellschaft: die paramilitären Verbände. Das Reichsbanner Schwarz-Rot-Gold, Bund republikanischer Kriegsteilnehmer und Der Rote Frontkämpferbund* (Braunschweig: Report of lecture by Dr.

H.-U. Ludewig at "Historisches Seminar," Technische Universität Braunschweig, Summer 2001).

149. Vogel, *Kampfverbände*, 226, 228–229, 234.

150. Whitney Smith, *Flags through the Ages and across the World* (Maidenhead: McGraw-Hill Book Co., 1975) 116–122; George L. Mosse, *Die Nationalisierung der Massen. Politische Symbolik und Massenbewegungen von den Befreiungskriegen bis zum Dritten Reich* (Frankfurt/M: Campus Verlag, 1993) 58; Hagen Schulze, "Die deutsche Nationalbewegung bis zur Reichseinigung," in Otto Büsch & James J. Sheehan (ed.), *Die Rolle der Nation in der deutschen Geschichte und Gegenwart. Beiträge zu einer internationalen Konferenz in Berlin (West) vom 16. bis 18. Juni 1983* (Berlin: Colloquium Verlag, 1985) 107; Bleuel & Klinnert, *Studenten*, 113–115.

151. Rohe, *Reichsbanner*, 229–230.

152. Michalka & Niedhart, *Die ungeliebte Republik*, 72, 255–256; Philip Bernard Wiener, "Die Parteien der Mitte," in Werner Mosse (ed.), *Entscheidungsjahr 1932. Zur Judenfrage in der Weimarer Republik* (Tübingen: J. C. B. Mohr (Paul Siebeck), 1966) 318–319; Werner Jochmann, "Die Funktion des Antisemitismus in der Weimarer Republik," in Brakelmann & Rosowski (ed.), *Antisemitismus*, 159; Kauders, *German Politics*, 180–181.

153. Hitler, *Mein Kampf*, 551–557.

154. Marx, Karl, *Manifest der kommunistischen Partei* http://gutenberg.spiegel.de/buch/ (Paris: 1848) "III. 1c. Der deutsche oder "wahre" Sozialismus"; Peter Pulzer, *The Rise of Political Anti-Semitism in Germany & Austria* (Cambridge, Mass.: Harvard University Press, 1988) 303; Clemens, *Martin Spahn*, 118–133; Dühring, Eugen, *Cursus der Philosophie als streng wissenschaftlicher Weltanschauung und Lebensgestaltung*, http://archive.org/details/ (Leipzig: L. Heimann's Verlag, 1875) 325; Berding, *Antisemitismus,* 94; Klaus von See, *Die Ideen von 1789 und die Ideen von 1914. Völkisches Denken in Deutschland zwischen Französischer Revolution und Erstem Weltkrieg* (Frankfurt/M: Akademische Verlagsgesellschaft Athenaion, 1975) 113; Sontheimer, *Denken*, 341–353; Barton, X. *Sources of Prejudice*; Emberland, *Religion*, 23.

155. Piper, *Rosenberg—Chefideologe*, 150.

156. Richard Hamilton, *Who voted for Hitler?* (Princeton, NJ: Princeton University Press, 1982) 249–250; Wiener, "Parteien," 289–306; Reinhard Rürup, "Emanzipation und Krise. Zur Geschichte der "Judenfrage" in Deutschland vor 1890," in Werner E. Mosse (ed.), *Juden im Wilhelminischen Deutschland 1890–1914* (Tübingen: J. C. B. Mohr (Paul Siebeck), 1976) 54, with note 149; Vogel, *Kampfverbände*, 303. Besides, in 1918 von der Goltz had contributed considerably in saving Finland from Bolshevik takeover.

157. Piper, *Rosenberg—Chefideologe*, 424.

158. Vogel, *Kampfverbände*, 235, 342.

159. Rohe, *Reichsbanner*, 202, 206, 288–289, 296–297.

160. Rohe, *Reichsbanner*, 147–148.

161. Vogel, *Kampfverbände*, 246–248; Rohe, *Reichsbanner*, 290.

162. Bracher, *Auflösung*, 144; Josef & Ruth Becker, *Hitlers Machtergreifung. Dokumente vom Machtantritt Hitlers 30. Januar 1933 bis zur Besiegelung des Einpartei-*

enstaates 14. Juli 1933 (Munich: Deutscher Taschenbuchverlag, 1983) 415–416; 418, 420; Rohe, *Reichsbanner*, 222, note 2; Jürgen Aretz, *Katholische Arbeiterbewegung und Nationalsozialismus. Der Verband katholischer Arbeiter- und Knappenvereine Westdeutschlands 1923–1945* (Mainz: Matthias-Grünewald-Verlag, 1982) 62–63, with note 122; William L. Patch, *Christian Trade Unions in the Weimar Republic, 1918–1933. The Failure of "Corporate Pluralism"* (New Haven: Yale University Press, 1985) 208–209.

163. Rohe, *Reichsbanner*, 377; Volk, *Episkopat*, 67; *Historisches Lexikon Bayerns*, Entry, "Bayernwacht."

164. Vogel, *Kampfverbände*, 280–282, 284–285.

165. Pridham, *Hitler's Rise*, 155.

166. Vogel, *Kampfverbände*, 299–300, 302–303, 342–350.

167. Vogel, *Kampfverbände*, 308–309; Jonathan R. C. Wright, *"Über den Parteien," Die politische Haltung der evangelischen Kirchenführer 1918–1933* (Göttingen: Vandenhoeck & Ruprecht, 1977) 99–100, 237.

168. Benöhr-Laqueur, Susanne, *Generation des Unbedingten. Das Führungskorps des Reichssicherungshauptamtes* (Book review of Michael Wildt) http://hsozkult. geschichte.hu-berlin.de/rezensionen/NS-2003-1-062 (Hamburg: HISVerlag, 2002).

169. Cremer, "Kulturkampf," 1; Aretz, *Arbeiterbewegung*, 45–4.

170. Aretz, *Arbeiterbewegung*, 45, note 3; Alfred Rosenberg, *Kampf um die Macht. Aufsätze von 1921–1932* (Selected articles from *Völkischer Beobachter*) (Munich: Franz Eher Nachfolger, 1937) 379.

171. Aretz, *Arbeiterbewegung*, 12, 17, 29–30, 32–33.

172. Steigmann-Gall, *Reich*, 43.

173. Michael Schneider, *Die Christlichen Gewerkschaften 1894–1933* (Bonn: Verlag Neue Gesellschaft, 1982) 126–127, 457–458, 628–633, 771; Patch, *Trade Unions*, 22.

174. Buchheim, *Parteien*, 402.

175. Patch, *Trade Unions*, 188–194.

176. Patch, *Trade Unions*, 194.

177. Patch, *Trade Unions*, 195–196.

178. Patch, *Trade Unions*, 196, 199, 205, 209–211.

179. Kaiser, *Democracy*, 43, 62–63; Wiener, "Parteien," 292–297.

180. Conway, M., "Catholic Politics," 237.

181. Hubert Jedin, "Kirche und Katholizismus im Deutschland des 19. Jahrhunderts," in Anton Rauscher (ed.), *Entwicklungslinien des deutschen Katholizismus* (Munich: Ferdinand Schöningh, 1973) 75; Walser Smith, *Conflict*, 44; Guenther Lewy, The *Catholic Church and Nazi Germany*. (Boston: Da Capo Press, 2000) 4–5; Barbara Schellenberger, *Katholische Jugend und Drittes Reich. Eine Geschichte des Katholischen Jungmännerverbandes 1933–1939 unter besonderer Berücksichtigung der Rheinprovinz* (Mainz: Matthias-Grünewald-Verlag, 1975) XXIII, 5; Hans Maier, "Zum Standort des deutschen Katholizismus in Gesellschaft, Staat und Kultur," in Rauscher, *Entwicklungslinien*, 46.

182. Spuler, *Regenten. Bd. 4,* 71–73, 131–132, 295–296, 419–420, 474–477, 646–647.

183. Pulzer, *Anti-Semitism*, 267; H. Roos, "Katolsk politisk teori," in Svend Erik Stybe (ed.), *Politiske ideologier. Fra Platon til Mao* (Copenhagen: Politikens Forlag, 1979) 54–55.
184. Liepach, *Wahlverhalten*, 114.
185. Thomas Fandel, *Konfession und Nationalsozialismus. Evangelische und Katholische Pfarrer in der Pfalz 1930–1939* ((Munich: Ferdinand Schöningh, 1997) 93.
186. Rohe, *Reichsbanner*, 309; Wiener, "Parteien," 292–306; Walser Smith, *Continuities*, 178.
187. Rohe, *Wahlen*, 68.
188. Martin Greschat, "Friedrich Weissler. Ein Jurist der Bekennenden Kirche im Widerstand gegen Hitler," in Büttner & Greschat (ed.), *Die verlassenen Kinder*, 105, note 34; Olaf Blaschke, *Katholizismus und Antisemitismus im Deutschen Kaiserreich* (Göttingen: Vandenhoeck & Ruprecht, 1999) 217; Mosse, *Crisis*, 135, 193; Norbert Kampe, *Studenten und "Judenfrage" im Deutschen Kaiserreich. Die Entstehung einer akademischen Trägerschicht des Antisemitismus* (Göttingen: Vandenhoeck & Ruprecht, 1998) 138.
189. Walser Smith, *Conflict*, 121, 125–126; Hans Kohn, *The Mind of Germany, the Education of a Nation* (N. Y.: Charles Scribner's Sons, 1960) 287.
190. Kohn, *The Mind*, 61–62, note; Daniel Jonah Goldhagen, *Hitler's Willing Executioners. Ordinary Germans and the Holocaust* (London: Abacus, 1997) 83; Bleuel & Klinnert, *Studenten*, 30.
191. Fritz Bolle, "Darwinismus und Zeitgeist," in Schoeps (ed.), *Zeitgeist*, 287.
192. Buchheim, *Parteien*, 285; Mosse, *Crisis*, 219–220.
193. Werner E. Mosse, "Der Niedergang der Weimarer Republik und die Juden," in W. Mosse, *Entscheidungsjahr*, 7–8.
194. Rudolf Morsey, "Die katholische Volksminderheit und der Aufstieg des Nationalsozialismus 1930–1933," in Gotto & Repgen (ed.), *Die Katholiken*, 16.
195. Hermann Greive, *Theologie und Ideologie. Katholizismus und Judentum in Deutschland und Österreich 1918–1935* (Heidelberg: Verlag Lambert Schneider, 1969) 207.
196. Hannot, *Tagespresse*, 126, 238; Pridham, *Hitler's Rise*, 156, 160; Childers, *Nazi Voter*, 189, 325, note 225; Aretz, *Arbeiterbewegung*, 238.
197. Hannot, *Tagespresse*, 133–134.
198. Piper, *Rosenberg—Chefideologe*, 183, 189–191; Rosenberg, *Mythus*, 71, 77–78, 614.
199. Francois Bédarida, "Nationalsozialistische Verkündigung und säkuläre Religion," in Michael Ley & Julius H. Schoeps (ed.) *Der Nationalsozialismus als politische Religion* (Bodenheim bei Mainz: Philo Verlagsgesellschaft, 1997) 162; Baumgärtner, *Weltanschauungskampf*, 260; Rosenberg, *Mythus*, 618, 701.
200. Spicer, *Priests*, 78–81, 88, 93, 97, 160, 257–258.
201. Falter, *Hitlers Wähler*, 189.
202. Pridham, *Hitler's Rise*, 162; Piper, *Rosenberg—Chefideologe*, 186.
203. Rosenberg, *Mythus*, 84–85, 129, 183, 397.

204. Steigmann-Gall, *Reich*, 98–99.
205. Piper, *Rosenberg—Chefideologe*, 409; Pridham, *Hitler's Rise*, 162; Letter to the author from Professor Anders Kjøstvedt May 26, 2010.
206. See chap."CHRISTIAN YOUTH ASSOCIATIONS AND NAZISM"; Steigmann-Gall, *Reich*, 91–94, 120, 125, 131, note 86; Iber, *Glaube*, 153–167.
207. Hannot, *Tagespresse*, 125–126; Pridham, *Hitler's Rise*, 156, 161; Breuning, *Vision*, 171.
208. Berding, *Antisemitismus*, 208.
209. Piper, *Rosenberg—Chefideologe*, 187.
210. Ernst Piper, "Alfred Rosenberg—der Prophet des Seelenkrieges. Der gläubige Nazi in der Führungselite des nationalsozialistischen Staates," in Michael Ley & Julius H. Schoeps (ed.), *Der Nationalsozialismus als politische Religion* (Bodenheim bei Mainz: Philo Verlagsgesellschaft, 1997) 115–116; see chap."The Protestant Church and the Third Reich."
211. Pridham, *Hitler's Rise*, 163.
212. Morsey, "Volksminderheit," 17; George L. Mosse, "Die Deutsche Rechte und die Juden," in W. Mosse (ed.), *Entscheidungsjahr, 15;* Gerhard Besier, *Die Kirchen und das Dritte Reich. Bd. 3. Spaltungen und Abwehrkämpfe 1934–1937* (Berlin: Propyläen Verlag, 2001) 222; Walter Hofer, *Der Nationalsozialismus. Dokumente 1933–1945* (Frankfurt/M: Fischer Bücherei, 1957) Dok. 65, 128; Nowak, *Evangelische Kirche*, 314; Schäfer, *Württemberg*, 105; Pridham, *Hitler's Rise*, 164; Meier, *Evangelische Kirche*, 46–47; Fandel, *Konfession*, 42.
213. Pridham, *Hitler's Rise*, 164; Morsey, "Volksminderheit," 12; Meier, *Evangelische* Kirche, 44.
214. Fandel, *Konfession*, 27–28.
215. Greive, *Theologie*, 198–199; Scholder, *Kirchen. Band 1.* 1977, 195–197; Müller, "Anticipated," 6, note 4, 13–38; Morsey, "Volksminderheit," 12–14; Volk, *Episkopat*, 23–25; Pridham, Hitler's Rise, 167.
216. Volk, *Episkopat*, 44; Wolf, *Papst*, 170.
217. Volk, *Episkopat*, 31.
218. Volk, *Episkopat*, 32.
219. Volk, *Episkopat*, 33; Wolf, *Papst*, 170–172.
220. Rosenberg, *Kampf*, 716–719.
221. Rosenberg, *Mythus*, 6–7, 9.
222. Fandel, *Konfession*, 35–39; Altgeld, *Katholizismus*, 43.
223. Breuning, *Vision*, 160.
224. Morsey, "Volksminderheit," 17; Kjøstvedt, *Hitler's Metropolis*, 256; Childers, *Nazi Voter*, 258–259.
225. Volk, *Episkopat*, 44–45.
226. Volk, *Episkopat*, 48; Pridham, *Hitler's Rise*, 178–179.
227. Müller, *Kirche*, 43.
228. Müller, *Kirche*, 43.
229. Aretz, *Arbeiterbewegung*, 59, 61–62.
230. Müller, *Kirche*, 6, note 5, 23, 42; Schellenberger, *Jugend*, 23–26, 28–30.

231. Heinrich Küppers, *Der katholische Lehrerverband in der Übergangszeit von der Weimarer Republik zur Hitler-Diktatur* (Mainz: Matthias-Grünewald-Verlag, 1975) 93–95, 99–101, 120, note 44.

232. Marjorie Lamberti, "German Schoolteachers, National Socialism, and the Politics of Culture at the End of the Weimar Republic," in *Central European History*, Vol. 34, No. 1 ((Riverside Cal., 2001) 64–68. 79–80; Küppers, *Lehrerverband*, 104–105, 107, with note 103.

233. Müller, *Kirche*, 6–7.

234. Fandel, *Konfession*, 49–51.

235. Müller, *Kirche*, 7–8, with note 11.

236. Scholder, *Kirchen. Band 1.* 1977, 194.

237. Liepach, *Wahlverhalten*, 174–176, 201–206.

238. Scholder, *Kirchen. Band 1.* 1977, 197.

239. Scholder, *Kirchen. Band 1.* 1977, 195.

240. Christ, *Protestantismus*, 105.

241. Conway, J., "National Socialism," 137–138.

242. Nowak, *Kirche*, 210–215, 294, 308–30.

243. Falter, *Hitlers Wähler*, 1; Nowak, *Kirche*, 297; Scholder, *Kirchen. Band 1.* 1977, 194, 199–212.

244. Conway, J., "National Socialism," 137–138.

245. Schäfer, *Württemberg*, 39–272; Nowak, *Kirche,* 297–303.

246. Bringeland, *Martin Dibelius*, 3.

247. Mensing, *Pfarrer*, 110; Bringeland, *Martin Dibelius*, 5.

248. Steigmann-Gall, *Reich*, 67–68; Nowak, *Kirche*, 317–318.

249. Scholder, *Kirchen. Band 1.* 1977, 199.

250. Scholder, *Kirchen. Band 1.* 1977, 201, 209–210; Mensing, *Pfarrer*, 68, 144.

251. Raimund Baumgärtner, *Weltanschauungskampf im Dritten Reich. Die Auseinandersetzung der Kirchen mit Alfred Rosenberg* (Mainz: Matthias-Grünewald-Verlag, 1977) 206.

252. Nowak, *Kirche*, 304.

253. Kjøstvedt, *Hitler's Metropolis*, 147; Barton IX, "The Protestants"; Nowak, *Kirche*, 304.

254. Mensing, *Pfarrer*, 112–114, 130, 142; Schäfer, *Württemberg*, 52–271.

255. Jantzen, *Faith and Fatherland*, 17–18, elaborated 18–31, 37–42.

256. Jantzen, *Faith and Fatherland*, 48–49, 60–61, 64–66, 133, 135, 175–176, 198.

257. Fandel, *Konfession*, 78.

258. Emberland, *Religion*, 23, 25; Fandel, *Konfession*, 78; Scholder, *Kirchen. Band 1.* 1977, 200–201; Meier, *Hakenkreuz*, 20–21; Mensing, *Pfarrer*, 102–124.

259. Mensing, *Pfarrer*, 118, 126-127, 135-137, 145-146

260. Mensing, *Pfarrer*, 178–179; *Der Theologe 4*, 44.

261. Schäfer, *Württemberg*, 234, 460.

262. Hans-Joachim Kraus, "Die evangelische Kirche," in W. Mosse (ed.), *Entscheidungsjahr*, 260; Steigmann-Gall, Reich, 39.

263. Fandel, *Konfession*, 136; Gaede, "Stellung," 416; Mensing, *Pfarrer*, 14, note 22; Stribrny, "Kirche," 164–167; Lewy, *Catholic Church*, 4; Kraus, "Die evangelische Kirche," 266; Dahm, *Pfarrer*, 88–89; Scholder, *Kirchen. Band 1*. 1977, 204.

264. Scholder, *Kirchen. Band 1*. 1977, 205; Harald Iber, *Christlicher Glaube oder rassischer Mythus. Die Auseinanderstzung der Bekennenden Kirche mit Alfred Rosenbergs: "Der Mythus des 20. Jahrhunderts"* (Frankfurt/M: Peter Lang, 1987) 207-209; Bracher, *Auflösung*, 320–328; Schäfer, *Württemberg*, 275; Mensing, *Pfarrer*, 62–64, 276.

265. Scholder, *Kirchen. Band 1*. 1977, 210.

266. Dahm, *Pfarrer*, 209–210.

267. *BBK*; Konukiewitz, Enno, "Hans Asmussen: ein lutherischer Theologe im Kirchenkampf," in *Die lutherische Kirche, Geschichte und Gestalten, Bd. 6*, www.kirche-christen-juden.org/dokumente (Gütersloh: Gütersloher Verlagshaus Mohn, 1984); Alfred Chandler, *Rosenberg's Nazi Myth* (N. Y.: Ithaca, 1945) 109; Mosse, "Rechte," 216; See further chap. *"Protestants and the Third Reich: Chaotic and Complex Situation."*

268. Iber, *Glaube*, 40–41; Baumgärtner, *Weltanschauungskampf*, 200–206.

269. Schäfer, *Württemberg*, 103–104.

270. Iber, *Glaube*, 41.

271. Rosenberg, *Mythus*, 10–11.

272. Scholder, *Kirchen. Band 1*. 1977, 211–212; Pridham, *Hitler's Rise*, 164–169, 171; Nowak, *Kirche*, 313.

273. Nowak, *Kirche*, 318–320.

274. Letter to the author from Kjøstvedt May 26, 2010; Kjøstvedt, *Hitler's Metropolis*, 254–261.

275. Schäfer, *Württemberg*, 159–172; Nowak, *Kirche*, 328.

276. Schäfer, *Württemberg*, 224–229.

277. Kraus, "Die evangelische Kirche," 267–268; Kurt Nowak, "Christuskreuz gegen Hakenkreuz. Die Ideologie des Nationalsozialismus im Urteil der Kirchen" in Heydemann & Kettenacker (ed.), *Kirchen in der Diktatur*, 224.

278. Schäfer, *Württemberg*, 256.

279. Beckmann, "Geschichte," Doc. 35, 68–69.

280. Scholder, *Kirchen. Band 1*. 1977, 199.

281. Nowak, "Christuskreuz," 219–220.

282. Nowak, *Kirche*, 221–222; Arve T. Thorsen, *The Gospel of the Fatherland. Christianity, Universality and National Thought in France and Germany in the Early 20th Century* (Oslo: Acta Humaniora, 2007) 439–440, note 976.

283. Bringeland, *Martin Dibelius*, 15.

284. Becker & Becker, *Machtergreifung*, Doc. 23, 56; Schäfer, *Württemberg*, 253–254.

285. Schellenberger, *Jugend*, 27.

286. Küppers, *Lehrerverband*, 102; Hömig, *Zentrum*, 276.

287. Becker & Becker, *Machtergreifung*, Doc. 39, 71–73.

288. Breuning, *Vision*, 177, note 6; Aretz, *Arbeiterbewegung*, 72; Küppers, *Lehrerverband*, 102; Becker & Becker, *Machtergreifung*, Doc. 46, 82, 418; Hömig, *Zentrum*, 276; Hannot, *Tagespresse*, 47–53.

289. Aretz, *Arbeiterbewegung*, 72–73; Clemens, *Martin Spahn*, 214–215; Küppers, *Lehrerverband*, 103; Ulrich von Hehl, "Das Kirchenvolk im Dritten Reich" in Gotto & Repgen (ed.), *Die Katholiken*, 96; Gerhard Binder, *Irrtum und Widerstand. Die Deutschen Katholiken in der Auseinandersetzung mit dem Nationalsozialismus* (Munich: Pfeiffer, 1968) 77.

290. Schäfer, *Württemberg*, 251, note 17.

291. Becker & Becker, *Machtergreifung*, Doc. 55, 91, Doc. 57 pp. 92–93; Günter Plum, "Übernahme und Sicherung der Macht," in Martin Broszat & Norbert Frei (ed.), *Das Dritte Reich. Ursprünge, Ereignisse, Wirkungen* (Frechen: Komet, 1983) 30.

292. Ernst Forsthoff, *Deutsche Geschichte seit 1918 in Dokumenten* (Leipzig: Alfred Kröner Verlag, 1935) 257.

293. Fandel, *Konfession*, 114.

294. Müller, *Kirche*, 64.

295. Haffner, *Jekyll*, 157–158.

296. Breuning, *Vision*, 177.

297. Dirk Erb (ed.), *Gleichgeschaltet. Der Nazi-Terror gegen Gewerkschaften und Berufsverbände 1930 bis 1933. Eine Dokumentation* (Göttingen: Steidl Verlag, 2001) Doc. 37, 146.

298. Becker & Becker, *Machtergreifung*, Doc. 91, 133–134; Clemens, *Martin Spahn*, 214–215; Küppers, *Lehrerverband*, 109.

299. Küppers, *Lehrerverband*, 124–130. Author's remark: The early surrender in Germany of the teachers' association might have encouraged Quisling in Norway to start with the Norwegian teachers' association in his project of transforming the country into a corporative state in 1942. To start with the social democratic trade union would have been hazardous. As it turned out, Quisling's ambitions ended as a total fiasco, and he turned his wrath against several hundred teachers, among them the author's father, Kjell Kolden, and sent them to a concentration camp in Kirkenes near the Eastern front.

300. Küppers, *Lehrerverband*, 185.

301. Schellenberger, *Jugend*, 32, with note 274; Müller, *Kirche*, 66

302. Becker & Becker, *Machtrergreifung*, Doc. 102, 141-143.

303. Scholder, *Kirchen. Band 1. 2000*, 346–358; Joachim Fest, *Hitler. En biografi* (Oslo: Gyldendal Norsk Forlag, 1979) 337–338, 340; Becker & Becker, *Machtergreifung*, Doc. 124, 170–172.

304. Detlef Junker, *Die deutsche Zentrumspartei und Hitler 1932/33. Ein Beitrag zur Problematik des politischen Katholizismus in Deutschland* (Stuttgart: Ernst Klett Verlag, 1969) 187–188, note 113.

305. Junker, *Zentrumspartei*, 231, 234–235.

306. *Verhandlungen des Reichstags. VIII. Wahlperiode 1933, Bd. 457* (Berlin: Verlag der Reichsdruckerei, 1934) 37–38.

307. Müller, *Kirche*, 73–78.

308. Volk, *Episkopat*, 69–71.

309. Lothar Kettenacker, "Hitler und die Kirchen. Eine Obsesssion mit Folgen," in Heydemann & Kettenacker (ed.), *Kirchen in der Diktatur*, 72; Fandel, *Konfession*,

119–120; Morsey, "Volksminderheit," 22–23; Ludwig Volk, "Nationalsozialistischer Kirchenkampf und deutscher Episkopat," in Gotto & Repgen (ed.), *Die Katholiken*, 53; Volk, *Episkopat*, 73; Aretz, *Arbeiterbewegung*, 79.

310. Scholder, *Kirchen. Band 1.* 2000, 362–363; Morsey, "Volksminderheit," 21; Hehl, "Kirchenvolk," 97.

311. Aretz, *Arbeiterbewegung*, 80, 83–84; Volk, *Episkopat*, 72, 78; Emma Fattorini, *Hitler, Mussolini, and the Vatican. Pope Pius XI and the Speech that was Never Made* (Cambridge: Polity Press) 105.

312. Spicer, *Priests*, 240–300.

313. John Zeender, "Germany: The Catholic Church and the Nazi Regime, 1933–1945," in Richard J. Wolff & Jörg K. Hoensch (ed.), *Catholics, the State, and the European Radical Right, 1919–1945* (N. Y.: Columbia University Press, 1987) 99; Binder, *Irrtum*, 198; Dieter Albrecht, "Der Heilige Stuhl und das Dritte Reich", in Gotto & Repgen (ed.) *Die Katholiken*, 26; Christoph Strohm, *Die Kirchen im Dritten Reich* (Munich: Verlag C. H. Beck, 2011) 31–32.

314. Scholder, *Kirchen. Band 1.* 2000, 541-546; Meier, *Hakenkreuz*, 205–208; Wolf, *Papst*, 175, 194, 196.

315. Fandel, *Konfession*, 162–205; Volk, *Episkopat*, 94–100, 119; Heinz Hürten, "Der katholische Episkopat nach dem Reichskonkordat," in Heydemann & Kettenacker, *Kirchen in der Diktatur*, 100.

316. Wolf, *Papst*, 200, 202.

317. Klaus Gotto, Hans Günter Hockerts & Konrad Repgen, "Nationalsozialistische Herausforderung und kirchliche Antwort. Eine Bilanz," in Gotto & Repgen (ed.), *Die Katholiken*, 189.

318. Ibid., 178–179.

319. Steigmann-Gall, *Reich*, 77; "Studien zum Mythus des XX. Jahrhunderts," in *Kirchlicher Anzeiger für die Erzdiözese Köln*, http://nsl-archiv.com/Buecher/ (Cologne: Erzbischöfliche Generalvikariat, J. P. Bachem, 1934); Baumgärtner, *Weltanschauungskampf*, 148–199; Ludwig Volk, "Nationalsozialistischer Kirchenkampf und deutscher Episkopat," in Gotto & Repgen, *Die Katholiken*, 56–57, 60, 62–63; Hehl, "Kirchenvolk," 98, 102–104, 108; Müller, *Kirche*, 240–241, 342–350; Barbara Schier, *Hexenwahn und Hexenverfolgung. Rezeption und politische Zurichtung eines kulturwissenschaftlichen Themas im Dritten Reich* (Munich: Bayerisches Jahrbuch für Volkskunde, 1990) 52–53; Lill, "NS-Ideologie," 146, 149; Piper, *Rosenberg— Chefideologe*, 217; Zeender, "Germany," 109, 115, note 46.

320. Meier, *Evangelische Kirche*, 85, note 51, 144.

321. Fandel, *Konfession*, 242–256; Besier, *Kirchen*, 126, 129, 141–142; Schellenberger, *Jugend*, 75, with note 359, 76, with note 370; Klaus Scholder, *Die Kirchen und das Dritte Reich. Band 2. Das Jahr der Ernüchterung 1934. Barmen und Rom* (Munich: Econ Ullstein List Verlag, 2000) 408, 411–413; Müller, *Kirche*, 240, 314–315, 328.

322. Anger, *Dokumenten*, chap. VI, Doc. 14, p. 50; Thomas Breuer, "Kirchliche Opposition im NS-Staat. Eine Basisperspektive," in Heydemann & Kettenacker, *Kirchen in der Diktatur*, 300–302; Gotto, Hockerts & Repgen, "Herausforderung," 180–182; Volk, "Kirchenkampf," 72–74.

323. Eggers, Kurt, *Rom gegen Reich. Ein Kapitel deutscher Geschichte um Bismarck* http://reichsarchiv.com (Berlin: Nordland Verlag, 1935) 31.

324. Konrad Repgen, "1938—Judenpogrom und katholischer Kirchenkampf," in Brakelmann & Rosowski (ed.), *Antisemitismus*, 117, 119, 122–123, 139, note 18 and 29; Martin Conway, *Catholic Politics in Europe 1918–1945* (N. Y.: Routledge, 1997) 66; Burkhard von Schewick, "Katholische Kirche und nationalsozialistische Rassenpolitik," in Gotto & Repgen (ed.), *Die Katholiken*, 159–160; Øyvind Foss, *Krystallnatten* (Oslo: Spartacus forlag, 2009) 115; Lill, "NS-Ideologie," 136–7.

325. Broszat & Frei, *Das Dritte Reich*, 121; Volk, "Kirchenkampf," 73–75.

326. Hehl, "Kirchenvolk," 113–114, 116; Fandel, *Konfession*, 415; Zeender, "Germany," 106.

327. Volk, "Kirchenkampf," 81–82; Steigmann-Gall, *Reich*, 202, 249; Tal, *Religion*, 70; Gotto, Hockerts & Repgen, "Herausforderung," 178–179.

328. Jeremy Noakes, "The Oldenburg Crucifix Struggle of November 1936" in Peter D. Stachura (ed.), *The Shaping of the Nazi State* (N. Y.: Croom Helm Ltd., Barnes & Noble Books, 1978) 310–332; Ian Kershaw, *Popular Opinion and Political Dissent in the Third Reich. Bavaria 1933–1945* (N. Y.: Clarendon Press, Oxford University Press, 2002) 331–357.

329. The title of a book by John Cornwell; Gotto, Hockerts & Repgen, "Herausforderung," 182–184; Repgen, "Judenpogrom," 120; Wolf, *Papst*, 65; Fattorini, *Hitler, Mussolini*, 125–127; Volk, "Kirchenkampf," 85–86.

330. Volk, "Kirchenkampf," 86–88; Schewick, "Rassenpolitik," 160–161, with note 34, 164, 166–168.

331. Schewick, "Rassenpolitik," 169, 171.

332. Repgen, "Judenpogrom," 12; Meier, *Hakenkreuz*, 212.

333. Baumgärtner, *Weltanschauungskampf*, 201.

334. Jantzen, *Faith and Fatherland*, 12–13, 82.

335. Chandler, *Nazi Myth*, 122; Meier, *Hakenkreuz*, 171; Steigmann-Gall, *Reich*, 56, 74–75.

336. Becker & Becker, *Machtergreifung*, Doc. 114, 156.

337. Becker & Becker, *Machtergreifung*, Doc. 114, 157.

338. Wolf, "Volk," 189–190; Meier, *Hakenkreuz*, 41–49.

339. Wolf, "Volk, " 190.

340. Beckmann, "Geschichte," 224–225; Wolf, "Volk," 190–191.

341. Scholder, *Kirchen. Band 1*. 2000, 509–540; Becker & Becker, *Machtergreifung*, Doc. 334, 376-377; Steigmann-Gall, *Reich*, 159–161.

342. Scholder, *Kirchen. Band 1*. 2000, 475–509, 588–700.

343. Scholder, *Kirchen. Band 1*. 2000, 782–786.

344. Wolf, "Volk, " 189; Meier, *Evangelische Kirche*, 53, 63.

345. Ulrich Kühn, "Die theologische Rechtfertigung der "Obrigkeit,"" in Heydemann & Kettenacker (ed.), *Kirchen in der Diktatur*, 246–249; Foss, *Krystallnatten*; Goldhagen, *Executioners*, 518, note 125 and 126; *BBK*, Entry, Niemöller, Wilhelm and Künneth, Walter; Steigmann-Gall, *Reich*, 34–36, 164, with note 45; Nowak, *Kirche*, 226; Chandler, *Nazi Myth*, 109; Christoph Weiling, *Die "Christlich-deutsche Bewegung." Eine Studie zum konservativen Protestantismus in der Weimarer Zeit*

(Göttingen: Vandenhoeck & Ruprecht, 1998) 326, note 13; Breuer, "Kirchliche Opposition," 308.

346. Iber, *Glaube*, 42, 45–46, 87–93, 110, 287; Baumgärtner, *Weltanschauungskampf*, 224, 231–250; Piper, *Rosenberg–Chefideologe*, 218–220; Gordon, *"Jewish Question,"* 256.

347. Iber, *Glaube*, 288.

348. Steigmann-Gall, *Reich*, 100–101.

349. Baumgärtner, *Weltanschuungskampf*, 228-231, 263; Iber, *Glaube*, 221–222.

350. Steigmann-Gall, *Reich*, 164, 181; Scholder, *Kirchen. Band 1.* 1977, 281, 745; Besier, *Kirchen*, 104.

351. Scholder, *Kirchen. Band 1.* 1977, 814–823; Barton, Dennis, *Hitler's Rise to Power, Part 2*, Chapter "IX The Protestants," The Church in History Information Centre, www.church-in-history.org Access date. 05.13.2005; Fandel, *Konfession*, 260, note 11; *Der Theologe 4*, 42.

352. Steigmann-Gall, *Reich*, 166; Scholder, *Kirchen. Band 2*, 64–71.

353. Walser Smith, *Continuities*, 65; Scholder, *Kirchen. Band 1.* 1977, 273-274; Fandel, *Konfession*, 334–335, 342–343, note 50, 353–354, 365, 367, 374, 392; Spicer, *Priests*, 261.

354. Kettenacker, "Hitler und die Kirchen," 78; Steigmann-Gall, *Reich*, 186; Fandel, *Konfession*, 516–517, 599; Mensing, *Pfarrer*, 182–183, 186.

355. Zeender, "Germany, " 103, 108; Armin Boyens, "Die Stellung der Ökumene und der Bekennenden Kirche zum Problem von Krieg und Frieden während der Zeit des Dritten Reiches," in Huber & Schwerdtfeger (ed.), *Kirche zwischen Krieg und Frieden*, 435–436.

356. Steigmann-Gall, *Reich*, 187, note 166.

357. Leonore Siegele-Wenschkewitz, "Protestantische Universitätstheologie und Rassenideologie in der Zeit des Nationalsozialismus," in Brakelmann & Rosowski, *Antisemitismus*, 53.

358. Ursula Büttner, "Von der Kirche verlassen: Die deutschen Protestanten und die Verfolgung der Juden und Christen jüdischer Herkunft im "Dritten Reich,"" in Büttner & Greschat (ed.), *Die verlassenen Kinder*, 69.

359. Goldhagen, *Executioners*, 106-116; Becker & Becker, *Machtergreifung*, Doc. 137, 186, 143, 190–191.

360. Repgen, "Judenpogrom," 119–120.

361. Scholder, *Kirchen. Band 1.* 1977, 360.

362. Bringeland, *Martin Dibelius*, 2–3.

Chapter Three

The Postwar Period
Change of Mentality among Protestants

THE CONFESSIONS OF GUILT BY THE CHURCHES

The Catholic Church was the first to issue a confession of guilt after WWII. In August 1945, it "deplored in the deepest way" what members of the Church had been involved in, and what the Church as Church had failed to do.[1]

Some months later, the BK issued its *Stuttgarter Schuldbekenntnis*, which more directly accused the Church as an institution, and deplored that the churchgoers had not prayed enough. Two years later a new more all-embracing and thorough declaration was issued. It revealed a more profound self-knowledge in the way the Church and its people had failed. The most important paragraphs, § 2 and § 3 read,

> 2. We have been wrong when we started to dream the dream of a special mission, as if "das Deutsche Wesen" could heal the world. Through this we have prepared the field for the uninhibited use of political power and placed our nation upon the throne of God.
> 3. We have been wrong when we started to establish a "Christian front" against reorganizations, which had been necessary in the life of man in society (i.e. the Weimar Republic). We have paid heavily for the Church's association with the preservative powers of the old and original system. We have betrayed Christian freedom, which allows and encourages us to change ways of life where social life demands such changes. We have denied the right to revolution but tolerated and approved the development to absolute dictatorship.[2]

By using expressions such as, "We have failed . . . prepared the field" and common conceptions among Protestants in both the Empire and in the Interwar period, which were charged with particularly strong values such as "special mission," "*das Deutsche Wesen*," and "heal" (*genesen*), the declaration indicates that the Nazis primarily could thank Protestant church people for their position of power. The Catholic declaration is noticeably totally void of such words and concepts, which were irrelevant to them as a description of the German Church and cultural life. Hence, the two declarations are radically different. The Protestant declaration, however, despite its profound humility, does not deplore its submission to the Godless roots of Rosenberg's version of Nazism, which had been the main Catholic target of ideological accusation.

Generally, Protestant theologians were not much interested in dealing so soon after WWII with the role the Church played in the Third Reich. The exceptions were Karl Barth, Martin Dibelius and the philosopher Karl Jaspers, all of whom were concerned about the issue of guilt.[3]

Björn Mensing asserts that many of 110 retired Protestant clerics in Bavaria interviewed in the late 1980s reflected on their attitude during the Interwar period for the first time in their lives.[4]

THE FEDERAL REPUBLIC AND EUROPEAN INTEGRATION

After WWII the Allies banned Nazi organizations. It was hardly necessary because practically no one admitted to having been a Nazi any longer.[5] Not only did Goebbels' "total war" end in total defeat, but Protestant churchgoers obviously realized that "*das Deutsche Wesen*," *völkisch* idealism and Nazi totalitarianism had been a "Myth of the Twentieth century." Without any significant reservations the bulk of nonsocialist Protestants sided with the Christian democratic programs of the Zentrum/BVP, based on the ideas of 1789, which paved the way for the new CDU/CSU parties. The importance of the "Weimar" parties in post-WWII Germany was envisioned by the emigrants Sebastian Haffner in 1940 and Peter Viereck in 1942, the former asserting that, "the forces behind the Centre are relatively intact", and the latter who asserted that, "Germany's incessant cultural pendulum will surely turn westward again".[6] True, there were, as said, still some conservative clerics who clung to their old racist and *völkisch* illusions, but the common change of mentality was very broad. A sign of this was the absence of a new Protestant "DNVP," which had been a major opponent of the Zentrum/BVP. The Protestant shift in mentality was probably also due to a general and global shift in mentality in the wake of WWII. Thus, "*Stunde 0*" represented a fundamental transformation of the mentality among Protestant churchpeople from antimodernist to modernist political ideas, and the confessional gulf which had dominated German society for eons, seemed to have vanished. This also had connections with a general secularization following WWII.

A parallel phenomenon happened on the socialist side (in the Federal Republic), when communism, much because of the futile strategy of the KPD in the early 1930s and the Soviet policy of oppression in Eastern Europe, succumbed, and the followers turned to the democratic SPD. Even the third "Weimar" party, the DDP, reappeared as the FDP and became a more stable 5 percent party.

The dramatic change in Protestant mentality paved the way for Adenauer's long-standing Francophile ambition of rapprochement with France, and with SIPDIC's plan from 1932 about European economic integration. Already in his first year as chancellor, in March 1950, Adenauer proposed to establish a union between Germany and France with a common parliament.[7] This proposal was of course too radical at that time, but when the Schuman plan was introduced not much later, Adenauer, together with other European Catholic Christian democrats, became an eager instigator behind a development which ended in the EU. Adenauer's immediate response to Jean Monnet in May 1950 was, "I realize the French proposal is the most important task in my future. If I only get the opportunity to complete it, I think I have not thrown away my life."[8] In 1963, his last year as chancellor, he ultimately achieved his special *Élysée*-treaty with France, which has dominated the German-French relationship ever since, of which even a recent (Nov. 2019) opinion poll bears witness. On the question "Which country is the most or second most important partner for the German foreign policy?" 60 percent favored France as no. 1 or 2 (and 42 percent the USA as no. 1 or 2 as the next popular country), and on the question "Should Germany in the future have more or less cooperation with France?" 77% percent said more, again as the most popular country.[9]

The German-French Catholic and democratic mentality in the Rhine border areas has on the whole been so central to the European process of integration that the Dutch author Geert Mak introduces the concept "The model of the Rhineland," as a system based on a mixture of capitalism, social democracy and Christian democracy.[10] Two Norwegian social scientists, Stein Rokkan and Tore Nedrebø put it in this way:

> It is no accident that the Roman Law countries were the ones to take the lead . . . in the struggle for a supranational Europe. (Stein Rokkan)[11]
>
> The European Union was launched on its supranational path when these (Christian Democratic) parties, led mainly by statesmen from Caroliningian-Lotharingian Europe, dominated the governments of the six founding states from about 1945 to 1965. Their discourse in this regard was heavily informed by ideology rooted in the universalist European legacy, whose mainstay remains Catholic, continental and southern Europe.[12]

NOTES

1. Ludwig Volk, "Nationalsozialistischer Kirchenkampf und deutscher Epskopat," in Klaus Gotto & Konrad Repgen (ed.), *Die Katholiken und das Dritte Reich* (Mainz: Matthias-Grünewald-Verlag, 1990) 91, note 45.

2. Ernst Wolf, "Volk, Nation, Vaterland im protestantischen Denken von 1930 bis zur Gegenwart," in Horst Zillessen (ed.), *Volk—Nation—Vaterland. Der deutsche Protestantismus und der Nationalismus* (Gütersloh: Gütersloher Verlagshaus Gerd Mohn, 1970) 208.

3. Hans M. Bringeland, *Martin Dibelius' oppgjer med nasjonalsosialismen. Ei jamføring med andre teologar sin kritikk, særleg Bultmanns og Barths* (Unpublished manuscript for lecture for the PhD, University of Bergen, 12.15.2011) 14.

4. Björn Mensing, *Pfarrer und Nationalsozialismus. Geschichte einer Verstrickung am Beispiel der Evangelisch-Lutherischen Kirche in Bayern* (Göttingen: Vandenhoeck & Ruprecht, 1998) 226–227.

5. Golo Mann, "Der Nazistaat," in Hans-Adolf Jacobsen & Hans Dollinger (ed.), *Deutschland. Hundert Jahre Deutsche Geschichte* (Stuttgart: Fackerverlag Brugg, 1973) 157; Gerhard Schulz, *Faschismus—Nationalsozialismus. Versionen und theoretische Kontroversen 1922–1972* (Frankfurt/M: Propyläen Verlag, Verlag Ullstein, 1974) 158; Andreas Wirsching, "Weit entfernt von simplen Antworten," Interview mit A. W. in *SPIEGEL SPECIAL GESCHICHTE*, Nr. 1, 2008, 21

6. Sebastian Haffner, *Germany. Jekyll and Hyde. An eyewitness analysis of Nazi Germany* (London: Abacus, 2008) 188; Peter Viereck, *Nazismens rötter. En historisk och psykologisk överblick* (Stockholm: Natur och kultur, 1942) 19.

7. *Vårt Land*, May (date unknown) 1998; *Dagen*, March 8, 2003; Victoria Martin de la Torre, *Fryktens kontinent. Hvordan europeere begynte å stole på hverandre* (Oslo: Frekk forlag, 2016) 56.

8. Torre, *Fryktens kontinent*, 79.

9. Opinion poll "Einmischen oder zurückhalten?" https://www.koerber-stiftung.de

10. *Bergens Tidende*, June 25, 2012, Interview with Geert Mak.

11. Tore Nedrebø, *Past and Present Sources of European Union. A Comparative Historical-Institutional Analysis* (Bergen: Dissertation for the degree of *doctor philosophiae* (Dr. Philos.), University of Bergen, 2010) 53.

12. Nedrebø, *European Union*, xi.

II

THEMATIC

Chapter Four

Other Denominations and Nazism

The denominations besides the main Catholic and Protestant Churches were all relatively small. At the census in 1925, their 620,000 members made up only 1.1 percent of the population.[1]

Like the bulk of the members and leadership of the Protestant *Landeskirchen*, most members and leaders of the evangelical free churches regarded the Weimar Republic as an evil. The first-time comments about Nazism from them turn up, was after the "Putsch," and these were mainly negative to the Nazi movement, although some young Methodists showed their fascination. They were soon admonished, though.[2]

The original attitude among some members had been not to get involved in politics, but this attitude changed after the election in 1930. The first reaction in some denominations was hesitant, but after a while, clear statements were issued, most of them somewhat ambivalent. Some reacted against the anti-Semitism, others to the relationship to the Old Testament or to the rowdyism.[3]

Because they were so few and spread all over the country, it is hard to assess their election behavior in 1932, but a representative of an umbrella organization, the *Deutsche Evangeliumsgemeinden*, asserted in February 1933 that old members, if they were active politically, "primarily had worked in the CSVD and partly the DDP and similar parties. Among young people, especially academics, many had joined the Nazi party." In May 1933, a Methodist layman asserted similar opinions, and already before the Nazi takeover, a significant part of the Methodists had favored Nazism and a lot more did afterwards.[4] The takeover was welcomed by an umbrella organization of denominational youth comprising Baptists, Methodists, Pentecostals, the South German Mennonites and the *Evangelische Gemeinschaft*.[5] After a while, even their main denominations, together with at least one Lutheran one, followed suit by issuing resolutions of approval, but Zehrer does not specify whether these were issued before or after the election of March 5 or the introduction of dictatorship on March 23.[6] Some months later, three more Lutheran churches issued their resolutions.[7]

It seems that the Herrnhut Brethren was the only evangelical denomination which did not issue any resolution in 1933. However, this was most probably not due to resistance against the government, because in 1934 only four people voted against and 1034 in favor of Hitler's policy among the 1060 suffrage entitled voters in the village of Herrnhut.[8] Not only denominations hailed the new government. Recent research has revealed that a foreign mission association, the German department of Hudson Taylor's *China Inland Mission*, the *Liebenzeller Mission*, not only hailed the government, but was influenced by anti-Semitism.[9]

Although the denominations were small, several of them were departments of international Churches and so were useful for Hitler's propaganda to deny any maltreatment of opponents and Jews in 1933. Especially useful was the American Methodist Bishop John Nuelson. Protests from abroad gradually ceased, because of the confidence found in the statements of Church leaders.[10]

Even Rosenberg honored the "*Freikirchen*," which together with the Old Catholics and the Greek Catholics, banned criticism of the regime at ecumenical congresses. On the day of the inauguration of the DC cleric Ludwig Müller as *Reichsbishof* the *Evangelische Jugend* in Berlin together with the DC, "*Freikirchen*" and the *Salvation Army* arranged a mass assembly, according to Scholder.[11] Neither Rosenberg nor Scholder specifies which churches "*Freikirchen*" represented.

Some denominations later criticized the Nazi racist ideas and the persecution of opponents and therefore ran into trouble, but most of them tried to behave discreetly, and Methodists and Baptists even servilely at international conferences.[12]

Rosenberg's literature was also assessed by the denominations, whose verdicts were unanimously negative, but, like the Protestant main churches, the general opinion was that his works were private and not representative of the party.[13]

The *Ernste Bibelforscher* (*The Jehovah's Witnesses*) differed from all other denominations. Together with the Catholics, the group had already been an object of Rosenberg's wrath since the 1920s[14], and the denomination was prohibited in Prussia in 1933. They consequently were insubordinate to orders they found incompatible with their theology and were met with harsh measures.[15]

Unlike the mainstream Churches, the denominations hesitated to issue confessions of guilt. Some Churches "waited" until 1984 when the *Alliance of Evangelical Denominations* issued a statement of regret at a continental European Baptist conference.[16]

Karl Zehrer sums up the attitude and situation of the denominations during the Third Reich in the following way:

> There is reason to believe that the attitude of the denominations during the Third Reich to a great extent may be described as "the indecisive center" in the evangelical Landeskirchen which numerically was much greater, . . . The Churches have up until 1943, and partway into 1944 regarded Hitler as God-given Führer of the German Reich and assessed Nazi policy positively, as their incessant acclamations indicate. These were not forced on them in any way. With this attitude they have ended up dangerously close to what the Bible calls "false prophecy". . . . They neither would nor could see through the real attitude and intentions of the authorities and based their interpretations of the authorities' statements and orders on their hopes, desires and dreams, but not on the declared intentions and aims. In such ways they were victims of their own self-delusions. Therefore the intention of the denominations as to the institutions, ideas and intrigues in the Third Reich must largely be characterized as a miserably blind alley.[17]

Hence, it is possible to conclude that the denominations as a whole, except for *The Jehovah's Witnesses*, hardly showed an attitude any more resistant towards Nazism than the Protestant *Landeskirchen* did.

NOTES

1. Karl Zehrer, *Evangelische Freikirchen und das "Dritte Reich,"* (Göttingen: Vandenhoeck & Ruprecht, 1986) 183.
2. Zehrer, *Freikirchen*, 107–108.
3. Zehrer, *Freikirchen*, 13–15.
4. Zehrer, *Freikirchen*, 15.
5. Zehrer, *Freikirchen*, 25, 184.
6. Zehrer, *Freikirchen*, 16–17.
7. Zehrer, *Freikirchen*, 18–19.
8. Zehrer, *Freikirchen*, 17.
9. Helmuth Egelkraut, *Die Liebenzeller Mission und der Nationalsozialismus: Eine Studie zu ausgewählten Bereichen, Personen und Positionen. Mit Stellungnahme des Komitees der Liebenzeller Mission* (Münster: Lit Verlag, 2015).
10. Klaus Scholder, *Die Kirchen und das Dritte Reich. Band 1. Vorgeschichte und Zeit der Illusionen* (Frankfurt/M: Verlag Ullstein, 1977) 377, 385; Zehrer, *Freikirchen*, 17–18, 136.
11. Alfred Rosenberg, *Protestantische Rompilger. Der Verrat an Luther und der "Mythus des 20. Jahrhunderts"* (Munich: Hoheneichen Verlag, 1937) 73; Scholder, *Kirchen. Band 1.* 1977, 747.
12. Gary King, Ori Rosen, Martin Tanner & Alexander F. Tanner, "Ordinary Voting Behaviour in the Extraordinary Election of Adolf Hitler," in *Journal of Economic*

History, Vol. 68, No. 4, 2008, 64–67; Zehrer, *Freikirchen*, 19, 26; *Holocaust Encyclopedia*, Entry "German Churches and the Nazi State"; Armin Boyens, "Die Stellung der Ökumene und der Bekennenden Kirche zum Problem von Krieg und Frieden während der Zeit des Dritten Reiches," in Wolfgang Huber & Johannes Schwerdtfeger (ed.), *Kirche zwischen Krieg und Frieden. Studien zur Geschichte des deutschen Protestantismus* (Stuttgart: Ernst Klett Verlag, 1976) 433–434.

13. Zehrer, *Freikirchen*, 26–27.

14. Rosenberg, *Kampf*, Inhaltsverzeichnis 1925.

15. King et al., "Voting Behaviour," 64–67; *Holocaust Encyclopedia*, entry "German Churches and the Nazi State."

16. Zehrer, *Freikirchen*, 76–77, 170–171.

17. Zehrer, *Freikirchen*, 78.

Chapter Five

Agrarian Parties and Confessional Differences

The distinct difference between confessions which was expressed politically after 1871 through the Zentrum/BVP on the one side and the Protestant dominated liberal and rightist parties on the other side, is also clearly visible with the specifically agrarian parties. The collapse which happened to the "urban" Protestant parties in the 1930s, was even more prodigious among the corresponding agrarian parties. I have already mentioned the originally "liberal" Waldeck constituency and the state of Saxony. Another interesting Protestant small constituency is Rothenburg ob der Tauber. In 1928 the DNVP got 78.6 percent, but only 4.1 percent two years later, greatly surpassed by the agrarian *Landvolk* which carried almost half of the votes (49.5 percent). Only two more years later, in July 1932, this party suffered an even more devastating defeat when the Nazis carried 83 percent.[1] In November that year *Landvolk* carried 3 *votes*!

Several agrarian parties ran in the elections in the Weimar Republic, but only in two regional states, Bavaria and Wurttemberg, getting relatively continuous support. It is worth noticing that in both states the parties were pronouncedly confessionally based, but for different confessions. The *Bayerischer Bauernbund* (BBB) was almost as Catholic dominated as the BVP, whereas the *Württemberger Bauernpartei und Landbund* primarily was the party for Protestants.[2] Philip B. Wiener asserts that "the *Deutsche Bauernpartei*, the (*Christlich-Nationale Bauern und*) *Landvolk(Partei)*, and the *Landbund*, . . . all could look back to a powerful anti-Semitic tradition."[3] All three were Protestant dominated, and the *Landbund* was, together with the DNVP and the *Stahlhelm*, part of the *Kampffront Schwarz-Weiss-Rot*, the alliance partner of the Nazi party in the coalition government in 1933. The vice-chairman of the *Landvolk*, Günter Gereke, was in Hitler's first government, in spite of the fact that his party hardly existed anymore.[4]

In addition to the BBB, there was another Catholic dominated party, the *Badischer Landbund*, the latter being strongly anti-clerical and rightist, though, and it folded up in the 1920s when their supporters drifted to the DNVP and other parties and eventually the Nazi party in the 1930s.[5] The BBB, however, differed considerably from all other agrarian parties in several ways: its size, its continuity and relatively loyal followers, and, not least, its political profile. The party was markedly leftist and, typically, established in 1893 as a Catholic alternative to the strong rightist and Protestant dominated *Bund der Landwirte*. The profile of the party surfaced at the start of WWI when it was probably the only organization not to applaud the German participation in the war, and representatives of it were correspondingly relieved at the end of it. The party emphasized traditional values and, in addition, its ideology was a peculiar mixture of leftist radicalism and separatism. It was not supported by the Church, maybe because it had participated in the revolutionary government in Bavaria in the spring of 1919, and one of its representatives had taken part in an agrarian conference in Moscow in 1923. Clearly, the party moderated its profile as it participated in the BVP dominated governments from 1920 until 1933 and was the only agrarian party to support the *Reichsbanner*.[6]

For this reason, the BBB can be regarded as one of the "Weimar" parties with loyalty to the values of "1789." Its confessional basis can be ascertained statistically. In the strong BBB constituency, Lower Bavaria, there was only one minor rural constituency that was Protestant dominated, Sulzbach. In Sulzbach, the BBB got 0.2 percent of the ballot in November 1932 whereas it got an average of 13.5 percent in the 37 Catholic-dominated constituencies. Hans Mommsen considers that, in contrast to the position in Protestant areas, farmers in Catholic areas remained indifferent to anti-Semitism, though probably, this assertion needs to be modified somewhat, at least as to Bavaria.[7]

It can be concluded that there were certain parallel tendencies within the Christian and agrarian voters. On the Catholic side in rather urban areas, there was one great consolidated—relatively leftist—party for churchgoers, the Zentrum/BVP opposed by several more or less transient and more or less rightist parties dominated by Protestants. A corresponding situation arose in the agrarian field. Outside Bavaria, most Catholic farmers obviously voted the Zentrum, whereas in Bavaria the bulk of them voted for the relatively large, leftist, consolidated BBB. In the countryside, the Zentrum, the BVP and the BBB had to run against several more or less transient rightist agrarian parties in Protestant areas. Confronted with Nazism, the Zentrum and the BVP remained unscathed, whereas the BBB "only" lost half its voters until 1933. In 1932 and 1933 on the Protestant side there were, the DNVP excepted, very little remaining of both agrarian and other nonsocialist parties, even though the DNVP and some of the agrarian parties had enjoyed overwhelming support in some minor constituencies in the elections of 1928 and 1930.

NOTES

1. Geoffrey Pridham, *Hitler's Rise to Power* (London: Hart Davis, 1973) 141–142, with note 56; see further chap. "The Situation as to Mentality Groups c. 1930."
2. Election statistics of November 1932 compared with confessional distribution in the minor constituencies.
3. Philip Bernard Wiener, "Die Parteien der Mitte," in Werner E. Mosse (ed.), *Entscheidungsjahr 1932. Zur Judenfrage in der Weimarer Republik* (Tübingen: J. C. B. Mohr (Paul Siebeck), 1966) 321.
4. *Historisches Lexikon Bayerns*, Entry "Kampffront Schwarz-Weiss-Rot"; Bertold Spuler, *Regenten und Regierungen der Welt, Teil II.*, Bd. 4: *Neueste Zeit 1917/18–1964* (Würzburg: A. G. Ploetz Verlag, 1964) 152.
5. Oded Heilbronner, *Catholicism, Political Culture, and the Countryside. A Social History of the Nazi Party in South Germany* (Ann Arbor: The University of Michigan Press, 1998) 35–37, 40–42.
6. Derek Hastings, *Caholicism and the Roots of Nazism. Religious Identity and National Socialism* (N. Y.: Oxford University Press, 2010) 23; Helmut Walser Smith, *German Nationalism and Religious Conflict. Culture, Ideology*, Politics, 1870–1914 (Princeton, NJ: Princeton University Press, 1995) 165, note 108; Hans Fenske, *Konservatismus und Rechtsradikalismus in Bayern nach 1918* (Bad Homburg: Verlag Gehlen, 1969) 38–39, 43, 45; Karl Rohe, *Das Reichsbanner Schwarz-Rot-Gold. Ein Beitrag zur Geschichte und Struktur der politischen Kampfverbände zur Zeit der Weimarer Republik* (Düsseldorf: Droste Verlag, 1966) 313; Pridham, *Hitler's Rise*, 70; Spuler, Regenten. Bd. 4, 80–82.
7. Hans Mommsen, "Die Funktion des Antisemitismus im 'Dritten Reich,'" in Günter Brakelmann & Martin Rosowski (ed.), *Antisemitismus. Von religiöser Judenfeindschaft zur Rassenideologie* (Göttingen: Vandenhoeck & Ruprecht, 1989) 183; Rudolf Lill, "Die deutschen Katholiken und die Juden in der Zeit von 1850 bis zur Machtübernahme Hitlers," in Karl Heinrich Rengstorf & Siegfried von Kortzfleisch (ed.), *Kirche und Synagoge. Handbuch zur Geschichte von Christten und Juden. Darstellung mit Quellen (*Stuttgart: Ernst Klett Verlag, 1970) 385–386.

Chapter Six

Women and Nazism

In the election of March 1933, the ratio of male and female Nazi voters was almost 50–50. As the number of male voters among those Catholics who voted for the Nazis was considerably higher than the number of female voters, it means that relatively more Protestant women than Protestant men must have voted for the party.[1]

This trend among women voters became visible in the last elections in 1932 and 1933. Whereas the Catholic women's organizations not only had rejected Nazism, but also, as said earlier, participated in a mass declaration against the Nazi Party in February 1933, Protestant women's Christian organizations functioned as supporters of the Nazi Party at the same elections. The most important amongst these was the largest of them all, the *Evangelische Frauenhilfe*, and at least two others.[2] Michael Phayer asserts: "The fascination of Protestant women for the *völkisch* renewal anticipates Nazism. . . . Protestant women liked to look upon themselves as precursors of the Nazi *völkisch* renewal. . . . As to most female churchgoers, belief in Protestantism went hand in hand with the Nazi revolution." Protestant women had anticipated some of the educational and social programs in as much as they initiated a declaration about promoting differences in the boys' curriculum. They ought to have more teaching in scientific and mathematical subjects than girls. The Mothers' Organization (Protestant) was openly racist and favored eugenics, as did the Inner Mission.[3]

In 1933 all Protestant organizations for Christian women were united in an umbrella organization, the *Frauenwerk*. When this organization and the *Nationalsozialistischer Frauenbund* tried to get organizations for Catholic women to join their courses in racist ideology, their invitation was sharply rejected. Soon the Nazi organization was eager to incorporate the *Frauenwerk*. The leader of the latter, Agnes von Grone, fought obstinately against this - although she was a devoted Nazi - until she had to give in three years later after intervention by *Reichsbischof* Müller and other bishops. She also opposed Müller's incorporation of youth organizations into the *Hitlerjugend*.[4]

The aversion of Catholic women to Nazism can partly be in connection with a lecture at a Bavarian ecclesiastical conference in 1930 where one of the topics was Rosenberg's view of women. A priest, Anton Scharnagel, asserted that Rosenberg had given the impression that childless woman could no longer be regarded as a "full member of the fellowship of the people," and, if she were married, that she had no right to correct the adultery of her husband. At the directions of Cardinal Faulhaber, Scharnagel's comment was sent to all spiritual advisors in the Bavarian archbishopric.[5]

NOTES

1. Jürgen Falter, *Hitlers Wähler* (Munich: Beck'sche Verlagsbuchhandlung, 1991) 140–146.
2. Martin Durham, *Women and Fascism* (N. Y.: Routledge, 1998) 19–20.
3. Richard Steigmann-Gall, *The Holy Reich. Nazi Conceptions of Christianity, 1919–1945*. (Cambridge: Cambridge University Press, 2004) 203–205.
4. Steigmann-Gall, *Reich*, 140-142, with note 142, 205–207.
5. Raimund Baumgärtner, *Weltanschauungskampf im Dritten Reich. Die Auseinandersetzung der Kirchen mit Alfred Rosenberg* (Mainz: Matthias-Grünewald-Verlag, 1977) 145, 147.

Chapter Seven

Christian Youth Associations and Nazism

About 1930 there were many Protestant youth associations, such as the YMCA/YWCA, the Inner Mission organizations, scout groups and others, having about 700,000 members altogether. Catholic youth associations were merged in 1928 in an umbrella organization with as many as 1.3 million members, despite there being only half as many Catholics in Germany as Protestants.[1] As to the relationship to Nazism before the Nazi takeover Steigmann-Gall asserts:

> Here again, there were stark confessional difference in attitudes toward Nazism and the H(itler)J(ugend). Catholic Youth, as might be expected, stayed away, having been warned by one of its leaders that no member "who stands by the banner of Christ and by the young Catholic People's front can belong to (this) movement." There were only isolated cases of Catholics belonging to the "Kampfzeit" HJ. In fact, before 1933 the HJ was weakest in precisely those areas where Catholic religiosity and membership in Catholic Youth was strongest: Bavaria, the Rhineland, and parts of Silesia. This is accountable both to institutional centralisation of Catholic youth and to ideological opposition to Nazi racial thought.
> By comparison, Protestant youth groups were far more favourably inclined toward the Nazis. The League of Bible Circles, in particular, was supportive of Nazism, with many "alte Kämpfer" (i.e. "old warriors") among its ranks.[2]

A report in the Nazi paper *Der Angriff* (The Attack) in the spring of 1930 listed organizations from which the *Hitlerjugend* members in Berlin had been recruited. Among these, there were many bourgeois and politically neutral scout organizations and even the communist *Jung-Spartacus Bund*. At least two Christian associations were represented. An observer even asserted in 1931 that most Protestant Christian youth belonged to "either the Nazi party and its youth- or warrior-organizations, or, at least, were very favorable towards them."[3]

Some people, especially in the PNB, protested against Bishop Müller's incorporation of Christian youth associations in the *Hitlerjugend* in 1933. However, it is worth noticing that the opposition—like in the case of the *Frauenwerk* of von Grone—first and foremost was from the desire to keep the institutional independence, not for reasons of ideology. When the BK was established half a year later, it organized its own youth groups, often based on earlier associations that had had local loyal leaders. These groups were often harassed by the *Hitlerjugend*. Baldur von Schirach, the leader of the *Hitlerjugend*, respected Christian activity in the organization to a certain degree until 1938, when the mightily anti-Christian Martin Bormann put a ban on this.[4]

The Catholics had made sure they kept their youth organizations in the *Reichskonkordat*. But during the 1930s, this paper construct was more and more undermined through harassment until in 1939 the authorities finally put a ban on them, and all young people between ten and eighteen were forcibly recruited into the *Hitlerjugend*.

Not only Catholics, but also Protestants of all kinds, should normally have steered clear of the *Hitlerjugend*. In September 1933 the Vatican received a report of a song which was used in the organization filled with expressions as "We do not need any Christian virtue," "No Pope can prevent us from feeling like Hitler's children," "Not Christ do we follow," and "I am no Christian and no Catholic."[5] The song was even sung as the official song of *Hitlerjugend* at the *Reichsparteitag* in 1934, and von Schirach made sure to enhance the anti-Christain mood of the ideology of the organization when he announced: "Rosenberg's way is the way for German youth. I cannot understand why there should be confessional associations beside the *Hitlerjugend*. We cannot give up the principle that all young people belong to us. We are unwaveringly going to stick to this purpose, and crush any opposition. . ."[6]

Young Joseph Ratzinger's membership in the *Hitlerjugend* in 1944 can hardly have been the result of ideological fascination. Later in life, he became Pope Benedict XVI.

NOTES

1. Richard Steigmann-Gall, *The Holy Reich. Nazi Conceptions of Christianity, 1919–1945* (Cambridge: Cambridge University Press, 2004) 212; 1.5 million according to John Zeender, "Germany: The Catholic Church and the Nazi Regime, 1933–1945," in Richard J. Wolff & Jörg K. Hoensch (ed.), *Catholics, the State, and the European Radical Right, 1919–1945* (N. Y.: Columbia University Press, 1987) 99.

2. Steigmann-Gall, *Reich*, 212–213.

3. Anders Granås Kjøstvedt, *Hitler's Metropolis? The National Socialist Movement in Berlin 1925–1933* (PhD-thesis submitted to the Faculty of Humanities, University of Oslo 10.14.2009, 2010) 176; Steigmann-Gall, *Reich*, 213.

4. Steigmann-Gall, *Reich*, 215–216.

5. Hubert Wolf, *Papst und Teufel. Die Archive des Vatikan und das Dritte Reich* (Munich: Verlag C. H. Beck, 2012) 257–258.

6. Guido Müller, "Anticipated Exile of Catholic Democrats: The Sécretariat des Partis Démocratique d'Inspiration Chrétienne," in Wolfram Kaiser & Helmut Wohnout (ed.), *Political Catholicism in Europe 1918-45*, Vol. 1 (N. Y.: Routledge, 2004) 312.

Chapter Eight

The Relationship of Pius XI to Totalitarianism

Pius XI had been active politically right from his first year as pope, in 1922. He asserted that the peace settlements after WWI had been motivated more by revenge than justice. He was also dissatisfied with League of Nations, which he thought was the instrument of British and French politics. He did not disfavor the idea in itself but thought that *Summa Theologica* by Thomas Aquinas contained the doctrinal foundation for a real "Alliance of the Peoples." The pope even urged amicable relations with the new Soviet state, although communism as an ideology was condemned.[1]

In 1891 the encyclical *Rerum Novarum* had been issued. The next one, *Quadragesimo anno*, from 1931, became the most important one among the other encyclicals of the 1930s for establishing a Catholic political theory and emphasized the principle of subsidiarity, i.e. de-centralization, and a cooperative order of society.[2] More important in this connection, however, was the series of encyclicals with criticism of totalitarian regimes.

Already two years after the Lateran Treaty, in 1931, *Non Abiamo Bisogno* was issued as a criticism of Italian Fascism. It was followed in 1933 by *Dilectissima nobis* with criticism of the anticlerical Spanish Azana-regime, in 1937 by the anti-Nazi *Mit brennender Sorge* and the anti-communist *Divini Redemptoris* as a reaction to the situation in the Soviet Union.

These documents not only represented the personal opposition of the pope, but also the anti-totalitarian attitudes of his closest subordinates, the secretary of state, Eugenio Pacelli (Pius XII), and consensus among the Italian, German and Slavic bishops in the respective countries.

Rev. John J. Conley summarizes the quintessence of the encyclicals to Italy, Germany and the Soviet Union in this way:

> Pius XI, however, does not limit himself to prophetic advocacy on behalf of those persecuted by totalitarian governments. His trilogy studies the ideological errors that have given rise to the practical violation of rights. These encyclicals unmask the idolatry operative in each of these totalitarian movements. In absolutizing respectively state, race, and class, these regimes have placed a particular creature in the place of the Creator. Unmasking the idolatry embedded in each totalitarian movement identifies the theological source from which the destruction of rights flows. The restoration of a just social order requires a breaking of the religious spell over the counterfeit social order.[3]

A central criticism of Fascism, which very probably was significant for the making of the *Reichskonkordat* two years later, was the condemnation of the elimination of the Catholic youth organizations by the Fascists, both because it violated the freedom of organization, generally, and the right and responsibility of the family and Church for the upbringing and education. Behind this policy, Pius asserts, is a special kind of idolatry: the deifying of the state. As a substitute for the many Catholic celebrations and rituals, the Fascists introduced their own ones in their hope to satisfy the overwhelmingly Catholic Italian people. The pope's detestation of Fascism resulted in more Fascist than Nazi literature being put on the *Index*.[4]

Not all German Catholics disliked the Lateran Treaty, and Mussolini and Fascism were regarded more favorably. They had been viewed negatively after the ban in 1926 on the sister party of the Zentrum, the *Partito Popolare Italiano*. Even after the settlement of the pope in 1931, some Catholics, such as Adenauer, showed sympathy for Fascism.[5]

The pope did not have much confidence in the *Reichskonkordat*, except that it at least would be a prop against the total elimination of the Church. Secretary Pacelli had not hidden his disgust for the Hitler regime and, as mentioned, asserted that, "*a gun had been put to his head and he had no alternative.*" than accepting the concordat. He emphasized the persecution of the Jews and political opposition and the general regime of terror, which had been introduced. He did not at all share the optimism of those who hoped that the regime's fury would run out of steam after a while.[6]

The *Reichskonkordat* made the continued existence of the favored concerns of the Church possible: confessional schools, youth organizations and influence in the appointments to theological faculties. In addition, the Church was permitted to pursue a racial policy that was contrary to the secular one.[7] Some have thought that the dissolution of the Zentrum and the BVP was a part of the concordat negotiations, which is not true, only the clause that clergy was not allowed to get involved in politics. The eradication of the Zentrum and the BVP was a natural consequence of the totalitarian process.

The concordat was, of course, a great and prestigious international victory for the regime and it was exploited in every possible way to prove that the regime was pro-Christian. The pope was right, though, with his gloomy fears. He rarely had contact with the regime himself, but left that to his secretary, Pacelli, who complained about the number of cases from Germany, which made more work for him than from the rest of the world. Between September 1933 and August 1936, the Vatican sent 54 complaints with 335 pages in total.[8] After Rosenberg had been appointed national educator and the Protestant youth associations had been transferred to the *Hitlerjugend* in the winter of 1933/1934, the pope anxiously contacted the government, which Hitler—while Hindenburg still was alive—could not ignore. Hitler gave an audience to the bishops and, when he was confronted with complaints of harassment of Catholic youth, he asserted that the bishops should be patient with the Nazi youth because too many Marxists had joined the *Hitlerjugend* and the movement lacked competent leaders(!)[9] When the Nazis published "The Farmers' Calendar 1935" where Christian holy days were replaced by days for Teutonic gods, and Good Friday was a memorial day for the victims of the Christianization of Germany, the *Osservatore Romano* declared that atheist Bolshevism was less dangerous than Rosenberg's and Hauer's anti-Bolshevist Nazism.[10]

The immediate occasion of the encyclical *Mit brennender Sorge* from the spring of 1937 was the many striking violations of the concordat. During the New Year diplomatic audience 1935/1936, the pope had fiercely attacked the appalled German diplomat about the suppression of media and what he thought was the Nazi plans of *Nationalkirche*, and when the German tried to explain, the wrath of the pope waxed even stronger.[11]

In the encyclical the pope was especially concerned about the suppression of Christian schools and youth associations. But his primary anxiousness was what was the basic ideas behind the suppression, a cunning kind of manipulation in the way that the Nazi paganism, in opposition to Fascism—or communism for that matter—passed itself off as a kind of Christianity.[12] The pope also emphasized the special features of the Nazi racist paganism. It was pantheistic, created confusion about a God who was part of the biological world and created an aura which only was a mere blind for atheistic materialism. The Nazi neo-paganism was the devotion of an impersonal racist god who replaced the God of the Bible. As a counter-measure, the pope had demonstratively appointed especially many new colored bishops.[13] (The recent work of Chapoutot gives a learned and comprehensive survey of the Nazi pantheistic neo-paganism.)

In addition, the pope attacked the anti-Semitic desire to abolish the Old Testament; the *Führer* adoration, which is nothing but a fake Christology; the effort of establishing a *Nationalkirche*, and the reinterpretation of several Christian conceptions in racist understanding: "faith"=confidence in the national destiny, "immortality"=nothing individually, but the survival of a specific people, "grace"=the privilege of belonging to a Nordic race. All these misrepresentations of theological vocabulary transformed the tools of redemption to instruments of racism and nationalism. Throughout the encyclical, the pope emphasized that the conflict in Germany was of an ideological nature, and he spoke on behalf of the whole Christendom and the encyclical bore an ecumenical stamp.[14]

Hitler was obviously surprised by the publication of *Mit brennender Sorge*. Goebbels tried first to hush the encyclical up, but after the world press had learnt of it, revenge was swift. Riots flared up in Catholic towns, such as Freiburg and Münster.[15]

The pope employed a new strategy. Later in 1937 he asserted that the Nazi success in the ideological field was alarming and had to be countered by a continual anti-propaganda, which resulted in the mobilization of the global Church through lectures, articles, leaflets and other kinds of literature at Catholic universities and schools all over the world. In 1938, the institutions were ordered to fight various kinds of racism, the glorification of bloodlines and the state's ownership of the individual. In a new "Academy of Science," the pope had demonstratively appointed Jewish members, and when an anti-Semitic book of propaganda was published in Italy, it was soon placed on the *Index*. The Vatican offensive was so broad that the SS asserted that the Catholic Church had been led into a "United Front against totalitarian states, but especially against Nazism."[16]

Conley asserts that the weakness of the encyclicals was that they were too ecclesiacentric. Although the pope dealt with the freedom of families and associations, his primary focus was on the freedom of the Church. He was not too concerned about individual freedom of speech, media and organizations, despite his behavior at the New Year conference, and the situation about the Jews in Germany was not dealt with, not by him nor his successor, Pius XII.[17]

Much because of the Nazi harassment of Austrian bishops after the "*Anschluss*" and the opposition against the closer relationship between Nazism and Fascism and introduction of racist legislation in Italy, Pius showed a more tough standing towards the ideologies in his last year. An Austrian priest had been thrown out of a window, and the cardinal and his secretary were almost assassinated while the mob were crying, "Kill Innitzer!"[18]

Emma Fattorini concludes that Pius' condemnation of totalitarianism at the end of his pontificate is not due to a democratic or liberal attitude, but disappointment with the outcome of the dictatorships. Totalitarianism was the ultimate result of an ideology, rooted in the French revolution,[19] which means that man can live without God. In the 1930s, this was expressed through racism and atheism. Communism had never concealed its attitude and was regarded by the pope as a more passive kind of atheism than Nazism. In Nazi paganism, he saw a kind of Messianism from the very beginning, which excluded all other religious projects. As heir and interpreter of such atheism, Nazism responded to the human need of holiness. Hence, and paradoxically, liberalism offered a better guarantee for Christianity, not because of its ideology, but because of the situation it created.[20] Not all in the Catholic hierarchy were enthusiastic about this "liberalism." In 1938, the Portuguese nuncio asserted, "Our leaders are influenced by Jews and Freemasons, which explains the present leftist sympathy and the fact that, rather than securing our own interests, we waste time defending human rights and the rights of Jews. Such is now the situation in the churches in Italy, France, Germany and Spain."[21]

When the pope died in February 1939, the executive committee of the Jewish world congress expressed that they would never forget this "great pope because of his defense of freedom and human values, and because of his protection of the numerous victims of racist persecution."[22]

Based on the recent free access to the Vatican archives, Hubert Wolf and Emma Fattorini describe in detail how the curia in the 1930s, with and without support from clerics from Germany and other countries, discussed for long periods of time ways to react and strategies for the relationship to Nazism and other ideologies. Encyclicals, syllabi, *Index*-filing and other measures were proposed and totally or partly completed. For strategic or other reasons, only a few of them were published, however. Wolf describes Pius' course of action in this way:

> Pius XI had found a typical Roman compromise between dogma and diplomacy . . . For political reasons he was not prepared to mention "horse and knight" (i.e. Hitler) because he neither could nor would attack the Führer and chancellor personally. The Catholic thinking about authority can ultimately have prevented him in condemning Hitler by name and putting his work on Index. Maybe he also followed the advice of archbishop Gröber who had argued with the fact that the statements of Pius so far "prove sufficiently how strong our holy church condemns this movement as purely Satanic." Another "new negative measure by the curia" would not have any effect, Gröber thought.[23]

Before his death, Pius had planned a new strong anti-Nazi resolution, which was never published.[24] The German ambassador to the Vatican, Ernst von Weizsäcker, asserts that if the pope had lived a little longer there surely would have been a breach between the countries.[25]

NOTES

1. Frank J. Coppa, "The Vatican and the Dictators Between Diplomacy and Morality," in Richard J. Wolff & Jörg K. Hoensch (ed.), *Catholics, the State, and the European Radical Right, 1919–1945* (N. Y.: Columbia University Press, 1987) 201–202.
2. Philip Morgan, *Fascism in Europe, 1919–1945* (N. Y.: Routledge, 2003) 170.
3. John J. Conley, "Totality and Idolatry: Rereading Pius XI," Part II: Articles, Vol. VI, in *The Catholic Social Science Review*, 2001, 1.
4. Coppa, "Vatican," 207–209; Hubert Wolf, *Papst und Teufel. Die Archive des Vatikan und das Dritte Reich* (Munich: Verlag C. H. Beck, 2012) 280–281.
5. Wolfgang Schieder, "Fatal Attraction: The German Right and Italian Fascism," in Hans Mommsen (ed.), *The Third Reich Between Vision and Reality. New Perspectives on German History 1918–1945* (N. Y.: Berg, 2001) 44–45.
6. Barton, Dennis, "V. The Concordat and the Encyklical" in *Hitler's rise to Power. Part 2*; The Church in History Information Centre, www.church-in-history.org ; Coppa, "Vatican," 208; Wolf, [Papst], 201–202.
7. Dieter Albrecht, "Der Heilige Stuhl und das Dritte Reich," in Klaus Gotto & Konrad Repgen (ed.), *Die Katholiken und das Dritte Reich* (Mainz: Matthias-Grünewald-Verlag, 1990) 29.
8. Coppa, "Vatican," 210.
9. Repgen, "Judenpogrom," 127; Schellenberger, *Jugend*, 48–49.
10. Gerhard Besier, *Die Kirchen und das Dritte Reich. Band 3. Spaltungen und Abwehrkämpfe 1934–1937* (Berlin: Propyläen Verlag, 2001) 142–143. Pius has allegedly said that "only Hitler is worse than Stalin." A source for this statement lacks, unfortunately.
11. Besier, *Kirchen*, 686.
12. Emma Fattorini, *Hitler, Mussolini, and the Vatican. Pope Pius XI and the Speech that was Never Made* (Cambridge: Polity Press, 2011) 119.
13. Wolf, *Papst*, 259.
14. Albrecht, "Heilige Stuhl," 35; Ludwig Volk, "Nationalsozialistischer Kirchenkampf und deutscher Episkopat," in Gotto & Repgen (ed.), *Die Katholiken*, 73; Conley, "Totality," 1–3.
15. Volk, "Kirchenkampf," 72–74; Fattorini, *Hitler, Mussolini*, 123-125; Ernst Piper, *Alfred Rosenberg. Hitlers Chefideologe* (Munich: Karl Blessing Verlag, 2005) 413.
16. Konrad Repgen, "1938—Judenpogrom und katholischer Kirchenkampf," in Günter Brakelmann & Martin Rosowski (ed.), *Antisemitismus. Von religiöser Judenfeindschaft zur Rassenideologie* (Göttingen: Vandenhoeck & Ruprecht, 1989) 127–131; Rudolf Lill, "NS-Ideologie und Katholische Kirche," in Gotto & Repgen (ed.), *Die Katholiken*, 148.
17. Conley, "Totality," 5–6.
18. Fattorini, *Hitler, Mussolini*, 131–151; Michael R. Marrus, "French Protestant Churches and the Persecution of the Jews in France," in Carol Rittner, Stephen D.

Smith, and Irena Steinfeldt, *The Holocaust and the Christian World* (London: Kuperard, 2000) 127; Lill, "NS-Ideologie," 140; Coppa, "Vatican," 211–212.

19. After 1789, though. Author's remark.
20. Fattorini, *Hitler, Mussolini*, 169–171.
21. Fattorini, *Hitler, Mussolini*, 198.
22. Repgen, "Judenpogrom," 118.
23. Wolf, *Papst*, 304–305.
24. Michael Phayer, The *Catholic Church and the Holocaust, 1930–1965* (Bloominton: Indiana University Press, 2000) 1-4; Rittner, Smith & Steinfeldt, Christian World, 146–147.
25. Fattorini, *Hitler, Mussolini*, 1.

Chapter Nine

Conclusions as to Differences of Mentality among the Confessions

There seem to be several explanations for the confessional difference in attitude to Nazism. The speech of Vice-Chancellor von Papen in June 1934 in Marburg seems to indicate a basic difference in mentality between Catholics and Protestants that had significance for German voting behavior in the early 1930s. One of the ideological differences between the rightist Catholic von Papen, the Zentrum renegade, and the "Weimar Coalition," was the relationship to the ideas of 1789, the ideas of *modernity*, which von Papen, together with the bulk of non-socialist Protestants, rejected. So, it is relevant to claim that to a great extent the Catholics followed a social democratic modernist political course, whereas theologically, with their conservative dogmatism, they were anti-modernist. The Protestants, however, showed the opposite mentality. Because of their widespread acceptance of alien influences in their theology, they can be regarded as theologically modernist. Politically, most non-socialist Protestants were far less interested in democracy than Catholics, and hence can be regarded as anti-modernist.

The general difference between Catholics and Protestants in Germany was more profound than the mere modernist/antimodernist splits in theological and political mentalities. In fact the differences demonstrated a *cleavage of civilization*. They based their cultures on outlooks on two different civilizations.

In this way, the rightist Catholic von Papen, although he did not favor democray, was solidly rooted in the plinth of the "Weimar Coalition" in his desire of *unity built on a common European civilizing foundation*. This originated in "The Legacy of Antiquity," i.e. the amalgamation of the Greek-Roman and Judeo-Christian culture from the fourth century, and the development of this culture in Western Europe afterwards.

The German Protestants, on the other hand, since the time of Herder seem to have been more attracted by their *genetic North European, Teutonic roots*, a leaning which ultimately ended in the Protestant based rightist movement's narcissistic, racist and autarchic German-nationalism. This tendency was clearly opposite to the Catholic culture outlined above, and the radical nature of German-nationalism can possibly be explained by a more or less concealed inferiority complex in the face of the "Western" and "Southern cultures" and the need to distance themselves from them and for self-assertion.

Thus, the Protestant-German nationalism also differed from the rather Catholic-based French kind of nationalism. Among the Protestant clergy in the Weimar Republic, 70 to 80 percent can be classified as "conservative national," i.e. in accordance with the German version.[1]

The radicalization and the militant attitude in German nationalism developed after the defeat in 1918 because the Protestants to a far lesser degree were willing to accept the reality that the powerful Protestant dominated Hohenzollern state really *had* lost the war. In the churches, clergymen had preached that Germany fought a good and just war, and prayers for victory had been prayed, prayers which people believed would be answered. On top of it all: Germany had hardly seen an enemy soldier on German soil since the Russians had been driven back from East Prussia in the autumn of 1914. On the contrary, in November 1918, Germany still controlled parts of France, half of Belgium and the best agrarian areas of European Russia. In the light of these realities, the feelings that emerged within the Protestant confession are understandable: the resentment, humiliation, frustration, revenge, self-pity and lack of acceptance of the situation. Liberal Protestants originally accepted the "Weimar Coalition," but like the German liberalism of the nineteenth century with *Nationalliberale*, which from the 1860s gradually became rightist, a similar development happened with the liberals in the Weimar republic but more rapidly. The rightist tendencies in Naumann's leftist liberal camp had been discernible even before 1918. The German version of liberalism was in several ways a veneer of classical Western European social liberalism.

The adulation of *"das Deutsche Wesen"* was a part of the German Protestant nationalist syndrome. It implied that Germans as a race were especially sublime and superior people, both culturally and morally. This view may have helped promote the spread of racist anti-Semitism within the Protestant milieu. This *"Wesen"*-persuasion was predominant in church circles, including the CSVD.

An important precondition that prevented Catholics from adhering to the same introvert German-nationalist ghetto was, of course, their close attachment to the Roman Catholic Church with its extensive, universal and international network. For German Catholics in particular, the pronounced loyalty to the pope, Ultramontanism, was an important element. They were obedient to the *ex-cathedra* dogma from 1870, obedience which was enhanced during the

Kulturkampf. Ultramontanism would play an important role in the "contest" for authority between the Vatican and German authorities, the latter in the empire based on a clear uniform Protestant-nationalist program backed by the majority of the populace. When the pope introduced his peace proposal in 1917, contrary to the interests of German authorities, this possibly led to, consciously or unconsciously, the thought among Ultramontanists that it was time to end the war.

Among Protestants, there had not been any corresponding "contest" between Church and state before the "Weimar Republic." The state was intended to be the supporter and protector of the Church, and when the choice for the Protestants after WWI was between on the one hand, a secular social-democratic and Catholic-dominated Weimar coalition, and on the other hand a party—the Nazi party—claiming to be a friend of the Churches, the choice was not so difficult.

Catholics had obviously noticed the use by Protestants of *"das Deutsche Wesen,"* but if this term were to have any relevance for them, they wanted to fill it with universal Christian values.

Already early in the 1920s, Catholics reacted strongly to the neo-pagan tendencies in the Nazi party. Also Protestants reacted later. Normally, one would expect such a phenomenon to be detested by pietists, orthodox and other Bible-oriented clergy and lay folk. Some of them were, but they were neither numerous nor authoritative enough to challenge the predominant mentality, much because of the long German tradition of accepting a great variety of theological opinions, more or less influenced by theosophy, mythology and occultism. It is conspicuous, but also symptomatic, that the great Protestant duel with Rosenberg's *Mythus* took place five years after its publication, and it was first then that a considerable number of theologians realized that the Nazi "Positive Christianity" was becoming more and more in line with Rosenberg's ideas.

The Nazis' "Positive Christianity," the assurances of Hitler and other Nazis of pro-Christian attitudes and measures taken in regional state governments with Nazis in coalition before 1933, seem to have set the minds at rest for the great majority of Protestants as things overriding the neo-pagan tendencies. In politics, Germans were only too familiar with socialist hostility to Christians because it had been explicit, while the exceptionally strong identification among Protestants of nationalism and Christianity ever since the time of Schleiermacher, made it relatively easy for Nazis to conceal their intentions.

Catholics, being members of an old international institution, seemed to be more familiar than Protestants with subordinating themselves to international treaty obligations, whether they were felt just or unjust.

There were also Catholics among the great number of *völkisch* Nazis and other radical rightist and German-national notables since 1800, and the monk Lanz von Liebenfels is even regarded as one of Hitler's precursors. But common to these—and the rightist-oriented "Reform" and Old Catholics—was the fact that they were numerically extremely few and in the Catholic milieu absolutely marginalized.

It seems that large parts of the Protestant church milieu were guided in their voting behavior in the 1930s by naive confidence in both the excellence of "*das Deutsche Wesen*" and the potential of the Nazi party as a strong and resolute "minister" of this "*Wesen*." This "ministry" included reestablishment of the national honor lost in 1918 and 1919 and the recovery from the economic and social debasement. No Protestant church leader managed to see through and warn against the destructive ideology which Nazi policy was based on and enacted by the Nazis once in power. Rather than warning against them, local clergymen recommended people to vote Nazi instead.

When the Catholic resolutions appeared after 1930, these can be regarded as not only symptoms of cleavage of mentality, but even a *cleavage of civilisation*, between Ultramontanism and Nazism. A corresponding cleavage was absent on the part of the Protestants, as the lack of resolutions from them show.

As mentioned, Ian Kershaw regarded the election campaigns of social democrats and Catholics as partly successful because they were directed to their own electorate. In a way, the extensive appeal of several Catholic organizations in February 1933 can be regarded as just such an exertion. The appeal, (which probably was not instigated by the Zentrum) is even more significant as a mighty manifestation and demonstration of the dominating *mentality* within the Catholic electorate in a time of crisis than as a contribution that mobilized the voters. Probably the Zentrum would have achieved almost the same result without it. In a corresponding way, there is reason to speculate about the effects of the Church resolutions from 1930 to 1933. The Zentrum had made progress already in the 1930 election but only minor progress afterwards. The "*Zentrumsturm*" had probably been so closed, robust and socially controlled that election campaigns for the party were hardly necessary.

In 2012, the EU was awarded the Nobel Peace Prize, partly on the grounds of it functioning as a peace-promoting factor in the relationship between Germany and France. However, it is probably truer to say the EU is the result of a radical *change of mentality among German nonsocialist Protestants* in the post-WWII period. These abandoned their long-standing anti-French attitude and let Adenauer have great freedom for his Francophile goals. President van Rompuy said in his speech of thanks that people could not know for certain what the relationship between the Federal Republic and France would be like in a Europe without the EU. The prospects for a military confrontation between the countries after 1945, even in a Europe without the EU, do seem not very likely, though.

The development and change of mentalities have greatly impacted the people of Germany, making for a dramatic history, during the last 200 years.

NOTE

1. Thomas Fandel, *Konfession und Nationalsozialismus. Evangelische und Katholische Pfarrer in de Pfalz 1930–1939* (Paderborn: Ferdinand Schöningh, 1997) 63.

Defining of Terms

Protestant -s: the established churches of Lutheran, Reformed, and Union churches of Lutherans and Reformed (The term includes free denominations with a similar theology)

Social democrat -s, -acy: ideology/opinion group represented by SPD in the 1920s and 1930s

Socialist -s, -ism: ideology/opinion group represented by SPD in the Empire, and a group designation of SPD, KPD and a lot of minor parties with similar ideology in the 1920s and 1930s. ("Socialism" is also used by right-wing radicals, but with another meaning, which is commented on page 148.)

Ultramontanist, -s, -ism: Catholic fraction which emphasized the authority of the Vatican; Ultramontan = beyond the mountains, i.e. the Alps. In Italy, beyond the Alps as to Germany, was the spiritual authority. (The term was used derogatorily by Protestants.)

"*Völkische Bewegung*" (The Volkish (/Popular) movement): a Protestant dominated German and Austrian radical right-wing syndrome of culture and mentality

References

Abrahamsen, Olav A., and Andreas Aase. *Portal. Verden etter 1850*. Oslo: Det norske Samlaget, 2004.
Albrecht, Dieter. "Der Heilige Stuhl und das Dritte Reich." In *Die Katholiken und das Dritte Reich*, edited by Klaus Gotto and Konrad Repgen. Mainz: Matthias-Grünewald-Verlag, 1990.
Allen, William Sheridan. "Farewell to Class Analysis in the Rise of Nazism: Comment." In *Central European History*, Vol. XVII, No. 1. Atlanta, 1984.
Altermatt, Urs. *Katholizismus und Moderne. Zur Sozial-und Mentalitätsgeschichte der Schweizer Katholiken im 19. Und 20. Jahrhundert*. Zürich: Benziger Verlag, 1989.
Altgeld, Wolfgang. *Katholizismus, Protestantismus, Judentum. Über religiös begründete Gegensätze und nationalreligiöse Ideen in der Geschichte des deutschen Nationalismus*. Mainz: Matthias-Grünewald-Verlag, 1992.
Anger, Walter. *Das Dritte Reich in Dokumenten*. Frankfurt/M: Europäische Verlagsanstalt, 1957.
Anners, Erik. *Den europeiske rettens historie*. Oslo: Universitetsforlaget, 1998.
Arbeidernes Leksikon. Oslo: Pax, 1977.
Aretz, Jürgen. *Katholische Arbeiterbewegung und Nationalsozialismus. Der Verband katholischer Arbeiter-und Knappenvereine Westdeutschlands 1923–1945*. Mainz: Matthias-Grünewald-Verlag, 1982.
Arvidsson, Stefan. "Germania. Noen hovedlinjer i forskningen om fortidens germanere." In *Jakten på Germania. Fra Nordensvermeri til SS-arkeologi*, edited by Terje Emberland & Jorunn Sem Fure. Oslo: Humanist, 2009.
Ascher, Saul. *Die Germanomanie. Skizze zu einer Zeitgemälde*. 1815 http://gutenberg.spiegel.de/buch/2602/1.
Barton, Dennis. *Hitler's Rise to Power. Part 2*. The Church in History Information Centre. www.church-in-history.org.

Baumgärtner, Raimund. *Weltanschauungskampf im Dritten Reich. Die Auseinandersetzung der Kirchen mit Alfred Rosenberg*. Mainz: Matthias-Grünewald-Verlag, 1977.

Becker, Josef and Ruth Becker. *Hitler's Machtergreifung. Dokumente vom Machtantritt Hitlers 30. Januar 1933 bis zur Besiegelung des Einparteienstaates 14. Juli 1933*. Munich: Deutscher Taschenbuchverlag, 1983.

Beckmann, Klaus-Martin. "Zur Geschichte des Völkischen" und des "Nationalen" im Umkreis der Ökumenischen Bewegung." In *Volk—Nation—Vaterland. Der deutsche Protestantismus und der Nationalismus*, edited by Horst Zillesen. Gütersloh: Gerd Mohn, 1970.

Bédarida, Francois. "Nationalsozialistische Verkündigung und säkuläre Religion." In *Der Nationalsozialismus als politische Religion*, edited by Michael Ley and Julius H. Schoeps. Bodenheim: Philo Verlagsgesellschaft, 1997.

Benöhr-Laqueur, Susanne. Review of *Generation des Unbedingten. Das Führungskorps des Reichssicherungshauptamtes*, by Michael Wildt. Hamburg: HIS, 2002. http://hsozkult.geschichte.hu-berlin.de/rezensionen/NS-2003-1-062.

Berding, Helmut. *Moderner Antisemitismus in Deutschland*. Frankfurt/M: Suhrkamp Verlag, 1988.

Bergmann, Werner. "Völkischer Antisemitismus im Kaiserreich." In *Handbuch zur "Völkischen Bewegung" 1871–1918*, edited by Uwe Puschner, Walter Schmitz, and Justus H. Ulbricht. Munich: K. G. Saur Verlag, 1996.

Berntson, Lennart. *Politiska partier och sociala klasser. En analys av partiteorin i den moderna statskunskapen och marxismen*. Lund: Bo Cavefors Bokförlag, 1974

Besier, Gerhard. *Die Kirchen und das Dritte Reich. Bd. 3. Spaltungen und Abwehrkämpfe 1934–1937*. Berlin: Propyläen Verlag, 2001.

Binder, Gerhart. *Irrtum und Widerstand. Die deutschen Katholiken in der Auseinanderstzung mit dem Nationalsozialismus*. Munich: Pfeiffer, 1968.

Biographisch-Bibliographisches Kirchenlexikon. http://www.bautz.de/bbkl/.

Blaschke, Olaf. *Katholizismus und Antisemitismus im Deutschen Kaiserreich*. Göttingen: Vandenhoeck & Ruprecht, 1999.

Blavatsky, Helena P. *The Secret Doctrine. The Synthesis of Science, Religion, and Philosophy, Vol. II*. Theosophical University Press Online Edition, 1888. www.theosociety.org/pasadena/.

Bleuel, Hans Peter and Ernst Klinnert. *Deutsche Studenten auf dem Weg ins Dritte Reich*. Gütersloh: Siegbert Mohn Verlag, 1967.

Bolle, Fritz. "Darwinismus und Zeitgeist." In *Zeitgeist im Wandel. Bd. 1*, edited by Hans Joachim Schoeps. Stuttgart: Ernst Klett Verlag, 1967.

Borchert, Wolfgang. *Draussen vor der Tür und ausgewählte Erzählungen*. Hamburg: Rowohlt Taschenbuchverlag, 1972.

Boyens, Armin. "Die Stellung der Ökumene und der Bekennenden Kirche zum Problem von Krieg und Frieden während der Zeit des Dritten Reiches." In *Kirche zwischen Krieg und Frieden Studien zur Geschichte des deutschen Protestantismus*, edited by Wolfgang Huber and Johannes Schwerdtfeger. Stuttgart: Ernst Klett Verlag, 1976.

Boyer, John W. "Catholics, Christians and the Challenges of Democracy: The Heritage of the Nineteenth Century." In *Political Catholicism in Europe 1918–45, Vol. 1*, edited by Wolfram Kaiser and Helmut Wohnout. New York: Routledge, 2004.

Bracher, Karl Dietrich. *Die Auflösung der Weimarer Republik. Eine Studie zum Problem des Machtverfalls in der Demokratie.* Villingen/Schwarzwald: Ring-Verlag, 1964.

Brakelmann, Günter. "Der Krieg 1870/71 und die Reichsgründung im Urteil des Protestantismus." In *Kirche zwischen Krieg und Frieden. Studien zur Geschichte des deutschen Protestantismus*, edited by Wolfgang Huber and Johannes Schwerdtfeger. Stuttgart: Ernst Klett Verlag, 1976.

Breuer, Thomas. "Kirchliche Opposition im NS-Staat. Eine Basisperspektive." In *Kirchen in der Diktatur. Drittes Reich und SED-Staat*, edited by Günter Heydemann and Lother Kettenacker. Göttingen: Vandenhoeck & Ruprecht, 1993.

Breuning, Klaus. *Die Vision des Reiches. Deutscher Katholizismus zwischen Demokratie und Diktatur (1929–1934)*. Munich: Max Hueber Verlag, 1969.

Bringeland, Hans M. "Martin Dibelius' oppgjer med nasjonalsosialismen." Unpublished manuscript for lecture for the *Doctor philosophiae* degree at the University of Bergen Dec. 15, 2011. Kindly permitted for use as reference in e-mail to the author April 14, 2020. (Published as extended and revised article "Martin Dibelius og nasjonalsosialismen" in *Teologisk tidsskrift*. No. 1, Vol. 2, 2013. Free access to Norwegian article and English abstract on www.idunn.no).

Broszat, Martin and Norbert Frei. *PLOETZ. Das Dritte Reich. Ursprünge, Ereignisse, Wirkungen.* Frechen: Komet, 1983.

Bruck, Arthur Moeller van den *Das dritte Reich.* 1922/33. http://nsl-arciv.com/Buecher/.

BT (the Norwegian daily *Bergens Tidende*).

BTMAGASINET, March 19 and 29, 2008 (A weekly magazine of *Bergens Tidende*).

Buchanan, Tom. "Great Britain." In *Political Catholicism in Europe, 1918–1965*, edited by Tom Buchanan and Martin Conway. Oxford: Clarendon Press, 1996.

Buchheim, Karl. *Geschichte der christlichen Parteien in Deutschland*. Munich: Kösel Verlag, 1953.

Bugge, Heuch. "Rettsordningen i det nye Tyskland." In *Norsk Rikskringkasting. Foredrag om det nye Tyskland.* Oslo: J. M. Stenersen, 1940.

Burger, Christoph. "Der Wandel in der Beurteilung von Frieden und Krieg bei Friedrich Schleiermacher, dargestellt an drei Predigten." In *Kirche zwischen Krieg und Frieden*, edited by Wolfgang Huber and Johannes Schwerdtfeger. Stuttgart: Ernst Klett Verlag, 1976.

Butler, Rohan d'O. *The Roots of National Socialism 1783–1933*. London: E. P. Dutton, 1942.

Büttner, Ursula. "Von der Kirche verlassen.: Die deutschen Protestanten und die Verfolgung der Juden und Christen jüdischer Herkunft im "Dritten Reich." In *Die verlassenen Kinder der Kirche. Der Umgang mit Christen jüdischer Herkunft im Dritten Reich*, edited by Ursula Büttner and Martin Greschat. Göttingen: Vandenhoeck & Ruprecht, 1998.

Calvin, Jean *Institutio Religionis Christianae, Book II*. English version, Grand Rapids: Wm. B. Eerdmans Publishing, 1989.
Cancik, Hubert. "Erbschaft jener Zeit." In *Religions-und Geistesgeschichte der Weimarer Republik*, edited by Hubert Cancik. Düsseldorf: Patmos Verlag, 1982.
Cancik, Hubert. "Neuheiden" und totaler Staat. Völkische Religion am Ende der Weimarer Republik." In *Religions-und Geistesgeschichte der Weimarer Republik*, edited by Hubert Cancik. Düsseldorf: Patmos Verlag, 1982.
Casper, Bernhard. "Gesichtspunkte für eine Darstellung der katholischen Theologie im 19. Jahrhundert." In *Entwicklungslinien des deutschen Katholizismus*, edited by Anton Rauscher. Munich: Verlag Ferdinand Schöningh, 1973.
Catholic Encyclopaedia. catholic.org.
Chamberlain, Houston Stewart. *Die Grundlagen des Neunzehnten Jahrhunderts, II. Hälfte*. Munich: Verlagsanstalt F. Bruckmann, 1907.
Chandler, Alfred R. *Rosenberg's Nazi Myth*. New York: Ithaca, 1945.
Chapoutot, Johann. *Das Gesetz des Blutes. Von der NS-Weltanschauung zum Vernichtungskrieg*. Darmstadt: Philipp von Zabern, 2016.
Childers, Thomas. *The Nazi Voter. The Social Foundations of Fascism in Germany*. Chapel Hill: University of North Carolina Press, 1983.
Childers, Thomas. "Who, Indeed Did Vote for Hitler?" In *Central European History*, Vol. XII, No. 1, Atlanta 1984.
Christ, Herbert. *Der politische Protestantismus in der Weimarer Republik. Eine Studie über die politische Meinungsbildung durch die evangelischen Kirchen im Spiegel der Literatur und die Presse*. Bonn: PhD dissertation, Friedrich-Wilhelm Universität, 1967.
Class, Heinrich (pseudonym: Daniel Frymann). *Wenn ich der Kaiser wär. Politische Wahrheiten und Notwendigkeiten.* Leipzig: Dieterichs'chen Verlagsbuchhandlung, 1913. http://reichsarchiv.com/Buecher/.
Clemens, Gabriele. *Martin Spahn und der Rechtsradikalismus in der Weimarer Republik*. Mainz: Matthias-Grünewald-Verlag, 1983.
Conley, John J. "Totality, and Idolatry: Rereading Pius XI." In *The Catholic Social Science Review,* Part II: Articles, Vol. VI. 2001.
Conway, John S. "National Socialism, and the Christian Churches during the Weimar Republic." In *The Nazi Machtergreifung*, edited by Peter D. Stachura. Boston: George Allen & Unwin, 1983.
Conway, Martin. *Catholic Politics in Europe 1918–1945*. New York: Routledge, 1997.
Conway, Martin. "Catholic Politics or Christian Democracy? The Evolution of Interwar Political Catholicism." In *Political Catholicism in Europe 1918–45, Vol. 1*, edited by Wolfram Kaiser and Helmut Wohnout. New York: Routledge, 2004.
Conway, Martin. "Introduction." In *Political Catholicism in Europe, 1918–1965*, edited by Tom Buchanan and Martin Conway. Oxford: Clarendon Press, 1996.
Conze, Werner. "Deutschland" und "deutsche Nation" als historische Begriffe." In *Die Rolle der Nation in der deutschen Geschichte und Gegenwart. Beiträge zu einer internationalen Konferenz in Berlin (West) vom 16. Bis 18. Juni 1983*, edited by Otto Büsch and James J. Sheehan. Berlin: Colloquium, 1985.

Conze, Werner. "Zum Verhältnis des Luthertums zu den mitteleuropäischen Nationalbewegungen im 19. Jahrhundert." In *Luther in der Neuzeit. Wissenschaftliches Symposion des Vereins für Reformatinsgeschichte*, edited by Bernd Moeller. Gütersloh: Gerd Mohn, 1983.

Coppa, Frank J. "The Vatican and the Dictators Between Diplomacy and Morality." In *Catholics, the State, and the European Radical Right, 1919–1945*, edited by Richard J. Wolff and Jörg K. Hoensch. New York: Columbia University Press, 1987.

Cramer, Kevin. "The Cult of Gustavus Adolphus. Protestant Identity and German Nationalism." In *Protestants, Catholics and Jews in Germany, 1800–1914*, edited by Helmut Walser Smith. New York: Berg, 2001.

Cremer, Douglas J. "To avoid a new Kulturkampf": The Catholic Workers' Associations and National socialism in Weimar-era Bavaria. In *Journal of Church and State*, Sept. 1999. http://www.highbeam.com/doc/.

Dagen. (Norwegian daily).

Dahm, Karl-Wilhelm. *Pfarrer und Politik. Soziale Position und politische Mentalität des deutchen evangelischen Pfarrerstandes zwischen 1918 und 1933*. Cologne: Westdeutscher Verlag, 1965.

Dantine, Wilhelm. "Frühromantik-Romantik-Idealismus." In *Kirche und Synagoge. Handbuch zur Geschichte von Christen und Juden*, edited by Karl Heinrich Rengstorf and Siegfried von Kortzfleisch. Stuttgart: Ernst Klett Verlag, 1970.

Darnstädt, Thomas. "Mephisto als Untertan." In *SPIEGEL SPECIAL*, no. 1, 2008.

Darré, Richard Walter. *Neuadel aus Blut und Boden*. Munich: J. F. Lehmann, 1943.

Das ökumenische Heiligenlexikon. heiligenlexikon.de.

Der Theologe Nr. 4. http://www.theologe.de/theologe4.htm .

Deutsche Biographie. deutsche-biographie.de.

Didriksen, Synnøve. *Steriliseringsloven av 1934—et ledd i norsk befolkningspolitikk*. Dissertation for *Candidatus philologiae*, University of Bergen, 1995 (Available at Bergen University Library).

Dietrich, Donald J. *Catholic Citizens in the Third Reich: Psycho-Social Principles and Moral Reasoning*. Piscataway New Jersey: Transaction Publishers, 1988.

Dietrich, Donald J. "Catholic Theology and the Challenge of Nazism." In *Antisemitism, Christian Ambivalence, and Holocaust*, edited by Kevin P. Spicer. Indianapolis: Indiana University Press, 2007.

Die Wahlen zum Reichstag am 20. Mai 1928, Heft II. Berlin: Reimar Hobbing, 1930

Die Wahlen zum Reichstag am 6. November 1932, Teil II. Berlin: Verlag für Sozialpolitik, Wissenschaft und Statistik, 1935.

Dirks, Walter. "Das Defizit des deutschen Katholizismus in Weltbild, Zeitbewusstsein und politischer Theorie." In *Religions-und Geistesgeschichte der Weimarer Republik*, edited by Hubert Cancik. Düsseldorf: Patmos Verlag, 1982.

Dohnke, Kay. "Völkische Literatur und Heimatliteratur 1870–1918." In *Handbuch zur "Völkischen Bewegung" 1871–1918*, edited by Uwe Puschner, Walter Schmitz, and Justus H. Ulbricht. Munich: K. G. Saur Verlag, 1996.

Dörner, Andreas. *Politischer Mythos und symbolische Politik. Sinnstiftung durch symbolische Formen am Beispiel des Hermannsmythos*. Opladen: Westdeutscher Verlag, 1995.
Durham, Martin. *Women and Fascism*. New York: Routledge, 1998.
Dühring, Eugen. *Cursus der Philosophie als streng wissenschaftlicher Weltanschauung und Lebensgestaltung*. Leipzig: L. Heimanns Verlag, 1875. http://archive.org/details/.
Egelkraut, Helmuth. *Die Liebenzeller Mission und der Nationalsozialismus*. Münster: Lit Verlag, 2015.
Eggers, Kurt. *Rom gegen Reich. Ein Kapitel deutscher Geschichte um Bismarck*. Berlin: Nordland Verlag, 1935. http://reichsarchiv.com.
Elvert, Jürgen. "A Microcosm of Society or the Key to a Majority in the Reichstag? The Centre party in Germany." In *Political Catholicism in Europe 1918–45, vol. 1*, edited by Wolfram Kaiser and Helmut Wohnout. New York: Routledge, 2004.
Emberland, Terje. *Religion og rase. Nyhedenskap og nazisme i Norge 1933–1945*. Oslo: Humanist, 2003.
Encyclopaedia Britannica. 1968.
Erb, Dirk. *Gleichgeschaltet. Der Nazi-terror gegen Gewerkschaften und Berufsverbände*. Göttingen: Steidl Verlag, 2001.
Eriksen, Trond Berg, Håkon Harket, and Einhart Lorenz. *Jødehat. Antisemittismens historie fra antikken til i dag*. Oslo: Cappelen Damm, 2009.
Evans, Ellen Lovell. *The Cross and the Ballot. Catholic Political Parties in Germany, Switzerland, Austria, Belgium and the Netherlands, 1785–1985*. Boston: Humanities Press, 1999.
Falter, Jürgen. *Hitlers Wähler*. Munich: Beck'sche Verlagsbuchhandlung, 1991.
Falter, Jürgen, Thomas Lindenberger, and Siegfried Schumann. *Wahlen und Abstimmungen in der Weimarer Republik. Materialen zum Wahlverhalten 1919–1933*. Munich: C. H. Beck, 1986.
Fandel, Thomas. *Konfession und Nationalsozialismus. Evangelische und katholische Pfarrer in der Pfalz 1930–1939*. Munich: Ferdinand Schöningh, 1997.
Fattorini, Emma. *Hitler, Mussolini and the Vatican. Pope Pius XI and the Speech that was Never Made*. Cambridge: Polity Press, 2011.
Fenske, Hans. *Konservatismus und Rechtsradikalismus in Bayern nach 1918*. Bad Homburg: Verlag Gehlen, 1969.
Fest, Joachim C. *Hitler. En biografi*. (Norwegian publication) Oslo: Gyldendal, 1979
Fichte, Johann Gottlieb. *Reden an die deutsche Nation*. Leipzig: Philip Reclam Jun., 1878. http://gutenberg.spiegel.de/buc/.
Fichte, Johann Gottlieb. *Der geschlossene Handelsstaat Ein philosophischer Entwurf als Anhang zur Rechtslehre und Probe einer künftig zu liefernder Politik*. Berlin, 1845. http://www.zeno.org/Philosophie/.
Fichte, Johann Gottlieb. *Das System der Rechtslehre*, 1812. www.textlog.de/fichte
Fischer Lexikon. Frankfurt/M, 1982.
Flasche, Rainer. "Religionsmodelle und Erkenntnisprinzipien der Religionswissenschaft in der Weimarer Zeit." In *Religions-und Geistesgeschichte der Weimarer Republik*, edited by Hubert Cancik. Düsseldorf: Patmos Verlag, 1982.

Forsthoff, Ernst. *Deutsche Geschichte seit 1918 in Dokumenten*. Leipzig: Alfred Kröner Verlag, 1935.
Foss, Øyvind. *Krystallnatten*. Oslo: Spartacus forlag, 2009.
Frech, Kurt. "Felix Dahn. Die Verbreitung völkischen Gedankenguts durch den historischen Roman." In *Handbuch zur "Völkischen Bewegung" 1871–1918*, edited by Uwe Puschner, Walter Schmitz, and Justus H. Ulbricht. Munich: K. G. Saur Verlag, 1996.
Freston, Paul. *Protestant Political Parties A Global Survey*. Burlington: Ashgate Publishing, 2004.
Friedmann, Jan. "Macht Platz, Ihr Alten." In *SPIEGEL SPECIAL*, no. 1, 2008.
Frøland, Carl Müller. *Nazismens idéunivers*. Oslo: Vidarforlaget, 2017.
Gaede, Reinhard. "Die Stellung des deutschen Protestantismus zum Problem von Krieg und Frieden während der Zeit der Weimarer Republik." In *Kirche zwischen Krieg und Frieden*, edited by Wolfgang Huber and Johannes Schwerdtfeger. Stuttgart: Ernst Klett Verlag, 1976.
Gennrich, Paul-Wilhelm. *Gott und die Völker. Beiträge zur Auffassung von Volk und Volkstum in der Geschichte der Theologie*. Stuttgart: Evangelisches Verlagswerk, 1972.
Giles, Geoffrey J. "National Socialism and the Educated Elite in the Weimar Republic." In *The Nazi Machtergreifung*, edited by Peter D. Stachura. Boston: George Allen & Unwin, 1983.
Glaus, Beat. "The National Front in Switzerland." In *Who were the Fascists?*, edited by Stein Ugelvik Larsen, Bernt Hagtvedt, and Jens P. Myklebust. Oslo: Universitetsforlaget, 1980.
Goebbels, Josef. *Wetterleuchten. Aufsätze aus der Kampfzeit 82. BAND "Der Angriff)*. Munich: Franz Eher, 1939.
Goldhagen, Daniel J. *Hitler's Willing Executioners. Ordinary Germans and the Holocaust*. London: Abacus, 1997.
Golücke, Friedhelm. *Studentenwörterbuch*. Graz: Styria, 1987.
Gordon, Sarah. *Hitler, Germans, and the "Jewish Question."* Princeton NJ: Princeton University Press, 1984.
Gotto, Klaus, Hans Günter Hockerts, and Konrad Repgen. "Nationalsozialistische Herausforderung und kirchliche Antwort. Eine Bilanz." In *Die Katholiken und das Dritte Reich*, edited by Klaus Gotto, and Konrad Repgen. Mainz: Matthias-Grünewald-Verlag, 1990.
Graf, Friedrich Wilhelm. *God's Anti-Liberal Avant-Garde. New Theologies in the Weimar Republic*. London: German Historical Institute London Bulletin, 2010.
Greive, Hermann. "Die gesellschaftliche Bedeutung der christlich-jüdischen Differenz. Zur Situation im deutschen Katholizismus." In *Juden im Wilhelminischen Deutschland 1890–1914*, edited by Werner E. Mosse. Tübingen: J. C. B. Mohr, 1976.
Greive, Hermann. *Theologie und Ideologie. Katholizismus und Judentum in Deutschland und Österreich 1918–1935*. Heidelberg: Verlag Lambert Schneider, 1969.
Greschat, Martin. "Friedrich Weissler. Ein Jurist der Bekennenden Kirche im Widerstand gegen Hitler." In *Die verlassenen Kinder der Kirche. Der Umgang mit*

Christen jüdischer Herkunft im "Dritten Reich," edited by Ursula Büttner and Martin Greschat. Göttingen: Vandenhoeck & Ruprecht, 1998.

Greschat, Martin. "Protestantischer Antisemitismus in Wilhelminischer Zeit. Das Beispiel des Hofpredigers Adolf Stoecker." In *Antisemitismus. Von religiöser Judenfeindschaft zur Rassenideologie*, edited by Günter Brakelmann and Martin Rosowski. Göttingen: Vandenhoeck & Ruprecht, 1989.

Groh, Dieter. "Der Umsturz von 1918 im Erlebnis der Zeitgenossen." In *Zeitgeist im Wandel. Zeitgeist der Weimarar Republik*, edited by Hans Joachim Schoeps. Stuttgart: Ernst Klett Verlag, 1968.

Grolleg-Edler, Charlotte. *Die wehrhafte Nachtigall—Ottokar Kernstock (1848–1928)*. Graz: Universitätsverlag, 2006.

Grünthal, Günter. *Reichsschulgesetz und Zentrumspartei in der Weimarer Republik*. Düsseldorf: Droste Verlag, 1968.

Haeckel, Ernst. *Die Welträtsel. Gemeinverständliche Studien über Monistische Philosophie*. Bonn: Emil Strauss, 1900.

Haffner, Sebastian. *Germany: Jekyll and Hyde. An eyewitness analysis of Nazi Germany*. London: Abacus, 2008.

Hagelstein, Bengt. Report of lecture by Dr. H.-U. Ludewig. *Die Militarisierung der Gesellschaft: die paramilitären Verbände. Das Reichsbanner Schwarz-Rot-Gold, Bund republikanischer Kriegsteilnehmer und Der Rote Frontkämpferbund*. Historical seminar at Technische Universität Braunschweig (Brunswick), Summer 2001.

Hagen, William W. "Murder in the East: German-Jewish Liberal Reactions to Anti-Jewish Violence in Poland and other East European Lands." In *Central European History,* Vol. 34, No. 1. Atlanta, 2001.

Hahn, Hans Joachim. *German Thought and Culture from the Holy Roman Empire to the Present Day*. Manchester: Manchester University Press, 1995.

Hamilton, Richard. *Who voted for Hitler?* Princeton NJ: Princeton University Press, 1982.

Hannot, Walter, *Die Judenfrage in der katholischen Tagespresse Deutschlands und Österreichs 1923–1933*. Mainz: Matthias-Grünewald-Verlag, 1990.

Harnack, Adolf von. *Das Wesen des Christentums*. Leipzig: J. C. Hinrichs'che Buchhandlung, 1908.

Hartung, Günter. "Völkische Ideologie." In *Handbuch zur "Völkischen Bewegung" 1871–1918*, edited by Uwe Puschner, Walter Schmitz, and Justus H. Ulbricht. Munich: K. G. Saur Verlag, 1996.

Harwell, Jonathan. *Myth and Monument: Memory of the Great War in Britain and Germany,* chap.s 2 and 4. Dissertation Williamstown, Mass., 1999.

Harvey, Elizabeth. "Visions of the Volk: German Women and the Far Right from Kaiserreich to Third Reich." In *Journal of Women's History,* Vol. 16, No. 3, John Hopkins University Press, 2004.

Hastings, Adrian. *The Construction of Nationhood Ethniciy, Religion and Nationalism*. Cambridge: Cambridge University Press, 1997.

Hastings, Derek. *Catholicism and the Roots of Nazism. Religious Identity and National Socialism*. New York: Oxford University Press, 2010.

Heckscher, Eli F. *Industrialismen. Den ekonomiska utvecklingen sedan 1750.* Stockholm: Kooperativa förbundets bokförlag, 1944.
Heer, Friedrich. "Weimar—Ein religiöser und weltanschaulicher Leerraum." In *Religions-und Geistesgeschichte der Weimarer Republik*, edited by Hubert Cancik. Düsseldorf: Patmos Verlag, 1982.
Hehl, Ulrich von. "Das Kirchenvolk im Dritten Reich." In *Die Katholiken und das Dritte Reich*, edited by Klaus Gotto, and Konrad Repgen. Mainz: Matthias-Grünewald-Verlag, 1990.
Heiber, Helmut, "Hitler, die Partei und die Institutionen des Führerstaates." In *PLOETZ, Das Dritte Reich*, edited by Martin Broszat and Norbert Frei. Frechen: Komet, 1983.
Heiden, Konrad. *A History of National Socialism.* New York: Octagon Books, 1971.
Heilbronner, Oded. *Catholicism, Political Culture, and the Countryside. A Social History of the Nazi Party in South Germany.* Ann Arbor: The University of Michigan Press, 1998.
Heilbronner, Oded. "Long live Liberty, Equality, Fraternity and Dynamite": The German Bourgeoisie and the Constructing of Popular Liberal and National-Socialist subcultures in Marginal Germany. In *Journal of Social History* 39.1, 2005.
Heither, Dietrich. *Burschenschaften.* Cologne: Papy Rosa Verlag, 2013.
Helle, Knut. "Rettsoppfatninger og rettsendringer. Europa og Norge i middelalderen." In *Festskrift til Historisk institutts 40-årsjubileum 1997*, edited by Geir A. Ersland, Edgar Hovland, and Ståle Dyrvik. Bergen: Historisk institutt, Universitetet i Bergen, Skrifter 2, 1997.
Herder, Johann Gottfried. *Ideen zur Philosophie der Geschichte der Menschheit.* 1784–1791. http://textlog.de/herder/.
Hieronimus, Ekkehard. "Zur Religiosität der Völkischen Bewegung." In *Religions-und Geistesgeschichte der Weimarer Republik*, edited by Hubert Cancik. Düsseldorf: Patmos Verlag, 1982.
Historisches Lexikon Bayerns. www.historisches-lexikon-bayerns.de.
Hitler, Adolf. *Mein Kampf.* Munich: Franz Eher, 1940.
Hobson, Rolf. Review of *Dolchstosslegende und politische Desintegration. Das Trauma der deutschen Niederlage im Ersten Weltkrieg 1914–1933*, by Boris Barth. Düsseldorf: Droste Verlag, 2003.
Hofer, Walter (ed.). *Der Nationalsozialismus. Dokumente 1933–1945.* Frankfurt/M: Fischer Bücherei, 1957.
Höfele, Karl Heinrich. *Geist und Gesellschaft der Bismarckzeit (1870–1890).* Göttingen: Musterschmidt Verlag, 1967.
Holocaust Encyclopaedia. United States Holocaust Memorial Museum. encyclopedia.ushmm.org.
Hömig, Herbert. *Das preussische Zentrum in der Weimarer Republik.* Mainz: Matthias-Grünewald-Verlag, 1979.
Horn, Daniel. "Reform and Revolution in German Education, 1890–1935." In *History of Education Quarterly*, Vol. 19, No. 4, 1979.
Hoyt, Robert. *Europe in the Middle Ages.* New York: Harcourt, Brace & World, 1966.

Huber, Wolfgang, and Theodor Strohm. "Protestantismus—soziale Organisation und der Friedensauftrag der Kirche." In *Kirche zwischen Krieg und Frieden. Studien zur Geschichte des deutschen Protestantismus,* edited by Wolfgang Huber and Johannes Schwerdtfeger. Stuttgart: Ernst Klett Verlag, 1976.

Hüppauf, Bernt. "The Birth of Fascist Man from the Spirit of the Front. From Langemarck to Verdun." In *The Attraction of Fascism,* edited by John Milfull. New York: Berg, 1990.

Hürten, Heinz. "Der katholische Episkopat nach dem Reichskonkordat." In *Kirchen in der Diktatur. Drittes Reich und SED-Diktatur,* edited by Günter Heydemann and Lothar Kettenacker. Göttingen: Vandenhoeck & Ruprecht, 1993.

Iber, Harald. *Christlicher Glaube oder rassischer Mythus. Die Auseinandersetzungen der Bekennnenden Kirche mit Alfred Rosenbergs "Der Mythus des 20. Jahrhunderts."* Frankfurt/M: Peter Lang, 1987.

Iddeng, Jon, Christine Amadou, Geir Atle Ersland, Per Strømholm, Brita Pollan, Ole Bjørn Rongen, Øystein Sjaastad, and Mona Ringvej. *tid og tanke. Historie og filosofi 1.* Oslo: H. Aschehoug & Co., 2008.

Irlenbusch-Reynard, Michael. "Interaksjon mellom vitenskap og ideologi? Tre perspektiver på den gamle norrøne kultur og litteratur i Tyskland fra 1850- til 1940-årene." In *Jakten på Germania. Fra Nordensvermeri til SS-arkeologi,* edited by Terje Emberland and Jorunn Sem Fure. Oslo: Humanist forlag, 2009.

Jacke, Jochen. *Kirche zwischen Monarchie und Republik. Der preussische Protestantismus nach dem Zusammenbruch von 1918.* Hamburg: Hans Christians Verlag, 1976.

Jacobs, Manfred. "Die Entwicklung des deutschen Nationalgedankens von der Reformation bis zum deutschen Idealismus." In *Volk—Nation—Vaterland. Der deutsche Protestantismus und der Nationaliismus,* edited by Horst Zillessen. Gütersloh: Gerd Mohn, 1970.

Jahr, Christoph. "Schleichendes Gift." In *SPIEGEL SPECIAL,* no. 1, 2008.

Jantzen, Kyle. *Faith and Fatherland. Parish Politics in Hitler's Germany.* Minneapolis: Fortress Press, 2008.

Jedin, Hubert. "Kirche und Katholizismus im Deutschland des 19. Jahrhunderts." In *Entwicklungslinien des deutschen Katholizismus,* edited by Anton Rauscher. Munich: Verlag Ferdinand Schöningh, 1973.

Jochmann, Werner. "Struktur und Funktion des deutschen Antisemitismus." In *Juden im Wilhelminischen Deutschland 1890–1914,* edited by Werner E. Mosse. Tübingen: J. C. B. Mohr, 1976.

Jochmann, Werner. "Die Funktion des Antisemitismus in der Weimarer Republik." In *Antisemitismus. Von religiöser Judenfeindschaft zur Rassenideologie,* edited by Günter Brakelmann and Martin Rosowski. Göttingen: Vandenhoeck & Ruprecht, 1989.

Jung, Walter. *Ideologische Voraussetzungen, Inhalte und Ziele aussenpolitischer Programmatik und Propaganda in der deutschvölkischen Bewegung der Anfangsjahre der Weimarer Republik—Das Beispiel Deutschvölkischer Schutz-und Trutzbund.* PhD dissertation at Georg-August Universität Göttingen, 2001.

Junker, Detlef. *Die deutsche Zentrumspartei und Hitler 1932/33. Ein Beitrag zur Problematik des politischen Katholizismus in Deutschland*. Stuttgart: Ernst Klett Verlag, 1969.

Kaiser, Wolfram. *Christian Democracy and the Origins of European Union*. Cambridge: Cambridge University Press, 2007.

Kampe, Norbert. *Studenten und "Judenfrage" im Deutschen Kaiserreich. Die Entstehung einer akademischen Trägerschicht des Antisemitismus*. Göttingen: Vandenhoeck & Ruprecht, 1988.

Kater, Michael. *Studentenschaft und Rechtsradikalismus in Deutschland 1918–1933. Eine sozialgeschichtliche Studie zur Bildungskrise in der Weimarer Republik*. Hamburg: Hoffmann und Campe Verlag, 1975.

Kauders, Anthony. *German Politics and the Jews Düsseldorf and Nuremberg*. Oxford: Clarendon Press, 1996.

Kershaw, Ian. "Führer und Hitlerkult." In *Enzyklopädie des Nationalsozialismus*, edited by Wolfgang Benz, Hermann Graml, and Hermann Weiss. Munich: Deutscher Taschenbuch Verlag, 1998.

Kershaw, Ian. "Ideology, Propaganda and the Rise of the Nazi Party." In *The Nazi Machtergreifung*, edited by Peter D. Stachura. Boston: George Allen & Unwin, 1983.

Kershaw, Ian. *Popular Opinion and Political Dissent in the Third Reich. Bavaria 1933–1945*. New York: Oxford University Press, 2002.

Kertzer, David I. *Die Päpste gegen die Juden. Der Vatikan und die Entstehung des modernen Antisemitismus*. Munich: Ullstein Buchverlage, 2004.

Kettenacker, Lothar. "Hitler und die Kirchen. Eine Obsesssion mit Folgen." In *Kirchen in der Diktatur. Drittes Reich und SED-Staat*, edited by Günter Heydemann, and Lothar Kettenacker. Göttingen: Vandenhoeck & Ruprecht, 1993.

King, Gary, Ori Rosen, Martin Tanner, and Alexander F. Wagner. "Ordinary Voting Behaviour in the Extraordinary Election of Adolf Hitler." In *Journal of Economic History*, Vol. 68, No. 4, 2008.

Kjellén, Rudolf. *Die Ideen von 1914. Eine weltgeschichtliche Perspektive*. Leipzig: S. Hirzel, 1916 http://archive.org/details/.

Kjøstvedt, Anders Granås. *Hitler's Metropolis? The National Socialist Movement in Berlin 1925–1933*, PhD dissertation at University of Oslo, Oct. 14, 2009.

Klee, Ernst. *Personenlexikon zum Dritten Reich*. Frankfurt/M: Fischer Verlag, 2005.

Kocka, Jürgen. "Probleme der politischen Integration der Deutschen 1867 bis 1945." In *Die Rolle der Nation in der deutschen Geschichte und Gegenwart. Beiträge zu einer internationalen Konferenz in Berlin (West) vom 16. Bis 18. Juni 1983*, edited by Otto Büsch and James J. Sheehan. Berlin: Colloquium Verlag, 1985.

Kohn, Hans. *The Mind of Germany, the Education of a Nation*. New York: Charles Scribner's Sons, 1960.

Köhn, Rolf. "Kirchenfeindliche und antichristliche Mittelalter-Rezeption im völkisch-nationalsozialistischen Geschichtsbild: die Beispiele Widukind und Stedinger." In *Mittelalter-Rezeption*, edited by Peter Wapnewski. Stuttgart: J. B. Metzlersche Verlagsbuchhandlung, 1986.

Kolden, Ingvar. "Konfesjonstilhørighet og oppslutning om NSDAP i Tyskland". In *Historisk Tidsskrift*, Bd. 77, Nr. 3. Oslo: Universitetsforlaget AS, 1998.

Konukiewitz, Enno. *Hans Asmussen: ein lutherischer Theologe im Kirchenkampf*. In *Die lutherische Kirche, Geschichte und Gestalten*, Bd. 6. Gütersloh: Gütersloher Verlagshaus Mohn, 1984. www.kirche-christen-juden.org/dokumemte.

Kracht, Klaus Grosse. Review of *Vom Gottesrecht zum Menschenrecht. Das katholische Staatsdenken in Deutschland von der Französischen Revolution bis zum II. Vatikanischen Konzil (1789–1965)*, by Rudolf Uertz. Munich: Ferdinand Schöningh Verlag, 2005.

Kratz, Peter. *"Alles schon mal dagewesen!" Zehn Thesen zu New Age und Faschismus.* Manuscript of lecture Dec. 8 and 9 1989, published on http://home.snafu.de/biffNA0.htm.

Kraus, Hans-Joachim. "Die evangelische Kirche." In *Entscheidungsjahr 1932. Zur Judenfrage in der Weimarer Republik*, edited by Werner E. Mosse. Tübingen: J. C. B. Mohr, 1966.

Kreuzer, Marcus. "Parliamentarization and the Question of German Exceptionalism: 1867–1918." In *Central European History, Vol. 36, No. 3*, Atlanta, 2003.

Kühn, Ulrich. "Die theologische Rechtfertigung der 'Obrigkei.t.'" In *Kirchen in der Diktatur. Drittes Reich und SED-Staat*, edited by Günter Heydemann, and Lothar Kettenacker. Göttingen: Vandenhoeck & Ruprecht, 1993.

Kupisch, Karl. "Bürgerliche Frömmigkeit im Wilhelminischen Zeitalter." In *Zeitgeist im Wandel. Bd. I. Das Wilhelminischen Zeitalter*, edited by Hans Joachim Schoeps. Stuttgart: Ernst Klett Verlag, 1967.

Kupisch, Karl. "Der Protestantismus im Epochenjahr 1917." In *Zeitgeist im Wandel. Bd. II. Zeitgeist der Weimarer Republik*, edited by Hans Joachim Schoeps. Stuttgart: Ernst Klett Verlag, 1968.

Kupisch, Karl. "Die Wandlungen des Nationalismus im liberalen deutschen Bürgertum." In *Volk—Nation—Vaterland. Der deutsche Protestantismus und der Nationalismus*, edited by Horst Zillesen. Gütersloh: Gerd Mohn, 1970.

Küppers, Heinrich. *Der katholische Lehrerverband in der Übergangszeit von der Weimarer Republik zur Hitler-Diktatur*. Mainz: Matthias-Grünewald-Verlag, 1975

Kværne, Per and Kari Vogt. *Religionsleksikon. Religion og religiøsitet i vår tid.* Oslo: Kunnskapsforlaget, 1992.

Lächele, Rainer. "Protestantismus und völkische Religion im deutschen Kaiserreich." In *Handbuch zur "Völkischen Bewegung" 1871–1918*, edited by Uwe Puschner, Walter Schmitz, and Justus H. Ulbricht. Munich: K. G. Saur Verlag, 1996.

Lagarde, Paul de. *Schriften für Deutschland*. Stuttgart: Alfred Kröner Verlag, 1933.

Lamberti, Marjorie. "German Schoolteachers, National Socialism, and the Politics of Culture at the End of the Weimar Republic." In *Central European History*, Vol. 34, No. 1, Atlanta, 2001.

Langbehn, Julius. *Rembrandt als Erzieher*. Leipzig: C. L. Hirschfeld, 1922 http://gutenberg.de/buch/.

Langner, Albrecht. "Diskussionsbericht." In *Entwicklungslinien des deutschen Katholizismus*. edited by Anton Rauscher. Munich: Verlag Ferdinand Schöningh, 1973.

Langner, Albrecht. "Katholizismus und nationaler Gedanke in Deutschland." In *Volk—Nation—Vaterland. Der deutsche Protestantismus und der Nationalismus*, edited by Horst Zillesen. Gütersloh: Gerd Mohn, 1970.

Leisen, Adolf. *Die Ausbreitung des völkischen Gedankens in der Studentenschaft der Weimarer Republik*. PhD dissertation at Ruprecht-Karl Universität Heidelberg, 1964.

Levenda, Peter. *Unholy Alliance. A History of Nazi Involvement with the Occult*. New York: Continuum, 2002.

Lewy, Guenther. *The Catholic Church and Nazi Germany*. Boston: Da Capo Press, 2000.

Liepach, Martin. *Das Wahlverhalten der jüdischen Bevölkerung in der Weimarer Republik*. Tübingen: J. C. B. Mohr, 1996.

Lill, Rudolf. "Der heilige Stuhl und die Juden." In *Kirche und Synagoge. Handbuch zur Geschichte von Christen und Juden*, edited by Karl Heinrich Rengstorf and Siegfried von Kortzfleisch. Stuttgart: Ernst Klett Verlag, 1970.

Lill, Rudolf. "Die deutschen Katholiken und die Juden in der Zeit von 1850 bis zur Machtübernahme Hitlers." In *Kirche und Synagoge. Handbuch zur Geschichte von Christen und Juden*, edited by Karl Heinrich Rengstorf and Siegfried von Kortzfleisch. Stuttgart: Ernst Klett Verlag, 1970.

Lill, Rudolf. "NS-Ideologie und Katholische Kirche." In *Die Katholiken und das Dritte Reich*, edited by Klaus Gotto and Konrad Repgen. Mainz: Matthias-Grünewald-Verlag, 1990.

Linse, Ulrich. "Völkisch-rassische Siedlungen der Lebensreform." In *Handbuch zur "Völkischen Bewegung" 1871–1918*, edited by Uwe Puschner, Walter Schmitz, and Justus H. Ulbricht. Munich: K. G. Saur Verlag, 1996.

Lohalm, Uwe. *Völkischer Radikalismus*. Hamburg: Leibniz, 1970.

Lot, Ferdinand. *The End of the Ancient World and the Beginnings of the Middle Ages*. New York: Harper & Row, Publishers, 1960.

Lübcke, Paul (ed.). *Politikens filosofi leksikon*. Copenhagen: Politikens Forlag, 1995.

Maier, Hans. "Zum Standort des deutschen Katholizismus in Gesellschaft, Staat und Kultur." In *Entwicklungslinien des deutschen Katholizismus*, edited by Anton Rauscher. Munich: Verlag Ferdinand Schöningh, 1973.

Mann, Golo. "Der Nazistaat." In *Deutschland. Hundert Jahre deutsche Geschichte*, edited by Hans-Adolf Jacobsen and Hans Dollinger. Stuttgart: Fackelverlag Brugg, 1973.

Marrus, Michael R., "French Protestant Churches and the Persecution of the Jews in France." In *The Holocaust and the Christian World*, edited by Carol Rittner, Stephen D. Smith, and Irena Steinfeldt. London: Kuperard, 2000.

Maxwell-Stuart, Peter G. *Pavene. Pavedømmet gjennom 2000 år*. Oslo: Forsythia, 1998.

Mazura, Uwe. *Zentrumspartei und Judenfrage 1870–1933*. Mainz: Matthias-Grünewald-Verlag, 1994.

Meier, Kurt. *Evangelische Kirche in Gesellschaft, Staat und Politik 1918–1945. Aufsätze zur kirchlichen Zeitgeschichte*. Berlin: Evangelische Verlagsanstalt, 1987.

Meier, Kurt. *Kreuz und Hakenkreuz. Die evangelische Kirche im Dritten Reich.* Munich: Deutscher Taschenbuchverlag, 2008.
Mensing, Björn. *Pfarrer und Nationalsozialismus. Geschichte einer Verstrickung am Beispiel der Evangelisch-Lutherischen Kirche in Bayern.* Göttingen: Vandenhoeck & Ruprecht, 1998.
Meyers Konversationslexikon. Leipzig: Bibliographisches Institut, fifth publ. 1897, sixth publ. 1904.
Michalka, Wolfgang and Gottfried Niedhart. *Die ungeliebte Republik.* Munich: Deutscher Taschenbuchverlag, 1981.
Michalsen, Dag. *Romerrettsideologi.* Oslo: Pax forlag, 2008.
Mogge, Winfried. "Religiöse Vorstellungen in der deutschen Jugendbewegung." In *Religions-und Geistesgeschichte der Weimarer Republik*, edited by Hubert Cancik. Düsseldorf: Patmos Verlag, 1982.
Mommsen, Hans. *Die Deutschen und der Holocaust.* Bonn: Friedrich Ebert Stiftung, 2006.
Mommsen, Hans. "Die Funktion des Antisemitismus im 'Dritten Reich.'" In *Antisemitismus. Von religiöser Judenfeindschaft zur Rassenideologie*, edited by Günter Brakelmann and Martin Rosowski. Göttingen: Vandenhoeck & Ruprecht, 1989.
Mommsen, Wilhelm. *Deutsche Parteiprogramme.* Munich: Olzog, 1960.
Montgomery McGovern, William. *From Luther to Hitler The History of Fascist-Nazi Political Philosophy.* London: George G. Harrap & Co., 1947.
Morgan, Philip. *Fascism in Europe, 1919–1945.* New York: Routledge, 2003.
Morsey, Rudolf. "Der deutsche Katholizismus in politischen Umbruchsituationen seit dem Beginn des 19. Jahrhunderts."In *Entwicklungslinien des deutschen Katholizismus*, edited by Anton Rauscher. Munich: Verlag Ferdinand Schöningh, 1973.
Morsey, Rudolf. "Die katholische Volksminderheit und der Aufstieg des Nationalsozialismus 1930–1933." In *Die Katholiken und das Dritte Reich*, edited by Klaus Gotto and Konrad Repgen. Mainz: Matthias-Grünewald-Verlag, 1990.
Mosse, George L. "Die deutsche Rechte und die Juden." In *Entscheidungsjahr 1932. Zur Judenfrage in der Weimarer Republik*, edited by Werner E. Mosse. Tübingen: J. C. B. Mohr, 1966.
Mosse, George L. *The Crisis of German Ideology.* New York: Howard Fertig, 1998.
Mosse, George L. *Die Nationalisierung der Massen Politische Symbolik und massenbewegungen von den Befreiungskriegen bis zum Dritten Reich.* Frankfurt/M: Campus Verlag, 1993.
Mosse, George L. *The Fascist Revolution. Toward a General Theory of Fascism.* New York: Howard Fertig, 2000.
Mosse, Werner E. "Der Niedergang der Weimarer Republik und die Juden." In *Entscheidungsjahr 1932. Zur Judenfrage in der Weimarer Republik*, edited by Werner E. Mosse. Tübingen: J. C. B. Mohr, 1966.
Müller, Guido. "Anticipated Exile of Catholic Democrats: The Sécretariat International des Partis Démocratiques d'Inspiration Chrétienne." In *Political Catholicism in Europe 1918–45*, edited by Wolfram Kaiser and Helmut Wohnout. New York: Routledge, 2004.

Müller, Hans. *Katholische Kirche und Nationalsozialismus. Dokumente 1930–1935.* Munich: Nymphenburger Verlagshandlung, 1963.
Nedrebø, Tore. *Past and Present Sources of European Union. A Comparative Historical-Institutional Analysis*, PhD dissertation at University of Bergen 2010.
Neumann, Sigmund. *Die Parteien der Weimarer Republik.* Stuttgart: W. Kohlhammer, 1977.
Nipperdey, Thomas. *Religion im Umbruch. Deutschland 1870–1918.* Munich: C. H. Beck, 1988.
Nirenberg, David. *Antijudaism. The History of a Way of Thinking.* London: Head of Zeus, 2013.
Noack, Winfried. *Die NS-Ideologie*, Frankfurt/M: Peter Lang, Europäischer Verlag der Wissenschaften, 1996.
Noakes, Jeremy. "The Oldenburg Crucifix Struggle of November 1936. A Case Study of Opposition in the Third Reich.. In *The Shaping of the Nazi State*, edited by Peter D. Stachura. New York: Barnes & Noble Books, 1978.
Nolte, Ernst. *Die faschistischen Bewegungen. Die Krise des liberalen Systems und die Entwicklung der Faschismen.* Munich: Deutscher Taschenbuch Verlag, 1969.
Norden, Günter van. "Der deutsche Protestantismus zwischen Patriotismus und Bekenntnis." In *Kirchen in der Diktatur. Drittes Reich und SED-Staat*, edited by Günter Heydemann and Lothar Kettenacker. Göttingen: Vandenhoeck & Ruprecht, 1993.
Nordisk Familjebok. Stockholm: Nordisk Familjeboks Förlag, 1908–1926.
Nowak, Kurt. "Christuskreuz gegen Hakenkreuz. Die Ideologie des Nationalsozialismus im Urteil der Kirchen." In *Kirchen in der Diktatur. Drittes Reich und SED-Staat*, edited by Günter Heydemann, and Lothar Kettenacker. Göttingen: Vandenhoeck & Ruprecht, 1993.
Nowak, Kurt. *Evangelische Kirche und Weimarer Republik. Zum politischen Weg des deutschen Protestantismus zwischen 1918 und 1932.* Göttingen: Vandenhoeck & Ruprecht, 1981.
NRK. (Norwegian Broadcasting Corporation).
O'Loughlin, John, Colin Flint, and Luc Anselin. *The Political Geography of the Nazi Vote. Context Confession and Class in the 1930 Reichstag Election*, Research paper 9323 (Year omitted, but probably 1993).
Patch, William L. *Christian Trade Unions in the Weimar Republic, 1918–1933.* New Haven: Yale University Press, 1985.
Paucker, Arnold. "Der jüdische Abwehrkampf." In *Entscheidungsjahr 1932. Zur Judenfrage in der Weimarer Republik*, edited by Werner E. Mosse. Tübingen: J. C. B. Mohr, 1966.
Paul, Ina Ulrike. "Paul Anton de Lagarde." In *Handbuch zur "Völkischen Bewegung" 1871–1918*, edited by Uwe Puschner, Walter Schmitz, and Justus H. Ulbricht. Munich: K. G. Saur Verlag, 1996.
Payne, Stanley G. "The Concept of Fascism." In *Who were the Fascists? Social Roots of European Fascism*, edited by Stein Ugelvik Larsen, Bernt Hagtvedt, and Jens Petter Myklebust. Oslo: Universitetsforlaget, 1980.
Payne, Stanley G. *A History of Fascism 1914–1945.* London: UCL Press, 1995.

Peters, Michael. "Der Alldeutsche Verband." In *Handbuch zur "Völkischen Bewegung" 1871–1918*, edited by Uwe Puschner, Walter Schmitz, and Justus H. Ulbricht. Munich: K. G. Saur Verlag, 1996.

Phayer, Michael. *The Catholic Church and the Holocaust 1930–1965*. Bloomington: Indiana University Press, 2000.

Philipp, Franz-Heinrich. "Protestantismus nach 1848." In *Kirche und Synagoge. Handbuch zur Geschichte von Christen und Juden*, edited by Karl Heinrich Rengstorf and Siegfried von Kortzfleisch. Stuttgart: Ernst Klett Verlag, 1970.

Piper, Ernst. "Alfred Rosenberg—der Prophet des Seelenkrieges. Der gläubige Nazi in der Führungselite des nationalsozialistischen Staates." In *Der Nationalsozialismus als politische Religion. Studien zur Geistesgeschichte*, edited by Michael Ley and Julius H. Schoeps. Bodenheim: Philo Verlagsgesellschaft, 1997.

Piper, Ernst. *Alfred Rosenberg. Hitlers Chefideologe*. Munich: Karl Blessing Verlag, 2005.

Plum, Günter. "Übernahme und Sicherung der Macht." In *Das Dritte Reich. Ursprünge, Ereignisse, Wirkungen*, edited by Martin Broszat and Norbert Frei. Frechen: Komet, 1983.

Preuschen, Erwin. *Kirchengeschichte für das Christliche Haus/die Christliche Familie*. Reutlingen: Ensslin & Laiblins Verlagsbuchhandlung, 1905.

Pridham, Geoffrey. *Hitler's Rise to Power*. London: Hart Davis, 1973.

Pulzer, Peter. "Die jüdische Beteiligung an der Politik." In *Juden in Wilhelminischen Deutschland 1890–1914*, edited by Werner E. Mosse. Tübingen: J. C. B. Mohr, 1976.

Pulzer, Peter. *Jews and the German State. The Political History of a Minority*. Cambridge US: Blackwell, 1992.

Pulzer, Peter. *The Rise of Political Anti-Semitism in Germany & Austria*. Cambridge, Mass.: Harvard University Press, 1988.

Puschner, Uwe. *Die völkische Bewegung im wilhelminischen Kaiserreich. Sprache—Rasse—Religion*. Darmstadt: Wissenschaftliche Buchgesellschaft, 2001.

Puschner, Uwe, Walter Schmitz, and Justus H. Ulbricht (eds.). *Handbuch zur "Völkischen Bewegung" 1871–1918*. Munich: K. G. Saur Verlag, 1996.

Rengstorf, Karl Heinrich. "Der Kampf um die Emanzipation." In *Kirche und Synagoge. Handbuch zur Geschichte von Christen und Juden*, edited by Karl Heinrich Rengstorf and Siegfried von Kortzfleisch. Stuttgart: Ernst Klett Verlag, 1970.

Repgen, Konrad. "1938—Judenpogrom und katholischer Kirchenkampf." In *Antisemitismus. Von religiöser Judenfeindschaft zur Rassenideologie*, edited by Günter Brakelmann and Martin Rosowski. Göttingen: Vandenhoeck & Ruprecht, 1989.

Repgen, Konrad. "Entwicklungslinien von Kirche und Katholizismus in historischer Sicht." In *Entwicklungslinien des deutschen Katholizismus*, edited by Anton Rauscher. Munich: Verlag Ferdinand Schöningh, 1973.

Riedl, Joachim. "Der lange Schatten des Kreuzes. Von Golgotha zur Svastika." In *Der Nationalsozialismus als politische Religion*, edited by Michael Ley and Julius H. Schoeps. Bodenheim: Philo Verlagsgesellschaft, 1997.

Rittner, Carol, Stephen D. Smith, and Irena Steinfeldt (eds.), *The Holocaust and the Christian World. Reflections on the Past. Challenges for the Future*. London: Kuperard, 2000.

Rohe, Karl. *Das Reichsbanner Schwarz-Rot-Gold. Ein Beitrag zur Geschichte und Struktur der politischen Kampfverbände zur Zeit der Weimarer Republik.* Düsseldorf: Droste Verlag, 1966.
Rohe, Karl. *Wahlen und Wählertraditionen in Deutschland. Kulturelle Grundlagen deutscher Parteien und Parteiensysteme im 19. Und 20. Jahrhundert.* Frankfurt/M: Suhrkamp Verlag, 1992.
Roon, Ger van. "The Dutch Protestants, the Third Reich and the Persecution of the Jews." In *The Holocaust and the Christian World. Reflections on the Past. Challenges for the Future*, edited by Carol Rittner, Stephen D. Smith, and Irena Steinfeldt. London: Kuperard, 2000.
Roos, H. "Katolsk politisk teori." In *Politiske ideologier. Fra Platon til Mao*, edited by Svend Erik Stybe. Copenhagen: Politikens Forlag, 1979.
Rosenberg, Alfred. *Der Mythus des 20. Jahrhunderts. Eine Wertung der seelisch-geistigen Gestaltenkämpfe unserer Zeit.* Munich: Hoheneichen, 1942.
Rosenberg, Alfred. *Kampf um die Macht. Aufsätze von 1921–1932.* Munich: Zentralverlag der NSDAP, Franz Eher Nachf., 1937.
Rosenberg, Alfred. *Protestantische Rompilger. Der Verrat an Luther und der "Mythus des 20. Jahrhunderts."* Munich: Hoheneichen, 1937.
Rost, Hans. *Gedanken und Wahrheiten zur Judenfrage. Eine soziale und politische Studie.* Trier, 1907 http://archive.org/details/.
Rürup, Reinhard. "Emanzipation und Krise. Zur Geschichte der "Judenfrage" in Deutschland vor 1890." In *Juden im Wilhelminischen Deutschland*, edited by Werner E. Mosse. Tübingen: J. C. B. Mohr, 1976.
Ryland, Glen P. *Translating Africa for Germans: The Rhenish Mission in Southwest Africa for Germans*, PhD dissertation at University of Notre Dame, Ind., April 2013.
Salomonsens Konversationslexikon. Copenhagen: J. H. Schultz, 1927.
Schäfer, Gerhard. *Die evangelische Landeskirche in Württemberg und der Nationalsozialismus. Eine Dokumentation zum Kirchenkampf. Bd. 1 Um das politische Engagement der Kirche 1932–1933.* Stuttgart: Calwer Verlag, 1971.
Scheffel, Johann Victor von. *Der Trompeter von Säckingen.* Leipzig: Philip Reclam jun., 1901–1917 http://gutenberg.spiegel.de/buch/.
Schellenberger, Barbara. *Katholische Jugend und Drittes Reich. Eine Geschichte des Katholischen Jungmännerverbandes 1933–1939 unter besonderer Berücksichtigung der Rheinprovinz.* Mainz: Matthias-Grünewald-Verlag, 1975.
Schellong, Dieter. "Ein gefährlichster Augenblick." Zur Lage der evangelischen Theologie am Ausgang der Weimarer Zeit." In *Religions-und Geistesgeschichte der Weimarer Republik*, edited by Hubert Cancik. Düsseldorf: Patmos Verlag, 1982.
Schewick, Burkhard van. "Katholische Kirche und nationalsozialistische Rassenpolitik." In *Die Katholiken und das Dritte Reich*, edited by Klaus Gotto and Konrad Repgen. Mainz: Matthias-Grünewald-Verlag, 1990.
Schieder, Wolfgang. "Fatal Attraction: the German Right and Italian Fascism." In *The Third Reich between Vision and Reality. New Perspectives on German History*, edited by Hans Mommsen. New York: Berg, 2001.

Schier, Barbara. *Hexenwahn und Hexenverfolgung. Rezeption und politische Zurichtung eines kulturwissenschaftlichen Themas im Dritten Reich*. Munich: Bayerisches Jahrbuch für Volkskunde, 1990.

Schmidt, Ute. *Zentrum oder CDU. Politisicher Katholizismus zwischen Tradition und Anpassung*. Opladen: Westdeutscher Verlag, 1987.

Schneider, Michael. *Die Christlichen Gewerkschaften 1894–1933*. Bonn: Verlag Neue Gesellschaft, 1982.

Schnurbein, Stefanie. "Die Suche nach einer "arteigenen" Religion in "germanisch-" und "deutschgläubigen" Gruppen." In *Handbuch zur "Völkischen Bewegung" 1871–1918*, edited by Uwe Puschner, Walter Schmitz, and Justus H. Ulbricht. Munich: K. G. Saur Verlag, 1996.

Schoeps, Julius H. "Deutsche und nichts anderes. Von Patriotismus deutscher Juden." In *SPIEGEL SPECIAL: Juden und Deutsche*, No. 2, 1992.

Scholder, Klaus. *Die Kirchen und das Dritte Reich, Bd. 1. Vorgeschichte und Zeit der Illusionen*. Frankfurt/M: Verlag Ullstein, 1977; Munich: Econ Ullstein List Verlag, 2000.

Scholder, Klaus. *Die Kirchen und das Dritte Reich, Bd. 2. Das Jahr der Ernüchterung 1934. Barmen und Rom*. Munich: Econ Ullstein List Verlag, 2000.

Schöndorf, Kurt. "Für Christus und Deutschland—Gegen Hitler und die Neuheiden." In *Saarpfalz. Blätter für Geschichte und Volkskunde*, No. 41, Homburg, 1994.

Schönhoven, Klaus. *Die Bayerische Volkspartei 1924–1932*. Düsseldorf: Droste Verlag, 1972.

Schulz, Gerhard. *Faschismus—Nationalsozialismus. Versione und theoretische Kontroversen 1922–1972*. Frankfurt/M: Propyläen Verlag/Verlag Ullstein, 1974.

Schulze, Hagen. *The Course of German Nationalism. From Fredrick the Great to Bismarck*. Cambridge: Cambridge University Press, 1990.

Schulze, Hagen. "Die deutsche Nationalbewegung bis zur Reichseinigung." In *Die Rolle der Nation in der deutschen Geschichte und Gegenwart. Beiträge zu einer internationalen Konferenz in Berlin (West) vom 16. Bis 18. Juni 1983*, edited by Otto Büsch and James J. Sheehan. Berlin: Colloquium, 1985.

See, Klaus von. *Die Ideen von 1789 und die Ideen von 1914. Völkisches Denken in Deutschland zwischen Französischer Revolution und Erstem Weltkrieg*. Frankfurt/M: Akademische Verlagsgesellschaft Athenaion, 1975.

Sieferle, Rolf Peter. "Rassismus, Rassenhygiene, Menschenzuchtideale." In *Handbuch zur "Völkischen Bewegung" 1871–1918*, edited by Uwe Puschner, Walter Schmitz, and Justus H. Ulbricht. Munich: K. G. Saur Verlag, 1996.

Siegele-Wenschkewitz, Leonore. "Protestantische Universitätstheologie und Rassenideologie in der Zeit des Nationalsozialismus." In *Antisemitismus. Von religiöser Judenfeindschaft zur Rassenideologie*, edited by Günter Brakelmann and Martin Rosowski. Göttingen: Vandenhoeck & Ruprecht, 1989.

Simon-Ritz, Frank. "Die freigeistige Bewegung im Kaiserreich." In *Handbuch zur "Völkischen Bewegung 1871–1918*," edited by Uwe Puschner, Walter Scmitz, and Justus H. Ulbricht. Munich: K. G. Saur Verlag, 1996.

Smith, Whitney. *Flags through the Ages and across the World*. Maidenhead: McGraw-Hill Book, 1975.

Sontheimer, Kurt. *Antidemokratisches Denken in der Weimarer Republik. Die politischen Ideen des deutschen Nationalismus zwischen 1918 und 1933*. Munich: Nymphenburger Verlagshandlung, 1964.
Spenkuch, Jörg L. and Philipp Tillmann. "Elite Influence? Religion and Electoral Success of the Nazis." In *American Journal of Political Science*, August 10, 2017.
Spicer, Kevin P. *Hitler's Priests. Catholic Clergy and National Socialism*. DeKalb, Ill.: Northern Illinois University Press, 2008.
Spicer, Kevin P. "Working for the Führer: Father Dr. Philipp Haeuser and the Third Reich." In *Antisemitism, Christian Ambivalence, and the Holocaust*, edited by Kevin P. Spicer. Bloomington: Indiana University Press, 2007.
Spuler, Berthold. *Regenten und Regierungen der Welt, Teil II, Bd. 3. Neuere Zeit 1492–1918*. Würzburg: A. G. Ploetz Verlag, 1962.
Spuler, Berthold. *Regenten und Regierungen der Welt, Teil II, Bd. 4, Neueste Zeit 1917/18–1964*. Würzburg: A. G. Ploetz Verlag, 1964.
Stachura, Peter D. "German Youth, the Youth Movement and National Socialism in the Weimar Republic." In *The Nazi Machtergreifung*, edited by Peter D. Stachura. Boston: George Allen & Unwin, 1983.
Stachura, Peter D. "The Nazis, the Bourgeoisie and the Workers during the *Kampfzeit*." In *The Nazi Machtergreifung*, edited by Peter D. Stachura, Boston: George Allen & Unwin, 1983.
Steigmann-Gall, Richard. *The Holy Reich. Nazi Conceptions of Christianity, 1919–1945*. Cambridge: Cambridge University Press, 2004.
Steigmann-Gall, Richard. "Rethinking Nazism and Religion: How Anti-Christian were the 'Pagans?'" In *Central European History*, Vol. 36, No. 1, Atlanta, 2003.
Stephenson, Jill. "National Socialism and Women before 1933." In *The Nazi Machtergreifung*, edited by Peter D. Stachura. Boston: George Allen & Unwin, 1983.
Stögbauer, Christian. *Wählerverhalten und nationalsozialistische Machtergreifung. Ökonomische, soziokulturelle, räumliche Determinanten sowie kontrafaktische Politiksimulation*. St. Katharinen: Scripta Mercaturae, 2001.
Store Norske Leksikon. Oslo: Kunnskapsforlaget, 1978.
Stribrny, Wolfgang. "Evangelische Kirche und Staat in der Weimarer Republik." In *Zeitgeist im Wandel. Zeitgeist der Weimarer Republik*, edited by Hans Joachim Schoeps. Stuttgart: Ernst Klett Verlag, 1968.
Strohm, Christoph. *Die Kirchen im Dritten Reich*. Munich: Verlag C. H. Beck, 2011.
"Studien zum Mythus des XX. Jahrhunderts." In *Kirchlicher Anzeiger für die Erzdiözese Köln*. Cologne: J. P. Bachem, 1935. http://nsl-archiv.com/Buecher/.
Tal, Uriel. *Religion, Politics and Ideology in the Third Reich. Selected Essays*. New York: Routledge, 2004.
Tal, Uriel. "Theologische Debatte um das "Wesen" des Judentums." In *Juden im Wilhelminischen Deutschland 1890–1914*, edited by Werner E. Mosse. Tübingen: J. C. B. Mohr, 1976.
Tanner, Klaus. *Die fromme Verstaatlichung des Gewissens. Zur Auseinandersetzung um die Legitimität der Weimarer Reichsverfassung in Staatswissenschaft und Theologie der zwanziger Jahre*. Göttingen: Vandenhoeck & Ruprecht, 1989.

Thorsen, Arve T. *The Gospel of the Fatherland. Christianity, Universality and National Thought in France and Germany in the Early 20th Century*, Thesis submitted for the dr. Art degree, Faculty of Humanities, University of Oslo. Oslo: Acta Humaniora, 2008.
Tilgner, Wolfgang. "Volk, Nation und Vaterland im protestantischen Denken zwischen Kaiserreich und Nationalsozialismus (ca. 1870–1933)." In *Volk—Nation—Vaterland. Der deutsche Protestantismus und der Nationalismus*, edited by Horst Zillesen. Gütersloh: Gerd Mohn, 1970.
Töpner, Kurt. "Der deutsche Katholizismus zwischen 1918 und 1933." In *Zeitgeist im Wandel. Zeitgeist der Weimarer Republik*, edited by Hans Joachim Schoeps. Stuttgart: Ernst Klett Verlag, 1968.
Torre, Victoria Martin de la. *Fryktens kontinent. Hvordan europeere begynte å stole på hverandre*. Oslo: Frekk forlag, 2016.
Treitschke, Heinrich von. *Ein Wort über unser Judentum*. Berlin: G. Reimer Verlag, 1880. http://nsl-archiv.com/Buecher/.
Udolph, Ludger. "Völkische Themen in der sorbischen Literatur." In *Handbuch zur "Völkischen Bewegung" 1871–1918*, edited by Uwe Puschner, Walter Schmitz, and Justus H. Ulbricht. Munich: K. G. Saur Verlag, 1996.
Ugelvik Larsen, Stein, Bernt Hagtvedt, and Jan Petter Myklebust (eds.). *Who were the Fascists? Social Roots of European Fascism*. Oslo: Universitetsforlaget, 1980.
Unruh, Karl. *Langemarck. Legende und Wirklichkeit*. Bonn: Bernard & Graefe Verlag, 1997.
Viereck, Peter. *Nazismens rötter. En historisk och psykologisk överblick*. Stockholm: Natur och kultur, 1942.
Verhandlungen des Reichstags. VIII. Wahlperiode 1933, Bd. 457. Berlin: Druck und Verlag der Reichsdruckerei, 1934.
Vogel, Wieland. *Katholische Kirche und nationale Kampfverbände in der Weimarer Republik*. Mainz: Matthias-Grünewald-Verlag, 1989.
Volk, Ludwig. *Der Bayerische Episkopat und der Nationalsozialismus 1930–1934*. Mainz: Matthias-Grünewald-Verlag, 1966.
Volk, Ludwig. "Nationalsozialistischer Kirchenkampf und deutscher Episkopat." In *Die Katholiken und das Dritte Reich*, edited by Klaus Gotto and Konrad Repgen. Mainz: Matthias-Grünewald-Verlag, 1990.
Völkische Bewegung 1871–1918, edited by Uwe Puschner, Walter Schmitz, and Justus H. Ulbricht. Munich: K. G. Saur Verlag, 1996.
Wahlen in der Weimarer Republik, http://www.gonschior.de/Wahlergebnisse (Statistics for elections in German states in the Interwar period. Used as source except for the *Reichstag*-elections in 1928 and Nov. 1932, or when otherwise is stated.)
Walser Smith, Helmut. *The Continuities of German History. Nation, Religion, and Race across the Long Nineteenth Century*. New York: Cambridge University Press, 2008.
Walser Smith, Helmut. *German Nationalism and Religious Conflict. Culture, Ideology, Politics, 1870–1914*. Princeton NJ: Princeton University Press, 1995.
Walter, Franz. *Soziale Akademiker—und Intellektuellenorganisationen in der Weimarer Republik*. Bonn: Friedrich Ebert Stiftung, 1990.

Warmbrunn, Werner. *The Dutch under German Occupation 1940–1945*. Stanford, Cal.: Stanford University Press, 1963.
Wehler, Hans-Ulrich. *The German Empire, 1871–1918*. Leamington Spa/Dover NH: Berg Publishers, 1985.
Weiling, Christoph. *Die "Christlich-deutsche Bewegung." Eine Studie zum konservatien Protestantismus in der Weimarer Republik*. Göttingen: Vandenhoeck & Ruprecht, 1998.
Weinzierl, Erika. "Austria: Church, State, Politics and Ideology, 1918–1938." In *Catholics, the State, and the European Radical Right*, edited by Richard Wolff and Jörg K. Hoensch. New York: Columbia University Press, 1987.
Weiss, John. *The Politics of Hate. Anti-Semitism, History, and the Holocaust in Modern Europe*. Chicago: Ivan R. Dee, 2003.
Westermann Grosser Atlas zur Weltgeschichte. Braunschweig: Georg Westermann, 1972.
Wiener, Philip Bernhard. "Die Parteien der Mitte." In *Entscheidungsjahr 1932. Zur Judenfrage in der Weimarer Republik*, edited by Werner E. Mosse. Tübingen: J. C. B. Mohr, 1966.
Windell, George G. *The Catholics and German Unity 1866–1871*. Minneapolis: University of Minnesota Press, 1954.
Winkler, Heinrich August. *Weimar 1918–1933. Die Geschichte der ersten deutschen Demokratie*. Munich: C. H. Beck, 1994.
Wippermann, Wolfgang. "Antislawismus." In *Handbuch zur "Völkischen Bewegung" 1871–1918*, edited by Uwe Puschner, Walter Schmitz, and Justus H. Ulbricht. Munich: K. G. Saur Verlag, 1996.
Wirsching, Andreas. "Weit entfernt von simplen Antworten." Interview with A. W. in *SPIEGEL SPECIAL GESCHICHTE*, No. 1, 2008.
Wiwjorra, Ingo. "Die deutsche Vorgeschichtsforschung und ihr Verhältnis zu Nationalismus und Rassismus." In *Handbuch zur "Völkischen Bewegung" 1871–1918*, edited by Uwe Puschner, Walter Schmitz, and Justus H. Ulbricht. Munich: K. G. Saur, Verlag 1996.
Wiwjorra, Ingo. "Arkaisme og krisen i det moderne." In *Jakten på Germania. Fra Nordensvermeri til SS-arkeologi*, edited by Terje Emberland and Jorunn Sem Fure. Oslo: Humanist forlag, 2009.
Wolf, Ernst. "Volk, Nation, Vaterland im protestantischen Denken von 1930 bis zur Gegenwart." In *Volk—Nation—Vaterland. Der deutsche Protestantismus und der Nationalismus*, edited by Horst Zillesen. Gütersloh: Gerd Mohn, 1970.
Wolf, Hubert. *Papst und Teufel. Die Archive des Vatikan und das Dritte Reich*. Munich: C. H. Beck, 2012.
Wolff, Richard J. and Jörg K. Hoensch. *Catholics, the State, and the European Radical Right, 1919–1945*. New York: Columbia University Press, 1987.
Wright, Jonathan R. C. *"Über den Parteien." Die politische Haltung der evangelischen Kirchenführer 1918–1933*. Göttingen: Vandenhoeck & Ruprecht, 1977.
Wusten, Herman van der, and Ronald E. Smit. "Dynamics of the Dutch National Socialist Movement (the NSB): 1931–35." In *Who were the Fascists? Social Roots of*

European Fascism, edited by Stein Ugelvik Larsen, Bernt Hagtvedt and Jens Petter Myklebust. Oslo: Universitetsforlaget, 1980.

Zander, Helmut. "Sozialdarwinistische Rassentheorien aus dem okkulten Untergrund des Kaiserreichs." In *Handbuch zur "Völkischen Bewegung" 1871–1918,* edited by Uwe Puschner, Walter Schmitz, and Justus H. Ulbricht. Munich: K. G. Saur Verlag, 1996.

Zeender, John. "Germany: The Catholic Church and the Nazi Regime, 1933–1945." In *Catholics, the State, and the European Radical Right,* edited by Richard J. Wolff and Jörg K. Hoensch. New York: Columbia University Press, 1987.

Zehrer, Karl, *Evangelische Freikirchen und das "Dritte Reich."* Göttingen: Vandenhoeck & Ruprecht, 1986.

Zernack, Julia. "Anschauungen vom Norden im deutschen Kaiserreich." In *Handbuch zur "Völkische Bewegung" 1871–1918,* edited by Uwe Puschner, Walter Schmitz and Justus H. Ulbricht. Munich: K. G. Saur Verlag, 1996.

Zmarzlik, Hans-Günter. *Wieviel Zukunft hat unsere Vergangenheit? Aufsätze und Überlegungen eines Historikers vom Jahrgang 1922.* Munich: R. Piper & Co. Verlag, 1970.

Index

Aachen, 187
"Academy of Science," 238
Action Francaise, 52
Adenauer, Konrad, 56, 132, 217, 236, 246
"Adler," 71
Adolf Hitler Leibstandarte SS, 188
Africa, 28, 61, 73, 90
Agrarian parties, 66, 157, 225, 226
Alemannic law, 72
Alldeutsche Vereinigung, 49
Alldeutscher Verband, 48, 49, 55, 60, 116, 135, 158, 159
Allgemeine Evangelisch-Lutherische Kirchenzeitung, 172
Alliance of Evangelical Denominations, 222
Alsace, 86
Altgeld, Wolfgang, 33, 34, 39, 45
Althaus, Paul, 79, 121, 173
Altkatholiken (Old Catholics), 21, 42, 54, 87, 91, 92, 161, 193, 222, 246
American, 51, 56, 222
Ammon, Otto, 59–61
Andersen, Friedrich, 135
Anners, Erik, 66
Anschluss, 78, 87, 148, 238
anthroposophy, 30, 31, 122
anti-modernist, 37, 93, 171, 216, 243

antiquity, 61, 64, 69, 74, 83, 90, 141, 243
Antirevolutionaire Partij (ARP), 43, 128, 132
Antisemitische Volkspartei, 68
anti-Semitism, 26, 29, 32, 33, 36, 42-60, 63, 64, 68, 73, 77, 84–93, 134–139, 144, 149, 153, 157, 158, 168, 171, 174, 191, 221, 222, 225, 226 238, 244
anti-Slavism, 58, 59
Antiultramontaner Reichsverband, 44
Apologetische Abteilung des Volksvereins für das katholische Deutschland, 54
Aquinas, Thomas, 24, 25, 64, 118, 195, 235
Aretz, Jürgen, 181
"Ariertum," 55
Ariosophy, 59
Aristotle, 64
Arminius ("Hermann"), 73, 74, 76, 146
Arndt, Ernst Moritz, 33, 36, 75, 76
ARP. *See Antirevolutionaire Partij*
Artamanen, 62
Arteigenes Christentum (Race-Specific Christianity). *See* Nationale Religion (national religion)
Aryan, 30, 31, 55, 59, 60–62, 84, 89, 92, 130, 139, 141, 148

Aryan paragraph, 189–192
Ascher, Saul, 45, 46
Asmussen, Hans, 176, 192
atheism, 117, 122, 139, 146, 149, 170, 237, 239
Augsburger Postzeitung, 78
Augustine, 24, 195
Austria, 115, 118, 119, 131, 147, 148, 150, 154, 185, 238
autarchy, 31, 66, 130–132, 157, 244
awakening, 6, 74, 91, 118, 148, 171
Azana-regime, 235

Bachem, Karl, 184
Baden, 22, 50, 67, 82, 117, 127, 156, 178
Baden, Max von, 133
Badischer Landbund, 226
Balduin of Trier, 140
Balkans, the, 71
Baptists, 25, 221, 222
Barmen, 124, 191, 192
Barth, Boris, 134
Barth, Karl, 26, 37, 51, 52, 124, 134, 175, 179, 180, 190–192, 216
Baumgarten, Otto, 124
Baumgärtner, Raimund, 190
Bausch, Paul, 176
Bavaria, 12, 22, 37, 43, 50–52, 56–58, 66, 68, 69, 78, 82, 115–117, 120, 125, 135–141, 143, 147, 151, 152, 154, 159, 163, 164, 173–175, 184–186, 188, 193, 194, 216, 225, 226, 230, 231
Bavink, Bernhard, 62
Bayerische Volkspartei. See BVP
Bayerischer Bauernbund. See BBB
Bayerischer Christlicher Bauernverein, 57
Bayernwacht, 150, 151
BBB, 2, 115, 146, 225, 226
Bea, Augustin, 139
Bebel, August, 42, 43
Bédarida, Francois, 161
Beelzebub, 166

"Beer Hall Putsch," 136–138, 141, 144, 145, 152, 221
Bekennende Kirche (BK) (Confessing Church), 23, 63, 78, 121, 124, 132, 171, 175, 176, 189–194, 215, 232
Bekentnis zur Wahrung des Rechts und der Verfassung, 180, 181
Belgium, 6, 24, 37, 116, 131, 244
Benedikt XV, 22, 52, 115, 116, 245
Berding, Helmut, 60
Berg Eriksen, Trond, 89, 135
Bergmann, Ernst, 32
Berlin, 47, 56, 71, 73, 74, 86, 126, 137, 140, 144, 165, 177, 188, 189, 192, 193, 222, 231
Berliner Tageblatt, 64, 159, 169
Berning, Wilhelm, 189
Berntson, Lennart, 4
Bertram, Adolf, 78, 145, 151, 164, 165, 188, 189
"*Berufsverbot*," 49, 50, 86
Bethge, Eberhard, 124
Bibelkreise, (The League of Bible Circles), 81, 231
Bible, 28, 30, 83, 92, 121, 136, 223, 237, 245
Biblical, 34, 161, 178
Billot, Louis, 52
Bismarck, Otto von, 22, 41–43, 59, 76, 90, 125, 127, 130, 148, 157, 187
BK. *See Bekennende Kirche*
black-red-yellow/gold, 38, 116, 119, 146–148
black-white-red, 38, 48, 146–148
Blavatsky, Helena, 31, 59, 77
Bleuel, Hans Peter, 83
"Blut und Boden" (Blood and Soil), 66, 69, 72, 73, 176
Bodelschwingh, Friedrich von, 76, 77
Böhme, Jakob, 30
Bolshevism, 151, 173, 174, 181, 237
Bonhoeffer, Dietrich, 26, 27, 127, 152, 191, 192, 195
Bonifacius, 75
Borchert, Wolfgang, 133

Bormann, Martin, 232
Bose, Herbert von, 118
bourgeois, 2, 3, 4, 5, 10, 15, 24, 48, 80, 81, 85, 87, 89, 122, 131, 134, 146, 148, 149, 153, 155, 156, 157, 159, 231
Bracher, Karl Dietrich, 13, 150, 184
Braun, Walter, 176
Bremen, 147
Breslau, 78, 164
Britain, 128, 176
British, 6, 126, 235
Bringeland, Hans M., 171, 179
Bruck, Moeller van den, 83
Bruderschaft sozialistischer Theologen Deutschlands, 175
Brüning, Heinrich, 13, 128, 129, 143, 160, 167, 169, 178, 184, 185
Brunstäd, Friedrich, 73, 123, 124, 190
Brunswick, 50, 163, 177
Brussels, 71
Buchberger, Michael, 166
Buchenwald, 128
Buchheim, Karl, 130
Buddhist, 30
Bultmann, Rudolf, 26, 179, 180
Bund der Landwirte, 49, 226
Bundesrat, 117
Bund für Deutsche Kirche, 190
Bündische Jugend, 80, 81
Bürgerliches Gesetzbuch, 66–68
Burgundians, 34
Burnham, Walter, 3, 4, 159
"*Burschenschaft*," 37
Buttmann, Rudolf, 163
Büttner, Ursula, 120, 194
BVP, 1–4, 10–12, 47, 22, 56–58, 66, 78, 82, 115, 125, 126, 129, 136–139, 142, 147, 150, 151, 155, 169, 178, 182, 184, 185, 216, 225, 226, 236, 237

Calvin, Jean, 46
Calvinist (Reformed Church), 11, 36, 37, 46, 118, 190

Canon Law, 67
capitalism, 46, 77, 217
Caritas, 62, 189
Carolingian-Lotharingian Europe, 217
Carolingians, 74, 75
Casti Conubii, 63
Catholic Congress. See *Katholiktag*
Catholic parties in, 217;
    Austria, 24
    Belgium, 24
    Hapsburg monarchy, 131
    Netherlands, the, 24
CDU, 56, 57, 216
Celle, 71
Central-Africa, 116
Centralverein, 50, 56, 57, 151
Chamberlain, Houston Stewart, 31, 61, 64, 88, 89, 92, 139, 161, 162, 175, 192
Chandler, Alfred R., 89
Chapoutot, Johann, 5, 237
Chardin, Pierre Teilhard de, 89
Charlemagne, 36, 73
China Inland Mission, 221
Christ, 162, 165, 231
Christ, Herbert, 170
Christian democracy, 131, 155, 216, 217,
Christlich-Deutsche Bewegung, 85
Christlich-deutsches Volk marschiert, 180
Christlicher Pilger, 168
Christliche Volkspartei, 126
Christliche Welt, 120, 171, 175
Christlichsoziale Arbeiterpartei (CSAP), 43, 46, 47, 53, 68, 116, 127, 128, 153, 154, 158
"Ciamac," 150
Civil Code ("*Code Napoleon*"), 67, 68
Class, Heinrich, 48, 55, 64
Clovis, 120
Cologne, 164
COMINTERN, 154, 155, 187
Comité de Genève ("The Black International"), 42
commissar, 191, 190

communism, 116, 117, 123, 130, 131, 134, 141, 149, 151, 155, 157, 163, 164, 165, 171, 173, 175, 177, 180, 181, 188, 217, 231, 239
Compiegne, 116
concordat, 82, 163, 168, 184–186, 232, 236, 237
confessional difference, 2, 3, 6, 8, 13, 21, 33, 41, 74, 84, 90, 194, 225, 231, 243
"Confessional-Lutherans," 122
confession of guilt, 215, 222
Conley, John J., 236, 238
conservative, 34, 42, 47, 58, 74, 79, 83, 88, 90, 117, 122, 124, 125, 127, 143, 145, 169, 171, 180, 190, 192, 216
"Conservative-National" group, 122
Constituent Assembly, 2, 65, 123
Conway, John S., 170
Conway, Martin, 85, 131, 156
Conze, Werner, 33, 43
Corpus Juris Civilis, 66
crucifix, 129, 161, 188
CSAP. See *Christlichsoziale Arbeiterpartei*
CSP, 77, 150
CSU, 66, 216
CSVD (*Christlichsozialer Volksdienst*), 3, 31, 60, 73, 127–130, 132, 143, 154, 174–176, 185, 221, 244
curia, 52, 239
CV, 85, 87, 136, 137, 170, 174, 176, 178, 185
Czechoslovakia, 85, 131, 194

Dachau, 194
Dahm, Karl-Wilhelm, 78, 122, 128
Dahn, Felix, 30, 60
Danzig, xi, 1, 2, 12, 14, 15, 85, 156
DAP, 91, 92, 135, 136
Darré, Walter, 67–69, 72, 75, 174
Darwin, 21, 22, 26, 30, 36, 44, 59, 61, 83, 89, 158
"*das Deutsche Wesen*." See "the German essence"

Das Wesen des Christentums, 88
Das Zentrum, 160
DC. See *Deutsche Christen*
DDP, 10, 14, 56, 82, 87, 119, 120, 122, 123, 127, 128, 132, 142, 155, 157, 158, 159, 169, 182, 184, 185, 216, 217, 221
"Democratic-Liberal" group, 122
Der Angriff (The Attack), 144, 231
Der Fels, 54
Der Mythus des 20. Jahrhunderts (The Myth of the 20th Century), 27, 60, 61, 69, 73, 89, 143, 161, 162, 163, 165, 171, 172, 176, 192, 193, 216, 245
Der Stürmer, 142
Deuerlein, Ernst, 169, 182
Deutsche Arbeiterpartei (DAP, in Bohemia), 48
Deutsche Arbeiterpartei (DAP, in Gernany). See DAP and Nazi party
Deutsche Bauernpartei, 225
Deutsche Christen (DC), 34, 51, 73, 122, 173, 176, 177, 183, 189–194, 222
Deutsche Demoktratische Partei. See DDP
Deutsche Evangelische Kirchenzeitung (*German Evangelical Church Magazine*), 35, 46, 47, 133
Deutsche Evangeliumsgemeinden, 221
Deutsche Glaubensbewegung (German Faith Movement), 32, 193
Deutsche Reformationspartei, 142
Deutsche Reformpartei, 48, 54, 68
Deutsche Vaterlandspartei, 60, 116
Deutsche Volkspartei. See DVP
Deutscher Bauernbund, 49
Deutscher Evangelischer Kirchenausschuss (DEKA), 119, 121, 152, 178, 181, 194
Deutscher Gewerkschaftsbund (DGB), 154
Deutscher Handlungsgehilfen-Verband (DHV), 154

Index

Deutscher Lehrerverein, 83, 167
Deutscher Sprachverein (German Language Association), 35
"*Deutscher Tag*," 137
Deutsches Pfarrerblatt, 79
Deutschkatholiken (German-Catholics), 21, 54, 92
Deutschnationaler Arbeiterbund, 154
Deutschnationale Volkspartei, See DNVP
Deutschsoziale Partei, 62, 157
"*Deutschtum*" (German-ness), 33, 37, 75, 76, 82, 83, 86, 89
"*deutschvölkisch*," 135, 138
Deutschvölkische Freiheitspartei (DVFP), 122, 135, 141, 142
Deutschvölkischer Schutz und Trutzbund (DSTB), 51, 134, 135, 145
dialectic theology, 124
Dibelius, Martin, 26, 171, 179, 180, 195, 216
Dibelius, Otto, 47, 51, 88, 119, 120, 121, 170, 171, 176, 190, 192
Didriksen, Synnøve, 62, 63
Die Eiche, 120
Die Welträtsel, 88
Dilectissima nobis encyclical, 235
Dinter, Artur, 139, 141, 142, 163, 176
Dirks, Walter, 166, 169, 170
Divini Redemptoris encyclical, 235
DNSAP, 77
DNVP, 9, 82, 117, 122, 127, 128, 129, 142, 148, 151, 155, 157, 174, 175, 216, 225, 226
doctrine, 22, 24, 93, 118, 140, 150, 161, 164, 165, 170, 192, 195
Doehring, Bruno, 133, 142
dogma, -tism, -tic, 21, 23, 24, 25, 26, 28, 30, 72, 88, 142, 143, 165, 195, 239, 243, 244
"*Dolchstosslegende*." See "Stab-in-the-Back-Legend"
Dollfuss, Engelbert, 119
Döllinger, Ignaz, 31, 91
Donar Oak, 74, 75

Dreilager thesis, 2, 156
DSTB. See *Deutschvölkischer Schutz und Trutzbund*
Dühring, Eugen, 59, 88, 149
Dutch, 43, 128, 132, 217
DVFP. See *Deutschvölkische Freiheitspartei*
DVP, 122, 127, 146, 148, 157

Eastern Europe, 217
East Friesland, 11
East Prussia, 11, 71, 182, 244
Eckert, Erwin, 175
Eckhardt, Dietrich, 135, 136
ecumenical, 64, 121, 194, 222, 238
Edda, 30, 74
EEC, 131
Eggers, Kurt, 187
Ehrenberg, H. Ph., 124
Einstein, Albert, 116
Eigengesetzlichkeitsthese (Separate Jurisdictions Dogma), 24–26, 125, 126, 152, 192, 195
Eiserne Front, 150
Elert, Werner, 121
Ellstätter, Moritz, 50
Élysée-treaty, 217
Emberland, Terje, 90, 148
encyclical, 24, 82, 117, 156, 235–239
Engels, Friedrich, 58, 59
Enlightenment, 6, 42, 44, 46, 73, 124
Epp, Franz Ritter von, 184
Erasmus of Roterdam, 25
Erlangen, 13, 141, 175
Ernste Bibelforscher (The Jehova's witnesses), 222, 223
Erzberger, Matthias, 115–117, 133, 135
ethnic cleansing, 63, 64, 90
EU, 217, 246, 247
eugenics, 61, 62, 91, 191, 229
euthanasia, 60, 61, 63, 188
evangelical, 170, 177, 178, 190, 191, 221, 223
Evangelische Arbeitervereine, 49, 153
Evangelische Frauenhilfe, 229

Evangelische Gemeinschaft, 221
Evangelische Jugend, 49, 222
Evangelische Volkspartei, 128
Evangelischer Bund (The Evangelical Association), 39, 44, 49, 120, 142, 170, 190
Evangelisch-Sozialer Kongress, 88
ex cathedra dogma, 21–24, 28, 244

Falter, Jürgen, 3–5, 7, 8, 10
Fandel, Thomas, 193
fascism, -t, 5, 6, 46, 57, 68, 71, 118, 131–133, 142, 150, 154, 165, 192, 235–238
Fattorini, Emma, 238, 239
Faulhaber, Michael (archbishop of Bavaria), 12, 56, 61, 63, 75, 116, 137, 138, 140, 141, 151, 185, 188, 194, 230
FDP, 217
Feder, Gottfried, 135
Fehrenbach, Konstantin, 55, 146
Fenske, Harald, 124, 125
feudal, -ism, 67, 68, 75
Fichte, Johann Gottlieb, 33, 34, 36, 46, 61, 63, 88, 132, 193
"*First Reich*," 71
Flint, Colin, 3, 4
Flottenverein, 44
Fortschrittliche Volkspartei. See Progressive party
France, 4, 6, 35, 37, 38, 41, 46, 66, 67, 77, 115, 117, 118, 128, 131, 142, 176, 217, 239, 244, 246
Franconia, 139, 141
Francophile, 217, 246
Franco-Prussian War, 38
Frankfort, 71
Frankfurter Zeitung, 169
Franks, -ish kingdom, 34, 75, 120
Frauenwerk, 229, 232
Freemasons, 52, 73, 134, 164, 239
Freiburg, 13, 164, 238
Freie deutsche Jugendbewegung, 49, 80–82

"*Freikirchen*," 222
Freisinnige Partei, 48
Freisinnige Vereinigung, 157
French, 5, 33, 34, 36, 38, 45, 52, 61, 73, 75, 83, 137, 217, 235, 246
French Empire, 38, 67
French nationalism, 33, 43, 45, 72, 243
French Revolution, the, 6, 33, 67, 72, 123, 128, 239
"French spirit," 39
Frick, Wilhelm, 85
Friedmann, Jan, 84
Friedrich, Hans E., 172, 179
Fries, Jakob, 45, 63
Fridtjov statue, 73, 76
Fritsch, Theodor, 62, 139
Frøland, Carl Müller, 5, 33, 34
"*Fronterlebnis*" ("front experience"), 31, 128, 132, 133
Führer principle/myth/adoration, 14, 47, 70, 71, 76, 79, 80, 143, 162, 166, 189, 190, 191, 223, 238
Führerhauptquartiere, 71
Fulda (archsee and northern bishops' conference), 42, 75, 145, 150, 164

Gaia, 30
Galen, Clemens von, 63, 188
Galton, Francis, 61
genocide, 63, 64, 90
Gerecke, Karl, 51
Gereke, Günter, 225
German-Catholics. See *Deutschkatholiken*
"*Germanentum*," German-ness. Germanism. See Deutschtum
"German essence," ("das deutsche Wesen"), 55, 60, 83, 88, 90, 91, 181, 215, 216, 244, 245, 246
German Federation (Deutscher Bund), the, 38, 43
German-nationalism, 244
Germania, (paper), 52, 126
Germania, (by Tacitus), 74
Germanism. See "*Deutschtum*"

Gesamtverband der christlichen Gewerkschaften (GcG), 153, 154
Gestapo, 162, 187
Gierke, Otto von, 68
Giles, Geoffrey, 14
global, 216, 238
Gobineau, Arthur de, 59, 91
Goebbels, Josef, 12, 35, 76, 85, 123, 129, 160, 162, 216, 238
Goering, Hermann, 70, 162, 164, 181, 182
Goethe, Johann Wolfgang von, 30
Gogarten, Friedrich, 124
Golz, Rüdiger, Graf von der, 149
Gorki, Maxim, 116
Görres, Josef, 91
Goslar, 71
Gotto, Klaus, 186
Graf, Friedrich, 80
Greek Catholics, 222
Grimm, Jakob, 36
Gröber, Conrad, 239
Grone, Agnes von, 229, 232
Grüber, Heinrich, 51
Grundlagen des 19. Jahrhunderts, 88, 175
Gundolf, Friedrich, 27
Günther, Hans, 85
Gurlitt, Ludwig, 80–82
Gustav Adolf Verein, 39, 44

Haeckel, Ernst, 30, 60–62, 88–90
Haecker, Theodor, 78
Haeuser, Philip, 140
Haffner, Sebastian, 129, 130, 182, 216
Hahn, Hans Joachim, 27
Hamburg, 13, 50, 133, 135, 147
Hannot, Walter, 160
Hannover, 13
Hannoverians ("*Welfen*"), 38, 39
Hanseatic, 147
Hapsburg, 25, 48, 131
Harket, Håkon, 89, 135
Harmsen, Hans, 62
Harnack, Adolf von, 30, 52, 88, 90

Harrer, Karl, 136
Harzburg, 129, 154, 182, 183
Harzburg front, 9
Hastings, Adrian, 65
Hastings, Derek, 77, 80, 91, 135–137, 140, 141
Hauer, Johann Wilhelm, 32, 193, 237
Heberle, Rudolf, 3
Hegel, Friedrich, 33, 34, 36, 46, 58, 67
Heiler, Friedrich, 176
Heimdall, 31
Heimwehr, 154
Held, Heinrich, 56, 115, 137, 138
Hentschel, Willibald, 62
Herder, Johann Gottfried von, 33, 36, 46, 60, 67, 243
Hermann. *See Arminius*
Herrnhut, 129, 222
Herrnhut Brethren, 129, 222
Hess, Rudolf, 28
Hessen, 50, 75, 117, 156
Heuss, Theodor, 79
Hildebrandt, Rudolf, 35
Himmler, Gebhard, 91
Himmler, Heinrich, 28–30, 75, 91, 188
Hindenburg, Paul von, 1, 12, 13, 77, 119, 128, 154, 167, 191, 193, 237
Hindu, 30
Hirsch, Emmanuel, 79, 121, 124, 173
Historische Zeitschrift (*Historical Magazine*), 35
Hitler, Adolf, 1, 6, 12, 13, 26, 30, 31, 47, 56, 58, 60, 63, 66, 71, 73, 76–81, 136–138, 140, 142–145, 148, 151, 154, 159–163, 166, 168, 170, 171, 173, 174, 175, 177, 180, 182, 184, 185, 191, 193, 194, 222, 223, 225, 236–239, 245
Hitlerjugend, 79, 137, 162, 193, 230–232, 237
Hitler's Pope, 189
Hobson, Rolf, 134
Hochland, 136
Hockerts, Hans Günter, 186
Hohenzollern, 26, 43, 244

Holl, Karl, 191
Holy Roman Empire, 22, 24, 25, 35, 71
homo singulus/privatus, 74
"Hour zero," 92
Huber, Christian Josef, 161
Hudson Taylor, 222
Hugenberg, Alfred, 127, 159
Hülser, Gustav, 154
Hungary, 131
Hüppauf, Bernt, 133

Iber, Harald, 176, 192
Idealism/idealism, 34, 37, 64, 216
"ideas of 1914," 40
"ideas/values of 1789," 35, 40, 82, 83, 118, 123, 128, 151, 156, 159, 216, 226, 243
idolatry, 61, 236
Ihmels, L., 122
Index Librorum Prohibitorum, 24, 32, 59, 89, 236, 238, 239
Indo-Europeans, 59
Ingolstadt, 143
Innere Mission (the Inner Mission), 23, 29, 62, 158, 193, 229, 231
Innitzer, Theodor, 188, 238
Instructio, 164
inter-confessional, 54, 84, 125, 131, 147, 153, 167, 168
International Catholic Union, 115
"International Commission for fighting Fascism," The, 150
International Court of Justice, the, 69
Internationale Démocratique, 132
internationalism, 31, 64, 66, 121, 136, 145
"internationals," 31, 45, 48, 149, 153; Black international, the, 31, 42, 45, 48, 149, 151, 153, 188; Golden/Yellow international, the, 31, 45, 48, 149, 153; Grey international, the, 31; Red international, the, 31, 45, 48, 149, 151, 153, 188; "white international," 135

Interwar period, 42, 66, 131, 156, 215
Israelit, 57
Italian, 5, 6, 34, 73, 131, 132, 165, 235, 236
Italy, 6, 35, 52, 57, 71, 115, 118, 131, 137, 236, 238, 239, 261

Jacke, Jochen, 120
Jahn, Friedrich Ludwig, 33, 36, 75
Jahr, Christoph, 84
Janssen, Johannes, 86
Jantzen, Kyle, 173, 174, 190
Jaspers, Karl, 216
Jebb, Eglantyne, 116
Jehova's Witnesses, The. See *Ernste Bibelforscher*
Jesuit, -ism, 29, 45, 54, 89, 92, 134, 139, 149
"Jewish menace," 121
Joos, Josef, 132, 152–154, 185
Judaism, 35, 44, 45, 46, 60, 88, 121
"*Judenschutztruppe*," 147
Jugendbund, 137
Jungdeutscher Orden, 144–147, 151, 152, 155, 157
Jung, Edgar, 118
Jung, Rudolf, 161
Jungmännerverband, 180, 184
Jungmännerverein, 139
Jungreformatorische Bewegung, 73, 132, 176, 189–191
Jung-Spartacus Bund, 231
Junker, Detlef, 184

Kaas, Ludwig, 56, 165, 180, 184
Kahr, Gustav von, 138, 139
Kaiser, Wolfram, 65
Kampfbund, 137–139
Kampffront Schwarz-Weiss-Rot, 148, 155, 225
Kant, Immanuel, 30, 46
Kapler, Hermann, 194
Kareski, Georg, 54, 165
Karwehl, Richard, 79, 80, 179

Katholiktag (Catholic Annual Congress), 42, 153
Katholische Arbeiterbewegung (KAB), 152, 153
Katholische Fraktion, 57, 58, 125
Katholische Jugend und Jungmännerverein Deutschlands, 145
"*Katholische Kanzlei Schwarz-Weiss-Rot*," 168
Katholische Parole, 168
Katholische Volksvertretung, 11
Kernstock, Ottokar, 77
Kerrl, Hans, 162
Kershaw, Ian, 4, 246
King, Gary, 3–5, 10
Kirchenbundesamt, 172
Kjellén, Rudolf, 40
Kjøstvedt, Anders G., 63, 84, 177
Klausener, Erich, 118, 187
Kleinschmidt, Samuel P., 62
Klinnert, Ernst, 83
KLVdDR, 167, 183
Koblenz-Trier, 139
Köln-Aachen, 139
Kolonialverein, 48
Konservative Partei (KP), 48, 62
KPD (the Communists), 7, 56, 130, 155, 187, 217
Kreisleiter, 84
Kreuzscharen, 150
"*Kristallnacht*," 187–189
Krone, Heinrich, 57
Kulturkampf, 22-24, 39-43, 45, 53, 54, 57, 64, 81, 86, 91, 92, 120, 125, 126, 145, 156, 189, 245
Künneth, Walter, 51, 121, 124, 171, 176, 190, 192
Kupisch, Karl, 41, 86, 88, 119, 124
Kuyper, Abraham, 43
KV (*Kartellverband*), 79, 85, 87, 136, 181
Kyffhäuserverband, 49, 86, 158

Labor Party, 126
Lächele, Rainer, 89

Lagarde, Paul de, 29, 31, 36, 45, 49, 62, 64, 80, 82–84, 88, 161, 162
Lammers, Heinrich, 71, 180
Lamparter, Eduard, 52
Landbund, 225, 226
Landeskirchen, 65, 119, 221, 223
Landvolk, 157, 158, 225
Langbehn, Julius, 30, 31, 36, 37, 49, 80, 82–84
Langemarck, 86, 132, 133
Lateran Treaty, 143, 154, 235, 236
League of Bible Circles, The. *See Bibelkreise*
League of Nations, 59, 69, 120, 129, 132, 150, 235
"*Lebensborn*," 61, 62
"*Lebensraum*," 59, 90
leftist, 117, 131, 133, 142, 143, 148, 150, 154, 157, 226, 239
leftist-liberal, 116, 117, 119, 123, 128, 131, 156, 157, 158, 169, 171, 175, 179
left-wing, 129, 133
Leipzig, 37, 76
Leo XIII, 24, 42, 117
Lerchenfeld, Hugo Max von, 140
Levenda, Peter, 77
Levy, Robert S, 56
liberal, 116, 117, 118, 120, 121, 122, 124, 125, 130, 131, 135, 147, 149, 156, 157, 158, 159, 171, 179, 225
liberal theology, ian, 21, 22, 25, 29, 35, 86, 88, 171, 175
liberalism, -t, 5, 29, 31, 35, 46, 58, 68, 116, 123, 124, 125, 132, 157, 158, 159, 166, 239
Liberation War. *See* Wars of Liberation
Lichtmenschen, 72
Lichtwark, Alfred, 82
Liebenfels, Jörg Lanz von, 31, 59, 246
Liebenzeller Mission, 222
Lieber, Ernst, 52, 53, 57, 58
Lietz, Hermann, 82
Lilje, Hanns, 190
Lill, Rudolf, 53, 120, 188

Lind, Emil, 193
Lippe, 9, 11, 12, 28
List, Guido von, 31, 59, 77
Lithuania, 6, 14, 15, 131
Lombards, 34
Lorenz, Einhart, 89, 135
"*Los-von-Rom*" ("Away from Rome"), 31, 40, 141
Lot, Ferdinand, 70, 71
Lower Bavaria, 139, 226
Lübeck, 147
Luden, Heinrich, 63
Ludendorff, Erich, 32, 137, 138, 141, 142, 163
Ludendorff, Mathilde, 32
Lutheran, ism, 11, 23, 25, 26, 35, 36, 37, 46, 79, 122, 135, 146, 162, 171, 173, 188, 190–192, 221, 222
Luther, Martin, 25, 27, 29, 30, 37, 46, 88, 89, 162

Machiavelli, 24, 158
Mahraun, Artur, 145
Maler, Hans, 44
Mainz, 164, 177
Mak, Geert, 217
Manichhaean, 60
"*Männerbund*," 71
Mann, Thomas, 29
Marburg speech, 243
March Revolution/the 1848 Revolution, 24, 35, 38, 41, 116, 118, 123, 147
Mark, 132
marxist, 3, 4, 72, 136, 145, 148–150, 157, 165, 166, 237
Marx, Karl, 58, 59, 130, 148
Marx, Wilhelm, 12, 55, 146
Masaryk, Thomas, 29
Master Eckhardt, 30
Masuria, 11, 14, 15, 39, 59
materialism, 121, 140, 166, 237
Mausbach, Josef, 65
Mazura, Uwe, 58
Mecklenburg, 133, 139, 177
Meier, Kurt, 189

Meinecke, Friedrich, 158, 159, 184
Mein Kampf, 60, 141, 142, 174
Meiser, Hans, 47, 51, 120, 193
Mensing, Björn, 141, 173, 174, 216
mentality, 1, 7, 11, 35, 36, 40, 53, 55, 59, 68, 72, 81, 83, 84, 86, 120, 129, 132, 133, 142, 159, 160, 167, 172, 175, 192, 216, 217, 143, 245, 246, 249
Messianism, 79, 80, 239
Methodists, 221, 222
Michelangelo, 83
Mierendorff, Carlo, 175
Migration Period/kingdoms, 70, 71
Mit brennender Sorge, 187, 235, 237, 238
Mitteldeutscher Bauernverein, 49
modernist, 53, 65, 93, 144, 216, 243
Molotov-Ribbentrop Pact, 188
Mommsen, Hans, 188, 226
Mommsen, Theodor, 46, 86
monarchy, 75, 86, 117, 125, 131
monism, 30, 47, 60, 61, 90
Monistenbund, 90
Monnet, Jean, 217
Montesquieu, 118
Montgomery McGovern, William, 68
Morsey, Rudolf, 184
Mosaic law, 72
Moscow, 149, 226
Mosse, George, 6, 31, 35, 45, 72, 76, 80, 82–84
Mother's Organization, The, 229
Muckermann, Hermann, 61, 62
Mulert, Hermann, 124, 179
Müller, Adam, 118
Müller, Hans, 168
Müller, Ludwig, 175, 191, 193, 222, 230, 232
Müller, Otto, 181
Mumm, Richard, 128
mundium, 70
Munich, 12, 13, 31, 56, 57, 71, 79, 85, 91, 92, 129, 135, 136, 138, 139
Munich-Freising (archsee and southern bishops' conference), 42, 145, 146

Münster, 187, 188, 238
Mussolini, Benito, 73, 78, 80, 137, 154, 236

Napoleon, 25, 33, 34, 37, 63, 66, 67, 72, 73, 118, 147, 193
Napoleon III, 77
National assembly. *See* Constituent assembly
"National bloc," 2, 3, 5, 142
Nationale Religion (national religion), 28–30, 36, 89
Nationalkirche (National Church), 54, 147, 161, 164, 168, 173, 177, 192, 193, 237, 238
Nationalliberale (National Liberals), 42, 48, 57, 157, 244
Nationalsozialer Verein, 149, 158
Nationalsozialistischer Frauenbund, 229
Nationalsozialistischer Verein, 149
Nationalsozialistische Volkswohlfahrt, 62
naturalism, 89
natural law/rights, 25, 30, 60, 65, 67, 69, 118, 178, 195
Nauen, 173, 174, 190
Naumann, Friedrich, 29, 128, 149, 158, 159, 244
Nazi Party (NSDAP), vii, viii, 2, 4, 6–11, 14, 22, 24, 31, 32, 48, 60, 62, 66–78, 81, 84, 117, 122 127–129, 132, 135–139, 141, 143–145, 149, 151, 152, 154, 155, 157, 159, 160, 162, 163–168, 171, 172, 173, 176, 177, 178, 184, 185, 193, 194, 221, 225, 226, 229, 231, 245, 246
Nedrebø, Tore, 131, 217
neo-occultism, 90
neopaganism. *See* paganism
Netherlands, the, 5, 24, 35, 70, 127, 128, 131, 189
Neudeutschland, 80
New Testament, 51, 161
Nibelungenlied, 74

Niemöller, Martin, 51, 176, 190, 192, 193
Niemöller, Wilhelm, 176, 192
Nietzsche, Friedrich, 24, 30
nihilism, 140
Nipperdey, Thomas, 23, 25, 88, 127
Nobel Peace Prize, 69, 157, 246
Non Abiamo Bisogno encyclical, 235
Norden, Günther van, 120
Nordic, 35, 61, 63, 73, 143, 161, 192, 238
North German Federation (Norddeutscher Bund), 53, 57, 147
Norway, 5, 26, 59, 61, 73, 76, 128, 131, 171, 217
Nowak, Kurt, 122, 144, 179
NSZ Rheinfront, 169
Nuelson, John, 222
nulla poena sine lege principle, 70
nullum crimen sine poena principle, 70
nuncio, 164, 189
Nuremberg, 77, 137, 139, 142

Obersalzberg, 71
occult, 30, 59, 77, 90, 121, 135, 136, 245
Old Catholics. *See Altkatholiken*
Oldenburg, 11, 156, 178, 188
Old Testament, 29, 30, 51, 53, 83, 88, 91, 136, 139, 161, 162, 178, 192, 221, 238
"*Ordnungstheologie*," 191
Orsenigo, 189
orthodoxy, 21, 32, 45, 59, 91
Osservatore Romano, 163, 237
"ostic" race, 61

Pacelli, Eugenio (Pius XII), 11, 82, 91, 138, 164, 186, 189, 235, 236, 237
pacifist, 61, 116, 129, 132, 157
Paderborn, 164
pagan, 28, 29, 32, 45, 75, 77, 78, 83, 139, 144, 161, 174, 175, 237, 239, 245
Palatinate (Pfalz), 168

pan-Europeanism, 66, 130, 131, 157
pantheism, 60, 90, 237
Papen, Franz von, 62, 79, 118, 167, 185, 243
"*Papphelm*," 146
paramilitary organizations, 144, 148, 150, 152, 155, 182
Paris, 149
parliamentarism, 24, 117, 123, 128, 130, 135, 145, 154, 160, 171, 184, 191
Parsee sun-cult, 77
Partei der Arbeit, 126
particularism, 64–66
Parti Démocrate Populaire (PDP), 131
Partito Popolari Italiano (PPI), 131, 132, 236
Patch, William, 154
Patriotenpartei, 2, 66
Pax Romana, 132
Payne, Stanley G., 4, 8, 43
Pazifistischer Studentenbund, 87
Peace Resolution/Resolution of Peace, 115, 133, 155, 158
Pentecostals, 221
Persian religion, 31
Petersen, Peter, 127, 128
Pfalzwacht, 150
Pfarrernotbund (PNB), 132, 176, 189, 191, 232
Pfleiderer, 86
Phayer, Michael, 229
Pieper, August, 137
Pieper, Lorenz, 78, 137, 138, 145
pietism, 32–35, 78, 89, 128, 178, 245
Piper, Otto, 124
Pirna, 173, 174, 190
Pius IX, 42, 65
Pius X, 22, 52
Pius XI, 32, 52, 63, 65, 78, 143, 164, 165, 166, 184, 185, 186, 187, 189, 235, 236, 237, 238, 239
Pius XII, 79, 82, 189, 238. *See* also Pacelli
Ploetz, Alfred, 60, 61
Poland, 71, 120

Poles, 11, 38, 39, 57–59, 126
Pope, 22, 24, 41, 89, 138, 169, 232, 244
political confessionalism, 3, 4, 159
"*Politische Theologie*," 121
"positive Christianity," 140, 143, 146, 149, 166, 174, 175, 183, 245
Potempa, 177
Prague, 71
Preuschen, Erwin, 22, 29
Preysing, Konrad von, 188
Pridham, Geoffrey, 143
Probst, Adalbert, 187
Progressive party (*Fortschrittliche Volkspartei*), 93, 115, 119
Protocols of the Elders of Zion, 45
Prussia, 3, 9–12, 33, 37, 38, 45, 50, 58, 59, 66, 82, 89, 117, 126, 127, 129, 134, 145, 147, 148, 156, 177, 178, 180, 183, 191, 222
Pulzer, Peter, 43, 44, 47, 72, 73, 148
puritan, 160
"Putsch." *See* "Beer Hall Putsch"

Quadragesimo anno encyclical, 235
Quervain, Alfred de, 124
Quickborn, 80, 81
Quidde, Ludwig, 157

race, 28, 31, 33, 47, 49, 53, 59–61, 64, 66, 75, 90, 136, 137, 139, 140, 149, 168, 178, 191, 192, 222, 231, 236, 237, 238, 239
Rade, Martin, 122, 124, 179
Radikaldemokratische Partei, 157
Rafael, 83
Rafaelsverein, Saint, 189
Ranke, Leopold von, 35
Rathenau, Walter, 87, 135
rationalism, 6, 21, 75, 92, 121, 123, 124,
Ratzel, Friedrich, 90
Ratzinger, Joseph (Benedikt XVI), 232
Ravensburg, 174, 190
reconfessionaliism, 21
Reformation, the, 24, 25, 33, 37, 45, 51, 59, 116, 176

Reformed Church. *See* Calvinist
Reformkatholiken (Reform Catholics), 22, 31, 42, 47, 51, 54, 85, 87, 91, 92, 135, 136, 246
Regensburg (Ratisbon), 166, 177
Reichsbanner, 57, 87, 131, 146, 147, 150, 152, 155, 157, 182, 226
Reichsbischof, 175, 191, 193, 222, 230
Reichsideologie, 118
Reichskonkordat, 82, 232, 236, 237
Reichsparteitag, 232
Reichsstatthalter, 71
"*Reichstheologie*," 62
Reichsverband Deutscher Zentrumsstudenten, 85
Reichsverband gegen die Sozialdemokratie, 44
Reichwein, Adolf, 175
"Religious Socialist" group, 122
Rembrandt, 83
Repgen, Konrad, 186, 189, 195
Republikanischer Schutzbund, 150
Republikanisches Studentenkartell, 87
Rerum Novarum encyclical, 24, 235
Rettet die Ehre, 120
Reventlow, Ernst zu, 162, 174
revolutionary, 35, 51, 56, 77, 80, 82, 117, 119, 125, 136, 147, 149, 154, 155, 157, 172, 226
Rheinische Mission, 51, 60, 64
Rhineland, 37, 52, 66, 67, 74, 182, 217, 231
rightist, 116, 117, 118, 123, 126, 128, 133, 138, 142, 147, 150, 151, 152, 155, 157, 175, 179, 225, 226
right-wing, 117, 129, 131, 134, 135, 138, 144, 145, 146, 149, 151, 152, 183
Ring Katholischer Deutscher Burschenschaften, 85
Ritschl, Albrecht, 25
Röder, Adam, 55
Rohe, Karl, 2, 3, 8, 142, 150, 155, 156
Röhm, Ernst, 118, 187
Rohrbach, Paul, 90

Rokkan, Stein, 217
Roman law, 60, 66–74, 89, 118, 123, 217
Romanticism, 34, 43, 90
Rome, 78, 89, 120, 138, 161, 162, 185, 187
"*Römlinge*," 74
Rompuy, van, 246
Rosenberg, Alfred, 27, 29, 32, 35, 54, 57, 61, 68, 69, 70, 71, 73, 75, 77, 89, 121, 134, 137, 138, 142, 143, 149, 161–165, 171–177, 186, 187, 192, 193, 216, 222, 230, 232, 237, 245
Rost, Hans, 55, 78
Roter Frontkämpferbund, 147, 148, 155
Roth, Alfred, 135
Rothenburg ob der Tauber, 225
Roth, Josef, 135, 162
Rousseau, Jean Jacques, 117, 130
Ruhr, 137
Russia, 50, 58, 115, 166, 244

SA, 129, 144, 147, 177, 180
Saar, 1, 2, 12, 14, 126, 187
Sacher, Hermann, 79
Sacrum imperium. *See* Holy Roman Empire
Salvation army, 222
Sasse, Hermann, 179
Sasse, Martin, 188
Satanic, 239
Save the Children, 116
Savigny, Friedrich K. von, 70
Saxony, 33, 48 50, 74, 225
Saxony (Lower S.), 75
Schachleiter, Alban, 162
Schacht, Hjalmar, 132
Schallmyer, Wilhelm, 61
Scharnagel, Anton, 230
Scheffel, Josef Victor von, 72
Scheidemann, Philip, 133, 135
"Schicksal" theology, 195
Schirach, Baldur von, 86, 162, 232
Schlageter, Albert Leo, 77, 137, 143

Schleiermacher, Friedrich, 27, 33, 34, 36, 45, 46, 52, 88, 162, 245
Schleswig-Holstein, 3, 193
Schlund, Erhardt, 32, 56, 79, 140, 141
Schmidt, Ute, 4, 8
Schmitt, Carl, 70, 123
scholastic, 24, 64, 91
Scholder, Klaus, 13, 169, 172, 175, 178, 184, 222
Scholz, Gustav, 172
Schönerer, Georg von, 141
Schopenhauer, Artur, 30
Schöpfungsglaube (Creation Faith), 32, 63, 79, 121
Schreiber, Christian, 165
Schreiner, Helmuth, 176
Schrönghamer-Heimdal, Franz, 136
Schufo, 147
Schuman, Robert, 217
Schwarzburgbund, 85
Schweizer, Albert, 193
scout, 49, 231
Sebottendorff, Rudolf von, 59, 136
Sedan, 26, 41, 73, 76
Seeberg, Reinhold, 62
See, Klaus von, 40, 68
Seldte, Franz, 151
Separate Jurisdiction Dogma. See "*Eigengesezlichkeitsthese*"
separatism, 11, 38, 65, 66, 79, 226
Serf, 68, 69
Silesia, 59, 231
Simonyi, Zsigmond, 68
Simpfendörfer, Wilhelm, 128, 129, 132, 154
SIPDIC, 131, 132, 149, 217
Slavic, 235
social Darwinism, 22, 80, 89, 149, 159
social democracy, 7, 35, 38, 39, 40, 41, 44, 56, 61, 87, 120, 136, 137, 146, 147, 152, 153, 156, 159, 170, 173, 184, 217, 243
socialism, 2, 3, 4, 7, 8, 10, 14, 15, 31, 44, 45, 47, 50, 54, 57, 61, 64, 68, 89, 93, 119, 120, 122, 123, 124, 131, 143, 147, 149, 150, 152, 156, 157, 163, 164, 165, 171, 172, 173, 175, 179, 182, 217
socialism, Nazi conception of, 69, 148, 149
Sognefjord, 73
Sommer, Margarete, 189
Sonderweg thesis, 4, 5
Sontheimer, Kurt, 123
Sorbian, 58
South German Mennonites, 221
Southwest Africa, 64, 90
Soviet, 59, 186, 217, 235, 236
Spain, 6, 166, 239
SPD, 3, 4, 10, 13, 42–44, 48, 50, 53, 56, 57, 59, 64, 78, 82, 87, 93, 115, 117, 119, 122, 123, 126, 127, 130, 131, 133, 139, 142, 143, 149, 155, 160, 163, 168, 169, 182, 217, 249
Spengler, Oswald, 83
Spenkuch, Jörg L., xi, 4, 8
Spicer, Kevin, 161, 185
spiritism, 90
SS, 129, 188, 238
Staatslexikon, 65
Staatspartei. See DDP
Staatspolitische Arbeitsgemeinschaft der katholischen Verbände Deutschlands, 167
"Stab-in-the-Back-Legend"/"Dolchstosslegende," 119, 133, 134, 142, 194
Stachura, Peter, 80, 81
Stahlhelm, 133, 144–146, 148, 151, 152, 155, 225
Stegerwald, Adam, 131, 182
Steigmann-Gall, Richard, 28, 29, 231
Steiner, Rudolf, 30, 31
Sterilization Law, the, 62, 63
Stern, Fritz, 82
Stimmen der Zeit, 139
Stöcker, Adolf, 32, 43, 46, 47, 49, 52, 62, 68, 86, 88, 116, 127, 128, 153, 154, 158, 174
Stockholm Conference, the, 32

Stögbauer, Christian, 3, 5, 8, 10
Stöhr, Franz, 172
Stonehenge, 30
Strasbourg, 86
Strasser, Gregor, 35, 69, 160
Strathmann, Hermann, 141, 175
Streicher, Julius, 142, 143, 174
Stresemann, Gustav, 49, 146, 148, 157, 159
Stribrny, Wolfgang, 127, 129
Studententag, 85
Studies of the Myth of the 20th century, 187
"*Stunde 0*" ("Hour zero"), 92, 216
Sturzo, Luigi, 132
Stuttgarter Schuldbekenntnis, 215
Suarez, Francisco, 24
subsidiarity, 235
Sudetenland, 39
Sulzbach, 226
Summa Theologica, 235
summus episcopus status, 25
sun-worship, 90
swastika ("Hakenkreuz"), 10, 77, 78, 127, 129, 135, 148
Swede, 40
Swiss, 124, 132, 175, 190
Switzerland, 5, 35, 127, 128, 131
Sybel, Heinrich von, 35
syllabi, 239
syncretism, 76

Tacitus, 74
Tägliche Rundschau, 129
Talmud, 139
Tal, Uriel, 60, 80, 188
Tannenberg monument, 76, 77
Tanner, Klaus, 123
Teutoburger Forest, 30, 73, 74
Teutonic law/judicial systems, 66–71, 123
Teutonic religion. See *Nationale Religion*
theosophy, 30, 59, 90, 122, 245
Thimme, Friedrich, 178

Thorsen, Arve, 26, 36, 40, 41, 65
Thulegesellschaft, 136, 137
Thuringia/Thüringen, 85, 163, 188, 192, 193
Tilgner, Wolfgang, 119, 120
Tillich, Paul, 124, 175, 179
Tillmann, Philipp, xi, 4, 8
Tolzien, Gerhard, 133
Torregossa, Vasallo di, 164
totalitarian, 14, 34, 192, 195, 216, 235, 236, 238, 239
trade union, 31, 49, 57, 66, 116, 131, 153, 154, 180, 182, 183, 210
Traub, Gottfried, 179
Treitschke, Heinrich von, 46, 73, 86, 90
Troeltsch, Ernst, 29, 30, 51, 179
Trotha, Lothar von, 90

Ugelvik Larsen, Stein, et al., 5
Ultramontanist, 7, 22, 28, 29, 31, 35, 38, 39, 41, 42, 47, 48, 54, 65, 79, 87, 91, 120, 138, 244, 245, 246
umbrella organization, 48, 80, 85, 119, 125, 149, 152, 153, 172, 221, 229, 231
Union-Churches, 190
Unitasverband, 85
Universal Christian Council for Life and Work, The, 51
universalism, 36, 64–66, 69, 118, 217
Universities and high schools, 1, 13, 43, 50, 73, 79, 83-86, 133, 141, 169, 194, 238
Upper Bavaria, 139
Upper Silesia, 59, 120
U.S.A., the, 63, 128, 194, 217
USPD, 119, 122
Utrecht, 189

Vatican, 7, 9, 22, 24, 52, 92, 136, 138, 157, 163, 164, 186, 187, 189, 232, 237, 238, 239, 245
Veit, Friedrich, 141
Verband evangelischer Lehrervereine Deutschlands, 167

Verband Süddeutscher Katholischer Arbeitervereine, 152
Vereinigte Vaterländische Verbände (United Patriotic Associations), 39, 149
Versailles Treaty, 2, 9, 10, 14, 25, 119–121, 126, 128, 134, 158
Vienna, 71
Viereck, Peter, 216
Vitoria, Francisco, 24
Vogel, Wieland, 145
völkisch, 28–32, 34, 40, 45, 49, 50, 53, 58, 60–62, 65, 66, 69, 74, 75, 77, 78, 80, 82, 83, 84, 85, 87, 89, 90, 91, 117, 120, 121, 132, 134, 136–139, 141, 142, 145, 151, 153, 154, 158, 159, 161, 162, 171, 173, 176, 180, 191, 194, 216, 229, 246
"*Völkisch-Deutschgläubisch*" group, 122
Völkische Bewegung, 27, 29–32, 34, 36, 54, 68, 75, 78, 80, 91, 93, 138, 140, 142
Völkischer Beobachter (*VB*), 136, 137, 139, 165, 180
Völkisch(nationale)er Block, 10, 122, 127, 141, 142
Volksdienst, 60
Volksfront, 150, 159
"*Volksgeist*" (Spirit of the People), 33, 34
"*Volksreligion.*" See Nationale Religion
"*Volkstum*," 73, 175, 176, 191
Volksverein für das katholische Deutschland (The People's Association for Catholic Germany), 42, 54, 55, 137
Volk theology, 25, 30
Vormarsch, 152
Vorwärts, 78, 136

Wagner, Josef, 160
Wagner, Richard, 73, 161
Waldeck, 157, 225
Wallhalla monument, 76
Wall Street crash, 4, 5, 159
Walser Smith, Helmut, 2, 3, 5, 8, 43, 64, 90
Wandervogel. *See Freie Deutsche Jugendbewegung*
Warmia, 182
Wars of Liberation, 29, 37, 40, 76, 191
wars of Unification, 40, 41
Wartburg, 37, 46, 76
Wasmann, Erich, 89
Weber, Max, 8, 158, 159
Wehrverein, 44
"Weimar Coalition/parties," 10, 41, 49, 56, 115, 116, 119, 120, 123, 125, 131, 145, 146, 147, 149, 155, 156, 157, 216, 226, 243, 244, 245
Weimar constitution, 10, 25, 69, 73, 85, 93, 116, 117, 119, 123–125, 147, 148, 158, 180
Weismann, August, 61
Weizsäcker, Ernst von, 239
"Weltanschauung," 156
Weltfrömmigkeit (Piety of the World), 27
Weltpolitik, 90
Wenz, Adolf, 174
Weser-Ems, 11, 12
"the West"/Western (European culture), 37, 40, 50, 52, 60, 77, 83, 90, 117, 124, 130, 162, 188, 243, 244
Westdeutsche Arbeiterzeitung (*WAZ*), 152, 185
Westfahlen-Süd, 139
Westphalia/Westfahlen, 52, 146
Weymar, Erich, 83
Wichern, Heinrich, 62
Wichern, Johann H., 62
Widukind, 73, 74, 75
Wiener, Philip B., 225
Wilhelm II, 35, 73, 116, 127, 159
Wilson, Woodrow, 69
Windthorst, Ludwig, 42, 52, 53, 57, 58, 86

Windthorstbund, 80
Wingolfsbund, 85, 86
Winkler, Heinrich August, 122
Wirsching, Andreas, 79, 130
Wirth, Josef, 116, 145, 184
Wirtschaftspartei, 127, 146
"Wittenberg," 138
Wiwjorra, Ingo, 74
Wolf, Ernst, 191
Wolf, Hubert, 52, 239
Wolff, Theodor, 159
Wolfsschanze, 71
Woltmann, Ludwig, 59, 60, 61
Wotan, 78
Wuppertal-Elberfeld, 178
Wurm, Theophil, 47, 122, 175, 181
Wurttemberg, 117, 122, 127, 129, 156, 175, 178, 181, 225
Württemberger Bauernpartei und Landbund, 225
Würzburg, 13

YMCA/YWCA, 231
Young-plan, 85, 151, 152
Youth Movement, 36, 49, 80, 131, 186

Zehnhoff, Hugo am, 54
Zehrer, Karl, 221
Zentrum, 1, 2, 3, 4, 6, 7, 8, 10–15, 24, 25, 38–44, 48, 50, 52–59, 63–65, 80, 81, 84, 86, 87, 90, 92, 93, 115–117, 118–119, 123, 125, 126, 127, 129–133, 135, 138, 139, 142–150, 152, 154, 155, 158, 160, 163, 165–167, 169, 171, 177, 178, 180, 181, 182, 184–186, 216, 225, 226, 236, 237, 243, 246
"*Zentrumsprälaten*," 166
"*Zentrumsturm*," 42, 87, 152, 153, 156, 167, 168, 169, 181, 246
Zernack, Julia, 73
Zionist, 56, 165
Zmarzlik, Hans-Günther, 40

About the Author

Ingvar Kolden (born 1950) retired in 2017 after 37 years as a senior high school teacher. He published his first article about Nazism and the confessions in the Norwegian historical magazine (Historisk Tidsskrift) in 1998, and was awarded the degree of doctor philosophiae at the University of Bergen in 2014 with a thesis on the same subject on which this book is based.

www.ingramcontent.com/pod-product-compliance
Ingram Content Group UK Ltd.
Pitfield, Milton Keynes, MK11 3LW, UK
UKHW041147230326
11408UKWH00010B/302